WHO'S WHO
in the
MIDDLE AGES

JOHN FINES

BARNES
&NOBLE
BOOKS
NEW YORK

Quotations from: *The Wars of the Roses* by J. R. Lander, by permission of Martin Secker and Warburg Ltd.;

from *The Study of the Bible in the Middle Ages* by Beryl Smalley, by permission of Oxford University Press;

from *Feudal Society* by Marc Bloch, by permission of Routledge and Kegan Paul Ltd.;

from *Nibelungenlied* translated by A. T. Hatto, and from *Imitation of Christ* by Thomas à Kempis, translated by Leo Sherley-Price, by permission of Penguin Books Ltd.;

from the Loeb *Plutarch's Lives* VI translated by B. Perrin, by permission of William Heinemann Ltd.;

from *Edward of Carnarvon* by Hilda Johnstone, by permission of Manchester University Press;

from *The Court Baron* by F. W. Maitland, by permission of the Selden Society;

from *Dutch Civilisation in the Seventeenth Century and Other Essays* by J. H. Huizinga, by permission of William Collins Sons & Co. Ltd.

This edition published by Barnes & Noble, Inc., by arrangement with John Fines.

1995 Barnes & Noble Books

ISBN 1-56619-716-3

Printed and bound in the United States of America

M 9 8 7

INTRODUCTION

'. . . Years after the Revolution, a young man asked the old Merlin of Thionville why he had helped to condemn Robespierre. The old man kept silent, but seemed to be groping for words. Suddenly he rose up and said with a violent gesture: "Robespierre . . . Robespierre! If only you had seen his green eyes, you, too, would surely have condemned him." His green eyes! what better way of teaching us about true historical motives, of warning us to beware of reducing man, with all his hate, fury and delusion, to a bundle of political or economic drives! This little anecdote emphatically shows us that we may never know what strange quirks of human nature might in any case have been decisive.'[1]

The biographical approach to history has been sadly neglected of late, in fact it has an old-world, nineteenth-century air about it, and is felt by some historians to be not only outmoded, but also dangerous—bordering on that great sin of anecdotalism. Hazlitt's *Spirit of the Age*, Carlyle's *Heroes and Hero Worship* and Emerson's *Representative Men* are not just neglected, they are ostentatiously ignored. We use Leslie Stephen and Sidney Lee's great *Dictionary of National Biography* because we cannot ignore it—it is too useful. The reason for this despisal of the biographical approach, however, is more deep-rooted than just a matter of fashion: a century of horrific wars has taught us that 'great leaders' can often lead nations into unimaginable wickedness and destruction; the same century has shown us the importance of the masses, the 'unimportant', both in terms of political and social revolution, and of the growth of socialist ideals. Our immediate past warns us to beware of great men, and to devalue their inflated achievements.

This has been an important lesson for us, and it has revolutionised both the teaching and writing of history, but it has been carried too far. In trying to understand the complex and alien societies of the distant past the reader of history is often left without a key—without that intimate knowledge of personalities which can demonstrate that this was a real situation, impinging on real people, who responded to pressures and reacted to people in very much the same ways as ourselves. The study of biography is the motivation that makes possible the study of the larger field of history; it is only when our humanity is touched by that sudden mirror-glimpse of another human being in the toils and joys of life that we are willing to make the effort required to comprehend his way of life.

Without the interesting people, medieval history can often seem so wilfully complicated and obscure that we become bored and irascible, and the very word 'medieval' becomes for us a term of abuse. Yet the history books we use take little account of this fact: chronological and sociological accounts sweep on, building trends, recording the processes of decline, and mention individuals here and there, not as characters, but more as the cast-list. It is assumed somehow that we know them already, that there is no need to pause for more than a few lines to sketch the man in action; but if the reader does not know the man, how can he become interested in his action? And if he cannot quickly find out about his contemporaries, how may he judge that action, other than by a casual imagining of what *he* might have done in that character's place, long ago?

Few scholars have worked to remedy this fault. Incomparably the best, of course, was

[1] J. H. Huizinga, *Dutch Civilisation in the 17th Century and other Essays* (Fontana, London, 1968), p. 233.

Eileen Power, with her *Medieval People* (1925, reprint 1963), and following in her path, H. S. Bennet, *Six Medieval Men and Women* (1956). But their range of characters, though excellently drawn, was small, and more recently we have had A. B. Emden's massive *Biographical Registers* of the medieval members of the Universities of Oxford and Cambridge (Oxford Univ. Press, 3 vols., 1957–9; Cambridge Univ. Press, 1963). A glance in these volumes reveals the rich stores of material open to the historian using the biographical approach: we find an Oxford schoolteacher drowned in the Cherwell whilst cutting willows to beat his boys, and a more kindly headmaster (of Winchester) giving a boy a leaving present of a book of algebra in verse; a dwarf is allowed to carry out his academic exercises in private, to avoid the mocking of the insensitive; Nicholas Hogonona, 'un wilde Irisshman' wends his rowdy way through the schools, and David and Elias of Wales amuse themselves stealing pub-signs; John Austell hits the manciple's wife over the head with a fire-shovel at Beke's Inn, but two years later he is a well respected head of house. The rich pageant is all there, and there are academic, ecclesiastical and political triumphs recorded in plenty. This is the romance of history without the fictional element that in the end makes 'historical romances' unacceptable.

To turn from Dr. Emden's magisterial work (perhaps the most outstanding piece of its kind in our time) to the present humble contribution is hard. What has been attempted here is merely a beginning, an aid for the 'reader over my shoulder' who wants to start work on the Middle Ages as a period of study, or who just wants a simple guide to help him in his general reading on the period. Initially some three hundred characters were chosen as representatives—a small enough number, but even so some two hundred highly eligible people have been shouldered out by the hundred who remain. To give a character a chance to show himself, he must have some room. The men and women in this book have, then, almost chosen themselves, as interesting people, worthwhile characters, who show particularly well a facet of the society in which they lived, or are, quite simply, men for all time. My apologies to those who have been so unceremoniously pushed out.

It was a smaller world than ours, of course, and various factors made it even more compact. It was not just smallness of population that kept down the number of leading personalities, but a sense of closeness, which the dawn of the nation-state collapsed. The ideal of Christendom and the surviving remnants of belief in the Roman Empire made for a world that still revolved round Rome, where all the great ones met. However hard the way, the poor roads and the inadequate transport did not prevent people travelling. The international language of Latin, which ruled literature, the Church and diplomacy made it possible for men of a little learning to choose their abode out of all Europe, and to change it at will. Feudal wars and dynastic changes meant that barons trooped over half the world, and the great chose their wives from far-away nations. Missionaries travelled to farthest China with their urgent Gospel, and soldiers ended their days in peace or war in Palestine. The roads were full of people journeying to fame or fortune, and the competition was from all the known world. There are few great cosmopolitans.

For these reasons, a hundred representatives are enough to give the savour of medieval Christendom (viewed through English eyes, as it must be, however hard we try to quell our national bias). Their stories are briefly told, wherever possible from the best biographical material, and using available original sources in translation. These are noted at the end of each biography, for the intention of the author is not to summarise satisfactorily, but to tempt the reader to read in more detail. Naturally every effort has been made to preserve accuracy, but compression is always the enemy of accuracy in the wider sense, so that further reading is essential.

My hope for this book is that people will enjoy it sufficiently to go beyond it. Part of the historian's duty, since the days when historians were minstrels, has been to celebrate the past, to rouse people to a sense of all that on which they draw to have their being, and to make this process both pleasant and educational. As a teacher, I have been very concerned with what the Newsom report christened 'Half our Future', but who might more aptly be called the bored generation; as an historian my central concern is to rouse an interest in (for the Christian Era, at least) half our past—that great stretch of time between the fall of Rome and the Renaissance. It is a period that can teach us much, and can provide much pleasure, and I cannot do better than end by quoting from the man who began the biographical approach to history:

'I began the writing of my *Lives* for the sake of others, but I find that I am continuing the work and delighting in it for my own sake also, using history as a mirror and endeavouring in a manner to fashion and adorn my life in conformity with the virtues therein depicted. For the result is nothing else than daily living and associating together, when I receive and welcome each subject of my history in turn as my guest, so to speak, and observe carefully "how large he was, and of what mien", and select from his career what is most important and most beautiful to know . . .'

(Plutarch's *Lives*, Loeb edn., vol. vi, p. 261, trs. B. Perrin, Heinemann, London 1918.)

J.F.

CONTENTS

WHO'S WHO
in the
MIDDLE AGES

Abelard

Still on that breast enamour'd let me lie,
Still drink delicious poison from thy eye,
Pant on thy lip, and to thy heart be press'd;
Give all thou canst—and let me dream the
   rest.

So Pope imagined Heloïse's longings for
Abelard, and told a story that has enrap-
tured poets and historians alike through
the centuries; doubtless the greatest story
of the Middle Ages, though it is really a
timeless one, completely out of period.

Peter Abelard[1] was born in Brittany,
near Nantes, in 1079. His father was a soldier, but had received some education, and
he supported his eldest son in his decision
to abandon his birthright and devote himself to scholarship.

Abelard went first to Roscelin, the
daring Nominalist philosopher, who had
had his doctrines condemned in 1092. At
that time the philosophers were in a mighty
struggle over the nature of reality and
existence, the two sides in the dispute being
the Nominalists and the Realists. Briefly,
the Nominalists claimed that reality lay in
the individual, whilst the Realists claimed
that it only existed at the level of the uni-
versals, or generalisations, the essential
qualities found in things belonging to the
same species (thus a table only existed by
virtue of its table-ness).

After a year with the leading Nominalist,
Abelard left for the school of Paris, where
the leading Realist, William of Champeaux
ruled. Soon, however, he fell out with him,
and decided to set up his own school in the
royal fortress of Melun.[2] Being a teacher
in his own right was not sufficient for
Abelard, however, for he had to prove he
was the best, so he moved his school nearer
to Paris, to Corbeil.

After an interval of illness, when he
rested up at home in Brittany, he returned
to Paris, and finding that William had retired to the Priory of St. Victor, pursued
him there to continue the battle. After a
period of acrimonious dispute in which
each side used every tactic of dialectics and
politics to beat the other, William retired
to a bishopric, and Abelard was left, in
1113, to set up his school on the Mont Ste.
Geneviève, where for a time he ruled
supreme.

Abelard's success as a lecturer was
rooted in his character: he was young,
controversial, he had style and panache,
and was above all easy to understand: as he
said of other teachers at the time, they believed teaching to be mere 'declaration' of
established truths; he explained and
reasoned. John of Salisbury describes
himself as a student of Abelard 'drinking
in . . . every word that fell from his lips'.
Another describes how students came to
Abelard from every part of Europe: 'The
dangers of travel meant nothing to them—
they came believing that he could teach
them everything.' His literary skill can be
seen at a glance (as can his fervour) when
one reads the Latin hymns he composed in
later life.[3] His philosophy lay between the
two great schools, and may be called
conceptualist. He agreed with the Nominalists that existence lay primarily with the
individual, but, in that the human mind
could not function without making
generalisations, these generalisations had a
kind of existence. His mode of argument
was from the particular to the general, and,
in effect, he was enunciating Aristotelian
principles which the medieval world was
to accept later on, when the whole corpus
of Aristotle's writings became available.

Two causes now prompted Abelard to

---

[1] A recent writer gives the 37 spellings of Abelard's name he has encountered, but sticks to this one. (D. E. Luscombe, *The School of Peter Abelard*, Cambridge Univ. Press, 1969, p. 315).
[2] He missed out most of the latter part of his university studies by so doing. Later in his life, Abelard tried to remedy this lack of basic education by taking secret lessons in arithmetic. He found it im-possibly difficult.
[3] Helen Waddell, *Medieval Latin Lyrics* (Penguin, Harmondsworth, 1952) pp. 174–81 (with accompany-ing translations).

move his ground and become once more a student, this time in theology. First was ambition, for theology was the highest branch of study; the second was personal: his mother called him home to see her before she entered a nunnery (his father had already become a monk), and this turned his mind very much more towards religious matters. Though he always remained fundamentally a philosopher, from now onwards philosophy became only a means to an end—a method to be applied to theology, and a means of attracting students, so that he might then lead them on to theology—for the large majority wanted only the course in philosophy.

So at the age of 34 the man with the greatest mind of the age became a student once more. This need not surprise us, for in a period when the Jews were as much abominated as ever they were to be for another eight centuries, he attended a course of lectures in a synagogue on the book of Kings, and asked questions afterwards.[1] The teacher to whom he went was the finest theologian of the day, Anselm of Laon, but he, like all Abelard's teachers, so it would seem, had too much respect for tradition, and too little for reason, and soon they fell out. Abelard tells us, 'While he kindled a fire, he filled the room with smoke but not with light.'

Anselm's students grew angry at Abelard's behaviour (after all, they were paying for the best tuition in the world), and challenged him to do better. They gave him an obscure passage of Ezekiel to lecture on, and advised him to take his time; 'but I indignantly replied that it was not my custom to advance through practice but through talent', and he lectured the next morning. The lectures were successful, so Anselm's two brightest pupils persuaded him to forbid them, and Abelard had now to move back to Paris in order to continue.

There he achieved a wild success, with crowds of students, who made him a rich man with their fees. The success and the money turned his head, and the forty-year-old man who had devoted his life to scholarship now planned to ᴧ ᵛve success in worldly affairs too. Up until that point he had had almost nothing to do with women, but, typically ambitious, he picked on the most famous and beautiful woman to seduce—Heloïse, the niece of Abelard's fellow canon Fulbert.

Heloïse was learned as well as beautiful: in the course of her life she mastered not only Latin, but also Greek and Hebrew, and Gilson has shown how much of Abelard's later thinking was a development of Heloïse's ideas. At this stage, however, Heloïse was still learning, and when the cunning Abelard suggested to Fulbert that he would become his lodger and not only pay a good rent but also teach Heloïse free of charge, the silly old man not only agreed, but urged Abelard to use corporal punishment as well if it were needed.

Abelard tells us 'there was more kissing than teaching, my hands found themselves at her breasts more often than on the book . . . No sign of love was omitted by us in our ardour and whatever unusual love could devise, that was added too.' To fool Fulbert he hit her, but they were love-blows. In school he became tired and lazy, and simply re-read previous lectures; his students became deeply upset, but could not influence him. All he wrote were love-songs, composing words and music too, and soon they were 'pop-songs' all over France—Heloïse tells us that having got his name known to the whole of the learned world, at last even the illiterate knew him.

At last Fulbert found out what had been going on under his nose, and threw Abelard out of his house. The two lovers kept writing, for what had started as a cynical seduction ended as the most passionate love-affair the world has heard of. Then Heloïse wrote 'with exultation' that she was pregnant, and one night when Fulbert was away Abelard had her whisked away

[1] Beryl Smalley, *The Study of the Bible in the Middle Ages* (2nd edn., Oxford Univ. Press, London, 1952) p. 78.

to his sister's in Brittany to have their child, the boy Astrolabe.

Abelard went to Fulbert and promised to marry Heloïse, so long as secrecy was kept, for although it was legal for him to marry, he would lose his benefices and his reputation if the story spread. Heloïse didn't want him to marry her, indeed she prophesied that the marriage would bring disaster on both their heads: Abelard belonged to the whole world, not to one woman; a philosopher should never marry —remember Socrates' nagging wife Xanthippe; the child's crying and 'constant degrading defilement' would upset him, as would the silly lullabies of nurses. She would rather be his mistress than his wife, knowing that her charm kept him, rather than any marriage vows. She would rather be his mistress than the wife of the Roman Emperor.

Yet Abelard insisted, and they left the child in his sister's care and returned to Paris for a secret wedding. Immediately Fulbert began to tell everybody of the marriage, and became infuriated when Heloïse stoutly denied that it had ever taken place. The situation became so difficult that Abelard had her taken away from Fulbert's house and put in the nunnery at Argenteuil, close to Paris, where she had been educated.

Her relations were now convinced that Abelard had never meant to make a real marriage, and planned a terrible revenge. In the middle of the night, they bribed his servants, burst into his bedroom and castrated him. The next day all Paris came to see him, bewailing the tragic fall from greatness: 'I felt the embarrassment more than the wound' he says. He fled to hide his shame to the great Abbey of St. Denis to become a monk, and advised Heloïse to take the veil at Argenteuil.

Abelard never did anything by halves: if his life to this point had been a successful struggle for worldly acclaim, from now on he was to devote himself entirely to God, and Gilson talks convincingly of a conversion. He was shocked that all around

him did not show the same fervour as he, and was bitterly disappointed by the disorder and moral laxity of his fellow monks. He had soon made so many enemies that he had to be removed to an outpost of the abbey where he once more set up his school, in response to students' demands.

He now published his book on the Trinity, and his enemies, who hated the thought of anyone teaching who had not gone through the long gruelling course of instruction they had endured, pounced upon it with glee. This was unauthorised writing—it lacked the imprimatur—the writing of a man whose combative nature would lead to heresy. Though no one could stand up to Abelard in dispute, and few could follow his reasoning, most people felt that it was somehow imperative that he should be silenced.

So at Soissons a council was convened in 1121 and he was condemned unheard, his book unread; the mob outside, inflamed by his enemies, was threatening to stone him, and Abelard was forced to burn his book himself. He was sent for a brief spell to the Abbey of St. Médard, a sort of monastic reformatory, or Devil's Island, and was then returned to the Abbey of St. Denis.

At this point his personal devil took a hand once more. Instead of settling down to rebuild his reputation, and trying to get on with his fellow monks, he did the worst thing possible. The monastery revelled in the fact that it had been founded by the patron saint of France, St. Dionysius (Denis) the Areopagite, who, having been converted by St. Paul, became bishop of Athens, and then of Paris. The critical spirit in Abelard smelt a rat in this story, and when he found a note in a work by Bede that Dionysius the Areopagite had been Bishop of Corinth, and not of Athens (this being a totally different Denis), he was exultant, and spread the news around as fast as he could. The monks were furious, and planned to send Abelard to the king for summary justice. In the middle of the night he escaped, and fled to the territories of the Count of Champagne.

There he amused himself by building a hermitage near Troyes, and living in a wattle and reeds hut; but as he himself explains, he was no good at this desert-island kind of existence, and when his pupils found him once more, he gladly let them make his life more comfortable. For a while they lived in make-shift cabins, and in his lectures 'for tables they heaped up sods', but, utilising their spare time, they had soon built a neat convent of wood and stone, and Abelard consecrated it with the name of the Paraclete—the Comfort brought by the Holy Spirit.

For a while his existence there was idyllic, but soon he became troubled by fears of persecution: 'God is my witness that whenever I learned of a meeting of ecclesiastics, I supposed it was held to condemn me.' He particularly feared the attentions of the two great monastic reformers, Sts. Norbert and Bernard, though at this stage it is difficult to see why: the only dispute we have a note of is that Abelard had discovered a slightly different text of the Lord's Prayer (in fact it was a false text) and, quite typically, insisted on using it at the Paraclete, which slightly upset Bernard.

Whether his fears had any real foundation or not, when he heard in 1125 that he had been elected Abbot of St. Gildas, a monastery in the wildest part of Brittany, he gladly accepted. Civilised France had only meant trouble for him, and he had never been anything but a foreigner there: so he went with a missionary joy to barbaric Brittany, which was, after all, his home.

He was not the stuff of which missionaries are made, however, as he soon found out. For six years he led a most miserable existence: the monks were violent and unruly, robbers and would-be murderers; the best Abelard could do in the situation was to preserve his own skin, for they even went to the extent of putting poison in his chalice.

In 1128 came the first bit of good news for a long time: the convent at Argenteuil (where Heloïse was now prioress) was being taken over by the Abbey of St. Denis, which had just proved an ancient claim upon it, and the nuns were being dispersed. Abelard now set up Heloïse and the nuns who were faithful to her in the deserted buildings of the Paraclete. This was a new interest in life for him, and (at last) a constructive one: Heloïse, he tells us, inspired so much love in all around that she did more to build up the convent in one year than he could have done in one hundred.

Now he discovered, to his horror, that though he had converted his love to God after his castration and his entry into the monastery, Heloïse, though obedient to his command that she should make her profession, still loved him more than God. She wrote, 'The pleasures of loving which we have tasted together have been so sweet that I cannot despise them, nor even efface their memory without great difficulty. Wherever I turn, there they confront me with their eternal longing. Even in my sleep, their shadows pursue me. It is not until the time of Mass, when prayer should be purest, that the obscene imagining of these pleasures so completely overwhelms my poor soul that I yield to their shameful delectation rather than to prayer. I who should tremble at what I have done, sigh after what I have lost. Nor is it only what we have done but the very places, the moments when we have been together that are so deeply graven into my heart that once more I see them with you in all their plenitude . . .'

The true tragedy of the story now revealed itself in a respected prioress who knew exactly the meaning of what she was writing, telling her husband, an utterly unsuccessful abbot, that she would go before him into Hell if he so commanded. Abelard was deeply disturbed, and though his monks set bandits on the road to catch and kill him, he at last escaped from Brittany to go and join Heloïse again, to give her that spiritual instruction that might save her soul.

A few happy years were left, and in them Abelard once more took up teaching and writing—putting forth the results of a lifetime's study. In his books he tried to show that he had a deep respect for the authority of tradition, but that the authoritative statements had to be winnowed out from the accumulated chaff: he was not prepared to accept a disorganised mass of contradictions, for his motto was 'By doubting we are led to enquire, by enquiry we perceive the truth.' It was in this spirit that he composed his great treatise *Sic et Non*, wherein some 150 basic questions in theology were supported and opposed by statements culled from the accepted theological authorities, and were then resolved according to the rules of logic.

Though the critical methods he applied to his subject were by no means new, his fervent spirit and profound belief in the power of reason was; and everything Abelard stood for was by now in direct contradiction to the spirit of the age, seen most strongly in St. Bernard, whose mystical understanding of the power of faith, and conservative belief in the danger of all challenges to authority were to be the twin pillars against which Abelard unsuccessfully pushed in these last years of his life.

Bernard firmly held that monasticism was the one sure route to heaven, and had confirmed his view on a recent visit to the University of Paris, where he was deeply shocked by the unruly independence of the students, the squalor they were prepared to put up with in pursuit of earthly glory, and the immorality which was a concomitant of their daily lives. In a famous sermon he spoke to them: 'My little children, who is teaching you how to avoid the wrath to come? . . . I beg of you, have pity on your souls . . . Fly from Babylon, . . .

throw yourselves into places of refuge where you may do penance for the past, obtain grace for the present, and await with confidence the glory to come.'

He became increasingly certain that Abelard was leading a terrible process of perversion of the young, and Bernard throughout his life had had a passionate commitment to their salvation. He sat down and wrote to all who had the slightest influence, letters which show genuine fear of what Abelard stood for and of the evil influence he had gained over the young scholars of Europe: 'The faith of the simple is being held up to scorn, the secrets of God are being reft open, the most sacred matters are being recklessly discussed . . . He approaches the dark cloud which surrounds God not as Moses did, alone, but with a whole crowd of his disciples . . .' God's works, and the most holy doctrines are 'being discussed at the crossroads'.

Bernard's fear was paralleled by that of Abelard, who demanded the right to reply at the Council of Sens in 1140, but when his turn came to speak, he tells a friend, his mind went blank, his wits deserted him and he fled away to appeal to the Pope.[1] Perhaps he believed that Bernard had 'fixed' the council in advance, or that the crowd would mob him as they had threatened to do at Soissons; certainly he recognised that the whole council stood ready to condemn him.

Now the old scholar (for sixty was a great age then) began to walk to Rome, but he had only got as far as the great Abbey of Cluny when he heard that the Pope had already condemned him, his books had been burnt, and he had been ordered never to publish anything again. The Abbot, Peter the Venerable, took him in and looked after him with loving care. Abelard

[1] A disciple of Abelard, Berengarius Scholasticus, gives a largely different picture of the council, in which he describes its members as being so befuddled by drink that they sleep through the reading of Abelard's suspect writings. 'They only rouse themselves to cry "Namus" (we swim) when they hear the official shout of "Damnamus" (we condemn him), their heads still hanging over arms, knees and cushions on which they had rested in their drunken stupor.' (*P. Abaelardi et Heloisae opera*, ed. A. Duchesne, Paris, 1616, p. 302, quoted in J. C. L. Gieseler, *A Compendium of Ecclesiastical History*, Edinburgh, vol. iii, 1853, p. 288.

was sick and weary, and soon made his peace with Bernard. In 1142 he died.

Heloïse wrote to Peter to ask for a description of Abelard's last years, and Peter wrote back a kind and deeply understanding letter. Abelard had 'enriched us with a wealth beyond all gold' and 'he, who for his supreme mastery of learning was known well nigh over the whole world' became a pattern of humility. He was quiet, and 'constantly bowed over books'. Now that Abelard was with God, Heloïse could at last give her undivided love to God: 'him to whom you once clung in the union of flesh and later in that stronger, finer bond of divine affection . . . hath Christ taken to his breast to comfort him, till at the coming of the Lord . . . He shall restore him to your heart again.'

Heloïse wrote back in restrained terms, begging for the body (which Peter personally conveyed to the Paraclete), and for the deed of absolution to hang over his tomb. Finally she asked whether Peter could help find a benefice for their son Astrolabe. She died in 1164, and the story goes that when Abelard's tomb was opened for her burial with him, he opened his arms to receive her.

There are many valuable biographies, among the best being Helen Waddell's *Peter Abelard* (Constable, London, 1933) which is cast in the form of a novel; J. T. Muckle has published an excellent translation of Abelard's own story of his troubles (Pontifical Institute of Medieval Studies, Toronto, 1964). By far the most valuable work, however, is Étienne Gilson's *Heloïse and Abelard* (Univ. of Michigan Press, Ann Arbor, 1960); as Helen Waddell understands the man's point of view, so Gilson brilliantly shows the woman's; his book is a triumph of understanding based on the soundest scholarship, and very beautiful. Would that other medievalists wrote a quarter as well.

Adelard of Bath

One would like to know a great deal more about Adelard of Bath. Born in the late eleventh century, he studied and taught in France before going to Spain to learn Arabic, which enabled him to translate the *Elements* of Euclid. He went on to North Africa, Greece (where he again learned the language) and Asia Minor. He was back in England by 1130, and there wrote a handbook of scientific information learned from the Arabs, who had had the works of the ancient Greeks translated into their language, and had developed still further from the Greeks' high peak of scholarship. He also wrote a book of philosophy, in which he declared himself an avowed Platonist (he knew the *Timaeus*), a book on the astrolabe, which he dedicated to Henry Plantagenet (the future Henry II, whom he had met in Bristol), several treatises on mathematics (including one on the abacus), a translation of the *Almagest* of Ptolemy (which revealed the secrets of ancient astronomy to the medieval world), and a book on pigments and one on falconry, a sport popular in Sicily, where he had spent some time. His works relate a great diversity of experiments and ideas, and it is astonishing to read them in so early a source: he discusses gravity, the nature of the earthquakes he had experienced in Syria, algebra and trigonometry, music, a pneumatic experiment he had attended in southern Italy, and the fact that light travels faster than sound. He came back to England full of pride in the new fields of knowledge he had gained, and tells us that his nephew considered that he praised the 'Saracens' ' ideas shamelessly, and was too eager to point out the ignorance of the scholars of Christendom; but despite his doubting audience, he continued to refuse to let them get away with accounting for every natural event by the inexorable and incomprehensible will of God: nature 'is not confused and without system, and so far as human knowledge has progressed it should be given a hearing'.

In an age when reading was a high achievement, to have written a dozen books must have been a source of pride, and when a journey from one English town to another must have been a major undertaking, to have travelled as far as Adelard was wonderful.

Adrian IV

Adrian IV, the first and only Englishman to become Pope, was born as Nicholas Breakspear, probably at Langley, near St. Albans, where his father became a monk after leaving the royal service, where he had been a clerk. The boy was sent to Merton Priory, Becket's old school, and he later went to France in search of further education, ending up at Avignon.

He became a canon regular, and soon rose to be abbot; but his rule was strict, and the canons complained to Pope Eugenius III, who made peace between them and their superior. When they complained a second time, and Eugenius thoroughly investigated the case, he realised the true merits of the abbot, and made him a cardinal. In 1146 he was sent to Scandinavia to reorganise the Church there and was so successful in cementing its ties with Rome that when he returned in 1154 he was hailed as the 'Apostle of the North', and elected Pope.

He was a notable preacher, with a fine voice, scholarly and gentle; he believed implicitly in the powers and importance of the papacy, telling John of Salisbury that the Pope's tiara was splendid because 'it burned like fire'. He had tremendous problems to deal with at his accession: William I of Sicily was denying papal suzerainty over his kingdom, and the Romans, inspired by the fiery vision of Arnold of Breschia (the revolutionary disciple of Abelard), were all for a republic, and all against the Pope. When a mob attacked and severely injured a cardinal, Adrian showed his mettle, and for the first time in history put an interdict on the city. Denied the valuable tourist-trade of pilgrims, the townsmen gave in and agreed to expel Arnold.

Adrian now put his hopes on Frederick Barbarossa (q.v.), who was fast approaching with his German army to be crowned Holy Roman Emperor; when they met, however, Frederick refused to come forward to take the Pope's bridle, for he had as high an idea of the Empire as Adrian had of the Papacy, so the Pope refused to give him the kiss of peace. After two days of nerve-racking tension, the Emperor gave in, and agreed to meet the Pope again, leading his horse before the whole German army; he needed the coronation badly.

Adrian's triumph was short-lived, for although Frederick willingly used the threat of his army to ensure his coronation, he was not willing to risk starving his men (or killing them off with Roman fever) to subdue the Roman rebels for the Pope, or to defeat the Sicilians. So in 1156 Adrian made his peace with the Sicilian king, and from that point on was (in varying degrees) opposed to the great Emperor.

That same year Frederick had captured and imprisoned Adrian's old friend the Archbishop of Lund, holding him for ransom. Adrian sent two cardinals with a stiff letter to the Imperial Diet in 1157, pointing out that he had freely conferred the benefice of the imperial crown on Frederick, and deserved better treatment. Now the language in which this statement was couched was strict feudal terminology, and clearly implied that the Pope was the feudal overlord of the Emperor: there were angry demonstrations against the cardinals and they were sent straight home. Not only the German nobility, but also the bishops supported Frederick, and within three months he was ready to descend once more upon Italy. Adrian was forced to retract and in this, his worst hour, he wrote that he had used biblical terminology, not feudal, and so the Germans had mistaken his meaning.

The dispute got worse, Adrian even descending to the crude insult of sending beggars as his letter-bearers to the Emperor, and Frederick openly encouraged the Romans in revolt. Adrian withdrew to Anagni, to be nearer his Sicilian ally's protective power, and was ready to excommunicate Frederick and put himself at the head of the anti-imperial element in Italy when he died, late in 1159.

One can well imagine the sigh of relief breathed by Frederick Barbarossa.

Ælfric

Ælfric, Abbot of Eynsham, lived at the end of the tenth century and the beginning of the eleventh—a time of great trouble for England, when the land was besieged and devastated by the Danes. He suffered for a while under a bad teacher who barely knew Latin, before going to study under Æthelwold, Bishop of Winchester, a scholar of great ability, whose life he was later to write. His early struggles impressed him deeply, and for the rest of his life he was to be concerned about the education and morals of the secular clergy.

About 987 he was invited by Æthelmær, a great patron of revived monasticism, to become abbot of his new monastery at Cerne, and it was there that he wrote most of his English works and translations, many of them commissioned by Æthelmær. About 1005 he went as abbot to another newly founded monastery at Eynsham.

Ælfric's old English writings show the precise mind of a Latinist who nevertheless retains a profound respect for his own language. He wrote a Latin grammar and glossary, dedicated to the boys of England, and a reader to accompany it, wherein a master and his pupil hold conversations with various craftsmen; from this book we can find out a great deal about social conditions of his time, not only at the highest level, but right down to the humble ploughman. Schoolboys were not to have such an interesting and amusing reader provided for them until Erasmus adopted the same pattern, 500 years later. There is a translation from Ælfric's *Colloquies* in W. O. Hassall's *They Saw it Happen, 55 B.C.–A.D. 1485* (Oxford Univ. Press, London, 1957), pp. 25–32.

For those who could not learn Latin, he exercised his lucid style in the production of translations of parts of the Old Testament, the lives of the saints and two volumes of sermons for use on the most important days of the Church's year. In these sermons he followed Ratramn of Corbie in his denunciation of the doctrine of transubstantiation (which held that Christ was really present in the consecrated bread at Mass). This, along with his having translated from the Bible into the mother-tongue made him a great favourite with the Reformers, and he would have been surprised to see his work re-published in 1566 with testimonials from both archbishops and thirteen bishops, all delighted to be able to prove that England had always been solidly Protestant.

His skill as a writer in English was widespread, and he was commissioned to write pastoral letters for both the Bishop of Sherborne and the Archbishop of York. In these he feelingly expressed his ideas about what the priesthood should be at its best, and his ideals were obviously too high for an age where priests were married, illiterate, and for the most part scarcely distinguishable from the other villagers.

Aidan

Oswald of Northumbria had spent some years in exile in Iona, where he was converted to Christianity, and learned the language and culture of the Irish monks of St. Columba. When he became king of Northumbria in the year 637 he appealed for a mission; but the man sent to be his bishop was dour, and set high standards, and soon returned to Iona to tell of the impossibility of the job. The monks sat round in silence, but then Aidan spoke up: 'Were you not too severe with the unlearned hearers? Did you not feed them on meat instead of milk?' This was a shrewd judgement, not only on the man, but on Celtic missionaries in general, and Aidan shewed himself to be exceptional in his power to win people by his example rather than by his fervour and discipline.

He was sent to Northumbria as bishop, and chose as his base the tidal island of Lindisfarne, because it resembled Iona, and was close to the royal palace at Bamborough. At court he was soon a success, with King Oswald acting as his interpreter before he learned the language; presents were showered upon him, but these he gave away, and so endeared himself to the poor of Northumbria as well. He travelled the country on foot, stopping everyone he met to preach to them, and distributing charity to the poor; once, when the king had given him a horse to facilitate his missionary journeys, he found himself without anything to give, and so finally gave away the horse. Soon churches were rising on every hand, and Lindisfarne was filled with monks from Iona, and English boys eager for education,[1] which was largely in the form of a training for the mission-field.

In 642 Oswald was killed in battle by the heathen Penda of Mercia, and the enemy troops got as far as trying to burn Bamborough, but were foiled by Aidan's prayer to God to change the wind. Now two kings reigned in Northumbria: Oswin, who ruled Deira and Oswald's brother Oswiu who ruled Bernicia. Aidan grew very close to Oswin, and when he was killed by Oswiu in his fight to reunite Northumbria in 651, Aidan's heart broke, and a few days later, feeling death upon him, he had a hut built against the west wall of the church in Bamborough. There he died, leaning against a post put to buttress the wooden wall, perhaps recalling the death of his master Columba.

Aidan was an ascetic who did not care about his surroundings, so the Lindisfarne over which he ruled was a poor place: but it was to grow into one of the foremost religious and artistic centres of the Middle Ages, and still attracts crowds of visitors.

Alaric

Alaric the Visigoth, the most noted destroyer of the early Middle Ages, may be given the negative credit of inspiring St. Augustine's *De Civitate Dei* by his sack of Rome. Initially he was simply a marauder, seeking to capitalise on the chaotic situation in which the Empire found itself at the death of Theodosius. Later we have a dim vision of a man responsible for a huge body of men and desperate to get them provisions, willing even to abjure war in order to achieve this object. Certainly the Emperor Honorius comes out of the situation with more stains on his character than Alaric. Finally he had the grandest burial ever known.

In 390 Alaric, aged about twenty, took command of a band of Huns and Goths in an attack on Thrace. Two years later he led his followers to join the Roman army, but as his troops received no pay, and he didn't get the promised position, he returned to his primary role. Many historians suggest that the empire fell because it voluntarily took in so many barbarians that its population was finally outnumbered; one cannot know what might have happened if the proffers of co-operation made by the barbarians had been genuinely taken up.

In 395 Alaric was aiming for Constantinople, but having been bought off, he turned on Greece, sweeping through Attica and on into the Peloponnese. Again he was bought off, and given the territory of Epirus on which to settle his followers. There he re-armed his troops from Roman arsenals, and in 401 moved into Italy. There he met a match in Stilicho, the great Vandal general who served Rome so well, and the two compacted to re-take eastern Illyria for the Empire. In 406 they were ready to go, but Stilicho was recalled to deal with the rebellion of Constantine. Two years later Alaric again entered Italy

[1] Not all were, in fact. Reginald of Durham records for us the story of Haldene, a boy at Norham School, started by Aidan. Haldene threw the School doorkey into the river to avoid lessons and punishments, but (of course) the salmon that swallowed it was soon caught by a fisherman, and the key returned.

and demanded 4,000 pounds of gold as compensation for not having the Illyrian lands. This he was given, and he might well have left again (until the gold ran out) had not the Emperor Honorius executed Stilicho.

Alaric now invested Rome, sending embassies to Honorius asking what he would give him to go away. The situation over supplies was getting desperate, for Africa had been lost, and no grain was getting through. Honorius did nothing, so Alaric elevated a Roman noble, Attalus, to the emperorship. Attalus let the whole thing go to his head, and instead of organising an expedition to re-take the vital granary of Africa, tried to capture Honorius in order to mutilate him and rule alone. So Alaric deposed him, and sacked Rome; much of the worst of the bestialities involved in the sack of 409 were done by the freed slaves who joined Alaric's army as camp-followers: in general he treated Romans with respect and humanity.

Having got supplies, he moved south in order to sail to Africa, but his fleet was dispersed in a storm, and on his way back he died (410). The Goths forced the slaves to divert the river Basentus, bury Alaric and all his treasure in the old bed, and then divert the river back over him; then they killed all the slaves. Perhaps the Nibelung treasure that Hagen sank in the Rhine was a folk-memory of Alaric's:

'And now listen to some marvels concerning the treasure! It was as much as a dozen waggons fully loaded could carry away from the mountain in four days and nights coming and going thrice a day! It was entirely of gems and gold, and even if one paid all the people in the world with it, it would not have lost a mark in value! ... In among the rest lay the rarest gem of all, a tiny wand of gold, and if any had found its secret he could have been lord of all mankind!' (*Nibelungenlied*, trs. A. T. Hatto, Penguin, Harmondsworth, 1965, p. 147.)

Alcuin

Alcuin was born at York in 735, and attended the monastery school there, where his master was a man who had studied under Bede. His education was both wide and sound, and particular attention was paid to the works of Virgil as the arbiter of style. Having completed his studies he became a teacher in the same school, and quickly rose to the position of director, controlling also one of the greatest libraries in Western Europe.

Though his early career may have a hint of the parochial, it was a preparation for a great future. He three times went to Rome, and soon achieved such a reputation as England's finest scholar, that when he met Charlemagne (*q.v.*) in 781 he was immediately invited to come to direct the palace school at Aachen. Like many an English scholar tempted to America, he was to remain in his second home for the rest of his life.

He received a magnificent endowment of two abbacies, and set to work to build up the school both as an international centre of learning (Theodulph the poet came from Spain and Peter of Pisa the grammarian and Paul the Deacon the historian from Italy), and as a place of education for the royal family (including Charlemagne himself at times), and the sons of the nobility. Charles and Alcuin aimed to rebuild Athens in Francia, and though the intellectual level of the disputations at Aachen may have been low, their relative success was high. As if this were not enough, he also wrote all the text-books for the pupils, and busied himself with the development of education in other parts of the realm.

Not only was he 'Minister of Education', but he was also Charlemagne's chief adviser on English affairs, and in 790 went on a two-year mission to the court of Offa, King of Mercia. When he got back to Aachen he had to put on yet another hat and combat the Adoptian heresy which was spreading from Spain (these heretics claimed that Jesus the man was not the natural son of God, but the adopted son, a viewpoint that could lead to some very dangerous conclusions). He had, however, to moderate his ecclesiastical fervour by turning a blind eye to the activities of Charlemagne's daughters whom he could not bear to give away to husbands, and who therefore satisfied themselves at court.

In 796 Alcuin retired to the Abbey of St. Martin of Tours, where one might have expected him to take a well-earned rest. Instead he set to work to re-invigorate the abbey school there, and from its scriptorium came the fine Carolingian handwriting known as minuscule, on which the Renaissance scholars and printers based their italic hand and alphabet. In this hand were written better texts of the Bible and corrected liturgies.

He also continued to write treatises, biographies, poems, epigrams, acrostics and letters—232 of his letters survive to us and form one of the most valuable sources for the history of that time that we possess. He also wrote a notable life of his relative Willibrord, the missionary of Friesland.

Alcuin died in 804.

There is a biography by E. S. Duckett; *Alcuin, Friend of Charlemagne, His World and His Work* (Shoe String Press, Connecticut, 1951, reprint 1965).

Aldhelm

Aldhelm came of West Saxon royal stock, and was born about 640. He began his studies under Maildubh, an Irish scholar, who started a community at Malmesbury, which took its name from him. However in 669 an exciting event occurred, for Theodore of Tarsus arrived in England to take his place as Archbishop of Canterbury. He was a very learned man, the last known pupil of the schools of Athens, and he brought with him the Abbot Hadrian, an equal in scholarship, who had been born in Byzantine Africa, and had spent some years in South Italy.[1] Scholars flocked to the school they set up in Canterbury, anxious to learn Latin and Greek, music and mathematics, and the arts of writing poetry. Aldhelm describes Theodore surrounded by Irish scholars as 'an angry boar hemmed in by grinning hounds'.

Aldhelm stayed as long as he could at Canterbury, soaking up learning of all kinds (including Roman law, which was extremely difficult, though he had more trouble with arithmetic and 'the most difficult of all things, which they call fractions'). When he returned to Malmesbury to become abbot of the community in which he had gained his earliest knowledge, he brought with him skills that were to build him a continental reputation for scholarship. In his flowery and affected Latin prose he began to write a number of works, including riddles and poems, many of which were designed to show a pattern or a picture when written out, a fashion that has recently returned after 1200 years.

Although Aldhelm rejoiced in knowledge for its own sake, like his fellow scholars, he could not destroy his Anglo-Saxon roots, nor his commitment to religion as an absolutely primary obligation. He often describes himself and his colleagues as bees, busily gathering converts and storing up heavenly treasure in England. When he found his congregations getting a little thin, he would take up his stand on the main bridge of the town, and begin to sing popular songs of his own creation in the vernacular. Soon a crowd would gather, eager to hear the minstrel, and he would gradually change the content of his songs, bringing in sacred subjects. King Alfred is said to have been very partial to Aldhelm's English songs, and may

[1] Poor Theodore was delayed in Rome for four months before coming to England because he wore the Greek tonsure—a totally shaven head, and he had, somehow, to grow some hair round his crown, in order to conform with the Roman practice. At this time England was torn between the Celtic and Roman Church, and one of the main bones of contention was the tonsure: the Romans shaved the crown, the Celts the front part of the head; it would never do for the Archbishop of Canterbury to introduce a third element into the struggle. Luckily for England, Theodore's hair finally grew again.

well have taken note of his technique for gaining converts.

Aldhelm was also a great founder of monasteries and builder of churches (one of which, his little church of St. Lawrence at Bradford-on-Avon, survives today, though heavily restored in the tenth and nineteenth centuries. Possibly also a doorway in the church of Somerfield Keynes is his). In 687 he went to Rome to gain papal privileges for his monasteries, and on his return in 701 he was given a triumphal welcome by the West Saxon and Mercian kings.

In 705 a synod of West Saxon bishops was convened to try to deal with an ecumenical problem which is familiar to us today. Many Welshmen who were of the Celtic Christian faith had by now been incorporated into the West Saxon kingdom, and the synod was trying to find ways of persuading them to join the Roman Church; they deputed Aldhelm to carry out this task, and he wrote a treatise in the form of a letter to Geraint, King of Devon and Cornwall. He told Geraint how Welsh priests refused to eat with Catholics, and scraped and scoured out the dishes their fellow Christians had used. The Welsh gave them no greeting, neither kiss of peace, nor washing of feet, instead they insisted on Catholics making a forty-day penance before they would speak with them. Nevertheless instead of treating the Celtic Christians as worthless heretics, Aldhelm accorded a measure of respect to their opinions, and tried reasoning with them instead of hectoring. As a result his letter had a marked success.

In the same year he was made Bishop of Sherborne (a diocese that included the Celtic Christians within the West Saxon kingdom) and he began a series of missionary tours on foot, to win the Celts over to the Roman faith. It was on one of these trips, in 709, that he fell ill near Wells, and died.

Alexius Comnenus

Isaac Comnenus resigned the imperial throne of Byzantium in 1059, and retired to a monastery. His policies had not met with universal favour, and the consistent opposition to his military plans was too much for him. In Byzantium emperors came and went much as prime ministers today—and were 'kicked upstairs' into the monastery just as British leaders retire to the Lords. There was a deal of bloodshed and torture as well, of course, and the regular change of emperors had ensured that the majority of the leading families felt a vague right to the throne when the time came, and this led to tremendous plotting of unimaginable complexity.

After Isaac had resigned, the army was cut back, just at the time when they were most needed. In 1071 Byzantium lost her last outpost in Italy to the fast-rising Norman power there, as well as the battle of Manzikert, which was to ensure Turkish control of almost all Asia Minor. Croatia gained independence, and Dalmatia, Serbia and Bulgaria all made a fair bid to follow suit. From across the Danube the wild Hungarians, Cumans and Patzinaks came raiding.

Such was the prospect that faced the young nephew of Isaac, Alexius Comnenus, when he entered politics, pushed by his powerfully ambitious mother. As a general he had successes against both Turk and Norman to his credit, though he owed them to devious cunning rather than valour. He allied himself by marriage to the leading house of Ducas, and became the favourite of the Empress. The Emperor, ruling through eunuchs and having an empty treasury, keenly sought young men of promise and good family who would serve him, and the Comneni stood high in his favour.

In 1081, having reached that pinnacle of favouritism that involved in Byzantine politics either a leap for the Empire, or a fall before the onslaught of the envious, Alexius leapt, and won. The Emperor retired, and left his problems to a younger hand. Alexius was about 33. Immediately he had to face an invasion of his domains from the Normans of South Italy under the energetic leadership of Robert Guiscard and his son Bohemond. Lacking finance for an army, Alexius turned to diplomacy, sending Norman dissidents to raise revolt in Italy, making a truce with the Turks, angling for Papal and Imperial support, and buying Venetian aid in return for commercial privileges within his Empire. The military resistance he could offer was small, but the diplomatic barrage was immediately impressive.

During the years 1086–90 he had to face serious raids from Patzinaks, but he was able to halt these by buying Cuman aid in 1091. He next faced trouble in Serbia, and in 1094 the Cumans themselves began raiding, but by now Alexius had managed to restore the army sufficiently to halt them in the following year.

In Asia Minor, which the Turks had divided into three Emirates in 1085, Alexius was able to combine his own military attacks with diplomacy that set Turk against Turk, and he slowly began to win back territory, which he protected with castles manned by Anglo-Saxon mercenaries who had fled William the Conqueror's wrath in 1070. He also restored the navy, establishing a base on Cyprus.

All this activity involved constant travel, and a deep concern for organisation: Alexius trained his own troops, and led them in person, wisely fearing successful generals, who throughout Byzantine history had returned home to take the throne. Often enough he had to face plots from the discontented aristocracy, who were supported by the Church, which objected violently to Alexius's habit of dipping into ecclesiastical revenues as a last resort. But just as the Emperor was a fine international diplomat, he was thoroughly informed on domestic affairs, and a good judge of men. Usually he was able to scotch plots before ever they reached fruition.

Now he faced his biggest battles of all: he had to meet with the Crusaders. Rela-

tions between Byzantium and Western Europe had never been good, for they were two civilisations at different stages of development. The thrusting arrogant power of the West seemed young, brash and discordant to the heirs of the Roman Empire, guardians of a long tradition, who believed deeply in custom, and whose society was elaborately organised. Alexius had made many attempts to improve relations— especially with the Papacy—in the early part of his reign, but was totally unprepared for the influx of disorderly soldiers, hungry for land and careless of custom, which the Crusade was to bring. For the lands of the East looked to medieval Europeans much as the Western territories seemed to nineteenth-century Americans, and they were as careless of the inhabitants' rights as the pioneers were to be of the Indians'.

Anna, Alexius's daughter, describes how at the ceremonial oath-taking at the Emperor's court, one of the Franks sat down on the throne, and when Baldwin of Boulogne, the one diplomat among the Westerners, persuaded him to get up, the embarrassed Greeks, shocked to the core, heard him mutter 'What a peasant! He sits alone while generals like these stand beside him!' Later the Emperor spoke with him, only to hear him announce that he had challenged all the men of his own country to single combat, and none had dared take up the challenge. Here is the Westerner, firmly believing that might *is* right, facing the Greek who almost worshipped tradition.

Nonetheless, despite every provocation, Alexius persuaded the Crusaders to treat with him. In 1097, accepting the Western habit of the feudal oath, Alexius became the Crusaders' suzerain, offering protection and provisions, in return for the Latins' promise to return to him all Greek territories they might win back from the Turks.

For a while, all went reasonably well, though the Franks could not overcome their habit of pillaging wherever they went; but when Bohemond took Antioch in

October, he determined to keep it as his own principality. He excused himself by saying that Alexius had broken the bargain, and he had a grain of truth in his case. Alexius had been moving his forces up to Antioch when he met Stephen of Blois, commander-in-chief at Antioch (and father of king Stephen of England) hurtling home in mad panic. Stephen had seen a large Turkish army coming to the relief of the city, and had fled without waiting for the result. In fact the Turks were repulsed, but so lurid was Stephen's picture of the 'defeat' that Alexius was persuaded to withdraw.

Alexius now declared he would not aid the Crusade unless Antioch was given up to its rightful lord, and Bohemond's only reply was to make war on him, allied with Pisa. More and more crusaders came flocking through Byzantium, leaving a trail of destruction behind them, but by now the Turks, appreciating the danger, had united, and the new parties suffered crushing defeats. They also engaged Bohemond heavily, which gave Alexius the opportunity of taking back some of his lands.

Bohemond was now in a vice, clamped between Greek and Turk, and so in 1105 he announced his own death and had himself shipped home in a coffin to raise support. He naturally painted a black picture of the Emperor's conduct, making him the scape-goat for all the Crusaders' failure. In 1107 he shipped an army of 34,000 across the Adriatic to Valona (mid-way between Corfu and Durazzo) to begin his conquest of Alexius's empire.

But the Emperor was now an old hand, and was ready for him, besieging the tricky Norman in Valona, and keeping a strict naval watch to prevent supplies getting in. He spread dissension among the high command by allowing letters to be captured, letters which pretended to reply to Norman offers of treachery. In 1108 the starving army was forced to its knees, and Bohemond had to agree to the Emperor's every wish.

On the crest of a wave, Alexius now began negotiations in Italy, aimed at restoring Byzantine dominion there. In 1111 he treated with the Pisans, and the following year, taking advantage of the Pope's imbroglio with the Western Emperor, tried out the ground for his own candidature. It came to nothing, but the bid was a brave and ambitious one.

In 1114 he had to quell another Cuman invasion, and, using an elaborate phalanx formation of his own invention, organised a big push against the Turks, which was very successful. But he was now old and sick, and his last years were taken up with domestic affairs, preserving the dynasty. His ambitious daughter Anna wanted the throne for herself, and she had the strong support of her mother: both seem to have developed a bitter hatred for her younger brother John, the rightful heir. In 1118 the dying Emperor played his last diplomatic ruse, and got John proclaimed and crowned emperor, and hurried him to safety inside the Sacred Palace. Alexius died happy, whilst his wife Irene berated him for his duplicity.

Alexius was an intelligent and victorious ruler, a true Greek of the cast of Odysseus. He was passionately interested in philosophy and theology, and prone to organise great political debates in the middle of campaigns. He fostered education and Church reform, and worked mightily for orthodoxy. He rebuilt the army and navy from scratch into a powerful fighting force. There was little he could do about finance and the economy, for the exterior threats were too great: he simply reverted to fiddling—issuing copper coins himself, he insisted on collecting tax in gold. Above all he was a great politician, manipulating international and domestic politics, as well as his subjects and enemies, with masterly skill. In a dim age he was bright, in times of frightful crisis he kept his head.

His daughter Anna's biography, The Alexiad (Penguin, Harmondsworth, 1969), is a fascinating picture in depth. It has been edited and translated for Penguin Classics by E. R. A. Sewter.

Alfred the Great

We are lucky in knowing so much about Alfred the Great: first in that we have a contemporary biography of him by his friend and teacher Asser, and secondly that the same biography has survived the terrible attack made on it recently by Professor V. H. Galbraith, who denounced it as an eleventh-century forgery (his lecture, which he gave at a session of the Anglo-American Historical Conference, and which caused a wholly unnatural pandemonium there, is printed in his *Introduction to the Study of History* (C. A. Watts, London, 1964). A cogent reply was made by Professor Dorothy Whitelock, in the first annual Stenton Memorial Lecture, Reading, 1968).

Alfred has been justly named the Great, for he showed in himself a combination of virtues that had not been seen in Europe since the death of Charlemagne, and were all too rarely seen after his own death. Astonishingly, he also lacked the great vices that so often are found in great kings. He was patient and dogged, yet possessed of a great and idealistic vision, a notable war-leader, outwitting the military might that was shaking all Europe, he nonetheless found time to encourage learning by practical demonstration of what he, a latecomer to literacy, could do in that field; a deeply religious man, of almost mystical inclination, he was also able to utilise an inventive mechanical genius which astonished a world totally unused to novelty and discovery.

He was born in 849 at Wantage, the youngest son of the West Saxon king. He was plainly the favourite of the family, an attractive personality who outshone all his elder brothers. At the age of five he went to Rome, where he captivated Pope Leo IV, who indulged his fancy by making him a Roman Consul.[1] Two years later he accompanied his father to Rome again, and remained there a year, broadening his horizons in a way given to few in that age.

At home he loved Saxon songs drawn from the distant past, and this passion stayed with him for the rest of his life; he taught the same old songs to his children as an essential part of their education. But he had no formal teaching, and it was not until he was twelve that he learned to read, encouraged by his mother with the prize of a book of songs with a beautifully ornamental initial. Perhaps another part of his education lay in his father's re-marriage to the great-granddaughter of the Emperor Charlemagne, around whom his life seems to have inexorably modelled itself.

There was little time for thought or learning in Alfred's boyhood, for England stood under the mighty threat of ruin from the Danes. They had been raiding the country since 835, but in the years 850 and 854 great armies, numbered in the thousands, wintered over in England, and it was plain that something far more serious than simple plundering raids was to come.

In 865 the great army that everyone feared came, prepared to stay until it had drained the country of its resources. They got horses in East Anglia and set off on a tour of devastation: their plan was simple —they selected an easily defensible spot, built a strong fortress there, and then ravaged the country around until they were bought off; then they went to another part of the land and repeated the plan. In this way they reduced the kingdoms of Northumbria, Mercia and East Anglia (martyring its King Edmund in the process), and by 870 they were ready to take on Wessex.

Alfred's elder brother Æthelred had succeeded to the throne, and Alfred was serving with him as second-in-command when the army of Wessex moved forward to face the Danes. With their usual perspicacity, they had selected Reading as their fortress, building earth-works across the neck formed by the joining of the Thames and the Kennet; the Saxons flung themselves against the impenetrable defences and failed. The Danes were so overjoyed

---

[1] Some doubt has been cast on the authenticity of this first journey to Rome.

by their victory that they were tempted out to take up a position on the ridge at Ashdown, trying perhaps to defeat the Saxon forces whilst their morale was low. Both armies were drawn up in two battle-ranks, and Alfred joined battle before Æthelred, who refused to come until he had finished his prayers. Later on Asser visited the site, and recognised the stunted thorn-tree Alfred had described to him: 'Around this tree the opposing armies came together, with loud shouts from all sides, the one part to pursue their wicked course, the other to fight for their lives, their dearest ties and their country'. Perhaps the Danes were deceived into thinking they were fighting the whole Saxon army, for when Æthelred's fresh troops joined the fray, they fled.

Yet no battle, throughout the long years of war, was to be absolutely decisive; the Danes always had a stronghold to retreat to, and there were always reinforcements coming, in the early days from Denmark itself, but later from northern France and from the Danes already settled in England.

In April 871 Æthelred died, and Alfred succeeded, to be defeated almost immediately at Wilton. Asser explains: 'the Saxons had been worn out by eight battles in one year, against the pagans, of whom they had slain one king, nine earls and innumerable troops of soldiers, besides endless skirmishes, both by night and by day'. Alfred had to buy them off, an inauspicious beginning.

For four years there was some sort of peace, while the Danes reduced Mercia, installing a puppet king to look after it until they should need it. Then the army split in two, and one part went off to settle what is now Yorkshire, and the other, under the leadership of Guthrum and two other kings, went to Cambridge.

In 875 Guthrum invaded Wessex, but this time Alfred was ready for him, and despite his trickery, he was forced finally to leave and take up residence in the northern part of Mercia (Lincoln, Nottingham, Derby and Leicestershire). Not to be outdone, he came again, in a lightning

swoop in the early part of 878, and totally reduced the main part of Wessex. Up until this point the Danes had always kept camp during the Winter months (indeed the Saxons called them the 'Summer armies'), and the element of surprise was great. Alfred was forced to retire to one of the farthest parts of his kingdom, the marshy land of Athelney, where a false tradition credits him with burning cakes.

At this, the lowest point in his career, Alfred achieved his greatest success, which is a greater proof of his powers of leadership, his popularity and his military skill than any other evidence we have. Within seven weeks he had collected sufficient troops to burst out and totally defeat Guthrum at Eddington, force him to receive baptism, and agree to retire to East Anglia.

Yet while the Danes were in England, and on the high seas, there was to be no peace. In 884 another army landed, and Alfred had to take the field once more. This time his battles resulted in the occupation of London and the southern part of Mercia, and a treaty with Guthrum which established the boundary between Wessex and the Danes at Watling Street, as well as some sort of equality between Danes and English in Danish-held territory.

In 892 a further army came, under the leadership of Haesten, and Alfred was involved in a total reorganisation of his defences. An effective navy was built (the first recorded in English history), and the army was established on the basis that half the peasantry would be left at home whilst the other half was in the field, thus preserving a continuing force that would not disappear at harvest-time. Most important of all, Alfred learnt a lesson from the Danes and set up fortresses throughout his territory (we know of 25 in Wessex alone) to which the surrounding peoples could retreat in time of stress, and which the people were to keep up and garrison.

This war was the hardest Alfred fought, for the Danes had learned the value of forced marches at lightning speed—they seemed to be everywhere at once. Twice they were thrust out of Wessex, yet in 894 they were threatening London once more. Alfred dislodged them, and before he knew what was happening, they were at Bridgenorth, the other end of his kingdom, but at last, in 896, tired of continual defeat, though never absolutely routed, the great army at last dispersed.

Alfred had ridden out the various invasions, and had met them as the Roman Empire had failed to do, for he remained king in his own country, and with an enlarged domain as well, for he ruled Kent and southern Mercia. Nevertheless, whilst the rest of England (except the tiny kingdom of Bernicia in the far north) was under Danish rule, and whilst the Danes remembered their years of success, Wessex was not safe, and when he died in 899, his country remained on the defensive.

For Alfred, however, defence was not enough—he aimed also at restoration. In his introduction to his translation of the *Cura Pastoralis* he recalls 'what wise men there were formerly throughout England . . . and what happy times there were then; and how the kings who had power over the nation in those days obeyed God and his ministers; how they preserved peace, morality and order . . . I remembered also how I saw the country before it had been all ravaged and burned; how the churches throughout the whole of England stood filled with treasures and books.'

To restore this happy state, Alfred imported scholars from wherever they were to be found, from Mercia, Gaul, Saxony, and Wales, whence came Asser. Their first duty was to teach the king, and Alfred began to learn Latin in 887 in order to begin his great work of translation. He knew he could not begin the re-education of his people without books in the vernacular, for the teachers of Latin were too few for many to be able to learn that language at once.

He chose the first work for translation with some care: Pope Gregory the Great's guide to the duties of a bishop, a book which gave strong emphasis to the importance of education for the laity. Alfred aimed at having every free-born boy who could afford education (and who was unsuited to military service) being given the chance of learning to read English; those who did well, and wanted to progress should then be able to learn Latin. Asser clearly indicates that the royal children learned to read and write English and Latin in the palace school along 'with the children of almost all of the nobility, and many also who were not noble . . .'

To make sure that his translation had a good effect, a copy of the *Pastoral Care* was sent to each cathedral of his kingdom, each one clasped with a clasp worth 50 mancuses. Meanwhile Alfred was at work on his next translation, Orosius' *History of the World*, a history in the form of annals that may well have influenced the making of the Anglo-Saxon chronicles. Here Alfred added to the original notes and illustrations drawn from his experience which brought the book up to date. One such addition was the extensive account of the voyages into the farthest North made by Ohthere and Wulfstan, who had come to Alfred's court to tell of their wonderful experiences in Arctic waters.

The next book to be translated was Boethius's great work on the *Consolation of Philosophy*. This work, written by a great Roman statesman in the service of barbarians, facing a horrible death through no fault of his own, is the classic stoic account of the uses of adversity—how the true hero, the religious, thinking man, can take the fell chance of fate and make it serve as a purifying agent in the development of his soul. This was, without doubt, Alfred's favourite work, for had not fate dealt severely with him and his nation? So his nation must read it, and he must translate it for them to read.

The last translation was more of a commonplace-book than anything else. Asser describes how Alfred, when one of his scholars was reading, would pick out phrases to record and remember, and this book is very much the product of such activity. Based on a translation of Augustine's *Soliloquies*, it has a fund of quotations and everyday examples added by the king, all aimed at resolving the great problem of immortality. In the introduction Alfred describes himself as one gathering wood in a great forest, which is quite large enough for others to enter and gather for themselves materials for every kind of building one might imagine. This metaphor is strangely moving, for Asser describes Alfred as a bee, gathering honey from all sorts of flowers in all sorts of places, and storing it thickly in the comb. There is no doubt that both metaphors are apt, particularly in their reference to industry, for Alfred must have worked immensely hard on his translations, as well as on gathering materials to supplement them. He did not stand in any tradition of writing, for he was exploring a new medium in using the vernacular.

Alfred gave full support to the Church which meant so much to him, founding a monastery at Athelney (which he had to fill with foreign monks, because so few Englishmen were available), and a nunnery at Shaftesbury, of which his daughter became prioress.

He also issued a code of law, for the first time in England for a century, collecting the best laws from the codes of Wessex, Kent and Mercia. Emphasis was laid on the limitation of blood-feuds, the protection of the weak and loyalty to one's lord, but in other respects the code was strangely conservative.

Besides building the great fortresses for the defence of his realm, Alfred also built palaces, and encouraged artificers of all kinds to decorate and glorify them. He was plainly of an inventive and scientific turn of mind, though the only invention that has come down to us is his candle-clock, whereby six candles were marked with twelve divisions to show the passing of the day. When the wind howled in 'through the doors and windows of the churches, the cracks in the partitions, the plankings,

or the thin walls of a tent' and blew his candles out, he invented a wooden lantern with a horn window to protect them.

Alfred was a model of successful virtue. We read in Asser, however, of his one weakness: he was constantly troubled by a racking pain throughout his body that no doctor could diagnose; but it is plain from Asser's statements that the fear of this disease was a far greater difficulty for Alfred than the disease itself: he dreaded becoming blind, leprous or imbecile, and when the pains he thought about so much finally came, he was so glad that they were not what he had dreaded that the gloom that had brought them on disappeared. Today he would be called a hypochondriac.

For a biography see C. Plummer: *The Life and Times of Alfred the Great* (Oxford Univ. Press, 1902; Haskell House, New York, 1968).

St. Anselm

St. Anselm was born in 1033, at Aosta, at the foot of the Great St. Bernard Pass. His family were decayed nobility, and meant little to Anselm: he didn't get on with his father, and when his mother died about 1056, he left home and crossed the Alps into Burgundy. Three years later he had moved on to Normandy, to the abbey at Bec, where the teaching of Lanfranc had built up a flourishing school.

Lanfranc taught him logic, and gave him access to a good library of pure texts, and it was on the basis of dialectical and grammatical skill, and a wide and deep reading of the Fathers of the Church (particularly Augustine) that Anselm was to build his theological work of later years. But for ten years he seems to have written nothing, preferring to immerse himself in his vocation as a Benedictine: obedience lay at the heart of his thinking, and in it he found a deep joy.

When he began to write in 1070, it was to be a set of prayers for religious ladies (the first recipient being a daughter of William the Conqueror). These prayers and meditations showed a strong piety that was able to communicate its passion and urgency through the skilled use of elaborate imagery. The mind was exciting itself to a full knowledge of its own baseness and examining the high example of the saints, and particularly of the Blessed Virgin Mary.

In 1077 he began to work on his treatises on the nature of God and the proof of His existence. He determined to work in a new way: he would not choose the traditional pattern of commenting on established texts, nor would he prove his arguments by reference to authorities at all. Simply, he would meditate, as a philosopher, on a central problem, and use his intellect as a tool of faith. This process was disturbing, for he found his mind wandering from the monastic services, and he seriously wondered whether the questions he was trying to answer had been posed to him by the devil. Then, in the middle of Matins, the ontological proof of the existence of God came to him suddenly, as a revelation after many months of fruitless thought, and he was jubilant.

He defined God as 'that than which nothing greater can be thought', and then examined the proposition put forward by some that God does not exist outside of men's minds. He pointed out that others believed God to exist outside of men's minds, and plainly the 'God' they thought of was greater than the 'God' the unbelievers thought of. So, by definition, the God of whom the believers spoke was the true God, and when the unbeliever said there was no God, he was not speaking of the same thing. Therefore it is impossible to say with truth 'God does not exist outside of men's minds'.

He was to continue and expand this work on the nature of God after he became Archbishop of Canterbury, during the years 1097–8, in his book *Cur Deus homo*. In this work he tried to explain the necessity of the Incarnation—why God had to become man to work out his plan of salvation. It was in answer to contemporary questions that were being raised in the new schools of Europe, and was a novel approach to a difficult and controversial subject. Had he not been Anselm, with a European reputation, he might have found himself on a heresy charge for some of the statements he made here, for he denied the traditional doctrine of the Devil's rights in the world.

In 1093, on a visit to England, Anselm was chosen against his will to succeed his master Lanfranc as Archbishop of Canterbury. He tried every means to prevent the election and its confirmation—even keeping his fist closed when the pastoral staff was pressed to it. He had no interest, or, to be honest, ability, in the hurly-burly of the world outside the monastery, and in attempting to apply his principles of scrupulous obedience and rectitude, he found himself fighting for matters of no importance, whilst vital battles were lost.

As he said of the king, William Rufus, and himself, 'You are yoking a young bull and an old sheep to the same plough'. It was impossible that they should work in harness, and although the actual points on which they fought were of little importance, within four years Anselm was reduced to a state of helpless and hopeless depression. He could, so it seemed, do nothing for the Church without the King's aid and assent, and he could not gain that without bending his principles.

So Anselm went to Rome in the vague hope that the Pope could help him, though, as he himself said, his was simply a case of the wrong man for the job. Finding no assistance in Rome, he stayed with a friend in France, until he heard of Rufus's death in 1100, and returned to England in hope of a better sovereign.

Henry I welcomed Anselm, for he was in a weak position at the beginning of his reign; but although he was prepared to temporise for a while, as soon as he was strong enough he would be as autocratic towards the Church as Rufus had ever been. The battle was waged on a difficult ground: Urban II had recently extended his denunciation of lay control in the election and elevation of priests and bishops, to the ceremony of homage. Anselm, as literal-minded and obedient as ever, insisted that from the moment of his return to England, no bishop should do homage to a secular lord for his see.

This was no small point, for the Church's part in the feudal structure was an important one, and once the ceremony of homage was removed, the crown stood to lose a lot. So Henry opened negotiations with Rome to have the inconvenient reform suspended. The successor of Urban II appeared to be more pliable, and Anselm was put in the embarrassing position of insisting on a reform at the urgings of a papacy which now seemed to be quietly forgetting the whole thing. So he went to Rome to find out the truth of the matter, only to find himself defeated by Henry's infinitely more cunning diplomats, and now excluded from returning to England, unless he gave in to the king on the question of homage.

Anselm calmly settled once more in Lyons, amongst his friends, and many said that he was using this affair as a pretext for avoiding the duties of an archbishop. However, in 1105 Henry confiscated the archiescopal estates, and this stirred Anselm to action. He had a very simple view of his responsibility before God as archbishop: he had been handed a clearly defined bundle of rights, privileges and possessions which he held in trust, and which he must hand over to his successor complete and in good order. So he threatened the king with excommunication. Henry was at that moment heavily engaged in the taking of Normandy, and could not afford the odium of excommunication: he meekly gave back the estates.

It is typical of Anselm that he did not take this opportunity of pressing his other demands on the king, for he was no politician. The king was, and he had used his time well: by 1106 he had come to an agreement with the Pope whereby he was allowed to keep clerical homage. Anselm returned to England looking very foolish,

having gone into exile for a principle no one seemed to value, and suffering a mighty defeat in the office he meant to defend with his life. He died in 1109.

His career cannot have seemed impressive to the world in which he lived: as an archbishop he was patently a failure, and as a scholar, though he achieved a wide reputation, he had little influence until at least a century after his death. His theology, with its strong linguistic bias, has aroused considerable interest among philosophers of our own day. But in the long run, he lives for us because of the skill of his biographer Eadmer, the self-consciously English monk of Canterbury who, along with others, recorded the sweet conversation of the master they plainly loved. Anselm's conversation was the improvisation of a virtuoso philosopher, deep, yet embroidered with delicate imagery that charmed, and pithy statements that stood in the memory. Anselm was angry when he found that Eadmer was writing his biography, and ordered him to destroy it; but Eadmer, who so deeply respected his master's love of obedience and horror of even the mildest sin, was wise enough to make a copy before carrying out the instruction.

See R. W. Southern: *St. Anselm and his Biographer* (Cambridge Univ. Press, 1963). Professor Southern has also edited Eadmer's *Life of St. Anselm* (Nelson, Medieval Text Series, London, 1963; Humanities Press, New York, 1962).

St. Thomas Aquinas

St. Thomas Aquinas was born about the year 1225 in the castle of Roccasecca, near Aquino, halfway between Rome and Naples. His family were Norman knights in the service of Frederick II, by no means a likely ground for a great theologian to spring from. They enjoyed literature and song—one of Thomas's brothers was a troubadour of note—and his father willingly sent Thomas, his youngest child, to school in the Abbey of Monte Cassino when he was five. Here he received a thorough grounding in traditional religion and scholarship, but for a young man of boundless energy and free-flying imagination, an old Benedictine monastery was no home, and at the age of nineteen he removed himself to the new secular university at Naples.

Here was a fascinating new atmosphere, based partly on the emphasis on vocational education, but more importantly on the devoted study of the works of Aristotle and of the Arab scholars who had commented upon him. Aristotle was exciting not only because he gave new and fresh ideas to his medieval students, but also because there was so much of him, and not all his writings had yet been discovered and transmitted to the West. Indeed, it was only late in his career that Thomas was to get really good translations of the latest works from his protégé, William of Moerbecke. Aristotle was like a vein of pure metal that showed no signs of giving out, and promised great riches. So glorious was this promise that some scholars, like Siger of Brabant, were to become intoxicated by him, proclaiming that all truth lay in him. Siger paid the price, stabbed to death by his secretary when he was barely forty. This was the strength of Aristotle's influence.

What Aristotle did for the Middle Ages was to restore some faith in the real world, to give back respect to the evidence of the senses, to make the tangible seem worthy once more. For generations Christian scholars had elevated all that was spiritual and had debased the worldly and sensual. They had made everything man touched, saw or smelled a bogey of evil: the world and the flesh belonged to the Devil. How repressive such a doctrine can be for the whole world (though for the few it can be the opposite—a release) can be judged in the upsurge of enthusiasm and delight in the Western world at the rediscovery of the work of the ancient Greek.

All this was at Thomas's feet when he came to Naples, but he had the joy of making a second discovery—the Dominican order. To someone brought up in the cloistered seclusion of a Benedictine monastery this was joy indeed: for to the student revolutionaries of the thirteenth century Dominic was the hero Ché Guevara is now. His passionate evangelism, his ability to discard the petty comforts of a decadent civilisation, and his determination to be at the hottest front of the war all appealed strongly. Above all he was an intellectual who succeeded in the hurly-burly world: he listened respectfully to the heretic's argument, and then converted him by sheer weight of proof. Many longed to be like him, and put to use the book-learning so hardly won, which before had seemed irrelevant.

So Thomas must have felt, but not his family. His brothers caught him and locked him up to knock some sense into him. For a year they tried every ruse: they sent in a seductive young lady who did her best, but Thomas had a vision that cured all that. An angel appeared in the night and girded his loins so tightly that he cried out with pain and woke up. After that he never felt sexual desire. Perhaps this is one of the most fascinating miraculous visions of the Middle Ages for the psychologist to interpret, for Thomas was passionate for truth and only told the story to his confessor very late in life under a vow of secrecy.

His brothers gave up a hopeless case and Thomas journeyed on—on foot as a Dominican must—to Paris where Albertus Magnus was lecturing, working out his great scheme of interpreting Aristotle for the Latin West. Thomas became his devoted student and followed him to Cologne when he was called there to set up a Dominican school.

At 27, Thomas was recalled to teach in Paris, where the University was rent with faction: the secular and monastic teachers hated the increasing power of the mendicants, who seemed able to convert the leading professors with ease. A boycott was organised against Thomas and Bonaventure, the Franciscan professor, and was not broken until the Pope specifically intervened.

Thomas's teaching was brilliant and novel, and formed the foundation of all his writing. His aim was to introduce his pupils to the 'wonderfulness' of each topic; he held at least three disputations a week, often of the new kind of his own invention, where students flung in questions, comments and challenges for him to review and answer. Each argument was given a respectful treatment—what he called 'benevolent interpretation'—before he would turn to its dissection and possible demolition. To build the new structure he drew on biblical and patristic sources with consummate skill, and of course Aristotle; but other philosophers were held in high esteem—he makes considerable use of Platonic and Neoplatonic sources. At no stage, however, does he present the blockbuster of authority—each argument, from whatever source, is examined with minute care before it is put into its place in the entirely fresh edifice.

In 1259 he was recalled to Italy where he was busy setting up Dominican schools and advising the Pope on his great project of uniting the Latin and Orthodox Churches. In 1269 he was sent back to Paris, for there dispute was once again high: not only secular and regular against mendicant, but conservative against Aristotelian: Siger of Brabant had taken a hand. Aristotle was now seen as a great threat to the Church, where once he had been held to be a splendid aid, a witness for truth. The world regarded its new discovery with new eyes, as, in our own days, we began to see the possibilities of the splitting of the atom.

In these last years in Paris Thomas wrote with a fantastic energy, at all hours of the day and night. Indeed he was once the king's guest at dinner, and, having had a sudden inspiration, called loudly for his secretary, forgetting where he was. Many books flowed (his collected works in the printed edition fill thirty folio volumes) but the greatest was the *Summa Theologica*, that most comprehensive work that was to earn him the title of *Doctor communis*, the authority to whom everyone must turn.

In 1272 he was called home to Naples to work for the Dominicans there, and two years later, still journeying on foot, he died on the way to the Council of Lyons, for which he had done so much of the preparation. A few months before his death he had stopped writing, leaving his great *Summa* unfinished. He had had a vision of the truth after which he had searched all his short life with such busy concentration and compared with that 'everything I have written seems to me as straw'. To us his writings are the vision, especially his prayer 'to be serene without frivolity, and mature without self-importance'.

The biography by G. K. Chesterton: *St. Thomas Aquinas* (Hodder and Stoughton, London, 1933), is universally recommended, but I have used here Josef Pieper's *Introduction to Thomas Aquinas* (Faber and Faber, London, 1963). The Medieval sources for his life have been edited by K. Forster (Longmans, Harlow, 1959).

Attila

'The Scourge of God' explains very little about the nature of Attila the Hun: more particularly he was the scourge of Rome, for he represented the extreme of the ideals of barbarianism, and his thinking was the very opposite of that of the civilised Roman. A Roman ambassador said of him, 'his very great fortune and the power derived from good luck exalted him so that he could not endure just proposals unless he thought they came from himself.' This fine judgement of the man was given to Priscus, who himself went on an important embassy to Attila, and left a long and valuable account, from which we can gain a clearer picture than is possible of other barbarian leaders (a translation is given in C. D. Gordon's *The Age of Attila* (Univ. of Michigan Press, Ann Arbor, 1960)).

Attila was described by Jordanes as 'a man born to shake the races of the world'. Proud and haughty of carriage, looking sternly from side to side, short, but big-headed and broad-shouldered, with small eyes, flat nose, swarthy complexion and a scanty grizzled beard. Though a warlike man 'he was personally restrained in action, most impressive in council, gracious to suppliants, and generous to those to whom he had once given his trust'. Priscus notes his sternness at a banquet he attended, where a fool was brought on who convulsed everyone else: 'neither in speech nor action did he reveal that he had any laughter in him, except when his youngest son came in and stood before him. He pinched the lad's cheeks and looked on him with serene eyes.' Even this display of affection is explained by the fact that a soothsayer had foretold that Attila's race would fail, but would be restored by his youngest son.

As a ruler he expected absolute devotion, regarding all whom he had conquered or gained tribute from as his slaves absolutely. Anyone who had fled from his domains into the Empire had to be returned, or Attila would make war, and time and again the Romans were in the humiliating position of returning to Attila those who had fled for asylum, knowing the dreadful fate in store for them. Priscus tells with shame the details of the first treaty between Rome and Attila, whereby the Romans had to promise not only to return deserters and refugees, but also such Romans as had been made captive by the Huns, but had managed to escape home without ransom being paid. Amongst those who were sent back were two children 'Mama and Atakum, scions of the royal house. Those who received them crucified them in Carsum, a Thracian fortress, thus exacting the penalty of their flight.' There is little wonder that Attila inspired so great a hatred in his time.

Attila was left as joint ruler of the Huns with his brother Bleda, but he killed him in 445, and acceded to sole rule over tribes stretching from Austria to Persia. At first he dealt easily with the Western Empire, perhaps because its leading figure

Aëtius had been a hostage with the Huns, and knew them well. He gave the Romans troops, and they gave him a trained staff of secretaries and administrative officers, as well as a disguised tribute: his pay as a general of the Roman army. With the Eastern Empire he dealt more harshly, demanding from them vast sums of money, and continuously raising his demands on ridiculous pretexts (for example, that a bishop had dug up treasure chests from the Hunnish royal graveyard and made off with them) from 350 pounds of gold, to 700 pounds, to 2,100 pounds per year. The taxes that had to be levied to pay these imposts were so heavy in Constantinople that 'men who were formerly well-to-do displayed their wives' ornaments and their furniture in the market-place.'

The results for Attila were interesting, for we find him living in a luxury that was placed severely within the context of his hard Asiatic background. His palace was as large as any city, built with wooden boards and beams so well jointed that they seemed one complete and highly polished surface; there were towered feasting-halls, and a full-scale Roman bath, built of stone imported at great cost by a Roman captive (who had thought to buy his freedom by this act, but was made chief bath-man instead). When Attila arrived maidens went out in rows to meet him, bearing above their heads canopies of fine white linen. Priscus describes a feast he attended at the palace: at the door they were given cups of wine, with which to offer prayers before taking their seats. Along either wall were chairs, and at the top end were the couches of Attila and his notabilities, ranged in front of the steps that led up to his bed, with its fine white linen sheets and coloured embroidery hangings. Attila now began saluting those present in order of seniority by drinking to them out of an ivy-wood cup, and the man so toasted had to stand to receive this salute, and return it. Each guest had his own cup-bearer. After all these toasts, tables were brought in, and the guests ate sumptuous foods from gold and silver plate; but Attila ate only meat from a wooden dish. Priscus noted also how plain his dress was, and that he never wore gold or jewels. Between each course further toasts took place, everyone drinking to the health of Attila. As darkness fell, torches were brought in, and the barbarians sang songs in praise of Attila's victories, which roused the young, and brought tears to the eyes of the old. Finally two fools came on to entertain everyone but Attila, who plainly didn't care for such things. At this point the ambassadors left, though it was obvious the carousals would go on the whole night through.

But these riches were rapidly draining the Eastern Empire dry, and a crazy plot was laid to assassinate Attila. The Emperor's chamberlain tried to bribe Edeco, Attila's bodyguard, to murder him, promising a palace with a golden roof and a life of luxury as a reward. Edeco naturally told Attila all the details, and the embassy that was bringing the money to bribe the other guards was quietly relieved of its gold and sent home unharmed, after a good telling-off from Attila. This was a great insult, for the barbarian was showing all too clearly how he could brush off the puny efforts of Byzantium without any bother at all. He was at this time (c. 449) supremely self-confident, having had a sword discovered in his domains which was widely believed to be that of Ares, god of War: luck was on his side.

The year 450 placed him in a quandary, however, for he could not tell which of the two Roman Empires he should attack first. The feckless Theodosius II—ruler of the East—had died, and the much stronger Marcian had succeeded and refused at once to continue the tribute. However, he felt he had an even stronger case for invading the Western Empire, and there was more to gain there. The fact is that Attila believed in his rights and was very legalistic about his aggression, though it is difficult to understand why he made so much of what to others were small matters: he had

been, for example, absolutely furious with the Emperor Theodosius for not keeping his promise of a rich wife for Attila's Latin secretary Constantius. But the Western Empire's debt was to Attila in person: briefly, the Emperor's sister, Honoria, had been caught going to bed with her butler, and he had been executed, whilst she was deprived of her royal title and a steady marriage was planned for her. She also seems to have spent some time in the strict nunnery-like confines of the household of the imperial ladies-in-waiting at Constantinople. Being a woman of spirit, she sent her ring to Attila, promising herself and half the Western Empire if he would come and avenge and rescue her. Attila, though he had many wives, was deeply attracted by the scheme, and, not recognising this to be a silly woman's fit of pique immediately demanded what she had offered as a right.

He also had another debt to collect in Rome. Long ago, when he was ruling with Bleda, they had been besieging Sirmium, and the bishop of that city had contacted Attila's Latin secretary, giving him the golden bowls from the cathedral treasury, which were to be used to ransom him if the city fell, or, if he died, to ransom other citizens. The secretary took no account of his agreement, and after the city had fallen, being in Rome on business, deposited the golden bowls with Silvanus the manager of Armius' Bank there, in return for a loan. Bleda and Attila suspected Constantius of keeping back loot, and when he returned, they crucified him. Attila now demanded not only the return of the bowls, but also the bank-manager, whom he considered a thief of his property.

Valentinian III had an access of courage, a rare event. He refused Honoria, because his mother wanted her kept; he refused the bowls because they were sacred vessels and shouldn't fall into pagan hands; he even refused the bank-manager, because he had not acted as a thief. Attila, quivering with a sense of the injustice of this world, moved off to take what was his.

He met with more than he had bargained for. Other barbarian tribes had viewed his increasing power with deep concern, and flocked to the Roman standards, brought in by the subtle Roman general Aëtius, who had spent his youth as a hostage with the Huns, had commanded armies of Huns when he was on good terms with Attila, and so knew their ways. As Gibbon says, in 452 on the Mauriac plain in Gaul 'the nations from the Volga to the Atlantic were assembled', and the result, though perhaps nearer a draw, is accounted the last victory of the Western Empire.

Attila swayed off towards Rome, but famine and disease hampered his progress; also there was a rumour that the Eastern Empire was sending a large army west to fight him. Superstition also struck hard, for Attila remembered how Alaric had died shortly after sacking Rome. Perhaps, after all, Honoria (who was in her mid-thirties) and a terrified bank-manager were not worth the effort. Then came Pope Leo I to plead for Rome's safety. That was the last straw, and Attila withdrew. Naturally, the Church claimed the victory as hers alone.

Having cut his losses, Attila decided to take on the Eastern Empire instead, as he should have done in the first place. In high good humour he decided to take another wife, the beautiful young Ildico (who appears in the *Nibelungenlied* as Kriemhild). He gave a mighty feast on his wedding night, and then retired, dead drunk, to lie on his back. His nose began to bleed, and he to swallow blood. Next morning, late on, with hangovers, his followers found him dead, with Ildico still in her bridal veil, weeping, not having dared to move.

They pitched his silken tent in the middle of a great plain, and galloped round it, declaiming a paean of praise. A great grave was dug, and everyone got drunk: they put him in a coffin of gold, then into one of silver, and finally into one of iron. At night they buried him with all the trophies he had won in battle, and all his royal panoply; they had the grave half filled, then killed the diggers and buried them above him. Within a year the empire he had built up lay in ruins around his unmarked grave.

For a magnificently illustrated description of the treasures of the barbarians, see E. D. Philips: *The Royal Hordes* (Thames and Hudson, London, 1965).

St. Augustine of Hippo

'A race, curious to know the lives of others, slothful to mend their own. Why seek they to hear from me what I am . . . And how know they when from myself they hear of myself, whether I say true . . . ?'

These words of rebuke and warning come from the famous tenth book of the *Confessions* of St. Augustine of Hippo. Undeniably the greatest and most influential of the Church Fathers, he was also that great rarity, a saint who by introspection and great writing has conveyed to us in an autobiography of overwhelming power the essence of his fascinating personality. Written when he was in his late forties, the *Confessions* show deep self-examination, and feats of memory that allow him to write of his earliest childhood, even suggesting that the life in the womb was a part of his history, could he but recall it. His penetration and understanding is remarkable, especially in his picture of his earliest years, as a child struggling to master self-will sufficiently to obtain approval, and as an adolescent longing for friendship. He recalls the embarrassment he felt at his father's observing him at the baths for the traces of his growth to manhood, and the crazy vandalisms of his 'gang'. Above all he understands the atmosphere of fear that children and youths breathe daily, and rails at the cant about childhood innocence and joy: he recalls bitterly the beatings for laziness administered by people who indulged in laziness, and the laughter of adults who failed to understand the terror and bitterness they inspired. His work is a great text of educational psychology and reveals with immense literary skill much of what was 'discovered' and conveyed in such turgid ways fifteen centuries later.

He was born in 354 at Thagaste, which is now Souk Arrhas in Algeria. His father, Patrick, was a poor freeman of the town (though well-connected), and remained a pagan until shortly before his death. His mother, Monica, was a devout Christian, and utterly devoted to her son. Augustine recalled at her death her 'enslavement' to him, and would have wept like a child, were he not responsible for quietening the grief of his own son.

A wealthy relative helped to educate the young Augustine, and though he describes himself as a lazy and obstinate child, hating Greek, he was a natural scholar, who went from one success to another. A natural Latin stylist, his love for the classics and the sophistication of fine writing never left him. At Carthage he learned rhetoric, the oratorical skill of Cicero, as a preparation for the course in law, which would open to the ambitious provincial any of the high administrative posts of the Empire. But suddenly his father died, and family responsibilities made it essential for him to abandon his course and take up teaching, first in Carthage, but later in Rome and Milan.

He still hoped for high office, but dogged by the requirement of supporting his family, he was unable to do many of the things he had planned. He could not marry for the moment, for a high official such as a provincial governor had to have a wife of the same caste. So, following the normal practice of the day, he took a concubine, whom he seems to have loved dearly, and only put her away at the urging of his mother when it seemed (falsely as it turned out) that he might at last make a judicious marriage. She bore him a son, Adeodatus—the God-given—who showed great promise, Augustine himself standing 'in awe' of his talent, wit and intellect, but he was to die before he was out of his teens.

Meanwhile his agonising quest for a personal faith had continued. At first his mother's Church had seemed to present little of value: the young man trained in all the sophistication of the Roman classics found the Bible an illogical compendium of folklore, with nothing beautiful about it. He turned to the followers of Mani, who had created a kind of religious Esperanto— a universal religion combined of the best elements of East and West, which based itself on the simple description of the world as a war between good and evil— light and darkness. There were obvious ways, said the Manicheans, of increasing in oneself the power of light, and so driving out darkness. It was all very regular and orderly; sensible, yet also attractive—for the deep appeal of the East was combined skilfully with the logic and sophistication of the West.

Augustine remained a Manichean for nine years—at first with the hectic enthusiasm of youth, but became increasingly concerned at the inadequacy, the man-made-ness of his faith. It was a far more complicated matter than Mani had thought. There seemed to be no answer, until Augustine went to Milan in search of a higher posting, and met Ambrose. He felt a deep attraction to this cultured man— musician, scholar, orator of great power, heir to all the virtues of the Latin West, but one who believed in the Christianity of the Bible. With his sweet arguments he could gently dispose of all the doubts that beset Augustine.

In 386 Augustine was converted, struggling with himself in a terrible agony, which took place in his garden, alone but for his stout friend Alypius. The description of this scene, book eight of the *Confessions*, is one of the finest pictures of a soul struggling with itself and God in the whole of literature. The rather ordinary Alypius—whose only real struggle had seemed to be with his passion for the circus games of death—stood by, unable to help.

The following year Augustine was baptised by Ambrose, and his son Adeodatus with him. He declared for celibacy and, deeply influenced by the writers of the

Christian era who followed Plato, planned to set up a small community to discuss philosophical and allied religious questions. After the death of his mother, he returned, in 388, to his birthplace, there to set up his ascetical academy.

In 391, however, he visited Hippo, and there found a people who desperately needed his help: he, a learned man, a philosopher and budding theologian, and an African, was needed within the Church, not in a retired community. Despite his pleas to be allowed to return to Thagaste, he was forced to be ordained, and within four years he was made coadjutor bishop of the place.

Now his attention was forced towards the larger scale of Church order, to the problems of a world on the verge of collapse. Philosophy must be forgotten, except for spare moments, and friendly dispute must be replaced by real argument. Theology must take the centre of his thoughts. In these years he wrote his *Confessions*, clearing the ground for a new period of Biblical study and active churchmanship.

He was to face a series of monstrous problems, and his reactions to each showed a growing command which was to leave him at his death the most respected authority in the Church. The first difficulty he had to deal with was the Donatist Schism, almost a century old when he came to Hippo. This futile but intensely bitter dispute grew from an incident of the years of persecution, when Caecilian, a bishop of Carthage had, perhaps weakly, given up his books to the authorities in obedience to an imperial mandate. A puritanical faction of the African Church had seen this as base treachery to the faith, and, following Cyprian, had declared that an unworthy priest could not give valid sacraments. Many considered this an extremist viewpoint, and denounced the Donatists, who responded by withdrawing their obedience from all priests and bishops who drew their consecration from the hated Caecilian, and virtually set up their own church. The Donatist Church was practically identical with the Catholic, but so separate did the two become that they would not have contact with one another. This silliness was hardened into hatred by violence: illiterate followers of the Donatists began to make forays against the Catholics, who replied with persecution.

Religious strife this petty, embittered and insoluble is not unknown in our own times, and one can sympathise with Augustine, whose mind was trained to answer real heresies, as he tried to deal with this non-heresy. He argued, and wrote, he negotiated, but all to no purpose, and gradually he was dragged, protesting ever less strongly, into a position of condoning the violent answer of repression.

For violence was in the air, and was at that moment presenting much larger, less parochial problems. In 410 the barbarians sacked Rome, and crowds of noble refugees flocked to Africa, bewailing the end of the world: where was the protection a faith should offer—where were the answers to the many fervent prayers for help? The city that stood at the centre of the world, now lay crashing into ruins, and slowly the feeling spread amongst the more hysterical elements that this was divine retribution, not of the Christians' God, but the anger of the pagan gods whom they had rejected.

This was a problem Augustine could deal with, something one could argue out, and this he did in his noble work on *The City of God*. There is a city that is eternal, he wrote, and there is a city that is doomed to fall, not now, but at judgement day; the fall of Rome is merely an incident (full of significance, without doubt) on the road to the eternal city. Meanwhile the two cities are intermingled here below, and those who will be saved and those who will be damned must live side by side, and we cannot tell which are which, for appearances are deceptive. Augustine knew a man of 84 who had lived continent and pious for 25 years with his good wife, who went out marketing one day and brought home a slave-girl he had bought for his pleasure. Augustine's sense of shock may be, for us, slightly misplaced, but he certainly has a point. So he provides a discourse on how to live in this world before that day when the City of God should be finally separated from the city of man, and all will be revealed. In a sense he was harking back a little to his Platonist days, and providing for a collapsing world another *Republic*.

Next he was to face the menace of Pelagianism, a long dispute during which he crystallised his doctrine of grace, and hardened his views on predestination. Pelagius was a Briton, possibly a lawyer, who came to Rome and was deeply shocked by what he saw: the injustice, the license, the pouring away of resources in feckless waste, and the depression and purposelessness of the place. He had all the fire and passion of the Welsh preacher, and soon won converts—rich Roman widows, fanatical young law-students—by and large a motley crew of eccentrics. He himself was not an extremist, and it was the misguided interpretations his disciples put upon his ideas that really caused the trouble. They denied the existence of original sin, and the need for childhood baptism, when he had simply denied that Adam's sin was conveyed through the act of reproduction. They said he had declared man's perfectibility without the aid of God's grace, whereas he had postulated that man must make an act of will to do well, though he needs God's grace in doing so; he was attempting to defy the languid piety that sat still and did nothing. Whilst he pointed out to the rich that they were not conforming to Christ's expressed teachings, a British colleague was touring Sicily preaching an apostolic poverty that verged on communism, in his name.

Pelagius the Church might have tolerated, but not the bumptious Pelagians, and in answer to their doctrines (and indeed to those of Pelagius himself) Augustine dwelt on God's grace. He was hard and pitiless in enunciating the doctrine of predestination, but he urgently preached that his message was really one of overwhelming love. For all men are worthy of damnation—not one may be saved by his own will; men sunk in sin cannot turn towards God unless he moves them by his grace. And it is surely a wonderful act of mercy that he should turn to save some of those on the road to hell. Augustine had examined his own soul minutely, and knew that from babyhood he had been filled with sin. We may smile at his agonised memory of an expedition to steal pears—not to eat, but just for the sheer joy of wicked vandalism and theft. Yet he tells us that people are foolish to smile indulgently and call this childish innocence—it is sin: a child moves from sins involving 'nuts and balls and sparrows . . . to [those of] gold and manors and slaves, just as severer punishments replace the cane'.

Man does not choose to extricate himself from the mire of sin, God moves him of his bountiful mercy, and Augustine had felt himself moved in that garden in Milan. The corrolary is unavoidable, for if God is the prime mover in the matter of salvation, he must be the one who chooses, elects and predestines individuals to salvation. Those who cry 'favouritism' are acting as children: God's choice may not be criticised.

Augustine beat the Pelagians, but the world found his doctrine hard to accept, and the Church gradually modified it; but it remained a moving force, to shake many in the Middle Ages, and more at the time of the Reformation.

Towards the end of his life Augustine set about correcting and presenting his vast corpus of works as an aid to those who came later. He had 93 works to his name, but he was meticulous, and the great library he presented to the world remained a fund of orthodox theology to guide the footsteps of the weak. In essence, no later theologian could carry on his work without consulting Augustine, and few went further than he in this holy science; those who did were standing on his massive shoulders.

He stayed at his post in Hippo, though the Vandals pressed ever nearer, destroying and corrupting. Augustine was unmoved, and died in 430, just a year before his town was evacuated before the oncoming barbarians.

For a biography, see the study by Peter Brown: *Augustine of Hippo: A Biography* (Faber and Faber, London, 1967; Univ. of California Press, 1969). This is one of the most outstanding biographies produced in recent years, and has a worthy subject. The best translation of the *Confessions* is that by F. J. Sheed, but there are many available.

Roger Bacon

Roger Bacon was born in 1214 into a substantial English family. One of his brothers became a knight, and another was, like him, a scholar, and Roger himself claims that before he joined the Franciscans he had spent some £2,000 on books and experimental materials, so the family must have been wealthy indeed.

He studied first at Oxford, which was flourishing under the benign influence of Robert Grosseteste, taking the arts course, but never going very far into the higher reaches of theology. This was because he felt a profound disapproval for the methods of teaching, and indeed the whole approach of the theologians of his day. He considered that they ignored many important branches of study in the fields of philosophy and science which were necessary to a true understanding of theology.

He taught philosophy in both Oxford and Paris, continuing in his study of Aristotle, who was frowned upon in Paris at that time. He took his inspiration from a pseudo-Aristotelian work called *The Secret of Secrets*, which developed a system of mystical philosophy from the materials of the natural sciences, and offered to all who might penetrate the veil of secrecy, power and mastery in this world through scientific knowledge.

In Paris Bacon gave at least eight courses of lectures on Aristotle, but lectures in which his students had an active and intelligent part. He allowed them to chip in with ideas and suggestions, and to challenge his statements to the uttermost.

About the year 1250, Bacon returned to Oxford to more intensive study of the natural sciences, but after two years he joined the Franciscans. This was a strange decision for a tetchy and often selfish scholar, totally unaccustomed to discipline. But the Oxford convent may have offered peace and quiet, and it did have Grosseteste's library. He could continue to teach, which he plainly enjoyed, and if he hated the menial tasks the Franciscans insisted upon him doing, he liked their strict morality and genuine enthusiasm for getting a job done.

He now set out to prepare a great synthesis of all scientific knowledge, a task no one had seriously attempted since the days of his revered Aristotle. This involved him in learning subject after subject. The texts of Aristotle were corrupt and the translations were bad, so he had to learn Greek. Mathematics and alchemy had to be mastered, and a whole range of disciplines comprehended. Plainly he could not do it all himself, and he was for ever on the watch for helpers. He heard William of Rubruck's fascinating account of his travels in the East, and got permission from alchemists to attend their experiments. He himself carried out a number of experiments, mainly in the field of optics—it is rather charming to find the great and rather fearsome scholar blowing bubbles in order to study the rainbow effect!

At the same time as he was collecting this vast range of materials about science, he was working out the scheme into which it would fit; for he planned to use his battery of scientific knowledge and skills to revolutionise theology, to make the work of the Church more effective. He openly despised and derided the theologians of his own time (including the much-respected Franciscan master Alexander of Hales), calling them ignorant and worthless men, who had no grounds for their theorising.

Perhaps influenced by Joachim of Flora and the Spirituals, he believed that the coming of Antichrist was at hand, and that there was an urgent need for his new knowledge.

The Franciscans stood so much, and then no more, for Bacon appeared dangerously close to heresy here, and in any case was doing the order considerable harm by his vicious attacks on the theologians. So he was exiled to the Paris convent in 1257, and told that he could publish nothing without censorship. The menial tasks were piled on.

It was impossible to muzzle such a man completely. He continued his work in secrecy, and got into contact with one of the cardinals (who was shortly to become Pope Clement IV) in an attempt to get his superiors' decision rescinded. He sent John, his favourite pupil, to whom he had taught all he knew, to persuade the Pope to give his authority to and finance the writing of a massive encyclopaedia of science. Bacon was to direct the work, using the talents of all the foremost scientists of Europe.

Clement was interested, and received a number of writings from Bacon, but he died before he could do anything about it. The task in itself was too grandiose for that age, and Bacon now realised that he would not find another Clement. He reconciled himself with his superiors, and returned to England towards the end of the 1260s. He continued writing, and despite further opposition was still busily at work when he died in 1292. We should, in this age of Science, deeply honour him, for he forecast most of the scientific achievements of our own age, among them flying machines, powered boats and the horseless carriage.

See S. C. Easton: *Roger Bacon and his Search for a Universal Science* (Blackwell, Oxford, 1952).

John Ball

John Ball was England's earliest socialist, though he was so revolutionary in outlook one should really see him as a communist. He had a long career of trouble before ever getting involved in the Peasants' Revolt. He was probably ordained at York, where he was a priest in the service of the Abbey of St. Mary, and then he moved to the Colchester district, where we first find him in trouble in 1366. He was ordered to appear before the Archbishop of Canterbury, and people were strictly forbidden to listen to his sermons. The archbishop gave him a light sentence, for England was not used to heresy or radical priests, though it was to get some nasty shocks from John Wyclif soon enough. Ten years later we find another order for the arrest of John Ball who had been so bold as to say that one might refuse to pay one's tithes if the priest didn't appear worthy of them; worse still he seemed to be going about saying that all men were equal, and property should be shared out accordingly. Yet once more the Church dealt kindly with him, to their cost, for when the great Peasants' Revolt broke out in June 1381 he was in prison again, at Maidstone, and the army of the poor flocked up to release him.

He now became secretary, propagandist, inspirer, and religious leader to Wat Tyler's band of angry men—villeins and villains. He sent out letters urging other peasants to rise, composing strange rhymes and jingles so that the illiterate could carry the message more easily:

Jon the Mellore hath y grounden smal,
smalle, smalle:
The Kingis son of hevene shal paye for
alle;
Be ware or ye be wo,
Knoweth youre friende from your fo; ...
They crowded on to London, the numbers swelling all the way. At Blackheath Ball preached to them his famous sermon on the text

Whanne Adam Dalfe and Eve Span
Who was thanne a gentil man?

The poor were to go to harvest and root up the tares, killing all the lawyers (who prove men's bondage by producing documents), and all the principal lords of

Church and State. They could then start afresh on the basis of equality, and hold everything in common. There would be only one king and one bishop, and we can all guess whom the latter was to be!

Inside London, all their hopes seemed to be coming true, and Ball was involved in the rush on the Tower that resulted in the brutal murder of the Archbishop of Canterbury, Ball's old enemy. But at Smithfield the rebellion was broken by Richard II—a mere boy—who reminded the peasantry of their loyalty to the old estate of kingship. How John Ball must have hated the means of his defeat!

He fled to the midlands, and was finally discovered at Coventry, hiding in an old ruin. He was taken before King Richard at St. Albans, and there, on the 15th of July, was hanged, drawn and quartered in the presence of that hereditary establishment he so hated. It had been, for him, an exciting month.

Baybars I

The story of Baybars I of Egypt is straight out of the *Arabian Nights*, only this one is true. Born a Cuman, on the north-west shore of the Black Sea, he was sold into slavery by Bulgarians during the Mongol invasions. Having passed through several hands, at the age of eighteen he became the slave of the Sultan of Egypt.

For some years the Islamic world had been divided by religious and political factions that brought tremendous problems in their wake. In that a Muslim war was a holy war, it was necessary to have an army of pure believers, and as the sects grew wilder and more numerous, the number of possible candidates for the army dwindled. The answer was to import slaves who had no connections or loyalties in Egypt, and bring them up from early childhood in pure orthodoxy to make an army of Mamluks. In this process the contribution of Baybars was to prove outstanding.

The Sultan had a crack regiment called the Bahri, whom he was having trained in Mongol methods of warfare—fast riding and accurate shooting—in order to prepare for the inevitable and dreaded attack. Baybars joined this regiment, and had achieved the rank of colonel by the time he was 20, so great was his physical and military prowess.

In 1250 the Sultan died, but his son turned out to have none of his abilities, and treated the Bahri regiment very badly. So Baybars murdered him, only to find the next Sultan behaving far worse, trying to exterminate the Bahri, who fled to Syria to avoid his attentions. The news that the threatened Mongol invasion was about to materialise finally brought them back home to Egypt, and there Baybars was given command of the army.

The great horde rolled on, sweeping all before it, until it reached Gaza. There Hulugu heard of the death of Mangu Khan in central Asia, and hurried back with most of his forces to secure his succession. This was Baybars' chance, and he drove quickly forward, beating the Mongols at Ain Jalut in 1260, and driving them out of Syria.

He was not rewarded sufficiently, and so he assassinated the Sultan, taking the throne for himself. Immediately he set to work to make alliances with other Muslim states, with Byzantium, the Syrian Franks, the Armenians and the Khan of the Golden Horde to ensure that when Hulugu came back for revenge, at least he could rely on others' neutrality. When the invasion came in 1265 Baybars withdrew before it, practising scorched-earth tactics, until the Mongols were sufficiently worn down, and then he drove them before him out of his dominions.

He now turned on the Latin States of Palestine and Syria, and by building castles in territory he had conquered, exterminating all traces of Western rule and re-Moslemising the land, he had cleared all but a few coastal territories by 1268. Desperate attempts were made by the Papacy to unite Western Christendom, and even to gain the support of the Mongols in an attack on Baybars' now enormous empire; but Baybars was cunning: he was in treaty with the Venetians and with Charles of Anjou, and the threatened attack was transferred to Tunis.

By 1271, when Edward of England landed, Baybars had got really all he required: the Franks were practically limited to the cities of Tripolis, Tyre and Acre, and were in the position of tributaries of Egypt. The treaty he made in 1272 secured the rights of pilgrimage to Jerusalem, Bethlehem and Nazareth, so few could really complain.

Late in the same year Baybars heard that the Mongols were preparing another attack, so he moved up to meet them on the Euphrates, where he routed them in 1273. He systematically ravaged the border country between his own dominions and Mongol territory, making a no-man's-land as an aid to defence.

He turned south now, to engage on the conquest of Nubia, and soon the whole of the Sudan was incorporated into his empire in 1275. Two years later he moved north once more and into Asia-Minor where he beat a combined Mongol-Seljuq army, and ascended the Seljuq throne.

The Mongols got him in the end, however; returning from his victory in Asia Minor he paused at Damascus for a celebration, where he tried the Mongolian drink Kumis, and liked it too well. Suffering from a hangover of massive proportions he called his terrified doctors, who gave him such strong purgatives that he died.

A ruthless and brilliant soldier and a skilled organiser, Baybars succeeded primarily because his timing was so faultless. He always made sure that he kept his movements an absolute secret, and his efficient and speedy intelligence service kept him fully informed of the enemy's position, strength and plans; with these two aids to his generalship he showed the world that the Mongols could be beaten, not just once, but any number of times.

There is a biography of Baybars by S. F. Sadeque: *Baybars I of Egypt* (Oxford Univ. Press, London and New York, 1956).

St. Thomas Becket

'All sorts of interesting things have happened this week. For instance, on Tuesday a gentleman came over from Margate, bringing with him his son. He asked to be allowed to see the bones, and then said that the boy's eyesight was failing, and that as he had tried all the doctors in vain, he had brought him as a last resource to see what the bones of the saint would do for him. Austin was delighted at this, and told us with great satisfaction how the gentleman made the boy kneel down and put his eyes close into the sockets of the skull, saying to him, "Now, no doctors can heal you; you must pray for yourself." Don't you hope that he will recover?...'

The above, far from being written in the Middle Ages, is a part of a letter from the daughter of one Anglican canon of Canterbury Cathedral to the daughter of another; 'Austin' was the surveyor of the Cathedral; the date was 1888, when the discovery of bones thought (with some justice) to be those of St. Thomas Becket caused a flurry of medieval excitement in the quiet close. For the text of these letters and a detailed study of the probabilities of the case, see A. J. Mason: *What Became of the Bones of St. Thomas?* (Cambridge Univ. Press, 1920.)

The story of Becket is one of the great stories of the Middle Ages, and is still retold in popular films, plays (by Anouilh and Eliot), novels and scholarly studies. Even when all the false romance is cleared away (and this is a Herculean task) the true drama that remains is deeply compelling.

Thomas Becket was born in London to Norman parents in 1118. His father was a knight who had become a businessman, and attained eminence in the City; he probably over-awed the boy, who was to be a stammerer all his life, and who was much closer to his pious mother. He was a lively child, with an excellent memory and verbal skill, but no scholar. He much preferred hunting and hawking to book-work, but despite his gaiety he remained faithful to his mother's ideals and continued chaste and devout in his personal life. After finishing his education in Paris, he came back to London to work as a clerk for a relative whose business was now prospering more than his father's.

He endured this job for three years, and then joined the household of Theobald, Archbishop of Canterbury. This proved to be a very different kind of experience, for the clerks maintained by Theobald were not just humble secretaries carrying out routine duties, but more like members of an institute of higher learning, picked out for their brilliance and promise; there were future bishops, archbishops and cardinals, and even a future pope for a short while. The reaction of this group of eminent scholars (of whom John of Salisbury alone had spent at least a dozen years on his university education) to the breezy sportsman whose Latin was none too strong can well be imagined, and when they saw that he was rapidly winning the favour of their master, this reaction became ever more marked. The more diligently he worked for Theobald, the more favour he won, and he was soon rich enough to indulge his taste for display and extravagant generosity; he plainly enjoyed authority, and longed also to be popular, but all that his rich gifts won him was enmity.

The stakes were indeed high, for Theobald was influential to a degree, and when in 1154 the Chancellorship of England became vacant, he recommended his favourite Thomas. Here Becket showed the wisdom of the choice: he listened to all with care and attention, and deployed both his boundless energy and his matchless memory to produce efficient and speedy administrative and legal decisions. The magnificence of the state he kept lived up to his reputation—everything in his household was of the best, to parallel the quality of his work.

To the young King Henry II he was a joy, for he was not only a wise and efficient adviser, but also a gay and understanding friend, surely the ideal combination. William Fitzstephen records that they 'played together like two boys of the same age, in the hall, in the church, in court and in riding', by which he means that everything was like a game to them, to be done with joy, as a team, and to be played with the utmost skill.

The game was not to last, for in 1161 Theobald lay on his deathbed, and it became apparent that Thomas was the royal candidate to succeed him. Becket had not as yet taken high orders in the Church, and felt that the scholars he had met in the household of Theobald had a better claim to do the job well; above all he feared the future, for his gay life as chancellor must end, and he must take up a totally different one.

All great men are single-minded in one degree or another—if they take on a job, they must do it supremely well; Becket had been a fine chancellor, but his experience in government during those years had shown him that if he were to be an equally good archbishop, he would have to fight to protect the Church from the inroads that Henry planned to make on it. He would not just forsake the gay life for a serious one, he would lose everything.

The position looked simple from either side: Henry wished to regularise the judicial system, and one thing that militated against his orderly view of things was the fact that his courts had no element of control over anyone connected with the Church, which had its own courts. Henry didn't want too great a revolution—he didn't even suggest that the royal courts should judge clergy, only see to their punishment after ecclesiastical courts had condemned them. The picture from the Church's side was very different: for years it had struggled to free itself from a lay control which had once been so powerful that feudal lords had regarded their priests in almost the same light as they regarded their serfs. The Church did not belong to the world (indeed some churchmen in their fervour believed the opposite to be true) and each right they had won from the secular powers was held to be a shining jewel in the treasury, to be protected to the last. No matter how small, each bit of liberty was an essential brick in the edifice they were building for God.

So when Henry forced Thomas to accept the archbishopric, believing that his best friend would continue to further his wishes as he had so splendidly done for seven happy years, he was setting in train the inevitable conflict and its tragic end. In October 1163 he put his plans before the Council of Westminster, and Becket stood out against them.

For two months Henry worked to divide the bishops, to win their support away from his treacherous servant, tried to discredit Becket, and confiscated his lands and public offices. Then at the Council of Clarendon he tried again: the archbishop was under great pressure from all sides, was made to feel how unreasonable he was being, how unfriendly—he stood alone. For a moment his courage broke and he was ready to agree, but the king now learned what he had lost in his efficient chancellor, for the documents were not ready in their correct form for the archbishop to seal. As the clerks scribbled away in a corner, and the king fumed in another, Becket had time to regain his composure, and when the documents were presented, refused to assent.

The king now decided to crush the archbishop. A third council was arranged to meet at Northampton in October 1164, and it was plain that Becket would there be declared a traitor and imprisoned, so that the king could do what he liked. The bishops turned away from him, and at Northampton he fell violently ill, sweating and trembling in fear and despair.

But at that point his confessor told him that he had nothing to lose, and he was inspired to make a stand. He recovered, and, dressed in all his magnificence, and

carrying his cross, he walked steadily to the keep of the castle. Around the door were all the bishops, forbidden by Becket to join in the proceedings against him; Gilbert Foliot, who felt that he should have been archbishop, said in a loud voice 'He always was a fool and always will be', and Roger, Archbishop of York (who had been senior clerk in the household of Theobald and had good reason to remember Thomas) ostentatiously swept off with his retinue 'so as not to witness the terrible fate that lay in store for the archbishop'.

Thomas refused to go up to the angry barons for judgement, so they were forced to come down to the lower floor to condemn him, leaving the anxious king above: first the Earl of Leicester tried to make the speech of condemnation, but broke down in face of the silent and impressive archbishop who had the power to cut him off from all spiritual benefits; the Earl of Cornwall tried to take over, but then Becket rose and began to leave. The king's supporters cried out angrily and flung rushes (which then did duty for carpets) at him. As he reached the door, Hamelin, the king's illegitimate brother, took him by the sleeve, but Thomas shook him off, saying, 'You lout and bastard, if these were not priest's hands, you would feel their strength.'

He rode away by circuitous paths, finally reaching the sea, and went into exile; he could count himself lucky to have escaped. For a while he had to keep silence, for Pope Alexander II was at the height of his dispute with Frederick Barbarossa and his anti-pope, and could not afford to antagonise England. He now had time to study and repair his knowledge, and to submit his body to the harsh expiatory training that medieval belief demanded. He believed that it was in part his own weakness that had caused the battle to be lost: he longed too much for friendship and popularity, and when he was met by their opposites he had twice allowed himself to lose control. So he punished his body to harden his spirit, though one should remember that it was not physical fear he was trying to over-come—when he was chancellor and at peace with the world he had fought in battle as bravely as any member of Henry's army.

The situation grew steadily worse during the five years that followed the Council of Northampton: Henry confiscated all Becket's property and punished his friends and relations; Becket took every chance the Pope allowed him to excommunicate high-ranking Englishmen in both Church and State. In June 1170 the final insult came, when the king organised the coronation of his son (a common practice at this time to assure a peaceful succession) in the absence of the one man who can crown kings in England: he got Becket's old enemy the Archbishop of York to do it.

This confirmed Becket in his intention to return to Canterbury; he landed on the first of December, knowing that his return would provoke the king to the uttermost. Yet he was so happy he flushed with joy when he entered his cathedral, and he received a great welcome from the people of Canterbury. He had come home, but specifically to die, and Christmas Day was filled with solemn excommunications of his enemies, a desperate provocation offered to a notoriously evil-tempered king.

In Normandy the King's anger knew no bounds and he screamed out imprecations against Becket, and four knights, taking him at his word, came over, and about three o'clock on the 29th of December went into the room where Becket and his clerks had just finished dinner after high mass. He did not see them at first, and they sat at his feet, not knowing how to com-port themselves in such strange surroun-dings. When he saw them he coloured up (he had always been a great blusher), and an argument ensued: Becket was un-repentant, and told them (using a fine mili-tary simile that they would understand), 'It is useless to threaten me . . . You will find my foot set against yours in God's fight.' The knights bustled out to get their weapons, muttering imprecations and

telling the monks to keep Becket there, and he followed them to the door shouting 'Hugh, what was that you said? No one is going to run away—you will find me here.' He put his hand to his head, and returned to his seat, where John of Salisbury gently reproved him for his hasty words: 'You have always been like that . . . Not a soul wants to die here, excepting you.'

The monks, hearing the clatter of the armed knights, now began to drag Becket to the church, while he resisted every inch of the way, and complained of the cowardly nature of the monks. He refused to let them bar the door, and was with difficulty per-suaded to stay in the church, crowded as it was with monks and townsfolk. Then the knights came in, and blinded by the gloom, one of them called out in his lisping voice 'Where is Thomas Beketh, the traitor?' He came forward and they rushed him, one of them trying to carry him out of the church, but he shouted to Fitz-Urse, 'Leave go, you pimp,' and shoved him back so hard he nearly fell. He told them they must kill him there in church. As he commended himself to God, they struck, and at the third blow he fell onto his hands and knees, whispering 'I accept death in the name of Jesus and for the Church.' At the final blow he fell with his arms outstretched, his cloak decently covering his whole body.

The miracles came, and along with them thousands of pilgrims; the saint was adored, written about, pictured the length and breadth of Europe. And King Henry endured a public penance far more humilia-ting than that suffered by Emperor Henry IV at Canossa a century before.

It is not possible to say which side won in the dispute between Henry and Becket, but certainly the reputation of the saint and what he stood for grew and prospered in England and in Christendom, and when a later Henry (whose Wolsey was his Bec-ket) was at work destroying the old reli-gion in his realm, he was not satisfied with the mere destruction of Becket's shrine, but ordered that wherever his name appear-ed it should be scratched out. Manuscripts in all the great libraries show to this day with what thoroughness the order was carried out in every part of the land; but the fear that inspired the order, four hundred and sixty years after the martyrdom, was itself a convincing demonstration of the power to thrill that that name held and still holds.

There are many biographies of Becket, long and short, but none surpasses the brilliant study by David Knowles in his Raleigh Lecture for 1949, reprinted in the collection of his essays *The Historian and Character*, (Cambridge Univ. Press, 1953).

The Venerable Bede

Bede was born close to the new monastery of Wearmouth about the year 673, and at the age of seven was given into the charge of its abbot, Benedict Biscop, a learned man with refined tastes. Almost as much at home in Rome as he was in the wild lands of Northumbria, he imported from the South beautiful things and skilful people: books, silver, paintings and stone-masons might arrive in one consignment. He even persuaded the Pope to let him have the arch-chantor of St. Peter's itself to teach his rustics how to sing.

Thus the little Anglian was introduced to a large new world of scholarship, beauty and cosmopolitan attitudes. He became passionately attached to the monastic way of life, but his love of his own people was to remain almost as strong. Unlike Benedict he never left Northumbria, and it is perhaps significant that when a joint foundation was set up nearby at Jarrow under Ceolfrid, Bede went there. The influence of Benedict Biscop remained strong, however, in Bede's love of music: when a terrible plague reduced the choir-monks at Jarrow to the Abbot and Bede, they together laboured to continue the services, and trained others to support them.

Bede completed some 40 works in his busy life, and one can tell from his state-

ments that he would never shirk any of his monastic duties in order to get on with his writing. Perhaps to him his commentaries on Scripture and his hagiographical work were the most important, but to us his significance lies in his great *History of the English Church and People*. In this he is truly the father of English history, not just because he was the first English historian, but because even now he still ranks as one of the best.

The title of the book is interesting: written to celebrate the triumph of Christianity in this country, it is also a record—and in some senses also a celebration—of the triumph of the English themselves. Though Bede is very fair to the Celts and their branch of the Church, there is no doubt at all from what point of view he is writing.

His thoroughness and accuracy are his great qualities, and when one considers the difficulties under which he laboured, his achievement was incredible. It has been calculated that Bede actually consulted some 144 separate works for his writings, so far as quotation evidence goes. The papal archives were checked for him, and evidence was received from innumerable witnesses from all parts of England. The whole was carefully checked and assessed by Bede himself, and presented with a regard for truth that has rarely been paralleled; yet there is still room for the verve and imagination without which great histories cannot be written.

Historians are rarely saintly, but Bede plainly was. The account of his last hours written by one of his students, is one of the most moving documents in medieval history. Though suffering from shortness of breath and swollen feet, he remained cheerful and continued to teach, filling in the remaining hours with prayer and contemplation, singing psalms and vernacular hymns to his students. He quoted text after text to them, saying, 'Oh King of Glory, Lord of might, Who on this day ascended in triumph above all heavens, do not leave us orphans . . .' but here he broke down in tears. He continued to dictate two books on which he was working, and with his translation of the Gospel of St. John into English nearly finished, he felt death upon him. So he delivered his few treasures to his friends—a little pepper, incense and linen, and talked earnestly with them. Then his scribe, a boy called Wilbert, quietly reminded him that there was one sentence left to translate. He gave him the version, and asked to be placed on the floor of his cell where he had used to pray. He chanted the Gloria, and died.

Two hundred and eighty-five years later, in 1020, a Durham monk stole his bones from Wearmouth. At the Reformation the reliquary in which they were kept was spoiled, but the bones hidden, and in 1831 they were dug up once more. Bede the historian would have been amused.

For a biographical study, see A. Hamilton Thompson (ed.), *Bede: His Life, Times & Writings* (Oxford Univ. Press, London, 1933).

St. Benedict

St. Benedict was born at Nursia, in Umbria, about 480. He came from a good family, who sent him to Rome for his education. Like many another sincere Christian in this position, he found the license and worldliness in this rotten core of a decayed empire revolting in the extreme. It was not so much what went on (worse had happened in earlier days); it was the habit of mind that accompanied and produced the sinful life: 'Eat, drink and be merry, for tomorrow we die.'

He fled from Rome to an isolated cave in the Sabine Hills at Subiaco, and there he remained a penitent and thoughtful hermit for three years. Partly escapism, partly a period of mortification for his own sins, and partly a preparation for the future, this period of retirement 'in the desert' was a parallel with Paul's and Christ's—for Benedict had no genuine commitment to the solitary life. As disciples flocked in ever increasing numbers to him, he found himself pulled inescapably into the problems of community life.

He founded some thirteen monasteries in that area, before moving his own community to Monte Cassino about the year 520. He had plenty of experience in establishing and ruling monasteries, and he had read widely in the texts of the desert fathers, and of those who had brought monasticism to the West. During these last thirty years of his life at Monte Cassino, he set about the production of a 'little rule for beginners' about the monastic life, a rule which was to remain the basis of monasticism in Western Europe, and one which would teach the secular governors in their very similar tasks.

His rule is by no means austere—the monks are to have sufficient food and sleep, and a balanced life of prayer, manual labour and reading. The abbot is given supreme power, but terrible responsibilities; he must listen to advice, but he takes action for the community who are all sworn to obedience to him, and he is directly responsible to God for what he has done in their name. Benedict's advice to the abbot is very sound; one feels that no one following these gentle words of wisdom could go wrong, and the community would be a happy and stable one. For stability is above all Benedict's aim: that is what a monastery provides, a stable place in a world sliding into catastrophe, a stable routine that will gently support the soul concentrating on the road to God.

It is impossible to assess the results of Benedict's written example, spiritual, aesthetic and scholarly; these things are not to be quantified. His order was to provide for the Church 24 popes, 200 cardinals, and 5,000 bishops and archbishops.

For a useful study of St. Benedict, see J. McCann's biography, London, 1937.

St. Bernard of Clairvaux

A mystical conservative, single-minded to the point of narrowness, puritanical, opposing all forms of radical scholarship, combative and vehement to a degree, St. Bernard of Clairvaux is not likely to find a host of admirers in the liberal days in which we live. Yet there is no doubt at all that he was one of the greatest figures of the Middle Ages, and in many ways a deeply attractive person. Though he interfered in matters that might well have been considered none of his business over the length and breadth of Europe, his only aim was the salvation of souls, for which the preservation of the Faith was essential. He may have acted like the most domineering of popes, but he genuinely hated going out from his monastery, and his one desire was to remain with his monks and at his devotions. It was conscience, and an overpowering love that drove him out: when he was embroiled in the disputed election at York, he wrote with passion that he 'found life a burden in a world where such things went unpunished'. As we go through his life and feel our hackles rising, it is essential to remember that Bernard *had* to do the things he did.

He was born about 1090, to a knightly father and deeply religious mother. All her children were offered to God, and she brought them up on little food and rough clothing, putting them into training for their future achievements.

Bernard went early to school and made excellent progress, though he was a shy boy who loved to be alone, and even in early youth practised mortifications to test himself; these brought on massive migraines, forerunners of a life-time of illness. His mother died in his early adolescence, and the strong influence she had had upon him, combined with the increasingly devoted memories he had of her, turned his mind ever more to the contemplation of the Virgin Mary, to whose cult he was to contribute so great an impetus in later life.

He found it difficult to get on with others and, as his biographer tells us, had many 'stormy friendships'. His greatest problem lay with women, for they were deeply attracted to him, and constantly tempted him; his only recourse was to grit his teeth and immerse his body in ice-cold water. His mind turned increasingly towards the monastic profession, but his relations urged him to become a scholar instead, for his literary knowledge and skill was really outstanding. This never left him, and after a life-time of training himself to ignore all the beauties and sensations of this world in order to concentrate more readily on those of the next, he still wrote some of the finest and most polished prose of his day, and plainly enjoyed writing it.

But the lure of the new abbey of Cîteaux was far stronger than the pull of any school for Bernard. This monastery had been founded by a few monks who were united in the belief that monasticism had changed and developed through the ages since the time of St. Benedict so much that it no longer represented in the slightest his original intentions and ideals. So they planned an 'apostolic' life where they would keep the Rule of St. Benedict to the letter, and thereby rebuild a true monasticism, untainted by the luxurious living that had spoiled every other attempt at reform. They chose to live in the wilderness, and to be a self-supporting community, cut off from the world; they would wear undressed and undyed woollen habits, and worship in a simple, unornamented church. Their services should be as nearly as possible those used by St. Benedict: so they sent to Milan for hymns and to Metz for anthems; they sounded quite dreadful to the musician's ear, but they sang them with fervour because they believed them to be original. They went to great trouble to get a pure text of the Bible, too, for in generations of copying many inaccuracies had intruded; they did not hesitate to contact Greek and Jewish scholars for help in this project. They felt that there was a quality to the life they lived which was pure, authentic and original, and did not care that it was also cruelly hard.

Bernard decided finally what he must do whilst on the road to visit his brothers who were encamped with the Duke of Burgundy laying siege to a town. They were not to be soldiers long, for Bernard made good use of his persuasive tongue, and he had soon got them to agree to come with him, and his uncle too. He determined that he should go to Cîteaux with a large party, and for six months he used his father's house as a base from which to collect adherents. His missionary activities were touched with ruthlessness: he was quite willing to force someone to join his party by threatening them with sickness, for he was, after all, saving their immortal souls. As a result 'mothers hid their children from him, wives hid their husbands and friends kept back their friends'.

In 1113 Bernard led thirty companions to the gates of Cîteaux, and immediately began to build a convent to receive their wives, quite close at hand. He embraced the novitiate with unparalleled ardour, and set as his aim the abolition of his own curiosity; he believed that man's senses detract from his ability to concentrate, so he began to train his eyes not to notice inessentials, his tongue not to taste, and his body not to demand comfort, least of all enjoy it. He slept and ate the bare minimum, and forced himself to do heavy and boring work. Soon he attained a success it is difficult for us to understand: he could only distinguish water from other liquids, and even then it was not its taste he noticed, but its cooling effect; and he observed so little that he could not even remember how many windows the chapel had, despite the long hours he spent there. Every part of his body was dulled, except in the one direction of the appreciation of God.

All this was done at the expense of his health, which was permanently ruined; he was totally unable to digest solids, and was so frequently ill that a basin had to be sunk in the floor by his stall in the chapel. Constantly in pain, he refused to let up on his plans one iota.

Perhaps the Abbot (Stephen Harding, an Englishman) thought that a position of responsibility would make him lighten his personal mortifications in favour of action, so in 1115 he sent him off to found a daughter abbey at Clairvaux, a wild place, the haunt of brigands. There life was even harder, and frequently the monks had nothing to eat but beech leaves. At this stage Bernard's old father came to join him, and his sister, who had married well, came on a visit. Bernard refused to see her, and her only greeting was to be called a clod of dung, for her fine clothes and retinue offended the monks' ideals. At last Bernard saw her, and though she would not give up her husband as he wished her to, she did agree to give up her finery; she went home, and during two years became ever more unworldly, finally joining the convent that had been founded shortly after Bernard had gone to Cîteaux. Bernard had a high vision of womanhood, and a strong family feeling (he would not rest until nearly every relation he had was a Cistercian), but the ruthlessness with which he expressed himself in these matters puts us off.

With himself he was even more ruthless, and the Bishop of Châlons was so upset at seeing the physical condition to which he had reduced himself, that he hurriedly arranged to have the abbot put under his immediate control, so that he might forbid for a year the extreme privations that were killing Bernard, as well as force him to take some care and attention.

The bishop's sensible action no doubt saved Bernard's life (though his health was never to be improved), and enabled him to undertake the tremendous series of controversies in defence of the faith for which he is so famous.

The first battle was against the most powerful abbey in the world—Cluny, rich, worldly and successful—and Bernard began a large correspondence with the Abbot, his contemporary, Peter the Venerable, who had much of Bernard's ability and intellect, and not a little of his stature, to which he added dignity, gentleness and good humour, qualities Bernard lacked. They both half admired each other, and both disliked the system the other represented.

The trouble began when a young cousin of Bernard's found life too hard at Clairvaux, and fled to the easier pastures of Cluny. Bernard was plainly very fond of the boy, and his family feeling was deeply hurt that one of his 'set' should be lost to the luxury-loving 'enemy'. He wrote him a letter couched in the strongest terms, and in it let fall some highly actionable comments about Cluny. The reply came quickly—the Cistercians were new Pharisees, whose white clothing showed them to be more concerned with impressing others than they claimed to be. What if the monks at Cluny had a little comfort in which to perform their scholarly and artistic tasks—had not Christ preferred Mary to Martha? To this Bernard replies with a particularisation of the forbidden luxuries used at Cluny (including 'cat-fur bed rugs'), a telling description of the princely state in which the abbot travelled, and a stern denunciation of the gold and ornamentation used in their church.

Another prelate who had to endure the withering fire of Bernard's puritanism was the most important man in France after the king, Suger, Abbot of St. Denis. He was busy building a national cathedral which would rival in its beauty all the buildings of the known world. Now Bernard attacked him vigorously for the sumptuous decoration of the church he was building, and for the style of life of this eminent statesman-politician. Suger responded astonishingly well to Bernard's strictures, and became his firm friend, seeking his advice on many matters of importance.

Bernard's influence in public affairs developed rapidly, and was by no means restricted to France; whatever one may think about what he did (and more particularly how he did it) there is no doubt that the eminent in secular as well as religious affairs recognised in him a mind and heart of outstanding quality, whose services they needed. For seven long and bitter years he led the campaign against the schism which resulted in the election of two Popes—Innocent II and Anaclete (Peter the Lion);

and by his defeat of the latter preserved the only uniting force in Christendom. He was also called in to settle secular disputes, and was busy on such a mission at the end of his life.

Perhaps he is most famous, however, for his almost continuous disputes against those whom he considered to be attacking the Church by reducing its mysteries to the level of subjects for dispute in universities. The Faith was for Bernard something to be accepted, not with one's reason, but with one's heart: 'What does philosophy matter to me? My masters are the apostles; they didn't teach me to read Plato or untwine the subtleties of Aristotle, they taught me how to live. And, believe me, that is no little knowledge.' Perhaps he recalled his own struggles as a young man to reject a literary career, and knowing what monasticism had meant to him, he felt his decision had been wholly correct; and he believed its correctitude held good for all.

His attack on Abelard (*q.v.*) is all too reminiscent for us of the techniques used in our own century by political believers to annihilate their enemies; but we must remember that in our age there is an acceptable alternative to totalitarian rule; in Bernard's time there was no acceptable alternative to the rule of faith, by which Europe had slowly risen from the depths of barbarism towards a pattern of civilisation which was rooted in Christian principles of good order between people. Without it the world would inevitably slip back to the days of Attila the Hun, and there was no possibility of a revival of a universal empire such as had existed in the great days of Rome. Finally it is most important to remember that Bernard tried his hardest to bring down other scholars (such as Gilbert de la Porée) on charges of heresy, and failed: there was a great deal of support in twelfth-century Europe for radical ideas, and Bernard was attempting to turn this tide alone.

Bernard's last great project was the launching of the Second Crusade, and it must have caused the greatest trial of faith in the whole of his life that the Crusade he had launched with such fine oratorical skill should have led to abysmal failure. In 1145 the Pope commissioned him to give the cross to King Louis, and, standing on a platform amidst a gigantic crowd at Vézelay, he so worked on their emotions that they all chanted as one 'Give us the cross! Give us the cross!', and Bernard, having run out of crosses to give to so many, ended up tearing his cowl into strips for them. He told audiences all over Europe that this was a time unlike any before, when 'divine mercy was pouring from Heaven, and happy are we to be alive in this year of God's choice, this year of jubilee, this year of pardon.' He told them that God was willing to forgive the very worst of sinners for taking the cross, and 'what is it but an act of exquisite courtesy all God's own?' The soldiers he told to come, for here at last they had a cause for which they could fight without danger to their souls; and to the merchants he said 'let me point out the advantages of this opportunity. Do not miss them . . . The cost is small, the reward is great.'

After such a triumph of oratory, the failure of the Crusade was crushing, and many lost faith in Bernard and turned on him. Yet he still had influence to use, for a Cistercian had become Pope Eugenius III in the same year as the preaching of the Crusade, and he turned to Bernard at every stage for advice. The influence was to be used in many ways, but one may note in passing that Bernard tried as hard as he could to stop the vicious persecutions of the Jews that were one of the blackest parts of an age of violence.

In the end we must judge Bernard solely by what he claimed to be, a Cistercian monk. He personally admitted some 900 monks in his lifetime, and he lived to see Clairvaux, which had begun with twelve, bursting at the seams with 700 monastic inmates. By the time of his death his abbey had 68 daughter houses and 159 lineal descendants. One can be sure that if any-

thing lay happily on his mind when he lay dying in 1153, it was this achievement, not all the rest. For he believed that the monastery was the gate of heaven, and without doubt the innermost gate was of the order of Cîteaux.

The contemporary biography, by those who knew him, has been translated and edited by Geoffrey Webb and Adrian Walker: *Story of His Life in Vita Prima Bernardie* (Mowbray, Oxford, 1960; Newman Press, New Jersey, 1960). Perhaps the most satisfactory modern biography is by Watkin Williams: *St. Bernard, Man and His Message* (Manchester Univ. Press, 1944).

St. Boniface

St. Boniface was born most probably at Crediton, Devonshire in 675, to a family of free landowners. His given name was Wynfrid. As quite a young child he entered the monastery at Exeter and later removed to Nursling, between Southampton and Winchester. His education was excellent, deeply influenced by the ideas and style of Aldhelm (*q.v.*); it was also strongly in the Benedictine tradition, and Boniface was to become one of the best exponents of Wilfrid's (*q.v.*) strict and aggressive Romanism. In a Christendom where missionary activity and consolidation were the twin necessities, it was plain that the magnificent effort of the Irish, though much to be admired, had failed. It was far too individualistic, often perversely so; and it seemed to demand that the kingdom of heaven should appear on earth at once. Like shooting stars, the great missionary saints of Ireland had reached the heights, but after their deaths the stars had fallen fast. What was needed was common sense and practicality, the ability to see problems clearly and to take concerted and vigorous action which was designed to produce lasting results. Above all, it was necessary to recognise a unified command and a unified procedure.

So Boniface became a pronounced and devoted Romanist. After an abortive mission to Friesland in 716 he journeyed to Rome to receive the papal commission to preach to the infidel, and to receive his new Roman name—henceforth he was only rarely referred to as Wynfrid. In 722 he was back in Rome again to be consecrated bishop, when he swore absolute subjection to the papal authority. About the year 732 he returned once more to be consecrated archbishop. Throughout his thirty-six-year mission, Boniface constantly reported back to Rome, and asked for detailed instructions; his fight was to be against pagans, true, but also he struggled to win back to obedience the independent and unruly Christians he found in Frankish territories and beyond.

In 721 he left Friesland, which was already being preached by the English missionary Willibrord, and began to concentrate on central Germany where he had to struggle with great physical courage against entrenched paganism. He cut down the great Oak of Thor and used the timber to build a little oratory dedicated to St. Peter. The monasteries he set up were like castles in an alien land, and his converts often went in fear of their lives.

He received tremendous support from England, whence came crowds of scholars and missionaries to join him in his work. He managed to carry on correspondence with numerous friends there, and the survival of these letters casts a fascinating light on his work. The Bishop of Winchester wrote advising him on how to convert the heathen: don't argue about the genealogies of their gods, he says, accept that they were born like men, and so must be men; if they still doubt, ask them where their gods lived before the creation of the universe—that will stump them; if they claim that the universe has always been there, ask them how the gods came to rule it. These and many other cunning and convincing arguments are retailed, and enable us to get a picture of the eighth century missionary arguing steadily on until the poor pagan submits, or the missionary can prove him wrong.

It is instructive to see how many of Boniface's letters to England are appeals for books, for in that wholly illiterate and pagan territory in which he worked this eminent scholar suffered a parched thirst for literature. He had a close contact with the charmingly named Abbess Bugga of Minster on the Isle of Thanet, who signs her letters to him 'in love unfeigned'; she searches for books he wants, and works on a copy of the Epistle of St. Peter which she is doing for him in letters of gold, the material for which is supplied by Boniface. He carefully warns her not to start her pilgrimage for Rome as it is being threatened by the Saracens, and does not mind receiving from one of her nuns, Leoba, pieces of prose and verse for criticism and correction. Leoba was to be one of his closest and most helpful followers in later life. We find him writing to an old pupil for commentaries on the Epistles of St. Paul, other than *Romans* and *First Corinthians*—he has those; he asks the Bishop of Winchester for his old abbot's copy of the *Book of the Prophets*, for his eyes are failing, and he remembers how large and clear the letters are in that copy; and he writes three letters, each more appealing than the last, for copies of the works of Bede. Finally we find him writing to the Archbishop of Canterbury to ask him to look up a knotty point in the laws relating to marriage, and for a copy of Augustine's questions to the Pope, and Gregory's replies (perhaps the most significant document in the history of missions), for the Registrar at Rome can find no trace of them; could the Archbishop check their authenticity and date, please? Boniface himself had few things to send in return—copies he himself had made in his few leisure moments, and once a really rich gift—a copy of St. Gregory's letters that had been sent him from the Roman archives, a book he believed to be quite unknown in England.

Thus in the wilderness (and in an age when at best scholarship and respect for books was weak), Boniface subdued his longing for a good reference library such as that being built up at York, but not his scholarly instincts. He would write again and again to English libraries and to Rome to get his materials and check his references. A slow business, but what joy when a parcel of books finally did arrive!

In 738 Charles Martel conquered the Saxons of Westphalia, and Boniface wrote home excitedly to urge his people to pray for the conversion of their kinsfolk of 'the same blood and bone'. He was now papal legate for the whole area east of the Rhine and for South Germany. Anglo-Saxons flocked to his aid as he set up dioceses and appointed bishops, abbots and abbesses. One of his appointments, the Abbess Waldburg, would surely have been astonished at the association of her name with the traditional celebrations that fell on her festal day—Walpurgis Night, but this was to happen much later.

In 739 Willibrord died and Friesland now came under the authority of Boniface, making him overlord of the whole mission-field of the Roman church. With the death of Charles Martel, and the accession of his sons Carloman and Pepin, came also a very much greater degree of co-operation from the secular power. National synods were held aimed at the restoration and reformation of the Frankish Church, and the decrees of the synods were given the force of laws of the realm. Boniface now laid the basis of the Carolingian commitment to Rome.

Reformation was badly needed, for there was neither obedience nor order, sound morals nor proper canonical behaviour. Furthermore the wild and uncontrolled individualism that had been fostered in the Merovingian Church had led to a plethora of extraordinary heresies which Boniface had to deal with: for example one Aldebert claimed to have received strange relics from an angel (also a letter dropped from Heaven by Christ), and went about consecrating churches to himself, and distributing clippings from his nails and hair for veneration as holy relics. The task was not easy, and as Boniface forcefully pointed out to the Pope, it was made no easier when members of his flock visited Rome and saw the way the inhabitants there celebrated the New Year, eating and drinking all day, and singing in the streets, the men doing no work, and the women wearing bracelets on their arms and legs and offering them for sale.

Even when it came to be a straight case of applying a known law, Boniface often found himself at a loss; he writes sadly to the Archbishop of York about a difficult case of a priest 'with a record' who lives in an area where there are no other priests. If he acts according to the law and inhibits him from his priestly functions, he is imperilling the souls of countless people there. The difficulty of Boniface's problem illustrates well the almost superhuman tasks that faced the strict Romanists who went on missions in that barbarous age.

In 753 Boniface felt he had done as much as he could to organise the Church of Francia proper, and was able to turn back to his real calling as a missionary to the pagans; though he was a great administrator, if he had had any real liking for the work he would have stayed at home in England, preaching and teaching, and involving himself in church-state diplomacy.

Now he interviewed his most trusted assistants, begging them never to leave the land of their adoption to return to the comforts of home; and he set off for the dank lands of Frisia, dissected by waterways and haunted by mists. He had great success, christening converts in their thousands, and encamped for the winter with the sense of satisfaction of one who has returned to his oldest love.

The following year he set to work again, having the same success, when suddenly his little band was attacked by a crowd of angry pagans. He refused to allow his followers to show the least sign of resistance, as always conscious of the missionary's prime task of setting an example, and, perhaps, moved by the desire for a martyr's crowning.

The pagans cut him and his 53 followers

to pieces, and leaving the dead scattered around the fields, hurried off with their booty. They carried away Boniface's heavy chests, and finally set them down; but before they could be opened, a great quarrel sprang up about the division of the loot. A mad struggle ensued, culminating in the survival of the fittest few, and finally the chests were burst open. Instead of silver and gold, they found books, which they flung aside in fury, sure that at the bottom they would find riches: but each and every chest contained books—the library that Boniface had begged, steadily, book by book, throughout his long and weary life. In their rage they scattered the manuscripts, swinging madly at them with their swords, and of the three that were rescued for the library at Fulda (where Boniface himself was finally buried, according to his wish), one is almost completely cut through.

Wynfrid the Englishman gave his all for the conversion of Germany, struggling manfully against tremendous odds. A scholar at heart, he would have loved to stay in England, teaching the monks and nuns who longed to learn. Throughout his long years abroad he retained and built new friendships with English men and women, for his power to charm shines through the letters that he wrote. His friendliness was compounded of an innate attractiveness and an overwhelming desire to please—he loved people as a missionary should, but very rarely do we find a missionary with such depth of affection as his. At the busiest period of his life he finds time to write a letter commending a serf to a priestly friend, asking that he should aid him 'as if he were a free man', because he was getting married and needed help. Yet, if there is anything he sees wrong, Boniface is not found to be weakly amiable: he can write to the Archbishop of Canterbury denouncing the disorder in his archdiocese, drunkenness, foolishness in dress, lay interference in the Church, and the dangerous habit of English women going frequently to Rome: 'There are many towns in Lombardy and Gaul where there

is not a prostitute but she is from England. It is a scandal and disgrace to your whole church'. He can even reprove the King of Mercia for his immoral and irreligious life, pointing out that in the land of his fathers —pagan 'Old Saxony'—women who misbehave are punished horribly, whilst in the Christian lands of the Anglo-Saxons, the king himself leads women to sin. Boniface, as we have seen, could even rebuke the Pope, whom it was his life-work to make supreme. He was a muscular Christian who loved and was beloved but he was not soft.

The documents of Boniface's life have been edited and translated by C. H. Talbot in *The Anglo-Saxon Missionaries in Germany* (Sheed and Ward, London, 1954).

Boniface VIII

'May he rot in Hell'—thus Dante in the xxviith canto of the *Inferno*, speaking of Pope Boniface VIII. The hatred this man called forth knew no bounds—accused before and after his death of sodomy, heresy, blasphemy and free-thinking, quite apart from the more normal use of the office of Pope for self-aggrandisement that people had grown to expect.

He was born Benedict Gaetani, about 1235, probably in Anagni, the town of Innocent III. His family were gentlefolk: indeed, his great-uncle was a Pope, and an uncle a bishop. The young Benedict learnt Canon Law at Bologna, and soon entered papal service, going as a cardinal's secretary to France in 1265, and to England in 1268, where he served the legate Ottobono in his tiresome task of settling the problems of the 'disinherited' after the baronial revolt against Henry III had been crushed.

Gradually he rose through the ranks, becoming a papal notary, and cardinal deacon, and serving on various diplomatic missions. In 1292 on the death of the Pope the cardinals found themselves unable to elect: the Orsini and Colonna factions neatly balanced each other out. There was desperate need for a Pope, for the dreadful

War of the Sicilian Vespers between Aragon and the French House of Anjou continued to produce more contestants as it raged its unfruitful way forward. Soon there would be so many self-styled kings of Sicily no one would know who was fighting whom.

In desperation the conclave picked an outsider in July 1294: Peter Morrone, an eighty-year-old hermit of peasant stock with minimal learning, and less experience of high politics. It was a bid for a saint to save a situation politicians had created, but it was disastrous. Celestine V (as he became) had not the makings of a Pope, and quickly became the catspaw of Charles II of Naples, in whose service he made one gaffe after another.

The cardinals tried to show him how impossible the situation was: it was rumoured that Benedict Gaetani spoke to him through a megaphone at night, giving him 'heavenly' messages. Finally, in December, he stepped down, and Gaetani was elected as a strong man to take his place.

Boniface immediately went to Rome for a rich and sumptuous coronation, and promptly cancelled all Celestine's acts. The aged ex-Pope took to the hills, but Boniface had him captured and put away in a dark tower near Anagni, where he could do no more harm. This was to be a new era.

The Pope now began to make large claims in the world, and especially in the papal fief of Sicily, where he took a great part in the hectic struggle for power. He introduced the forces of Charles of Valois from France, making good use of them on their way to reduce Florence and Tuscany to his rule.

He was an immensely irascible man, who saw no reason to guard his tongue. As a lawyer he saw the position quite clearly: there was no room in the world for two supreme authorities, and the one who must rule over all was unquestionably the Pope. Methods did not matter too much; it was the cause that counted. He promoted himself with vigour, sending statuettes of himself in silver to anyone who would receive them. A more constructive measure was his effort in bringing up to date the book of canon law, issuing a sixth section to add to the five already published long before.

All opposition was seen as an act of treachery to the highest authority in the world—even when it was led by cardinals. The Colonna family, seeing Boniface elevating his own relatives to power and estate in the land, revolted and declared he had taken the papal tiara by fraud. Boniface declared a crusade against them and took their lands, razing their town of Palestrina and scattering salt over the site. Anagni was to be the princely centre.

In 1300 he gave ceremonial expression to his ideals, declaring a year of Jubilee, in which all who visited Rome would gain a plenary indulgence. Giotto and other painters, sculptors and architects were employed to set the scene, and the pilgrims came in their thousands—or as one authority claims, millions. All day and night two priests stood at St. Peter's altar with rakes, pulling in the money. So many came, Dante tells us (*Inferno* xviii), that a one-way traffic scheme had to be instituted.

Even before this date Boniface had begun that quarrel with the French King Philip IV which was to last his life. Philip, following the advice of counsellors trained in civil, rather than canon law, was building the secular state, and elaborating its theory. When Boniface issued his Bull *Clericis Laicos* in 1296 to stop secular taxation of clergy without papal permission, Philip forced the Pope to back down.

In October 1301 Philip arrested one of his bishops on a charge of (among other things) treason, and asked the Pope to unfrock him so that he could proceed to punishment. Boniface naturally insisted on an ecclesiastical trial, and an acrimonious correspondence blew up, which was made much worse by the circulation on both sides of forged letters, using even more disgraceful phrases. For example Philip is supposed to have written 'Philip, by the grace of God, King of the Franks, to Boniface who gives himself out for Supreme Pontiff, little or no greeting. Let your great fatuousness know that . . .'

The quarrel grew larger, pausing on the French side after their unexpected reverse at Courtrai in July 1302. Late in that year, however, Boniface issued the Bull *Unam Sanctam*, which made the largest claims ever for the place of the papacy: 'Both the spiritual and material swords are in the power of the Church, the latter indeed to be used for the Church, the former by the Church, the one by the priest, the other by the hand of kings and soldiers, but by the will and sufferance of the priest . . . it is for the spiritual power to establish the earthly power, and judge it if it be not good . . . We, moreover, proclaim, declare and pronounce that it is altogether necessary to salvation for every human being to be subject to the Roman Pontiff.'

This enormous challenge was taken up by Philip, under the advice of his chief Minister William Nogaret, who condemned the Pope as a heretic and usurper, and persuaded his King to call a General Council to depose him in March 1303. William was sent off to Italy, and plotted with the Colonna to capture Boniface. In September they attacked Anagni, and forced their way in to the Pope. The Colonna wanted to kill him, but Nogaret knew that this would prove disastrous to his cause, and so roughly made him prisoner. An observer of the scene, William Hundleby, wrote home to friends in Lincoln: 'he might have been our Geoffrey Ceco or Peter Stall, for all the respect he got from them.' The old man in his papal robes sat through the night muttering 'The Lord gave and the Lord has taken away.'

Throughout the next day, looting and drinking, the attackers argued what to do. On the following day the citizens decided for them: rallying to the Pope, they flung the invaders out, and brought Boniface out of prison into the market-place, 'And everyone could speak with the Pope, as with any other poor man. The women brought him wine and food, whilst the men played with the French banners, trailing them in the mud.'

The world was deeply shocked at the French action, and Boniface might have built on this for further victories; but his pride was broken, and on 12th October of that same year he died.

There is a biography by T. S. R. Boase: *Boniface VIII* (Constable, London, 1933). For a variety of viewpoints see *Philip the Fair and Boniface VIII*, ed. C. T. Wood (Holt, Rinehart and Winston, 1967).

Robert Bruce

'. . . so long as there shall but one hundred of us remain alive, we will never consent to subject ourselves to the dominion of the English.' (Declaration of Arbroath, 1320)

Robert Bruce was seven years old when his aged grandfather made his bid for the throne of Scotland in 1291. The royal line had failed with the death of Alexander III's daughter, and Edward I of England was then adjudging the various claims to the succession, the chief of which were those of John Balliol and Bruce. Balliol was fairly given the throne, his right was the stronger, but Bruce was not the sort of man to forget his own rights, which descended to his grandson.

Balliol was an ineffectual ruler, and Edward a demanding suzerain. In 1295 the Scots tried to take advantage of an alliance with France to throw off English overlordship, but Edward swooped down on the 'rebels', degraded the king, and took the Stone of Destiny, on which Scottish sovereigns were enthroned, back with him to Westminster. Two years later Scotland was in arms once more, under the inspired leadership of William Wallace, and Robert Bruce had his first taste of guerrilla warfare.

The rebellion was heroic, but plainly the English were in a position to repress it. Its aim was the restoration of John Balliol. These two factors account for Bruce's defection to the English in 1302; for four years he was apparently on Edward's side, though during the latter part of this period he was actively planning his rebellion. He had rich estates and titles in Scotland, but also a large English estate, with a town house in London, and a country seat at Tottenham. His family origins were as Anglo-Norman as any English baron's, and one brother, Edward, was in the household of the prince of Wales, whilst another, Alexander, was studying the liberal arts at Cambridge and showing himself to be a very gifted scholar. Few could have suspected what was in Bruce's mind in 1305.

Early in 1306 he went north to meet his fellow-plotters. At Dumfries he met 'Red Comyn' before the high altar of the Grey-friars' church and tried to persuade this important leader to join him. Comyn refused—there were harsh words, a scuffle, and Bruce mortally wounded him with his dagger. A bad and untypical beginning, for Bruce was a very pious man, usually calm and unruffled.

Revolutions cannot be stopped for remorse, and Bruce went on to his coronation at Scone. Edward's wrath, and the speed of his vengeance were unparalleled—within three months Bruce was a hunted fugitive, his family and supporters being given no mercy. His sister was suspended from the walls of Roxburgh castle in a cage, and the same treatment was proposed (but not in fact carried out) for his twelve-year-old daughter in the Tower of London.

Bruce escaped—perhaps to the Hebrides, more probably to Ireland. He was strong and capable of great endurance, and within the year he was back again as a guerrilla chief with few but hardy followers. But with Edward I dead, and only his son Edward II (*q.v.*), as an opponent, much more was possible.

Patiently he pushed on, taking ever larger areas into his control, never indulging in the folly of a pitched battle, husbanding his resources and making brilliant use of the techniques that were available to him. Castles he took by night—crawling with his men (covered in black surcoats) to their objective and then sending in skilled climbers (often miners) to open the way. Edinburgh was taken in this manner, using the services of a young man who had been brought up in the castle and had had plenty of experience climbing out at night to visit his girl in the town. Always Bruce was at the forefront, wading through icy moats and climbing the steepest walls, encouraging his men on.

The treasure-chest was kept full by raiding into England, and either marauding or levying protection—some £20,000 worth in all.

Meanwhile Edward II had done practically nothing to stop Bruce's advance, and by 1314, when Stirling alone remained in English hands beyond the Forth, the situation had reached a crisis. Much to Bruce's annoyance, his brother had bargained with the governor of Stirling that if a substantial English army had not come to its relief within a set time, it would be surrendered.

So in June Edward appeared south of Stirling with an army of some 20,000 foot and 2,500 cavalry, prepared for a set battle —the thing the Scots most feared. Bruce had barely 500 light cavalry, and some 6,000 foot. The road to Stirling lay through a forest, and here the Scots prepared themselves. Below was a small dry field, backed by boggy land, closely intersected with sluggish streams. The little village of Bannock stood by the largest of these burns.

Edward had no battle plans, and ignored what local information was available. Immediately on arrival, one contingent of cavalry was sent storming up to the woods, and was easily beaten off, with Bruce cleaving its leader's head in two. A second party tried to sneak off round the forest, but was beaten back by Moray's brigade, using the schiltrom formation. This manoeuvre was deadly to cavalry unsupported by archers. The Scots kept close formation, presenting a wall of spears to the enemy, aiming at the horses rather than the men.

The knights, angry at being unable to get at the Scots, threw their weapons at the schiltrom, doing little damage, and providing useful additional armament.

The English spent a confused night, preparing for the main battle the next day, but they had not learned the lesson of the first engagement. When the Scots moved out towards the enemy, the English archers were right at the back, and were brought forward only with difficulty, and much too late. In the restricted area of dry ground the cavalry could only get in the way. As the Scots pressed on carnage and confusion reigned, and the English were forced back into the bog behind them. The Scots morale grew as the English declined, and soon Edward II was led protesting from the slaughter to race for his life to the border, as the Scots commentator laconically remarks, not being able to pause to make water.

The incredible defeat of the English set Bruce firmly on the throne, but Edward II perversely refused to recognise him, and was backed in this by a complaisant Pope. The Scots ravaged the Marches, and invaded Yorkshire in an attempt to force the King of England's hand. Ireland was invaded, and Edward Bruce set up as king there (until his timely death and defeat at Dundalk in 1318) to provide a possible base for an invasion of Wales, and the setting up of a new Celtic, anti-English confederacy. Only in 1322 did papal recognition and a truce with England finally come, and Bruce had to wait for a new king in England for a final renunciation of England's suzerainty over Scotland, in 1328.

'Good King Robert' died the following year, having suffered from 'leprosy' (a common medieval designation for any skin disease) for some two years. A pious man—his closest allies had always been learned clergy—he had restored the kingdom from ruins, and given it peace. Castles were destroyed and replaced by manor houses, and Bruce's last years had been happily filled with the peaceful sports of sailing and boat-building—hobbies of Edward II. Scotland was established and renowned once more, and Bruce cannot be blamed for the failures of his son, and for the Stuart dynasty that sprang from his daughter Marjory.

There is a biography by G. W. S. Barrow: *Robert Bruce* (Eyre and Spottiswoode, London, 1965; Univ. of California Press, 1965).

Richard de Bury

Richard de Bury, author of the *Philobiblon*, was born in 1287. After some ten years of study at Oxford he entered the royal service, and soon rose to a position of importance in the household of the baby Prince Edward of Windsor, whom he probably tutored for some three years up till 1326. Two years later his prince became King Edward III, and Richard was made Keeper of the Wardrobe and of the Privy Seal. As a leading member of the administration, he was one of the chief promoters of the *coup d'etat* that made Edward king indeed, without the leading strings or hindrances of his mother and her lover. Richard was well rewarded: a long stream of ecclesiastical preferments led up to his appointment as Bishop of Durham in 1333, and to his consecration came the King and Queen of England and the King of Scotland. In 1334 he was made Treasurer of the Exchequer and Chancellor of England. Meanwhile he was also involved in frequent missions to the Popes at Avignon, the courts of France and Scotland, as well as into France and the Empire.

Yet this hard and ambitious politician is to be remembered chiefly for his overwhelming love of books. When he died in 1345 five large carts were needed to take his library away, and although some envious souls suggested that his scholarship was patchy, none could deny his fervour for learning, which even the great Petrarch had admired. He almost worshipped books, which could transport him anywhere in space or time—even to 'inspect the antarctic pole, which eye hath not seen, nor ear heard'; indeed, 'all the glory of the world would be buried in oblivion unless God had provided mortals with the remedy of books'. He was very distressed at the careless and the rough way people handled books, and strongly objected to the practice of pressing flowers. He also gives a convincing description of a priest's concubine rousting out his books and declaring them to be useless, and selling them off in order to buy fine clothes.

In the *Philobiblon* he tells us how he accumulated his collection: as a royal official he was constantly travelling, and would be gladly accorded permission to root about in the libraries he found; and of course, the more important he became, the more willing the monks and friars were to give him their books in order to win his influence on their behalf. So 'volumes that had slumbered long ages in their tombs wake up and are astonished'. On his many embassies he could view foreign collections, particularly in his 'Paradise'—Paris, where there were 'delightful libraries, more aromatic than stores of spicery' (Bury sounds to have been a book-smeller—a form of drug-addiction not unknown today). He gathered around him a 'family' of notable scholars—such as Bradwardine, Walter Burley and Robert Holcot, and also employed friars to seek out rare texts all over Europe and copy them for him: 'What leveret could escape amidst so many keen-sighted hunters?' They also brought him accounts of the latest academic controversies. Needless to say, the booksellers of England, France, Germany and Italy all knew his tastes and sent him what he wanted: plenty of poetry and grammar (specially Greek or Hebrew, which he aimed to foster), but no civil law or natural science.

The *Philobiblon* is in fact his will, in which he has the vision of a new hall at Oxford centring round his library: he lays down the rules and the loaning system in some detail, and gives his picture of an ideal library where 'boards of cedar with shelves and beams of gopher wood are most skilfully planed; inscriptions of gold and ivory are designed for the several compartments' and the books are carefully arranged to avoid over-crowding. But it was not to be: he had spent so much building up his library that his debts were too great to keep it, and his executors had to sell. Oxford awaited Duke Humphrey.

E. C. Thomas' translation of the *Philobiblon: Love of Books: the Philobiblon of Richard de Bury*, is available in the King's Classics edition (Delamore Press, London, 1903) from which the above quotations are taken. N. Denholm-Young has written about Richard de Bury in the *Transactions of the Royal Historical Society*, 4th Series, xx, 135–168.

St. Catherine of Siena

There are moments in history when women suddenly take the forefront of the stage usually occupied by men—usually times of crisis; one thinks of the great queens of the sixteenth century, the revolutionists of the late nineteenth and earlier twentieth centuries—and of the religious women of the late fourteenth and early fifteenth centuries. Amongst these last St. Catherine of Siena is one of the most interesting.

She was born in 1347, the twenty-third child of a dye-maker. Her mother was a rough and simple woman, who never had a moment to think about anything but looking after her children and grandchildren, until she reached old age, and Catherine's biographer approached her for her memories. She loved her daughter—the only child she had been able to suckle, so frequent had been her earlier pregnancies—but her love was a mindless devotion.

It was her father who understood Catherine, a quiet and patient man, a model of calm and self-restraint. Without his support her life would have been hard indeed. From a very early age she was much given to devout practices, and became obsessed by the Dominican ideal—indeed she contemplated disguising herself as a man in order to be able to join the friars in their work.

She had her first vision of Christ when she was just six years old, and soon began to practice abstinence: in such a large household it was easy for her to dispose of food onto her brother's plate, or to the cats beneath the table. Soon she was living on bread, salads and water alone. Throughout her life people marvelled at her ability to do without food, and criticised her for what they took to be ostentatious saintliness; to meet these criticisms she made valiant attempts to eat, but so used was she to fasting that eating caused her to become severely ill.

At an equally early age she took a vow of virginity, though she was too shy to reveal this to her parents. She was a presentable girl, though careless of her appearance, and when she reached the marriageable age of twelve her parents quite naturally looked around for a suitable groom. Her mother nagged her to dress up and look nice, and for a while she gave in (though she bitterly regretted this 'lapse' for the rest of her life). When it looked as though a suitor had been found, however, she cut off her hair to postpone the evil day.

Her parents took all this to be simple naughtiness, and punished her severely. Only when Catherine finally plucked up enough courage to tell them of her vow did her father agree to stop the wedding preparations. He must have been rather hurt by her secretiveness, but she had taken all the punishments as a part of her penances, probably guarding her secret until the last minute in order to encourage her parents to punish her. For Catherine had a profound sense of sin, and believed deeply in the power of expiatory penance: she wore an iron chain tight round her waist, slept on boards, and flogged herself daily with an iron chain. Her mother was convinced that Catherine was killing herself.

She now joined the Sisters of Penance of St. Dominic—an order usually reserved for widows. It was not an enclosed order, its members remained in their own homes, and for the next three years Catherine immured herself in her own room, speaking to no one but her confessor. In this period she developed her mystical theology out of an intensely personal relationship with Christ, whom she saw in ecstatic visions where her whole body became rigid, and she conversed freely with Him. She held herself as His bride, and throughout her life would constantly glance at His 'ring' on her finger—invisible to others, but clearly envisaged by her as being of gold, with a diamond set in pearls.

At the end of three years she received divine instruction to go out into the world and take part in daily life in order to save souls. She was obedient, but deeply hurt at not being allowed to continue with the life she had led and enjoyed so deeply. She busied herself with domestic chores, and with the relief of suffering in the town, secretly distributing food to the poor. So fearful did her family become of absolute ruin, that all but her father carefully locked up their possessions against Catherine's urge to give everything away.

She cared for a peevish old woman who was dying of leprosy, and brought comfort to the plague-stricken. In this work she had to overcome her own natural fastidiousness and strong sense of smell: she forced herself to undertake the most repulsive tasks in the service of the sick, and triumphed in her control.

Throughout she took great comfort from the Holy Sacrament, which she received as often as possible—much to the annoyance of the friars—for she would go into lengthy trances on receiving the host, and so prevented them from closing up the church at their accustomed hour. She had no concept of time, and often her followers were wearied by her enthusiasm—even her biographer admits to going to sleep once whilst she was talking to him, to be awakened by sharp taps on the shoulder.

It was indeed hard for people to understand a woman who saw the religious world with such sharp clarity. The Devil—whom she amiably referred to as 'Old

Pickpocket'—was constantly present, searching for a means of attack, and Catherine would laugh loud and long at his many defeats and undignified retreats. But it was Christ whom she saw most clearly, and with whom her relationship was most profound: she even believed that He played practical jokes on her. There are a number of examples of this, but the best comes from a period when she was very ill. She heard of a family on the verge of starvation, and, despite her weakness, determined to try to get food to them. All the way there the sack seemed very light, but at the last moment came the practical joke— after depositing the food in the doorway, she found herself unable to stir. It was getting light, and soon people would be on the move, and catch her in a generous act; so she spoke to Christ: 'Why, sweetheart, have you deceived me like this? Do you think it a nice thing to do to mock me and upset me by making me lie here?' She forced herself to crawl away, muttering, 'You'll move, even if I have to die for it.'

So, as her biographer says, 'I have at times seen an endless stream of men and women coming down from the mountains and country towns around Siena, as if summoned by an invisible trumpet, to see or hear Catherine . . .' She was surrounded with disciples, noble and poor, scholarly and ignorant, and her ready response to appeals for help, in Siena and elsewhere, built her a massive reputation. Her contacts were kept by a steady stream of letters (of which some 400 remain to us), and all who met her were deeply impressed. But such holiness, such closeness to God, inspired envy and back-biting as well, and many spread rumours against her, which were only dispelled by her presence.

In 1376 she visited Avignon to attempt to reconcile Pope Gregory XI with the dissident Florentines. She established a powerful influence over this timid Frenchman whom she called 'Daddy'. She urged him to act like a man, rather than a frightened child, and to move to resolve the manifold problems of the Church by the exercise of his power. She was bitterly hurt to see the Church so consumed with vice, and in a powerful image she told the Pope that he must cauterise the major wounds, not fearing the anguish of the operation. Just spreading ointment over them may please the patients, but will not cure. So convincing was she that she persuaded the Pope to end the Babylonish Captivity and return to troubled Rome, facing up to difficulties instead of running away from them.

She was also busy trying to stop the vicious feuds that were tearing Italy apart, and to encourage the soldiers to go on crusade. She wrote to Sir John Hawkwood (*q.v.*) himself and begged him to 'withdraw a little into yourself and consider' how short his time was, and how sinful his life of warfare against Christians. He liked war —well, fair enough, he could go and fight the Saracens. She had considerable success in converting some of the mercenaries— one of her letters to her mother refers to her friars gobbling up the souls of the free-lances until they got a belly-ache— but to no purpose, for the crusade did not materialise.

Her presence seemed to be required everywhere, but when she had gone again people fell into evil ways, and Catherine wrote heart-broken letters to win them back again. In an interval of peace in Siena in 1378 she found time to compose her *Dialogue*, a moving account of her talks with God; but soon she was called to Rome, where the Schism had broken out, and Pope Urban VI needed her support. She busied herself writing to the Kings of France and Hungary, the Queen of Naples, cardinals and bishops in an attempt to get them to support the true Pope, and in persuading the Roman populace to refrain from violence.

It was all to very little effect and in 1380 Catherine saw a Church in full decline. In bitter sadness she offered all she had left— her constancy in self-denial: she begged that she might expiate in her body some of the sins of the world that were the cause of the Church's decline, and, racked with terrible torments, she finally achieved her aim in death.

She had longed all her life for martyrdom, only once coming close to it, when a band of Florentine villains set out to murder her and found, to her regret, that they could not kill her. It is difficult for us to understand this great desire for death, but in Catherine's correspondence there survives a letter that goes far towards an explanation. It is an account of almost hysterical excitement and intensity induced by a personal experience of the purifying qualities of 'blood and fire'.

A young Paduan gentleman had unwisely criticised the Sienese government in some light words, and had been condemned to death. He was horrified at the injustice of this sentence, and reduced to black despair. Catherine went to visit him, and persuaded him to make a good death, accepting the axe as a gift of immeasurable grace, giving entrance to paradise before the young man could have expected it. She banished all his fear, and went with him to the block. She held, and received his head, and at that moment of execution had a vision of his soul entering Heaven.

Covered in blood she dashed off the letter to her confessor, ending 'Ah me! miserable! I will say no more. I stayed on the earth with the greatest envy. And it seems to me that the first new stone is already in place. Therefore do not wonder if I impose upon you nothing save to see yourselves drowned in the blood and the flame poured from the side of the Son of God. Now then, no more negligence, sweetest of my sons, since the blood is beginning to flow, and to receive the life.'

See George Lamb's translation of *The Life of St. Catherine of Siena by Blessed Raymond of Capua* (Harvill Press, London, 1960), and *Saint Catherine of Siena as seen in her letters*, ed. & trs. by Vida D. Scudder (Dutton, New York, 1905). (The letter referred to at the end is on pp. 109–14.)

Charlemagne

England is about to lose one of the last traces of the Emperor Charles the Great—Charlemagne—for it was he who established the system of reckoning in pounds, shillings and pence. He will also be remembered as the white-haired old king in the *Song of Roland*; but he was neither an economist nor the rather feckless character of the *Song*, being rather one of the ideal examples in European history of the man of action, a type that always spells danger.

He was born in 742, to Pepin the Short, who was Mayor of the Palace of Childeric III, the last of an ever degenerating line of Merovingian kings. In 751, with the support of the Pope, Pepin cut off Childeric's long hair, the mark of his kingship, and sent him to a monastery, arrogating to himself the royal power. He was an active ruler, imposing peace on his border-lands, and twice descending on Italy to protect the Pope from the Lombards, giving to him the duchy of Rome as his own state into the bargain.

In 768 Charlemagne and his brother Carloman succeeded to the joint rule of the Franks, but three years later Carloman died, and Charlemagne ruled supreme. He was as active as his father in defending and expanding his territories. In 773, when the Lombards were again putting pressure on the Pope, he crossed the Alps with astonishing speed and defeated the Lombards absolutely, putting their king in a monastery (by now a family habit) and assuming the 'Iron' Crown of Lombardy himself.

He now began a systematic campaign to conquer the Saxons, and ten years of the most bitter fighting ensued. The Saxons discovered an able leader in Widukind, and in 782, managed to wipe out a substantial army of Franks. Charlemagne had 4,500 Saxons beheaded at Verden in retribution, and went on to celebrate 'The Nativity of Our Lord and Easter as he was wont to do', says Einhard, his biographer. It took nearly three years to find Widukind, and he was then baptised—a clear declaration of submission; the rest of the Saxons gave little trouble in taking baptism, or obeying their new Frankish masters—they remembered Verden.

A feudal vassal of Charlemagne who should have learned a lesson from this was Duke Tassilo of Bavaria, but he preferred to behave as if he were independent of his overlord. Charlemagne gave him one chance to reform, but then found that he was plotting with his enemies, so in 788 he too was put into a monastery, and Bavaria was incorporated into the fast growing empire.

In Spain he was not so successful: he had been forced to call off his invasion in 778, for his troops were needed elsewhere, and anyway the Muslims turned out to be not as disunited as he had been told; it was in this retreat that Roland died. But in 793 the Muslims attacked over his borders, so he set up an enclave on the southern side of the Pyrenees to guard the area.

He now turned his attention to the Avars, relations of the Huns, who lived in the area of the middle Danube, and were phenomenally rich with tribute-money they had wrung from the Byzantine Emperors. Peaceful negotiations had failed to keep them from raiding Charlemagne's lands, and so he set out to conquer them. It was as hard a war as that against the Saxons, lasting from 791–9, and Charlemagne was wise to distribute the loot he gained from it to his war-weary people instead of keeping it for himself.

Since 476 there had been no Emperor in the West, and until recently the Popes had looked to the Byzantine Emperors for protection. In 800 the Pope was set upon and deposed, and Charlemagne had to go down to Rome and restore him. On Christmas Day of that year he was praying in St. Peter's when the Pope came up and crowned him as Emperor, taking him 'unawares'. Historians wrangle over the coronation of Charlemagne, and the results of their researches read like detective stories. Suffice it to say that Charlemagne must have known what was going to happen, but he was rather disturbed about

the whole thing afterwards; possibly he was upset at not having the fiat of the Emperor of the East (though a woman was reigning there at the time), possibly he felt the Pope had arrogated to himself too great a part in the coronation. Certainly he kept a very healthy respect for the Byzantine Empire, though he was not a man to fear another's power: he had good relations with Haroun-al-Raschid, the Caliph of Baghdad (who sent him a white elephant), and arranged protection for pilgrims visiting Jerusalem, in the heart of Muslim territory. In a less exciting area he developed good relations also with the various Anglo-Saxon states in England; and the first commercial treaty of which we have a record in English history is a letter from Charlemagne to Offa of Mercia, then the central Anglo-Saxon state, requesting more short cloaks, but not as short as the last batch, for when one was forced by the call of nature to get off one's horse, the cloak turned out to be a very draughty affair.

Einhard's biography gives us a fine picture of Charlemagne in the prime of his life: a large pleasant looking man, with rather a weak voice, who loved all forms of exercise, but excelled in swimming. He wore the ordinary dress of his nation, objecting strongly to having to dress in Roman fashion on the two occasions Popes requested it to impress the citizens in Rome. He ate and drank moderately, but had a passion for roast meat. He loved to hear music and to listen to readings from St. Augustine's *City of God*; he also delighted in the old songs of his nation, which his priggish son had destroyed after his death, because they were pagan. He plainly respected learning, and loved to be surrounded by learned people, but he probably didn't get very far in his own learning; he used to keep a copy-book under his pillow (for he suffered from insomnia) but he never really learned to write.

His palace at Aachen was the Versailles of the ninth century, beautiful and impressive, though it is a typically homely touch that he settled on this site because the swimming was good there, with natural hot springs to warm the water. The pictorial arts flourished under him, especially in the decoration of books, which themselves were written in the fine minuscule hand which was developed in his reign, and was to form the basis of the Renaissance italic hand. Schools were built up, modelled on the palace school, which was more of a university in that it served as a place for distinguished scholars to work, and a training ground for the sons of the nobility. Alcuin was called from England, and Peter of Pisa came, along with the best minds of the age. Monasteries built up huge libraries, and in their scriptoria multiple copies were made. By these means the riches of the literature of the ancient world were preserved for the modern, and not even the destructive power of the Norsemen could entirely root out the achievement. Although the full effect of this educational revolution was not to be felt until after the death of Charlemagne, when the whole of Europe began to build great edifices of stone, and Anglo-Saxons took the art of illumination and brought it to its highest point, and theologians and philosophers dared to reason, this was truly the Carolingian Renaissance, and owed a tremendous debt to the boundless vision and enthusiasm of Charlemagne himself.

In fact the cultural influences of the Carolingian state were to outlast by far the state itself. Having conquered territories, Charlemagne tended to do little but install Frankish counts there, introduce his elementary form of feudalism, and then occasionally add to the legal system such laws as were necessary. He sent round groups of 'Missi Dominici' to check on the administration of the counts, and held formal assemblies each year, which provided an elementary check on what was happening all over the Empire; but it was only while his dominant personality and military might were at the head of the system that it could work—the whole Empire was ready to spring apart into fragments when this was removed. It lacked the economic organisation necessary for unity, retaining the spirit of self-sufficiency which was the hallmark of medieval regionalism.

On his death in 814 his son Louis the Pious succeeded, but on his death in 840 civil war broke out between Louis' sons, and in 843 at Verdun the Empire was divided between the three of them, one taking the western strip, one the eastern and the third taking a central strip right down from the Low Countries to half-way down Italy—Germany was to go a separate way from that of France, the Low Countries and Burgundy were to aim at separate development, and all were to have an interest in what became of the Italian domains.

It is possible to place too much emphasis on the decisiveness of this treaty for the future history of Western Europe, but even so one should remember that the year before it was made when the two leaders of West and East met to make the preliminary arrangements, the one swore his oath in French and the other in German so that their followers could understand them.

The popular names for the rulers who followed in the wake of Charlemagne spell out for us the decline from greatness, Louis the Pious, Charles the Bald, Louis the Stammerer, Charles the Fat, Charles the Simple. Europe was to be divided, with disastrous results; but nonetheless people remembered the achievement of Charlemagne through the long terrible years of war and the terrible attacks from the Norsemen. They created the tradition of the *Song of Roland*, which was only outdone in popularity by the later re-workings of the predominantly national legends of the Germans and the Celtic lands. Perhaps it was not so bad that Arthur replaced Charlemagne in the end, for his like did not come to Europe again until the days of Napoleon.

The contemporary *Life of Charlemagne* by Einhard has been translated by S. E. Turner (Michigan Univ. Press, Ann Arbor, 1960).

Charles IV

Charles IV, Holy Roman Emperor (christened Wenceslas, but he took the name Charles when he was confirmed) was born in 1316, son of John of Luxembourg, King of Bohemia. His father was the son of the Emperor Henry VII, and had been elected king on his marriage to the daughter of the last of the Přemyslid line. John did not get on with the Bohemian nobles, or with his wife, and he left the country late in 1319, to return only for short visits to raise money for his schemes. The Czechs grumbled at his exactions, but enjoyed his long absences, secretly rather proud of the prowess of their jousting King, who flew about Europe doing deeds of prowess. He was never still—he could make the difficult journey from Prague to Frankfurt (255 miles as the crow flies) in four days, and was liable to pop up anywhere. He gained substantial additions to his kingdom—notably Silesia, for which his subjects were duly grateful.

Charles was brought up a Czech whilst his father fought to establish Lewis of Bavaria on the Imperial throne, though the Emperor was to prove very ungrateful for his fine services. In 1323 John took Charles to the French court to be educated in a new language and a fresh culture, whilst the king dashed off to crusade in Lithuania. From there he was invited to Italy to serve first as a mercenary, then as a ruler, building up a principality in Lombardy over which he set Charles as governor in 1331.

This strange addition to his crown was soon lost, however, and in 1333 Charles was entrusted with the government of Bohemia, where he showed himself to be a skilful and popular administrator. The years 1336–8 were spent trying to recover his brother's appanage of the Tyrol, which the Emperor Lewis had obtained by annulling the marriage of its Duchess with John Henry of Luxembourg, and marrying her to his son.

This was only the last of a long line of injustices inflicted on the House of Luxembourg by Lewis the Bavarian, who owed his very throne to them. He had conducted an enormous running war with the papacy, employing eminent political philosophers to write for him (see William Ockham), and had deposed a pope and raised another with his own hands. His plain desire to use his office as a means of enriching his own family and little else had antagonised many. The time had come for a showdown.

In 1342 Charles' old tutor had been elevated as Pope Clement VI, and he now worked hard in Charles' favour, succeeding in 1346 in persuading the Electors to depose Lewis and elect Charles King of the Romans. Charles agreed to the most abject terms and was thenceforward known as 'the priests' king.' He had little power to stand out against Lewis, who was in a good position to prevent Charles from taking up his rule.

That same year Charles and his father (who had been blind for many years now) dashed off to aid the French at Crécy. King John showed boundless gallantry in charging the English when all was lost, and the story goes that Edward III picked up his standard, three ostrich plumes over the motto 'Ich Dien', and gave it to the Black Prince to carry as a reminder of a great knight.

Charles was less addicted to fighting than his father. He was nervous (a great whittler of sticks) and often sick, but his diplomatic skill and his vision for his country of Bohemia mark him out as a greater man than his noble and energetic parent.

In October came a stroke of luck: Lewis the Bavarian died whilst hunting, and the field was now clear for Charles. As Emperor he succeeded to a strange position—an incredible clutter of states, united only in name, and devoted to nothing so much as internecine war. A total absence of order or regularity, no constitution or ordered array of customary law to look to. Above all a shambles of a financial system, where no one clearly knew who had rights to what, and all were determined to resist demands for money at all costs.

He was aided by the disunity and

ineffectuality of the heirs of Lewis the Bavarian—they were not able to unite against him. He used ruses where he could (imposing an impostor on Brandenburg for a number of years who claimed to be the last of the Ascanian line—a man who had died thirty years previously); and where these failed he purchased loyalty on the open market.

He was not in the least interested in the Empire's claims in Italy. When Cola di Rienzo visited him in Prague in 1350 to urge him to come and restore the old Roman Empire (having failed magnificently to revive the office of Tribune of the People for himself) the Emperor imprisoned him, and later handed him over to the Pope. Throughout, Charles showed a commendable desire to keep the promises he had made to Pope Clement in 1346, though this earned him the jeers of Europe. His visit to Rome for his coronation in 1355 lasted (as agreed nearly a decade before) for but one day, and his only other trip to Italy came ten years later, in a brave, but admittedly foolish attempt to restore the papacy to Rome from its Babylonish Captivity in Avignon.

Charles was a realist, and saw that his high title had little basic meaning. In the 'Golden' Bull of 1356 he attempted to regularise the position in the Empire, establishing clear rules for the election of Emperor. Thoughts of reviving ancient Roman rule—even when expressed by his friend Petrarch—were laughably anachronistic to Charles, and he saw himself as only a little more than the president of a league of states, working to preserve as much harmony as was humanly possible. If he could profit by it, so much the better.

Opponents were met with bland and subtle diplomacy, as usual. When Rudolf of Habsburg produced forged charters claiming grants to the Austrian house by Julius Caesar and Nero, Charles suppressed a smile, assessed his power, and made a treaty. If either of their two houses failed to produce an heir, the other family would succeed to their united kingdoms, and

many years later the Habsburgs did gain Bohemia, to their infinite disturbance in the Thirty Years War.

The opposition of Lewis of Bavaria's grandsons was even more skilfully treated, for Charles came out of that in 1373 with the much coveted Mark of Brandenburg, and the reversion of the crown of Hungary to his second son, Sigismund. Three years later he had persuaded the electors to set up his eldest son Wenceslas as King of the Romans in his own lifetime.

Charles used the Empire for his family, but he also had a high sense of duty towards his kingdom, and as his family prospered, so did Bohemia. He may not have been a very good Emperor (in the circumstances one might ask whether this was even a possibility), but there is no doubt at all when one turns to his kingdom. Bohemia was much enlarged during his rule by the additions of Brandenburg, Carinthia and the Tyrol, and it was given first place in the Empire in all things.

Charles worked strongly for the restoration of good order and justice in Bohemia, even passing a law which allowed people of the lower classes to prosecute their lords in courts of law. He encouraged agriculture and trade, and brought crowds of people to his capital, enlarging it with new buildings in the French style, and adorning it with the new University of Prague. Under him art and learning flourished, and although there were large numbers of Germans and Frenchmen involved, the style was very definitely evolving as Czech.

His deep interest in theology led him to take a large part in ecclesiastical affairs. He had persuaded the Pope to raise the See of Prague to archiepiscopal status in 1344, thereby releasing it from German domination. He encouraged movements for reform, patronising the immensely popular preaching of Conrad Waldhauser and John Milič. The latter was a kind of Czech St. Francis, preaching poverty and mysticism and winning large numbers of converts. He even converted a great crowd of prostitutes to the religious life, and Charles gave him a former brothel called 'Venice' to be their nunnery. John promptly changed the name to 'Jerusalem'. He could be tiresome —in a moment of hysteria he had pointed out the Emperor as Antichrist in one of his more public sermons, but Charles continued to support him and his movement for moral reform. As the state grew richer, more culturally refined and infinitely more powerful, it could not afford a corrupt and relaxed Church. The groundwork for Hus and his followers was being firmly laid.

Charles was a cultivated man—he spoke and wrote fluently Czech, French, Italian, German and Latin, and he corresponded with Petrarch, who visited him in Prague in 1356. But he was still, despite the Renaissance diplomacy, art and literature, a man of the Middle Ages. He collected relics and believed sincerely that his dreams could forecast the future. He also believed in poltergeists. Perhaps a charmingly modern feature of his character was his pride in the strength of his fourth wife, Elizabeth; he had her give demonstrations to the wondering courtiers of breaking thick chunks of wood, and tearing masses of parchment.

He died in 1378, leaving a kingdom well established and immensely grateful to his memory. The Archbishop of Prague spoke wisely at his funeral of 'bringing almost impossible things to a good ending'.

There is a biography by Bede Jarrett: *The Emperor Charles IV* (Eyre and Spottiswoode, London, 1935).

Geoffrey Chaucer

Geoffrey Chaucer was born in London about 1340, son of a wealthy vintner with court connections. He must have received a substantial early education, but we first hear of him in 1357 as a page in the household of the Countess of Ulster, wife of Lionel Duke of Clarence. There he met his future wife, Philippa, sister to Katherine Swynford, who was to become first mistress, then wife to John of Gaunt.

In 1359 he joined the expedition to France, and had rather an inglorious military career, for he had to be ransomed the following year, the king contributing £16. By 1367 he had become a yeoman of the king's chamber, and in 1372 he was promoted to squire. It was a gay court, travelling much, and fattened on the plunder of the French wars. Romantic jousts and courtly (and uncourtly) love gave it an Arthurian touch. Part of Chaucer's duties as squire consisted of the entertainment of the king, and he was already a productive poet. His first major work was for his good patron John of Gaunt, the *Death of Blanche the Duchess*.

Throughout the decade following 1370 Chaucer was active as a diplomat, often on a very high level. At least seven times he journeyed abroad, twice to Italy. There he came under the sway of Dante, Boccaccio and Petrarch. He probably met the latter in 1373. In 1379 he went to treat with Sir John Hawkwood (*q.v.*), and probably took the chance to renew his Italian acquaintances.

He was well rewarded with substantial annuities from the king and John of Gaunt (*q.v.*), and with two comptrollerships of customs, for which he speedily found deputies, taking the bulk of the salary for himself. He lived well, in a pleasant 'flat' in Aldgate Tower, and wrote prolifically—mainly translations from the Latin, French and Italian, as well as shorter poems of his own invention.

In 1386 an economising Council removed his synecures, and in the same year he lost his wife (and her annuity). These were hard times, and the poet was forced to raise cash on his own annuities. In 1387 he made his Canterbury pilgrimage, and during the next two years did the bulk of the work on his great poem. Like his admired Dante, he had discovered the ideal vehicle for the presentation of the whole of society, and the *Tales* celebrate as well as describe the medieval world at its ending, but before the chaos to come.

In 1389 things looked up once more,

financially, for Richard II grandiosely made him clerk of the royal works. He was by no means efficient (though the highway-robbery he endured in 1390 could hardly be blamed on him) and in 1391 he was relieved of the office. He went to live in Greenwich with his little love-child Lewis, for whom he wrote the *Treatise on the Astro-labe*, to satisfy the ten year old's scientific leanings.

In 1394 Richard granted Chaucer a further annuity, which he badly needed, being deep in debt. Soon his old patron's son was on the throne, and Henry IV substantially increased the poet's annuity, so that he could now move back into London, and lease a tenement close to Westminster Abbey (and 'nigh to the White Rose Tavern' too), in which to spend his last days. It was a good house—his rich son was to lease it later on.

In early summer 1400 Chaucer fell ill, and after some months in bed, died in October. Poets such as Gower and Hoc-cleve were clear in their belief that here was a master, the true founder of English literature, and soon readers by the hun-dreds, then thousands when printing came, recognised that he was a source of deep enjoyment too. Worthily, he was the first poet to be buried in the Abbey.

G. G. Coulton, *Chaucer and his England* (Methuen, London, 1963; Barnes and Noble, New York, 1963).

Christina of Markyate

The life of Christina of Markyate is remark-able in every respect. Most important of all is that we possess an excellent biography of her, written by one who knew her and her associates very well, which gives us a pic-ture that is clear and rings true throughout; much of the really personal information he gives must have been told to him by the people involved, particularly Christina her-self (there is an excellent edition and trans-lation by C. H. Talbot, Oxford Univ. Press, 1959). Secondly she is one of the few Anglo-Saxons we hear of in detail after the

Conquest. Thirdly she stands as a fas-cinating case-history of a medieval woman's attitude to sex.

She was born about 1097 into a rich Anglo-Saxon family in Huntingdon, des-cribed by her biographer as 'a family of ancient and influential English nobles and the whole of that district for miles around Huntingdon was full of her relatives.' Her father and mother, Autti and Beatrice, were deeply religious in their own way, being constantly in the priory church of St. Mary's Huntingdon, and visiting hermits around. Her brother became a monk of St. Albans, and her sister later joined her at Markyate. The area around was full of recluses and anchoresses, and Dr. Talbot has suggested (pp. 12–13) that the eremeti-cal movement at this time represented some sort of national division, whereby the Anglo-Saxons underlined their difference of race by withdrawing from the largely Norman-dominated monasteries.

In fact all seemed well for her to enter religion, but (as the constant attacks on her virginity show) she was stunningly beauti-ful, and a thoroughly outstanding sort of girl: the biographer clearly indicates that Autti gave her his keys (rather than to his wife) and she was in charge of his treasury and affairs. She was a pearl among women, and her parents were highly reluctant to see her disappear into what they viewed as religious nonentity and seclusion.

As a small girl she showed strong signs of her devotion, for when put to bed she would hold conversations with God at the top of her voice, believing that no one could hear her. When she realised that her family was laughing, she stopped this habit. She was taken on her birthday to visit the great abbey of St. Albans, where she was deeply impressed with the monas-tic life, and vowed secretly to preserve her virginity in order one day to make it her profession. She was supported in this by an old canon of St. Mary's Priory in Huntingdon, one Sueno, who had a deep influence on her thinking.

When she was sixteen, however, her

troubles began. Ranulph Flambard, the king's chief officer, and Bishop of Durham, had had as a mistress Christina's aunt, and they had several children. He had set her up with a husband who could support her in Huntingdon, and was in the habit of visiting her 'for old time's sake', whenever he was on the way north to Durham, or south to London. There one day he met Christina, and longed to have her. He arranged a wild party for the whole family, and while it was going on, withdrew to his room, which was hung about with rich tapestries, and ordered that Christina should be brought to him. When she arrived he ordered his servants to leave, and, catching her by her sleeve, began, as they say, to make advances. Christina, thinking what she could do, begged to be allowed to bolt the door, lest they should be discovered, and when he let her go, she ran out and bolted it on the other side. He came back again with silken garments and precious jewels, but could not persuade her; so he decided to plot her ruin, and arranged for a local celebrity, one Burthred, to ask for her hand in marriage.

Christina could not be persuaded to agree, and for a year her parents tried everything: they gave her presents, got her married friends to tell her what fun they had, and kept her firmly away from her religious friends in the priory. Finally they took her to the annual feast of the Gild Merchant in Huntingdon, where Autti was the leading figure, and made her act as cup-bearer. They made her remove her mantle, roll up her sleeves, and belt in her flowing garments to show off her figure: they hoped 'that the compliments of the onlookers and the accumulation of little sips of wine' would make her realise what gaiety she was missing.

At some stage in these machinations the family got her to agree to the betrothal by gathering all together in the priory church. We don't know what arguments they used, but as Thomas Becket was to be forced to change his mind in a similar situation, and under similar pressures later in the century,

we cannot blame her, for all were against her.

Burthred had built a fine new house to receive her, and longed only for the marriage day, but Christina put it off so often, her parents again decided to take a hand. They arranged for Burthred to enter her bedroom late one night: he found her fully dressed and waiting for him, and they sat out the night like brother and sister, whilst she persuaded him of the joys and rewards of chastity. The next morning her parents were furious, and called Burthred 'a spineless and useless fellow'. Twice more the same experiment was tried, but the first time Christina hid between the hangings and the wall, clinging to a nail, and the second she fled out of the door and leapt over the high spiked fence that surrounded the house, astonishing all by her agility.

Her father was in despair, and now took Christina to the Prior of St. Mary's to get him to persuade her. He explained that he realised why Christina wanted to remain chaste, but knew that he would become the laughing-stock of the neighbourhood if he let her flout his authority. 'Why must she depart from tradition? Why must she bring this dishonour on her father? Her life of poverty will bring the whole of the nobility into disrepute.' The Prior tried to persuade Christina of the holiness of the state of matrimony, but failed, and urged them to put the case before the Bishop of Lincoln, who was staying close by. The case was put, the bishop decided for Christina, and her father fell into a state of utter dejection at being so crossed.

All seemed well, but then some of Autti's friends came to him and pointed out that he couldn't have expected to win the case, as he hadn't bribed the bishop, who was notoriously greedy. He immediately cheered up, and sent large presents to the bishop, who promptly re-opened the case and decided against Christina. At last the parental authority had won, for surely the girl would not dare to go against the word of her bishop.

But she did, and Autti and Beatrice

seemed to go mad with rage. Autti once turned her out of the house naked, and then recaptured her again, and Beatrice once took her out from a feast and flogged her until she was weak, bringing her back again for all to taunt. Indeed, her mother now said that she didn't care who deflowered the virgin so long as someone did.

Christina was now closely watched by the servants and more particularly by her sister Matilda, but she managed to bribe them to allow her to have a few words with the hermit Eadwin. He agreed to help her, and went off to see the most famous hermit of the area, Roger of Markyate. Roger had met three angels at Windsor on his return from Jerusalem, and they had led him to the place he now kept as his hermitage; a monk of St. Albans (an abbey free of the bishop's control), he had official permission to reside as a hermit, and had a general control over all the hermits of the area.

But at first he would have nothing to do with the case, believing Christina to having ruined herself by agreeing to her betrothal. Eadwin went on, however, to see the Archbishop of Canterbury, who gave his general consent to Christina's wishes, and urged Eadwin to help her. On his return to Huntingdon he sent his servant Loric to Christina, and they planned her escape. The next time her parents went away to visit the hermit Guido, Loric would bring two horses to the fields outside the town at dawn.

When the time came, Loric wasn't there, and Christina walked around distracted; she met the town reeve who asked her whether she meant to escape and she told him yes. Back at home, whilst she sat miserably with the servants, she suddenly got the feeling that Loric was now there, and, dressing in male clothing, and covering herself with a large cloak, she went off to meet him. Her sister Matilda followed her, and as they went Christina let one of the full sleeves of her man's coat fall out from her cloak; Matilda came up and asked what it was. Christina told her she was going to pray, gave her a veil she

happened to be carrying, and also her father's keys, adding, 'And these, too, sweetheart, so that if our father returns in the meantime, and wishes to take something from the chest, he will not get angry because the keys are missing.' Frightened of her father's wrath, Matilda forgot her inquisitiveness, and fled off home.

The biography describes the moment of embarrassment when Christina realised she would have to ride like a man, but this soon passed, and they were off to Flamstead, covering the thirty miles in six hours. There the anchoress Alfwen clothed her in her habit, which was rough after the silks and furs she was accustomed to, and she retired to a tiny chamber to read the Psalms.

Meanwhile her parents had organised a massive search, ordering that anyone who had assisted her escape was to be killed. Her husband-to-be even visited Roger's hermitage, offering two shillings reward for any news of Christina. Roger had not yet heard of her escape, and sent Burthred off with a flea in his ear, shocked to think that anyone could imagine him receiving a fresh young girl into his hermitage.

But after two years with Alfwen, Christina did go to join Roger, for she longed to be taught his methods of contemplation. They tried always to avert their gaze from one another, but one day, stepping over her prostrate body in his chapel he turned for a quick glance, and found that she too was looking at him. He called her his Sunday daughter, and was plainly attached to her, but he had to keep her presence secret even from the hermits who lived with him. So for four years she lived in a tiny cell, with the door barred. Roger would come at night to let her out to satisfy the calls of nature, and the biography notes the agonies she endured when he was delayed, or absent-mindedly forgot.

Burthred now came to Roger and officially renounced his marriage with Christina, and the Archbishop of York (a friend of Roger's) who was staying nearby at the time, annulled the marriage, and arranged for Burthred to be allowed to re-marry. Then Roger died, and Christina was without a protector, so the archbishop had her go to join a high-born cleric he knew. It was an unfortunate arrangement, for both were subject to torments of desire, the man even coming naked before her to plead with her.

In worse agony of spirit than ever before, Christina fled back to Markyate, to occupy Roger's cell. There she was comforted by a strange and interesting vision. For a whole day Christ appeared to her in the shape of a little child which she cuddled and put to her breast, and at other times felt to be in her womb. Her other visions always showed Christ as a stunningly handsome and attractive man, and although it may seem a tasteless comment, there seems to be little doubt that in renouncing physical sex she had by no means put it behind her, but had incorporated it into her personal religion.

At last her persecutor the Bishop of Lincoln died, and she was enabled under the new bishop to make her monastic profession formally at St. Albans. Leading clerics from all parts of England, and on the Continent too, tried to ger her to come to head nunneries which they had founded; but although she was troubled by the reputation for sanctity she had built up in her own area (she performed some psychosomatic cures), she decided to stay at Markyate and build up a nunnery there.

The last man in her life was Abbot Geoffrey of St. Albans, with whom she had a deep and satisfying relationship in religion, though it provoked scandalous comments from many. This fascinating character had become a monk by mistake, almost: he had been a schoolmaster at Dunstable, and had had a fire in which were burnt some valuable copes he had borrowed from the abbey as costumes for a play. As compensation he had offered himself as a monk, and had risen fast because of his administrative skills, and his worldly know-how. He was completely captivated by Christina, whom he called his 'girl', and was constantly referred to by her as 'beloved'. He longed to be with her, and took no steps without her advice: she seemed to be able to know absolutely what he was doing, thinking—even wearing— when he was not with her. Indeed, the biography ends (the manuscript was damaged by fire and is incomplete) with a description of her fussing over him, and 'sensibly reproving him when his actions were not quite right . . .'

Because of the incompleteness of the text, we know almost nothing of Christina's last years. In 1155 she sent with the Abbot Robert (nephew, and next abbot but one at St. Albans to the Abbot Geoffrey) two mitres and a pair of sandals embroidered with her own hands as a gift to the Pope. Within a year she died.

It is impossible to sum up such a woman's life, instead let us leave her with one more story that shows her as a woman, rather than as a holy woman. One day at dinner she refused to eat a salad put on the table by Godit, one of her maidens, because it had come from the garden of a neighbour who had once refused her a sprig of chervil, out of miserliness. The embarrassment felt by all those at dinner with her, eating away while she fasted, is plain to read in her biographer's account, but it's nice to know that she too had quarrels over the garden wall.

Cnut

In 1041 the Archbishop of York made his sermon of the Wolf (a pun on his own name —Wulfstan—and a dire warning in itself) to the English: 'Beloved men, realise what is true: this world is in haste and the end approaches.' For some thirty years Æthelræd (nicknamed 'Unræd', which means ill-advised, not unready) had payed the Danes to go away, for he knew that he had not sufficient loyal men to fight them. The men described in the great Anglo-Saxon poem of the *Battle of Maldon* as fighting the Danes to the death, encouraging each other on:

'Thoughts must be braver, hearts more hard, and courage the greater as our strength grows less'—these were not typical: those shown running away in the poem represented the bulk of the English nation. And who can blame them, for the Vikings were both fearless and merciless. In the saga of the Jomsvikings we read of Bui, who when receiving a thrust which cuts off his lips and chin, simply spits out the loose teeth and says, 'The Danish women on Bornholm won't think it so pleasant to kiss me now.' Later, when forced to abandon ship, and having had his two hands chopped off, he sticks his stumps in the handles of his gold-chest and leaps overboard. When the Jomsvikings are caught, they face execution with a mere scientific curiosity, asking the executioner to note whether they continue to grip after death, and whether they pale at the last moment, 'for we have often spoken about that.' (*Saga of the Jomsvikings*, ed. N. F. Blake, Nelson, London, 1962.)

In 1013 Swein, King of Denmark, landed in England, determined to overthrow finally the weak remainder of Anglo-Saxon rule, and he brought with him his young son Cnut. The Danes already settled here flocked to his standards, and the rest of England meekly bowed before him. Æthelræd fled to Normandy, and Swein ruled the country, but only for a short time, for he died early in 1014. Cnut was eighteen years old, and was left in a perilous position of command, for the death of his father was a signal for the Anglo-Saxons to recall Æthelræd, and move against the hated Danes. So Cnut withdrew before them, to his elder brother's kingdom of Denmark.

In 1015 he returned to England, to contest the crown up and down the land with the weakening Æthelræd, and his valiant son, Edmund Ironside. Edmund was two years older than Cnut, and his equal in battle: in fact Cnut so respected him that, even after inflicting on the English a heavy defeat at Ashington, he still chose to meet Edmund and divide the land,

giving Edmund his ancestral domain of Wessex, and taking the rest for himself. Within weeks, however, Edmund died, and though there is no evidence of foul play, it was certainly within Cnut's character to have him killed.

For the new king carefully sought out the possible Anglo-Saxon heirs to have them killed, though he could not reach the Ironside's children in Hungary, or Æthelræd's two sons, safe in the protection of the Duke of Normandy. He solved the latter problem by marrying their mother, the redoubtable Emma of Normandy; it did not seem to matter to him that he already had a wife, Ælfgifu of Northampton, whom he had no intention of putting away. She was to be his Scandinavian Queen, whilst Emma was his English consort.

Cnut was a sea-king, with a standing fleet ever ready to whisk him back to Denmark, which he inherited on his brother's death in 1018, or to his conquest of Norway and parts of Sweden, or on his invasion of Estonia (his mother was half Polish, and he seems to have envisaged an enlargement of Denmark to the south and east, perhaps with a vague memory of possible claims he might have).

In 1027 he went to Rome, as Emperor of the Northern Seas, to attend the coronation of the Holy Roman Emperor. He was plainly proud to be received—the first Viking monarch to be so honoured—and was flattered by the attentions of the Pope and Emperor; but he was not overwhelmed—he kept his head, and negotiated substantial privileges for his dominions from both.

There was something more to his visit, however, than pure display and diplomacy: Cnut seems to have been genuinely attracted by at least the exterior elements of his adopted faith. In England he lavished attention and favours on the Church (which must have marvelled at so strange a benefactor) and issued a revised and conflated code of law, based almost entirely on previous Anglo-Saxon codes.

He died young, still under forty, in 1035. His two rather insignificant and dissolute sons succeeded him in quick succession, and the great empire of the North fell to pieces around them. They were succeeded by Æthelræd's and Emma's son, Edward the Confessor, the last Anglo-Saxon king.

There is a biography by L. M. Larson: *Canute the Great* (A.M.S. Press, 1912).

Constantine the Great

Constantine the Great was born about the year 274, in Dacia, a province of the Roman Empire roughly equivalent in modern times to Rumania. His father was Caesar in Gaul, and had the task of recovering Britain for the Empire after the revolt of the Roman commander Carausius. It was a responsible post, in an area where revolts had been common, and Constantine was sent to the court of Diocletian, partly as a hostage for his father's loyalty, partly to receive the education in government that his birth required.

It was thought that Diocletian was grooming Constantine as his successor, but at the last minute he changed his mind, and Galerius ruled in his place. Constantine wisely rejoined his father, and took part in the campaigns in North Britain. He must have impressed the army, for when his father died at York in 306, it was led by one of its barbarian commanders (charmingly named Crocus) in acclaiming him in his turn Caesar in Gaul.

He now ruled a quarter of the Empire, but for some time he showed little ambition to do more than that; for six years he engaged in warfare along the Rhine frontier, and established peace in his province. But in 312 he swooped down to take Italy. Winning the notable victory of Saxa Rubra, he saw in the sky a cross, with the motto 'In this sign conquer', and from this time forward this was to be the battle-cry that directed his mind and heart. Soon he was sharing the government of the Empire with Licinius, and by 323 he ruled it alone.

Constantine was to establish that coalition between Christianity and the Empire that was to be the main guiding force in the medieval world, and indeed in early modern times. The unity of Christendom, achieved by the combined efforts of State and Church, was the goal and challenge he set before the world. His real view of Christianity, on a personal level, is hard to assess, for it has been shrouded in the misty veils of hagiography. At most times a humble and pure-minded person, he none the less betrayed at certain periods of his life that ruthlessness we associate with the worst Roman Emperors: the executions for treason or imagined treason of his wife, son, nephew and brother-in-law stand witness against him. His slow, politic moves towards a full and public acceptance of Christianity are all too reminiscent of the relations of Charles II and the Church of Rome. In his last illness, Constantine put off the imperial purple robe, and took the white one of the Christian, going at last to his baptism, saying, 'Let there be no more ambiguity.'

There were, to be fair, many genuine and personal reasons for Constantine's promotion of Christianity, which, we must remember, was still very much a minority faith; but the chief reason, without any doubt, was that he recognised in this religion the essential bonding that the Empire needed, the mortar without which the wall must inevitably fall. He worked very hard indeed in his own bluff and soldierly way to heal the discords and schisms within the Church, and the squabbles between Arians, Donatists, orthodox and other branches must have been both puzzling and infuriating. When, in 325, he called a Council of all Christian bishops at Nicea, their first action was to present him with a great bundle of grievances against each other for his decision: he burnt the lot before their eyes, unread.

His second great and significant action was, of course, the movement of the capital. He found Rome an unfriendly place: the heirs of the republican tradition were shocked by the state he kept—nearer that of a sultan than that of a Roman Emperor—and they instinctively disliked his adoption of Christianity. In any case, Rome was fast becoming an anachronism, too far from the frontiers that mattered, and from the provinces that meant most to the Empire in financial terms. Constantine knew the Rhine frontier well, and he knew how fast it was decaying under the repeated blows of barbarian influx. The Danube and the Euphrates protected the richest provinces. At Byzantium the great trade routes that fed the Empire crossed; it was the most highly defensible position one could wish. So there he built his capital, New Rome, Constantinople, and it was to last a thousand years, the envy of the world.

Constantine's last years were peaceful, and his achievements were huge; when he died in 337, he could surely look back with satisfaction on his efforts. Even looking forward (the restrained privilege of historians) one can still accord him the worthy title of 'the Great'. But the financial cost of a re-unified Empire, with a new religion and a new capital city, was both uncalculated and incalculable. Money was to defeat Constantine's dream—though geography and human nature, over which the truly great can exercise a modicum of control, were to have their part to play.

There is a biography by A. H. M. Jones: *Constantine and the Conversion of Europe* (English Univ. Press, London, 1948).

Dante

Dante Alighieri was born in Florence in 1265, son of a small business man with noble connections. The city was rich—its very name synonymous with money—the florin—but the country was torn by the disputes between Emperor and Pope, and the feuds of townsmen and nobility. The spirit of Montague and Capulet ruled the land.

Dante's studies lay in the arts: he was a voracious reader of vernacular as well as classical literature, and he claimed to know the *Aeneid* by heart. He also studied painting and music. By 1287 he was at Bologna—possibly at the university, but his whole heart was set on poetry, and at this young age he dared to submit a sonnet for criticism to the leading poet of the age, Guido Cavalcanti. At the same time he led a rich social life, and (as was normal for young nobles of the time) twice appearing on the field of battle.

His first major work was the *Vita Nuova*, a striking piece of self-psychologising, set in the form of a critical exposition of his sonnets. These were concerned with his strange relationship with Beatrice, with whom he fell in love at the age of nine (she was only eight).[1] With all the devotion of Courtly Love that demanded purification through a kind of self-denial and worship usually accorded to the Divine, he pursued Beatrice with adoring glances, being rewarded with one famous salutation on the bridge.

His devotion, however, was obviously real, for when she died in 1290 he changed his mode of life considerably in reaction. He married and had children, and indulged in a certain amount of dissipation and free-thinking, which he much regretted in later years. He attended the Mendicants' schools and learnt philosophy; he was sufficiently impressed by Aristotle to quote him some 300 times in his own works, and he became more deeply interested in science and logic.

He also began his public career as a servant of his city in 1295. These were deeply troubled years for Florence, for the city was divided between the 'Whites' (Ghibelline, and in favour of the Emperor) and the

---

[1] This early experience was not as rare at this time as might be expected. Froissart comments, 'When they put me to school there were little girls who were young in my days, and I . . . would serve them with pins, or with an apple or a pear, or a plain glass ring; and in truth we thought it great prowess to win their grace . . . and then would I say to myself, "When will the hour strike for me, that I shall be able to love in earnest?" . . .' (Quoted in G. G. Coulton, *Chaucer and his England*, Methuen, London, 1963, p. 20.)

'Blacks' (Guelph, favouring the Pope). Dante remained impartial, serving as both a diplomat and an administrator (for a short period he was in charge of road-improvement projects).

In 1301 the city was threatened by the advance of Charles of Valois, and Dante went on embassy to the Pope to beg that he should do no harm to Florence. Whilst Dante was at Anagni, Charles entered the city, and organised a purge of the 'Whites'. The Blacks ruled triumphant, and Dante feared to go home, for he was suspected of 'White' sympathies, and was threatened with the stake should he return.

So began his sad exile, wandering around Italy, and longing only for Florence, which he dearly loved, though some of the bitter statements of his old age were to disguise his love. In this period he wrote his *Convivio* and *De vulgari eloquentia*, which expressed his deep feeling for the Italian language. The vernacular was to him not just a nationalistic expression, but a genuine poetic vehicle, and he did more than anyone in his own time or for many years afterwards to advance the claims of the vernacular as a literary language.

As the years of exile lengthened, Dante became more and more convinced that the only hope for Italy lay in the strength of the Emperor. Surrounded as he was by petty strife of all kinds that was sapping the vitals of his country, he saw clearly that concord could only be achieved by a universal secular arbiter. With concord would come that ideal political state of freedom, and one feels here the unspoken result: Dante could go home.

His last years were spent in Ravenna, where two of his sons and his daughter came to join him and make life a little more comfortable. He received acclaim—the laurel crown—for his poetic work. His great work, *The Divine Comedy*, occupied these last years—indeed, he only completed the final cantos of *Paradiso* on the night of his death, in 1321.

The *Comedy* is a supremely well told story, excellent in its variety and pace, and with a tense and exciting range of emotion. All Europe secretly longed to know the true story of the afterlife, and Dante did not let their interest down. This was a supremely well chosen vehicle for his survey of the tragic heritage and boundless possibilities of his homeland.

See T. G. Bergin: *An Approach to Dante* (Bodley Head, London, 1965).

St. Dominic

St. Dominic Guzman was born in 1170 in the little village of Calaruega, in the province of Burgos, where his father was hereditary royal warden. It was a religious family: his eldest brother became a Canon of St. James, the next, Mannes, was to follow Dominic into his order; he also had a sister.

At the age of seven Dominic was sent to an uncle who was a parish priest and kept a petty school. At 14 he went on to study at Palencia, not as yet recognised as a university, but a notable centre of study. He was a quiet and studious child, already showing that ready sympathy for the plight of others that was to characterise his life. On one occasion he sold his valuable collection of books, the margins covered with notes, to provide for the poor. He was also developing his taste for music, singing gaily with a sonorous voice. Already he was practising self-denial, going without wine, and sleeping on the floor for penance.

In 1195 he was ordained and took up the canonry at Osma that had provided for his needs during his theological studies of the last five years. An energetic and reforming bishop ruled over the canons, and they did a great service in the town and surrounding countryside, providing for parishes too poor to support a priest. Dominic advanced fast in the community, and within four years was made sub-prior.

The new century brought a new bishop, Diego d'Azevedo, who had been a close friend of Dominic's and now worked intimately with him. In 1203 they both went off to negotiate for a bride for the

King of Castille's son, and, stopping in Toulouse for a night, discovered the Albigensians. These heretics drew their doctrine from Bulgaria, but its seeds were deposited early in the Christian era. Essentially, they defined the material as evil and the spiritual as good, and suggested that everything that tended to produce or favour material things should be discouraged: thus marriage was condemned (along with most of the other sacraments of the Church), and suicide favoured. The devotees, known as the 'Perfect', ate the bare minimum of food, and endured heavy penances, but they recognised that not all could attain to such heights; so they encouraged followers who did not practice the doctrine to the full. The nobility followed eagerly, for Albigensianism involved the disestablishment of the Church. Many truly religious people followed because of the fine example the 'Perfect' offered. The poor followed because of the workshops and craft-training centres that were set up as vehicles of propaganda. The Roman Church was in such a sad state, and offered such a poor example, that it seemed the time was ripe for the laity to take a hand.

Diego and Dominic were deeply shocked at what they found, and even more disturbed when visits to the Pope and to Cîteaux revealed that every attempt at reconversion (even employing the tremendous preaching powers of St. Bernard) had failed. Undiscouraged, they set out on their own mission, trying different tactics.

Dominic had two distinct advantages: he spoke much the same language as the Albigensians, and possessed a trained mind, supremely capable of disputation. To these he was to add a third: he would beat the 'Perfect' at their own game of asceticism; barefoot, ill-clad, fasting and disciplining himself with a three-fold iron chain, he set an example that was hard to parallel. But he was not a miserable ascetic—he was gay and sang gladly, and retained an even temper; throughout his dangerous mission he did not show the least sign of fear.

He was physically attractive, and crowds of young women tried to 'mother' him, without much success. At the end of his life, when he felt himself to be boasting of his virginity, he reminded himself that he had ever taken more pleasure in the company of young women than in that of old.

He held long disputations with the leading 'Perfect', some of which lasted up to eight days. They were exciting occasions, for the crowd took a very full part, electing the chairman and the judges who would decide the winner, interjecting comments and questions, laughter and applause, and even occasionally voting on the result.

In 1207 Diego died, and Dominic was left as leader of a small band of missionaries. The following year the Church started the crusade against the heretics, deciding that at least an element of force must be tried. Dominic had good relations with the leader, Simon de Montfort, but did not believe in the usefulness of force. Though he did take part in some examinations of heretics, at no stage did he have anything to do with the Inquisition. Inquisitorial duties were imposed on his order after his death, and much against the will of the friars, whose whole aim lay in the field of rational persuasion.

Dominic saw how great a part the women played in the dissemination of heretical doctrines, and he now set up a convent of nuns at Prouille, which would act as a refuge for converted women, and as a school for the young. His followers had their headquarters there too, so that they could act as spiritual directors and defenders of the nuns.

In 1215, however, he was given a house in Toulouse where he could establish a community for men. Already he was seeing clearly the wider significance of his work; the Albigensian heresy was merely a heightened form of a malaise felt by all Christendom, which was rooted in the failure of the Church to provide a good example and sound preaching and teaching. So at Toulouse he built up a library, and took his brothers to the university, to hear the lectures of the English professor Alexander of Stavensby.

That same year the Pope heard him put his case at the Lateran Council, and in the following year the new Pope, Honorius III, confirmed his order, which was to put itself under the rule of St. Augustine. Whilst in Rome Dominic met Francis (*q.v.*), and they took a great liking to one another; their characters were very different, but their aims were the same.

During these two years the Crusaders had been pushed back by the resurgent Albigensians, and when Dominic's little group of friars welcomed him back from Rome, they must have expected a period of consolidation in Toulouse, ready for an all-out push against the enemy. Instead Dominic remained consistent with his inner vision, and demanded that they disperse, increase their knowledge and multiply their numbers. One party was sent to Spain and another to Paris. Only eight were to remain in Provence, whilst Dominic and a companion set off for Rome, preparatory for a trip to Tartary on mission (for which Dominic carefully grew a Tartar beard as a disguise. The mission was not to materialise in his lifetime, but he kept the beard).

The Paris house prospered, and won many recruits. In Rome Dominic set up a reformed house for nuns, and a substantial friary. He also sent off a party to Bologna which had an instant success, converting nearly all the professors. Dominic was like a magnet for the young, who snipped pieces from his garments as mementoes of their meeting. They came in crowds, especially the more intelligent, who had at last found a religious leader their minds could respect.

Things were not going so well with the friars in Spain, so Dominic next journeyed there, with the same magical effect. He set up convents at Segovia and Madrid. From there he went on to Paris, and insisted that the friars should disperse once more into five more French towns, leaving only a small nucleus behind.

Back in 1220 to Italy, where the first chapter-general of the order was held in Bologna. Dominic later had another meeting with Francis, and returned to Bologna worried that his own order did not have that high respect for poverty held by Francis and his immediate followers. He suggested that each convent should have a lay 'business manager' so that the friars should have no dealings with money, but was voted down. He did manage to stop the rebuilding of the Bologna convent, however, as it was only aimed at enlargement of the facilities, and not at expansion of numbers. He also insisted that the order should not receive estates, and publicly tore up the deeds of a gift of land.

Finally he reached Rome, where he presented his nuns with a little gift he had carried all the way from Spain—a cyprus-wood spoon for each. In Rome the conversions continued—Germans, Poles, Czechs and Hungarians, who would set out to establish convents far to the East.

Dominic's order introduced a totally new dimension into the work of the Church. In its very constitution it was modernistic—the election of superiors, and the representation of ordinary members in provincial councils, for example. While it continued the best traditions of monasticism, and emphasised the power of communal prayer, it established new principles of missionary work that joined teaching with preaching in a powerfully combined weapon. Its impetus to education in Europe is immeasurable.

Dominic died at Bologna on 6th August 1221. Nine days later the first Dominicans to reach England set up their convent where the town hall now stands in Oxford.

There is a biography by Bede Jarrett: *The Life of St. Dominic* (Burns and Oates, London, 1924; Benziger, New York, 1924).

Duns Scotus

When the Renaissance and Reformation combined to make revolution respectable, the students destroyed a lot of books, enjoying both the destruction and the virtuous feeling that they were stamping out all traces of a worthless and degenerate past. One of the authors for whom they felt a particular virulence was the pride of the Franciscans—John Duns Scotus—the word Scotist and the word Duns, or Dunce, was enough to set the students aflame with anger and scorn. Not that there was much in his writings to object to, compared with many others; the fact was that Duns wrote at great length, was very dry, and very difficult.

Born about 1265 in Roxburghshire, John was destined for his order, for his uncle was warden of the Dumfries convent of Franciscans, and the order's vicar-general for Scotland. He joined his uncle in 1278, and probably went from there to Cambridge, though in 1291 he moved to the much more important schools at Oxford. During the following years he showed his skill, and moved easily between the Universities of Oxford and Paris. His acceptance in both academic communities was to be useful, for he twice incurred the wrath of King Philip IV, and was forced to depart for Oxford rather hurriedly. He was an outspoken critic, and it rarely occurred to him that discretion is the better part of valour. His final move came in 1308, the year of his death, when his over-strong support for the doctrine of the Immaculate Conception made a move to Cologne seem wise.

The Franciscans revered his memory, mainly because much of his life was devoted to an expansion and critique of the work of the Dominican hero, St. Thomas Aquinas. He modified the emphasis of the common doctor on the unity of species, pointing out the element of uniqueness in every thing and quality, however similar it may be to others. More important, he reversed the trend of thinking that suggested that all may be explained by reason, and restored to God His freedom from the trammels of earthly rules of logic. He worked hard to establish proper bases for new thinking in theology, but died before being able to undertake a systematic demonstration.

St. Dunstan

St. Dunstan was born about the year 909, near Glastonbury, and was closely related to the royal family. Nearby was the royal palace at Cheddar which has only recently been excavated: it was a substantial hall which must easily have accommodated the large royal retinue. Dunstan went to school in Glastonbury Abbey, but in 923 he joined his uncle who had been translated from the See of Wells to that of Canterbury. This brought him close to the court of King Æthelstan, and over the next few years he was to spend much time there. Æthelstan was rich and powerful, and his court was thronged with embassies from all over Europe trying to prove by their magnificence and display that their monarchs were worthy of alliance by marriage with any one of his numerous daughters. The king had artistic tastes, was a great collector of beautiful things and the less beautiful but more valued relics of saints. He was, in the manner of the great Anglo-Saxon king, very generous in his dispersal of gifts from this ever growing collection.

Dunstan enjoyed the court, and responded readily to its artistic influences, learning drawing and metalwork, how to write poetry, singing and playing music. But he was bookish and withdrawn, preferring the company of old men who could tell him the heroic tales of the struggles against the Danes to that of his contemporaries. He was also a great dreamer, prone to nocturnal visions to which he attached great significance, and which (like many another) he could not resist communicating to those around him. The young and boisterous hunting, shooting and fishing set of Æthelstan's court found him very odd, and slowly the rumours grew. He was, they said, undoubtedly a witch.

The situation grew steadily worse, until Æthelstan acceded to the majority view, and sent him away from the court. His enemies followed after him and rolled him in the mud, and kicked him until they were tired. They had settled *his* hash for him, they thought, and that was the end of the matter.

Dunstan was 24, and returning home a failure, quite literally covered in disgrace. He wondered whether or not to become a monk: it was at that time no inviting prospect. The Danish invasions had hit the monasteries hardest of all, and though Alfred had worked hard to promote recovery, monastic life was petty, feeble and corrupt, bearing little relation to the way of life St. Benedict had established. The very fabric was crumbling: at the time of his vocation, Dunstan was nearly killed by a falling stone from the roof of the church in which he was praying; even towards the end of his life in 978 when the Witan met at Calne in an upper room the floor collapsed and Dunstan alone escaped injury by clinging to a beam.

So in 936 Dunstan entered Glastonbury as a monk, and began the work of re-establishing true monasticism that is known to historians as the 'tenth-century Reformation'.

In 939 Æthelstan died and the new king, Edmund, revoked the ban on Dunstan, but within a short while the witchcraft rumours began to spread once more, and he was banned a second time. Deeply hurt, he made ready to go to Germany, but the king was to have a dramatic change of mind. While out hunting, Edmund lost his followers in the headlong pursuit of a deer, and was thoroughly enjoying the chase when he realised with horror that his horse was making direct for Cheddar Gorge, and he felt himself to be going too fast to be able to stop before the brink. The thought flashed through his mind that if he were saved he would recall Dunstan and ever hold him in honour. He was, and he did—both remarkable facts. Dunstan was made Abbot of Glastonbury and helped to rebuild it as a centre for the revival of Benedictine monasticism in England.

Under Edmund and his successor Duns-tan and his programme flourished, but in 956 the feckless Eadwig came to the throne. At his coronation feast he suddenly left, and to everyone's acute embarrassment failed to reappear. Dunstan stalked off to find him, seated happily chatting with his wife and mother-in-law, and he had to use force to get him to resume the crown and return to the feast. He had made three deadly enemies, and wisely retired to Flanders where he found interesting movements of monastic reform to study.

England soon tired of Eadwig, and the following year the Northumbrians and Mercians raised his brother Edgar in his place. He summoned Dunstan and made him first Bishop of Durham, and, two years later, conferred the See of London on him as well. That same year Eadwig died, and Edgar the peaceful ruled supreme: he made his faithful and wise counsellor Archbishop of Canterbury.

He went to Rome to fetch the sign and confirmation of his office, the pallium, but quickly returned to aid the king. He created for him a splendid coronation service, ancestor of the one used today. He advised him on all matters of state, giving powerful support to his policy of peace and reconstruction, and to the imposition of justice on a land that was none too keen on the law. He was not a cruel man in any way, but one Whitsunday, when he was about to say mass, he heard that a sentence of loss of the right hand for illicit coining had been postponed because of the holy day. He insisted that it be carried out and postponed mass, tears pouring down his face, until he should receive confirmation of the execution.

In his work for monasticism Dunstan had two helpers of stature—Æthelwold at Abingdon, Winchester and Ely, and Oswald of Worcester. Both had personally experienced the work of the Cluniac revival at the Abbey of Fleury. Together the three leaders rebuilt and filled monasteries wherever it was possible, but one major problem was the rule. In the years of chaos all sorts of strange local customs had arisen in various parts of the country, and had become sanctified by traditional usage, so that practice in one monastery could vary widely from that in another. So they convened a council at Winchester and sent for advisers from Fleury and Ghent to attend, and hammered out the *Regularis Concordia*, the agreed rule for English monasteries. Based firmly on the work of St. Benedict, it took example from the best new developments in Europe; but the elaborate ceremonial of the continent was rejected in favour of simplicity. Many pleasant English traditions were kept, such as the ringing of bells at Christmastime, and the simple drama played out in church on Easter Sunday that was the forerunner of the mystery plays of the High Middle Ages.

The achievement of monastic revival was great, but it did not come without making enemies. The huge estates required to support each monastery withdrew wealth and power from a nobility which recognised no equal. When Edgar died in 975, Dunstan and his colleagues faced a determined band of opponents. Edgar's son by his first marriage, Edward, naturally succeeded, but the Queen, his step-mother, was fiercely ambitious for her own son Æthelræd. The nobles who opposed Dunstan clung closely to her.

In 978 King Edward came to Corfe, to visit his step-mother and half-brother. As he reached for the loving-cup at the gates of the castle, he was struck down.

His brother Æthelræd, known to history as the Unready, was to rule for forty years, but he never escaped the stigma of the reason for his accession, though he was far too young to have had anything to do with the murder, and even his mother is thought to have had no part in it. In 980 the Vikings returned, and for years to come folk saw them as vengeance for Edward's murder.

Æthelræd was 'Unræd'—he lacked counsel. Suspicious of everyone, unable to judge a man sufficiently well to trust him, he was forced to take his own advice and face his sea of troubles alone. Dunstan could not help him, and after the coronation retired from affairs of state to devote himself to the administration of his church. He was an old man, and died in 988 before Viking plunderers came drunk to Canterbury and murdered one of his successors.

The great reviver of the monasteries was well loved, for all the misunderstanding he had endured as a young man. His ardent conversation and story-telling was remembered long after his death. His interest in art had promoted a revival of its own which remains with us today in the great Benedictional of St. Æthelwold. Like St. Francis after him, he had employed his spare time in making decorations for the Church —working mainly in metal. His musical skill as a harpist encouraged developments in that field too—he must have been very proud of the great organ he revived in Winchester with its 700 pipes and 26 sets of bellows. He had done a great work in times when to do anything was hard enough, and remained human and lovable. But in his own self portrait he is entirely humble, and so very small.

There is a biography by E. S. Duckett: *St. Dunstan of Canterbury* (Collins, London, 1955; Norton, New York, 1955).

St. Edmund of Abingdon

St. Edmund of Abingdon, though not the greatest of the medieval Archbishops of Canterbury, was certainly among the best loved, and the most truly saintly. He was born about 1170 in the small town from which he took his name, though his family name was Rich. The great abbey of Abingdon must have been a formative influence on his life, but a stronger influence must have been his mother, nicely named Mabel. His father died when he was quite young, but his mother, who was famous for her devout way of life, pushed on with the education of her family. When the time came for Edmund and his brother to go to study in Paris, she packed for them, tucking in two hair-shirts as a 'breast-plate' against the devil. She had nothing to fear, for when an inn-keeper's daughter fell for Edmund, he took no notice of her 'signals, nodding and sighs'; and when she invaded his room and began to undress, he drove her away with a whip he had thoughtfully 'prepared for this purpose'. Whilst he was at his studies his fellows observed that, besides his books, there stood upon the table an image of the Blessed Virgin 'of the purest ivory, and of singular beauty, and all round her throne were shown, in wonderful carving, the mysteries of our redemption'. In any history of religion the mothers of the saints should surely play a notable part.

About the year 1195 Edmund returned to Oxford, where he lectured for six years in the arts. He was a good teacher, and his humility is shown in this rather long period of work in what was to the medieval mind a relatively low branch of study. However, he returned to Paris to scale the heights of Theology, and was soon teaching there as well. He was a kindly soul, who would sell his books to support poor scholars, and often spent great sums in gaining medical attention for them. Once, while engaged on giving a full course of lectures, he looked after a sick pupil in his own house, and sat up with him every night for five weeks.

In 1222 he became treasurer of Salisbury Cathedral—a recognition of his worth to the Church of England, but not entirely a wise appointment, for throughout his life he was inclined to give everything he had to the poor, and soon the account was in the red. Yet his virtue was plain, and soon everyone knew of it, for he became a very active preacher and 'his speech was as a fair face without spot or wrinkle'.

In 1223 there was considerable trouble in the election of a new Archbishop of Canterbury, and after three elections had been annulled, they chose a man spiritually suited to the job. Edmund was certainly worthy in this respect, but had not the worldly diplomacy and spirit of compromise necessary at that time. At once he began to denounce the wicked govern-

ment of Henry III, assuming the mantle of previous great archbishops. Within a week of his consecration he was threatening the king with excommunication. His life was henceforth to be taken up with the crusade against bad government, not because he was at all interested in politics, or vindictive by nature; rather he was following the example and precedents of men of the calibre of Becket and Anselm, who had made such work the job of the archbishop. It was not all warfare—Edmund above all things loved peace, and he spent many weary hours negotiating agreements between quarrelling parties in storm-tossed England.

Henry was no fool: he knew that the way to break Edmund's spirit was to form an alliance with the Pope. So the papal legate Otho was sent in 1237 to override Edmund in his own archdiocese, and to extort vast sums of money from the English Church (a large measure of which would end up in Henry's pocket). Edmund tried all means to resolve an impossible situation, but when he received a demand for 300 English benefices for Roman nominees of the Pope, he realised he was no longer strong enough to protect the English Church from the rapacious combination of King and Pope. He had been once to Rome to try to straighten matters out, but now in 1240 he set off again; but on the way through France he fell ill and shortly after died. Later, after the canonisation, Henry III was ill—so he went to pray for his recovery at the tomb; his maddening nature is typified by this act of wisdom after the event.

See Bernard Ward: *St. Edmund, Archbishop of Canterbury, His Life, as Told by Old English Writers* (Sands, London, 1903). There is a modern biography by C. H. Lawrence: *St. Edmund of Abingdon* (Oxford Univ. Press, London, 1960).

Edward I

Edward I was born at Westminster in 1239, and was named for his father Henry III's favourite saint, Edward the Confessor. He was heir to wide domains and many troubles, and he had an early taste of both. In 1252 he was given charge of the troublesome but lucrative Gascon territories. Two years later he was married to Eleanor of Castile—a political marriage, but one that was to turn into a love-match.

There was little time to enjoy it at first, for Edward was now pitched into the discords of the English baronial revolt. His father was neither a good leader of men, nor a good soldier, so the burden was thrust upon his young son. The barons' leader, Simon de Montfort, was Edward's uncle, and there is no doubt that the prince was both attracted to his uncle's ideas of government, and also deeply influenced by his military tactics. But after the defeat at Lewes, and a humiliating imprisonment, his admiration turned to hostility, which was only sated with the rout of Evesham in 1265.

In the next few years he acted as a moderating influence on his father's vindictive wrath, and saw to it that the settlement with the baronial opposition should not in itself provoke a further uprising.

In 1270 he was at last able to go off on crusade, when he brought relief to Acre. His military reputation now soared, and in 1272 he suffered an attack from an assassin, in which he was grazed by a poisoned dagger in the scuffle. He recovered, and was able to negotiate a ten-year truce before returning home, covered with honour.

On landing in Sicily he heard of his father's death, but he did not hurry to get back to England, spending a whole year settling his affairs in Gascony first. It was 1274 before England saw him. Once properly seated on the throne, however, he gave every evidence of his vigour and determination to rule. Within two months of the coronation, commissioners were scouring the land completing a survey as large and efficient as any that had been undertaken since Domesday. The commissioners enquired into encroachments upon royal rights, and into injustices committed by the king's servants; their detailed reports are known to historians as the Hundred Rolls, based as they were on the administrative unit of the hundred.

The evidence of the Hundred Rolls was to be the basis of Edward's legislative reforms. A long series of statutes, enacted at the enlarged parliaments introduced by Simon de Montfort, aimed at the improvement of justice at the local as well as the national level, and also tried to rationalise the bewildering array of jurisdictions (known as liberties) that feudal government had seen grow up. Edward had a genuine concern to see justice done, which gained for him the deep admiration of his subjects. He was also very well informed about the localities, for he was constantly on the move, covering distances of about 2,000 miles a year, with a court of perhaps a thousand horses lumbering behind him on the muddy and dangerous medieval roads.

Much larger groups travelled with him when he went to war, and Wales was the first to see his unwelcome visitation. Llewellyn, Prince of Wales, had rather foolishly refused to do homage for his lands at Edward's coronation, and in 1277 the King attacked and reduced his dominions by half. Five years later the Prince's brother David rose in rebellion, and Llewellyn was forced to join him, only to be killed in a petty foray. With no great leader left to them, the Welsh submitted to annexation, and saw gigantic castles rise in key-points such as Conway, Caernarvon and Harlech, castles that would prevent future revolt. Edward was an arrant colonialist, and typically brought back from Wales the great cross of Neath to carry in procession to Westminster for the service of thanksgiving. The Abbey was to see many more proud trophies plundered for its decoration and distinction.

Edward was eager to be off to Palestine once more, but the European situation prevented a new crusade: France and Aragon struggled over the body of Sicily, and the

Pope was hopelessly committed as a partisan. Edward now spent long months attempting to bring peace to Europe so that the Christian nations could unite in crusade.

His design for Europe was interrupted by troubles at home. In his prolonged absence corruption throve, and in 1289 the King was forced to conduct an enquiry which resulted (among other things) in the banishment of his chief justice. The same year he had to go north to convene the court that was to judge between the various 'competitors' for the throne of Scotland. The legalism fascinated him, but in the middle of this interesting judicial wrangle, his wife died. He was heartbroken, and as he accompanied the body from Lincolnshire to London, he ordered elaborate crosses to be set up wherever the cortège rested. The last was Charing Cross. A most beautiful monument was set up in Westminster Abbey, and those who view it can see something of Edward's loss.

Back in Scotland he finally adjudged John Balliol's claim for the crown to be the best, but forced him to accept vassal status as a *quid pro quo*. Years of trouble lay ahead: the French made war, the Welsh rebelled, and the Pope made life extremely difficult for the hard-pressed English king. He continued to demand Edward's presence on crusade—which he would have dearly loved, but found impossible; his only contribution was the expulsion of the Jews in 1290. Furthermore the Pope had suddenly issued a Bull declaring that the state had no right to tax the clergy, and Edward was desperately short of money for war on three fronts.

These difficulties explain but do not excuse the viciousness of his actions in the next few years. Scotland had refused to accept him as overlord, and he annexed the land, deposed Balliol, and removed the Stone of Scone to Westminster Abbey in 1296. When Wallace rose as a leader in Scotland, Edward increased the fury of his attack; the rebels received no mercy.

Gradually the King seemed to be achieving his aims. France was satisfied by his marriage to the sister of the French king, and by 1304 Scotland seemed well under his heel, controlled by a policy of ruthless savagery. Edward could at last turn his attention back to English affairs, where disorder was rampant. New justices were sent round on the 'Trailbaston' commission to seek out the unsavoury Robin Hoods of the land, and gradually order returned.

Imagine then the fury of the aged king when, in 1306, Robert Bruce, who had been his man for the past four years, suddenly went north and was crowned King of Scots. Old, tired, and sick, Edward moved up country to deal with this fresh menace to peace, but was taken very ill on the way. He had to direct the campaign from his bed, and vitriolic letters showered on his commanders accusing them of inaction and failure.

In a last tremendous effort the King got up and gave his litter to Carlisle Cathedral —a typical gesture, again—and set off on horseback. The progress was desperately slow—some two miles a day—but even that was too fast for the sick king, who quickly succumbed and died in July 1307.

Son and father of weak and ineffectual kings, Edward I had many fine qualities which seem to make nonsense of heredity. He was tall and strong, a fine horseman and a doughty warrior. A great leader of men, he was also able to lead to success. He was interested in government and law in a very genuine way. As a personality he was pious, but easily provoked to rage and often vindictive. He was fond of games—so passionately did he love his hawks that when they were ill he sent money to shrines to pray for their recovery. He was generous to the poor, and often a gay companion: he played chess, and loved music and acrobats; once he bet his laundress Matilda that she couldn't ride his charger, and she won! Every Easter Monday he paid a ransom to his maids if they found him in bed. He loved his two wives, and fussed over their health and that of his children with a pathetic concern—sometimes threatening the doctor with what would happen to him if his patient did not recover. His people feared, respected and remembered him.

There is a biography by L. F. Salzman: *Edward I* (Constable, London, 1968; Praeger, New York, 1968). The short biography by E. L. G. Stones: *Edward I* (Oxford Univ. Press, London, 1968), though written for schools, is interesting and clear.

Edward II

Edward II was one of the most disastrous failures in the history of kingship, yet the story of his reign is full of compelling interests. The stories of his horrible death make it impossible to be too hard in our judgment; and to a generation that is more ready to understand homosexuality, Edward and the picture Marlowe paints of him is more acceptable than he was to a generation whose history books were written by the Bishop of Oxford.

He was born at Caernarvon in 1284, and although he left Wales at the age of four months and did not return for sixteen years, this first English Prince of Wales was known as Edward of Caernarvon. Even as a baby he had a large household, the expenses exceeding £2,000 per year, exclusive of wine. Most of his youth was spent trailing around the country after his restless father, only staying in his house at King's Langley in the depths of winter. In the year 1292-3 he journied some 68 times.

He was a handsome, healthy boy, not over-addicted to his books (though on occasion he would borrow them from monastic libraries, and fail to return them). He was a capable horseman, but not at all interested in knightly pastimes. He followed his father to the Scottish wars on a number of occasions, and performed moderately well, but he was to prove himself a rash and incapable commander-in-chief later on.

He was fond of music, and once sent his Welsh harper, Richard the Rhymer, to Shrewsbury Abbey to learn to play a strange instrument called a crwth, a forerunner of the violin. He liked swimming and rowing, gambling and fooling about with simple folk. Once Robert, his fool, received compensation from him for injuries sustained 'through the prince in the water'. He fancied himself practical with his hands, designing a ship for his twelve-year-old bride from France; at moments of stress he reverted to estate management (a trait he shared with Gladstone, the Kaiser, and Winston Churchill), digging his own ditches and making fences.

He had a nice sense of humour. Writing to Louis of France in 1305: 'We send you a big trotting palfrey which can hardly bear its own weight, and some of our bandy-legged harriers from Wales, who can well catch a hare if they find it asleep . . . And, dear cousin, if you want anything else from our land of Wales, we can send you plenty of wild men if you like, who will know well how to teach breeding to the young heirs and heiresses of great lords.'

He met Piers Gaveston when he was about sixteen, a gay and attractive Gascon who had just escaped romantically from a French gaol. As careless as Edward, he was also as proud: he provided some element in life that Edward desperately needed, for whatever one may think of the relationship it was plain that Edward didn't just adore Gaveston—he could not bear to be without him. Indeed, when in 1305 young Edward had annoyed his father by speaking insultingly to his chief minister Walter Langton, one of his punishments was to be deprived of Gaveston's company.

However, the quarrel was made up, and in 1306 the King knighted his son, along with 200 others. Edward kept his vigil in Westminster Abbey, but there was so much noise from the hustle and bustle of the preparations for the following day that the monks could barely keep up their chant—one side of the choir could not hear the other. The next morning, so great was the press, that war-horses had to be put in to clear a path to the high altar. The feast that followed was of epic proportions—the eighty minstrels in their splendid attire cost Edward £130 alone.

Edward I had probably viewed his son's affection for Gaveston with an amused indulgence, recognising that such things happen in adolescence; but as Edward grew older his passion for Gaveston grew stronger, and when he approached his father in all seriousness to ask for either the County of Poitou or the Earldom of Cornwall for his favourite, the king knocked him down, and pulled his hair, exiling the unfortunate Gascon. It was the last spark of rage of an old man who recognises that the son he has cherished as his heir is a degenerate. In July 1307 he died, and Gaveston was back within the fortnight.

Edward gave his father a decent funeral, but it was rumoured that at his wedding to Isabella of France, Gaveston had the pick of the presents, and at the coronation he appeared 'so decked out that he more resembled the God Mars than an ordinary mortal.' Opposition grew fast: it was unbecoming to a king to behave so, and the snobbish and xenophobic English objected to seeing a petty foreigner risen so much above themselves. Soon Edward was forced to send Gaveston to Ireland, loading him with presents, including a parcel of blank charters, sealed with his own seal, to be used as royal grants in whatever way he wished.

Edward now raised Heaven and Earth to get Piers back, bribing the opposition with grants, promises and offices—careless of all cost. Yet when the favourite returned he put no restraints on him, and Gaveston treated the English earls like servants, and invented dirty nick-names for them.

In 1310 the lords formed a committee to promulgate ordinances for the reform of the government, and Edward fled north to join Gaveston under the pretence of carrying on his father's Scottish wars. By 1311 he was forced to return south by lack of funds, and faced ordinances under 41 headings, which demanded the exile of Gaveston, and a large measure of control over Edward's financial and governmental actions. Edward wept, complained that he was being treated 'like an idiot', and allowed Gaveston to go; but he quickly returned, and the unholy pair celebrated Christmas at Windsor openly in 1311, before dashing off north once more.

The Ordainers carefully planned a pincer movement to catch them, and whilst Edward was sheltering in York, Gaveston gave himself up to Pembroke, who swore on his oath no harm would come to him. He brought him south, intending to keep him in his castle at Wallingford whilst negotiations took place; but at Deddington, in Oxfordshire, a halt was called, as the prisoner needed rest. They stayed the night in the rectory, whilst Pembroke took advantage of the break to pay a speedy visit to his wife, who was in the area. In his absence, Warwick made a raid and snatched Gaveston away to his castle. Pembroke was acutely and genuinely distressed, for he had guaranteed his prisoner's safety, but he could do nothing, and within a few days the Earls had decided upon an execution, and Gaveston's headless body was carried into Oxford on a ladder by four cobblers.

Throughout England there was a sense of shock and horror at this murder of the King's dearest friend whilst under safe-conduct, and many people recoiled at such conduct, moving to support the King. It seemed as though civil war must break out immediately, and hectic negotiations continued through into the following year. To avoid the war, in October 1313, the lords made a public apology for their act in Westminster Hall. An uneasy truce reigned, but Thomas of Lancaster for one could never forget the humiliation of that moment.

During these years of turmoil, Robert Bruce had made great progress in undoing the work of conquest of Edward I in Scotland. By 1314 even Edward II realised that something had to be done, for the Scots were now raiding England with impunity. So he gathered a large army and went to the relief of Stirling. Bruce feared the invasion, for he had less than half the force England was bringing against him, but he chose his ground well, and prepared his tactics with skill. Edward relied on his cavalry, but the marshy ground at Bannockburn was not the place for set-piece battles. He forced the tired English on through sheer impatience, but their morale must have been low, for when they saw the camp-followers moving up behind the Scots they took them for re-inforcements, and the English turned to run—straight into the marsh, where they were slaughtered.

Edward barely escaped with his life: he had lost the only fighting force his country had, and in doing so made Bruce king indeed; the northern border was now his prey—and Ireland too, for in the following year his brother Edward invaded there, and was not to be defeated for three years.

Lancaster now had his chance for revenge. He insisted on his right as steward of the realm to purge the administration of Edward's friends, and to run the country almost without reference to the king. Edward moodily filled in the time by moving Gaveston's body to his favourite manor of King's Langley, where he held a solemn interment worthy of the translation of a saint. More time was spent rowing about on the Fens 'with a great company of simple people'.

The state of England grew from bad to worse. A disastrous harvest in 1315 had brought famine and huge rises in prices; there was universal misery, and it was said that lonely travellers were killed and eaten in the more deserted parts of the country. Lawlessness broke out all over, and gangs of bandits either took to the forests, or organised protection rackets—the citizens of Abingdon employed a gang of thugs to look after them, paying for it by taking a collection-box round the burgesses once a week. This was the time when the Robin

Hood stories were made up, but the true Robin was not the seventeenth-century 'rob the rich to pay the poor' saint of the highway, but more of a Chicago gangster.

Neither Edward nor Lancaster could run the country alone, and patently whilst both pulled lustily in opposite directions, the land was going to rack and ruin. Pembroke tried to create a middle party aimed at mediation and (as it were) coalition, but a disastrous failure to retake Berwick opened up old wounds.

Edward did not help: he now began to favour the Despensers, father and son, who were as rapacious a pair as Gaveston had been insolent. Lancaster once more organised the lords to force Edward to banish them, and began now to prepare for a complete take-over of the kingdom. But this time Edward was lucky: early in 1322 he prepared an army to move against Lancaster, and drove him north to Boroughbridge, where an army of veteran border warriors defeated him. He was caught and executed. Edward was triumphant, and barely noticed the reaction of the people of England: Lancaster had been neither a pleasant nor a saintly man, but he had been far better than Edward, and pilgrims began to flock to his tomb, to honour his memory, and pray for release.

Now Edward recalled his favourites, the Despensers, and they began to milk the land for all it was worth, depositing in their foreign banking accounts sums of up to £5,000 a time.

At last the Queen took a hand. She had been only twelve years old when Edward married her, and probably did not notice or understand much about the goings-on with Gaveston at first. After his death, she bore her husband four children, and was well provided for; but now that it looked as though a new Gaveston ruled, she determined on action, and used great cunning. She persuaded her husband to let her take their son, the heir to the throne, to France, there to do homage to the King for Gascony. Throughout their marriage Edward readily gave way to her. But once in France she announced that neither she nor her son would return until Edward gave up the Despensers, and to rub salt in the wounds, openly flaunted her liaison with Edward's enemy, Mortimer.

The King would not give in, so Isabella mounted an invasion from the Low Countries in September 1326. She was greeted rapturously in East Anglia, and quickly moved on to enter London, whence Edward had fled. London gave itself over to debauch and riot—which included executing the Bishop of Exeter with a butcher's knife in the street. Edward fumed hopelessly, for no one would rise to his support: he called his wife 'the she-wolf of France', carried a knife in his stocking to kill her with when they should meet, and boasted irrationally that if he had no other weapon, he would crush her with his teeth.

But Isabella moved on remorselessly, taking Bristol, and the elder Despenser, who was executed almost at once. Edward and the younger Despenser fled on with a handful of attendants, but were finally caught as they made their way through a heavy storm between Neath Abbey and Llantrissant Castle where they hoped to gain shelter. Edward was taken to Kenilworth, the Despenser party were winkled out one by one and executed, and a Parliament was convened in London. Edward was to be deposed in favour of his son. In mid-January 1327, a deputation came to Kenilworth and urged Edward to resign of his own free will, threatening that they would make their own king if he did not, and refuse to accept his son. With tears and sighs, he finally agreed, and his steward broke his staff of office and announced to all that the royal household was dissolved.

In April Edward was moved to Berkeley castle. Shortly after this move he was apparently rescued for a brief while by a party led by a Dominican friar, and they may have got as far as Corfe before they were captured. In September Mortimer heard of a new plot to rescue him, and decided that an ex-king was too dangerous

a luxury to afford. John Maltravers, William Ogle, and Thomas Gurney received certain instructions, and shortly afterwards it was announced that Edward was dead. It was said that, to avoid exterior signs, the murderers had inserted a red-hot iron into his bowels through the rectum. Three years later they were tried for his murder, found guilty, and allowed to escape abroad.

Isabella arranged a magnificent funeral for her husband at Gloucester, and, strange to relate, the pilgrims came there too, and offered so much money at the shrine of this oddly chosen local saint, that the monks could rebuild the choir with the profits. Of course some people said that Edward was still alive, in Lombardy of all places—but then people often thought such things.

There is no good biography of Edward, but Hilda Johnstone presents an excellent picture of his youth in *Edward of Caernarvon* (Manchester Univ. Press, 1946). For the rest of his life I have largely relied on Miss McKisack's Oxford History, *The Fourteenth Century*.

Edward III

Edward III was born in 1312 to a rough inheritance. In 1326 his mother Isabella and her lover Mortimer overthrew her husband, Edward II, and in the following year the King was foully murdered. England under Edward's grandfather, the first of that name, had been powerful and successful, but now it was in chaos. In 1328 Edward had to see France go to Philip of Valois, heir in the male line, whilst he himself was heir in the senior female line, and, worse still, he had to do homage for the few remaining shreds of English lands in France. In Scotland he had to face defeat (which brought him to tears), and was forced to accept the kingship of Bruce. Even his marriage—to Philippa of Hainault (who was to prove one of the best queens England ever had)—was in payment for the Count of Hainault's assistance to his mother.

No wonder then that he countenanced the overthrow and execution of his mother's lover in 1330, and took over personal rule. He turned first to Scotland, to win back the honour his father had lost at Bannockburn. In 1333 he supported the return of Edward Balliol, John Balliol's heir, to replace the infant David Bruce, Robert's heir. He won a great victory at Halidon Hill, and was once more suzerain of Scotland. He had learnt in the Scottish campaign to use Scottish tactics, protecting the flanks of his army with archers in open order, and using weapons rather than armour to defeat the enemy. The old days of knightly battle were over: no longer was weight to win, but manœuverability. The soldiers' chief weapon was that little dagger, the *misericord*, that hangs at the knight's belt on many an English brass: once the enemy knights in their cumbersome armour were down, the little poignard would find a crack through which to be driven home.

Edward next turned to France: having allied with the merchants of Flanders, desperate for English wool, and the German Emperor Lewis the Bavarian (whom he visited in 1338 with Geoffrey Chaucer's father in his train), he began the attack. At first it was a phoney war—landings here and there, and the only notable victory being the naval triumph of Sluys in 1340. His chief difficulties lay at home, in getting sufficient supplies. Edward had tried to continue the personal rule of the country that had brought his father down, and parliament objected; for a while there was trouble, but Edward's minister Stratford diverted the attack, and the king came to a truce with his subjects that was to continue until 1376.

In 1346 Edward attacked through Normandy, and at last came a great victory— Crécy. There English steadiness triumphed, and the French came on in disorder, the sun in their eyes, the fleeing Genoese archers in their way and the new guns firing against them. At least 4,000 French knights were killed, and among them the energetic King of Bohemia (father of Charles IV, *q.v.*), whose blindness did not prevent his joining the battle.

Edward went on to the year-long siege of Calais, to be encouraged by the news of the defeat of the Scots at Neville's Cross. David Bruce had returned to take the crown five years previously, but now he was an English prisoner, and was to remain one for eleven years. But Calais held up the English king for too long, and, in a rage, he demanded six burghers to hang. Only the Queen's pleading prevented this bestial act, but when Edward finally occupied the town he turned out all the Frenchmen and replaced them with English. Calais was to remain the chief English continental possession in France until it remained the only one, and finally fell in the reign of Mary.

A truce was made by two cardinals, but the spectre of plague was to enforce a temporary halt in warfare. The Black Death, most horrible of medieval plagues, appeared first in England in 1348, and killed a third of the inhabitants in the course of the following year. The terrible toll was worst among ecclesiastics, but none the less it also produced a serious shortage of manpower, and the government, scared of a steep rise in wages, and the resulting increase of power in the state to the lower elements, introduced the first wages legislation—the Statute of Labourers—in 1351, an enactment that tried to peg wages at the level of 1346, and one which was to be a major contributory factor in the Peasants' Revolt.

By 1355 England was ready to make war again, under the leadership of the Black Prince, who had already proved his worth at Crécy. His tactics of devastation produced results (not least among the French, who learnt from him, translating his aggressive tactics into defensive ones—a policy of scorched earth). At Poitiers the French suffered a smashing defeat in 1356: in three hours 15,000 died, and humble archers led away prisoners by fives and sixes. Ransoms of the order of £1,500 were possible—much was at stake; but the greatest French loss in this battle was their new king, John II, captured and taken to England by the Prince.

In France all the minstrels were forbidden to sing, and a terrible internecine war broke out, complicated by the social turmoils of the French Peasants' Revolt, the *Jacquerie*, and by the roving bands of ex-soldiers, the *Compagnies*—out of which was to grow the White Company of Sir John Hawkwood (*q.v.*).

In 1360 the two nations came to the peace table at Brétigny—a peace that gave all southwest France to England, along with a ransom for King John of 3 million gold crowns.

In a sense, part of the war with France was Edward's ecclesiastical policy, directed as it was at a French papacy, resident in Avignon. In 1351 the first Statute of Provisors limited the Pope's power to provide clerks of his nomination to English benefices, and increased the king's ability to reward his servants with ecclesiastical patronage. Two years later the first 'Statute' of Praemunire restricted appeals to the papal court, and both Statutes were re-issued and confirmed in 1365. The King also used Parliament to prevent the resumption of the payment to the papacy of 1,000 marks a year, begun when King John did homage for the realm. Similarly he opposed papal taxation of the English Church, using the services of John Wyclif (*q.v.*) in the negotiations at Bruges in 1374. These arguments were about the right to collect money in England, and not about religious matters at all; Edward was orthodox, if not terribly interested.

The French problem was by no means settled. In 1364 John II, who had conformed to chivalric law by replacing his second son in captivity in England after the Duke of Anjou's escape, died in London. Now Charles V, who was more interested in ruling than in chivalric law, succeeded to the throne. Dissident elements were reconciled, and every effort was made to foment rebellion in English

territories. Though the ruse of getting rid of the *Compagnies* by sending them under Du Guesclin to oppose Pedro the Cruel of Castile failed when the Black Prince followed and defeated them at Nájera, many good results came for France. The English armies, and the Prince himself, were worn down by sickness, and the French recognised the need for new tactics and organisation in the army. The abilities of the defeated Du Guesclin were recognised. The new armies rarely fought, but withdrew before the English, ravaging the land, so that the enemy could get no supplies. By 1375 the English, having lost the majority of their winnings, were brought back to an inelegant truce.

At home the affairs went as badly. The Black Prince, the nation's hero, was mortally sick, and the king, prematurely senile, was under the thumb of his mistress Alice Perrers, who had been one of the maids of the Queen, who had died of the plague in 1369. Parliament was thoroughly outraged, and searched for victims. When the king's chief minister, William of Wykeham, asked for further supplies for the French war in 1371, they demanded that he should be removed. Wykeham, who had risen from low status, via the practice of architecture, to the king's favour, was Bishop of Winchester, and founder of Winchester and New College, Oxford. A low-class prelate, made quickly rich, was an ideal scapegoat, for at a time when money was scarce, the wealth of the Church was undeniably attractive.

But in the next few years the corruption grew at court, and John of Gaunt (*q.v.*) seemed all-powerful. Gradually an opposition grew, led by Wykeham, Courtenay, Earl of March (who had married the daughter of Lionel Duke of Clarence, who had stood next in line of succession to the Black Prince until his untimely and suspicious death in Italy in 1368; from this marriage grew the Yorkist claim to the throne in the next century) and the Black Prince.

In 1376 the discord broke out in the

'Good' Parliament, where the opposition triumphed, using the Speaker, Sir Peter de la Mare, steward of the Earl of March. They demanded the presence of the true heir, Richard of Bordeaux, son of the Black Prince. In the next few months Gaunt managed to undo all the work of the Good Parliament (though he was forced to see Wykeham return in 1377); but Edward no longer bothered. For long enough affairs had been managed for him—privately by Perrers (banished from his presence by the Good Parliament, but soon to return), and publicly by Gaunt. The Black Prince had died in 1376, and his father followed him the next year. The victories had been so transient, the policies had been all of war; only disorder was to remain to the child heir.

Edward IV

Edward IV was born at Rouen in 1442, and as Earl of March served his father Richard Duke of York in prosecuting his claim to the throne as a descendant of the third son of Edward III (whereas the Lancastrians descended from the fourth son). With Warwick (*q.v.*) and Salisbury, he defeated the Lancastrians at Northampton in 1460, and on his father's death at Wakefield in the same year, he took over the leadership of the Yorkist cause, and won the throne for himself, defeating the Lancastrians at Towton, and forcing Henry VI and his family to take refuge in Scotland.

He was King by virtue of his claim, as also by his success in battle and his worthiness for the throne. In place of a spiritless lunatic, England now had a man tall, strong and handsome. He was gay, highly sexed (a notable mark of a popular English king), a fine dresser, and eminently approachable to all. If a man came to court and was too shy to speak, Edward would put a friendly hand on his shoulder to encourage him. He was business-like (nearer a merchant than anything else in cast of mind), shrewd and a quick thinker. He hated disorder and was willing to take hard measures to put it down; he could be cruel when he wished: in the Tower rested the new rack, pleasantly named the Duke of Exeter's daughter; he was willing to employ the hard Italianate Tiptoft (*q.v. sub.* 'Worcester') to put down disorder by terror.

His first years as king were spent defeating the Lancastrian survivors in the north and west, and he was helped in this by Warwick, who regarded himself as Mayor of the Palace, though Edward was soon to change things. Confrontation came over foreign policy and marriage. Warwick, the conservative baron, favoured an alliance with France, now ruled by his friend, the wily and able Louis XI. Edward, recognising the continuing hatred of France in England, and favouring the mercantile interest (for he himself was a great dealer in wool on the side) preferred to treat with Burgundy, a land naturally linked with England through its trade in wool.

Warwick was allowed to continue his negotiations for a French marriage in ignorance of the fact that Edward had already secretly married Elizabeth Woodville on 1st May 1464, and was not unnaturally furious when the marriage was revealed at Reading five months later. Her numerous family were to receive high promotion and estate, and Warwick had now to face a many-headed opposition.

The humiliated king-maker was to receive a worse blow in 1466 when plans to marry the king's sister to the future Duke of Burgundy were made, and cemented the following year in that gay court occasion when the Queen's brother jousted with the bastard of Burgundy. It was a splendid occasion, marred only by a dispute over fouling, which was the only joy Warwick got that year. In 1468 a 30-year treaty was made with Burgundy.

The following year Warwick took the King's brother, George Duke of Clarence, to Calais and married him to his daughter, using the services of his brother the Archbishop of York. The challenge was down. Clarence was a paranoic young man, easily swayed. He was the ideal tool. Together the two plotters returned in force to London, and Edward had to withdraw to Nottingham. Warwick had managed to raise the north by suggesting that Edward was illegitimate, and the northern and southern forces converged to capture the King.

Edward was too popular to be easily deposed, and the prospect of civil war unleashed fresh disorders which Warwick was unable to quell. He was forced to release the King on parole, and Edward promptly raised an army. After a last bid at fomenting rebellion in Lincolnshire Warwick finally left for France.

The King was now foolishly convinced that the Warwick menace was over, and happily left the Earl's brother, Montague, in charge of the north. Montague had served Edward well, but had been only skimpingly rewarded. Warwick had kept a substantial force, and now the King of France brought him and Margaret of Anjou together, plotting a Lancastrian restoration. Her husband, Henry VI, was already in London, in the tower, having been captured wandering around the North country. In September 1470 Warwick sailed again for England, and, with his brother acting as the northern arm of a pincer movement, took Edward unawares, forcing him to withdraw to East Anglia, and sail from there to Burgundy.

This speedy victory proved to be deceptive. Neither Warwick nor his policies proved popular, and the Lancastrian house had few fervent adherents. The 'Readeption' ended in March 1471, when Edward returned from Burgundy with a small force. Many of Warwick's supporters left him to rejoin the King—among them Clarence. At Barnet the two armies met in a fog, and Warwick was defeated and killed in a battle of high confusion. That same day Henry's wife Margaret and her son Edward had landed, and the King rapidly moved up to defeat them at Tewkesbury, killing the prince. Unfinished business was brought to a nasty conclusion with the murder of Henry VI (captured whilst wandering on the Northern border) in the Tower, and Edward ruled once more.

In 1475 Edward set off to make war on France, in pursuit of his lost domains, and in support of Burgundy; but he was no Henry V, and when Burgundian help failed to materialise, he treated with the French at Picquigny, happy to be bought off with a substantial pension, which was to support him in luxury for the rest of his life. Edward had a healthy respect for money, and had endured many years of penny-pinching economies; his last years were to be different.

Different indeed, for they were to be years of self-indulgence and shilly-shallying. One of his major problems—what to do about Clarence—exemplified his conduct. Clarence, having been pardoned for his outrageous alliance with Warwick, promptly began to bewail his lot, and point with envy to the rewards loaded on Richard of Gloucester, who had stuck by his brother the King. He gave vent to hysterical suspicions about poison-plots against his family, and after his wife's death demanded a rich Burgundian marriage. Every little villain who plotted against the crown found his ready ear. The King was told of his doings times without number before he allowed him to be put into the Tower and attainted of treason, but even then would not sign the death warrant. It was Elizabeth and Mary Queen of Scots before their time. Finally in 1478 Clarence was drowned—in his bath or the famous butt of Malmsey, and the problem was solved for Edward.

His behaviour over foreign policy was similar—playing with alliances with both Burgundy and France, but doing nothing about it, until in 1482, much to his mortification, the two warring nations at last agreed. He left his brother to manage the war with Scotland.

For the King was now fat and sleek, more eager to introduce new fashions than new laws. Hastings managed the country for him whilst he chased women, 'married and unmarried, noble and lowly', and they fell to his charms with ease. His greatest favourite was Jane Shore, wife of a city gentleman, gay, witty and intelligent, a woman to manage an aged king. Even the moralist Sir Thomas More found good words to say of her, for although she had great influence, she exercised it with discretion and charity. 'I doubt not,' he says, 'some shall think this woman too slight a thing to be written of and set among the remembrances of great matters. But meseemeth the chance so much the more worthy to be remembered, in how much she is now [c. 1513] in the more beggarly condition, unfriended and worn out of acquaintance, after good substance, after as great favour with the prince, after as great suit and seeking to with all those that those days had business to speed, as many other men were in their times, which now be famous only by the infamy of their ill deeds. Her doings were not much less, albeit they be much less remembered because they were not so evil. For men use, if they have an evil turn, to write it in marble; and whoso doth us a good turn, we write it in dust: which is not worse proved by her, for at this day she beggeth of many at this day living, that at this day had begged if she had not been.'

Edward died in 1483.

There is a biography by Cora L. Schofield: *Life and Reign of Edward the Fourth* (Longmans, Harlow, 1923).

St. Francis

The world has never ceased to give thanks for the existence of St. Francis, for he was that rare thing, a cheerful saint. Though his story really ends in tragedy, Protestants and atheists join with Catholics in a common response to his appeal, recognising in his example a culmination of all that is best in inspired human nature.

He was born about the year 1181 in Assisi, son of a dealer in woollen cloth. His father was away in France at the time— hence the name of the new baby. He was a gay youth, surrounded by friends, interested in fashion, music and clothes, and filled with the vague idealism of youth—in his case inspired by the songs and poems about courtly love and knightly courtesy that came into North Italy from that seat of fashion, France.

These ideals took a substantial beating when Francis, aged about twenty, went to war in his city's fight against Perugia, and when he joined briefly a band of mercenaries. Somehow soldiers didn't act like the knights in the poems, and Francis gave away all his rich armour to a penniless knight, and journeyed miserably home.

But he could not find the 'courtesy' he searched for in his father's business: just as coins dirtied his hands, he saw riches turning their owners into litigious money-grubbers, extorting more and more from buyers, and treating them mercilessly when they failed to pay. In great distress of mind he journied to Rome on pilgrimage. There he saw parsimony all around him, and in an angry gesture he flung down his full purse at the nearest shrine. He experimented by exchanging clothes with a beggar one day, and on the way home was moved to give a leper the kiss of peace. This must have cost him more than a purse-full of money: each age has the disease it fears and hates: the nineteenth century feared consumption, while today we fear cancer; in Francis's time leprosy seemed by far the worst.

Back in Assisi he busied himself in rebuilding ruined churches, singing newly invented songs of praise to the latest French jongleur tunes as he worked. He took cloth from his father's store to sell to get the money he needed: for a while this was overlooked, but when his father saw his son confirmed in his madness, he treated him like a lunatic, locking him up, and beating the evil spirit out of him. His mother released him, but the father, determined to cure the young man, pressed his case in the courts.

Now Francis knew what he was to do, and his sense of the dramatic rose to the occasion. In answer to his father's demands for restitution, he stripped himself naked before the court, and gave back all he possessed to his father; he would have walked out naked as well, had not the bishop covered him with his own cloak. He had cut himself off as effectively as he could: he was alone and penniless, able at last to build the new life he wanted.

It was not to be long before others joined him, for it seemed that poverty was the key to boundless joy. A wealthy man of Assisi and a learned lawyer sold all they had and gave the money to the poor, and came to Francis as his first Franciscans. Then came a peasant, who had nothing to sell, but who one day knelt down by Francis and said simply, 'Brother, I would be with you.' A knight sold his armour and came, and a famous jongleur—these two must have pleased Francis very much.

But to most people they were all madmen. There were plenty of monasteries about for them to join, instead of making a nuisance of themselves with their begging —and anyway, that cost the community money. The hard-headed northern Italian businessmen objected to rich men giving away all they had and promptly becoming a charge on the state. Anyway, Francis's attitude to money—their staple diet—was insulting—he wouldn't allow any of his followers even to touch a coin. They accepted only gifts in kind, and only as much as they needed—they weren't even a reputable charity organisation!

This opposition was to continue for many years, and the extraordinary irregularity of Francis's followers simply made for confusion. They accepted all who came, without any novitiate; there was the sketchiest of Rules—it barely went beyond stating the principles of poverty; the brothers had no stability—wandering about from this place to that; and there was no organisation at all. One is not surprised to read of the many occasions on which they were taken for heretics and madmen in the early years—with characters like the simpleton Brother Juniper collecting a congregation outside Rome by playing on a see-saw, and Francis himself preaching to the birds, who could blame those who denounced such indecorous

behaviour, and tried to put it down?

Luckily the Pope saw that there was more to the movement than madcap tricks and strange behaviour. Francis met Innocent III in 1210, and won his support. Innocent feared the popular heresies that were springing up in the south of France, and also recognised the desperate need for spiritual regeneration in the Church: he saw Francis and Dominic (q.v.) as the solution to both of these problems. The vigour and absolute faith of Francis would obviously do a great work for the Church, and do it quickly, for his appeal was very direct. He was a powerful speaker, who would often become so enthralled in his subject that he would girate as though dancing—an embarrassment in sophisticated circles, but not with ordinary folk. Though he could read, he was not learned, and his speech was homely. Indeed it did not appear to matter what he said, for as one contemporary recorded, 'I never remember what words he uses, and if I do they do not seem to me to be the same.' Often singing as well as 'dancing', his unconventional and extrovert approach brought people to him. Once there they felt the pull—the strange magnetism that made animals totally unafraid of him, and attached men so closely that they could never willingly let go.

They came in thousands, but the message was hard: absolute poverty was its core—a poverty so absolute that the 'little brothers' could not stay more than a few nights in one place, whatever it was, Etruscan tomb or dilapidated cow-shed, lest people should think of them, 'That is *their* place'. Yet the followers, even in the hardest conditions, seemed not just happy but cheerful as well. With Francis joking, laughing and singing, who could be miserable? They all worked—Francis making pots and carving wooden church-decorations—he was artistically gifted, and others giving their labour in return for kitchen-scraps. Only occasionally did the proud spirit of their leader break out in temper: once, when a brother preferred to pray rather than preach, Francis sent him to preach in Assisi in his underpants—if he was too ashamed to preach, let him preach with double shame, there was no room in the order for people obsessed with their own problems, everyone had to be totally concerned with the welfare of the rest of the world. Yet Francis's temper soon subsided, and he flung off his outer clothes and rushed down to Assisi to preach naked with his brother.

His total commitment to the unconventional may have appeared strange, but it made people sit up and think, and it enabled Francis himself to see more clearly the way ahead. His greatest revolution came when Clare, a daughter of one of the leading houses in Assisi, came to him requesting admission to the order. The medieval Church frequently saw women as merely the cause of the fall of man, and often showed itself not just afraid of them, but antipathetical as well. Certainly the male orders were fanatically careful about the exclusion of women. But Francis was never troubled by this, and frequently shocked his followers by the free and easy ways he had with women. He was not disturbed by Clare's application, for he recognised in her a true vocation, and a spirit on a par with his own. He cut off her hair, and found a place for her to stay. She was a Franciscan, and soon other women came to join her in the order for the Poor Clares. Francis visited them frequently, and used them as a power-house of prayer for the order.

If this was shocking, far worse was his friendship with a Roman widow who could not join the Clares because she had children to bring up. Francis saw no difference between her and his other friends 'in religion': he gave her on one occasion a lamb, and when he lay dying she arrived with frangipani cakes, and was with him to the end. Francis had a deep respect for women that stemmed from his kindly and understanding mother. He urged his followers that if one among them should exercise authority he should do it as a mother, caring for her family, and receiving that obedience that comes from love.

Once, when undergoing a personal crisis, he was observed to go out into a winter's night and make for himself a snow 'wife' and snow 'children', making concrete what he was imagining for himself, so that he could compare a life he had given up with the one he had. This is very typical of his level of thinking—making practical experiments, concrete exemplars of the abstract in order to examine them—but it also tells us much of the man.

In 1212 Francis went to Syria on a missionary journey, and in 1214 to Spain. He was very concerned that his order should undertake missionary work, and longed himself to be engaged at the frontier; whilst crusaders fought, he would preach. He would have been glad to know that within a century of his death there were fifty Franciscans in the environs of Peking.

Back in Italy in 1215, Francis attended the fourth Lateran Council, where his order received full official confirmation. He made many new friends there, among them Dominic, but the most important to him was Cardinal Ugolino, who was to take over responsibility for the order on the death of Innocent III that same year.

Ugolino and Francis had a deep and abiding respect for each other, but they were very different in character. Ugolino saw that an order as large and popular as the Franciscans badly needed some kind of organisation, if it were to succeed; Francis was all too well aware that organisation and regularisation meant a decline from the original standards of simplicity— it had happened with all the monastic orders, and he did not want it to happen to his own. Yet instinctively he knew that this must come—for he was a strong enough character to have fought Ugolino to the finish had he really been convinced he was wrong. Step by tragic step he was to give way to heart-rending changes that gradually reduced his original aims to nonsense; for his original aims could only work whilst he was in charge of a handful of people. Now there were thousands—and where was a new Francis to come from?

In 1219 there was a chapter meeting in Assisi, and 5,000 Franciscans came. Francis refused to make any preparations—for had not God once provided for the feeding of 5,000 other souls? The people of Assisi, already aware of the value of tourist attractions, got to work whilst he was away, and built a large meeting hall for them. When he returned he went up to the roof with a few companions and began to pull it down, but was restrained in the end: had these poor folk laboured to please only to have their gift thrown in their faces? In his youth he would have thrown it, but now he did not know what to do. He reminded the chapter of his call to simplicity, to the position of 'a fool in this world', and speeding Brother Giles off on his mission to Tunis, went himself to join the crusading armies in Egypt.

He was a missionary, not a partisan, and having preached in the crusader's camp, he set off for the tents of the enemy. He didn't know the language, and had made no advance preparations. The soldiers on guard gave him a hot reception—beating him about the head, and shoving him back towards the crusaders' camp, threatening worse if he did not go. But the gaunt figure with bloodshot eyes, and a body ruined by privation simply hid his head and kept on crying 'Soldan! Soldan!', and eventually the soldiers relented, taking the madman before the Sultan, who heard him preach, and sent him back with honour, saying, 'Pray for me, that God may deign to reveal to me that faith which is most pleasing to him.'

He went on to Palestine, and there heard that Ugolino and the brothers favouring his reforms were splitting the order. He returned, and found this to be true: his order, founded on the bedrock of poverty, now sported at Bologna a substantial and well-built convent, with a fully-equipped school attached. Francis turned them out on the streets, where they belonged, and went to meet Ugolino.

Some kind of compromise was reached, but it did not tip in Francis's favour. He retired to prepare a new Rule for the order, agonising over each compromise as a fall from grace, and knowing inwardly that it would not be acceptable when produced. Brother Elias, a reformer, now ruled as minister-general of the order, and in chapter Francis sat at his feet, twitching his robe to ask permission to speak. Those who supported the original ideas of the order must have been disturbed at Francis's humble conduct, and his refusal to move against the reformers; but he tried to explain that the essence of their life was in the giving of example and not in action. As he sat there in chapter, giving example as no one else could, and knowing it was not being followed, it was a bitter time for him too.

Brother Elias was determined to win, even to the extent of completely ignoring the founder of his own order. He insisted on absolute obedience being written into the new Rule, though Francis sensibly reminded him that this only existed in a corpse, and that forgiveness was the more urgent Christian virtue. He who had once given away the last Testament his order possessed to be sold for charity, now had to see convents endowed with huge libraries.

Seeing that he could effect little by present example, he retired with a few followers to a cave, where the true Franciscan life was lived. At Christmas he carried out another of his 'experiments', setting up a crib in the local church, and bringing in oxen, so that he could 'behold with bodily eyes His infant hardships'.

The following summer he retired to a deeper hermitage, to meditate, and prepare for death. When his few close friends brought him down from the hills he had to be taken to Clare to nurse. He was nearly blind, constantly sick, and his hands and feet were bandaged. He had in this time received the stigmata. Whatever one may think of other such revelations, it is impossible to doubt Francis, a more honest and straight-forward person did not exist—

he had those wounds. In the intensity of his vision of God, and thinking constantly on the sufferings of the betrayed (and he himself was being betrayed most deeply) he received a sign. It was his nature—he liked always to make the concrete significations for abstract problems which bothered him. To him, as he says in the Canticle of Brother Sun (composed at this time), the whole of the natural world is a signification of God. He feared pain—when the doctors came to him to cauterise his cheeks to relieve his eyes, he blenched, then said, 'Brother Fire, be courteous to me', before submitting to them. He needed to understand the highest pain, and so there in the mountains, without any physical interposition from himself or others, his mind and heart had conquered his flesh, and the stigmata had appeared. He had understood.

He travelled about for a little while, but when death was upon him in 1226, the citizens of Assisi sent an armed guard to fetch him home—they did not want his potentially valuable, miracle working body to become the property of any other town. On the way back the soldiers found difficulty in buying bread; Francis was amused, and explained to them how to beg, and they soon succeeded.

He was canonised within two years of his death, and his order did great work: but his immediate followers were finally hounded out—it was the reformed order that had the day, an order Francis would not have recognised. His philosophy may be summed up in a letter to his devoted Leo, telling him to come to him whenever he wanted to: 'My son, as a mother to her child, I answer "Yes." This word resumes our talks by the wayside, and all my opinions. . . . Whatever be the way in which you think you can please God, to follow his footsteps and live in poverty, take it. God will bless you, and I authorise you to it.'

T. S. R. Boase, *St. Francis of Assisi*; (Thames and Hudson, London, 1968; Indiana Univ. Press, revised ed. 1968).

Frederick Barbarossa

In some wild mountain, so legend tells us, there is a cave, and in it sits Frederick Barbarossa; his great red beard has already curled twice around the table before him. When it has finished its third orbit, he will arise and come out to fight his last battle, and the day of judgement then will come.

In 1152, at the age of 30, Frederick of Hohenstaufen, Duke of Swabia was elected Emperor: the Germany he was called to rule was no inviting prospect, torn as it was by dispute between the Welf Dukes of Saxony and Bavaria and his own family, who took the name of their castle of Waiblingen as a battle cry. (When the dispute was later fought out in Italy the names of the two parties were transmuted into Guelphs and Ghibellines.) Frederick, who was half Welf through his mother, had a great deal in his favour: he was physically strong and handsome (a contemporary said that he looked always about to burst into laughter), had had experience of warfare on the Second Crusade and was the epitomy of the chivalrous knight; he was intelligent, understood Latin, and enjoyed German poetry, and was interested in history and law; he was energetic and determined, and deeply concerned that justice should prevail.

It took him a bare two years to settle Germany to his own satisfaction: he dealt justly with the Welfs, giving them territories to rule over within his overlordship, and he established law in the land, and made sure it was kept, punishing infringements harshly, and inhibiting private warfare. He gained an unprecedented control over the Church, establishing his right to nominate bishops in a disputed election.

In 1154 he departed for Italy, to regain for the Empire the rich territories there which it had not controlled in fifty years. In the fast developing towns a strong spirit of independence had arisen, and they had frequently set up Republican or Communal government. Even Rome, under the stimulus of Arnold of Breschia, the disciple of Abelard, had responded to this call, and

Frederick had to use his forces to reinstate Pope Adrian IV (*q.v.*), in order that he might be crowned Emperor.

After a spell back in Germany to consolidate his position, Frederick returned once more to Italy in 1158 to attack the cities which still opposed him. He got doctors of law to lecture to the Diet on the doctrine of the absolute rule of the Roman Emperor, but this was not enough, and he was forced to besiege cities, using the best modern techniques, and the worst degrees of harshness. He tied prisoners of war to his siege engines to be shot at by their own side, razed cities to the ground which opposed him, and installed German governors to extract maximum obedience and profit.

In 1159 Pope Adrian died, and the College of Cardinals split, the minority favouring the imperialist side electing one Pope, the majority another, Alexander III. Alexander quickly won the allegiance of France and England, and Frederick soon found himself in a very tricky position. It was made far worse when his Pope died on him, and he foolishly agreed to the totally illegal election of another, which lost him the support of even his own bishops.

Not disheartened, he had his new Pope canonise the Emperor Charlemagne in 1165, and in the following year attacked Italy again. All went well, and in 1167 Rome was in his hands, and Alexander had fled. At this stage fate struck as hard as ever it could, and his army (and his leading generals and advisers) was decimated by a terrible pestilence. Frederick led the pathetic remnant of his conquering host through a prominently hostile North Italy, where the Communes had now organised themselves into the powerful Lombard League.

Back in Germany, all his plans were for another invasion of Italy, but he no longer had a united following, for he was now at odds with the leading Welf, Henry the Lion, who had been quietly building up his power in the North. Using his alliance with the Danes, and the knowledge of modern warfare he had gained from ex-perience with Frederick, he revived the 'Drive to the East', colonising the lower Elbe with Germans, Frisians and Flemings, setting up towns, encouraging trade, and developing agriculture by promoting new Cistercian and Premonstratensian monasteries there (for these monks were the finest farmers of the age). He also forcibly converted the Wendlish inhabitants, one of whose chieftains said to him 'There may be a God in Heaven, he is your God. You be our God, and we are satisfied. You worship him, we will worship you.' Such a powerful man was a man to be reckoned with, and Frederick unfortunately gravely insulted the Welf prince by buying Welf territories from the man's impecunious uncle.

So it was without the support of troops from North Germany that Frederick invaded Italy for the last time in 1174, and his army was so small that he was forced to try negotiations before giving battle at Legnano, where he was so completely routed that he even lost his shield and personal standard, and was forced to retreat to Pavia.

Frederick did not need telling twice that his cause in North Italy was now lost, and he set to at once to use diplomacy where arms had failed. He recognised Pope Alexander, made a six-year truce with the Lombard League, and a fifteen-year truce with Sicily. He was always a deeply emotional person, and deeply sympathetic in personal relations. When in 1177 the Doge of Venice led him to meet Pope Alexander in the square before St. Mark's to celebrate the signing of the treaty closing eighteen years of bitter warfare, he flung off his imperial mantle and prostrated himself, and Alexander, himself in tears, raised him up and led him into the church to give him his benediction.

Frederick now turned to the affairs of Germany once more, to settle with Henry the Lion, whose grasping and domineering ways had roused tremendous opposition. After a long trial, Frederick confiscated his lands and, cutting them into smaller parcels, distributed them amongst his own supporters (and among them the Wittelsbachs ruled Bavaria until 1918). Henry was banished to the court of his father in law, Henry II of England.

Frederick now used diplomacy as his strongest tool, developing his personal territories, and arranging peaceful settlements with his feudatories, forgetting his dreams of a personally dominated Empire in favour of a more federal structure. In 1183 he made peace with the Lombard League, recognising the Communes' rights of self-government in return for their recognition of his sovereignty. Diplomacy seemed to be paying more dividends than war, for he also arranged the marriage of his son Henry to Constance, the aunt of William II of Sicily.

Having arranged peace in his domains, and the possibility of his son Henry gaining what he dreamed of, he now allowed himself the luxury of a return to the East, which had exercised his imagination ever since he had been on the disastrous Second Crusade. Having sent Saladin a personal challenge, warning him that if he did not relinquish the Holy territories, he would have to deal with Frederick in person in a year's time, he set off with 20,000 knights. Having met with difficulties in Bulgaria, in Byzantium and in the Sultanate of Iconium, Frederick was pressing on towards his goal when, in 1190, he was mysteriously drowned at a river-crossing. No one knows the details, or probably ever will.

For a biography, see Peter Munz: *Frederick Barbarossa: A Study in Medieval Politics* (Eyre and Spottiswoode, London, 1969; Cornell Univ. Press, New York, 1969). Frederick's uncle, Otto of Freising, who had a great influence on his upbringing, was one of the foremost of medieval chroniclers, and his work has been translated as *The Deeds of Frederick Barbarossa* by C. C. Mierow (Norton, New York, 1966).

Frederick II

Frederick II, known to his friends as *Stupor Mundi*, the world-amazer, and to his many enemies by a great variety of inventive epithets, was born in 1194. His father Henry VI was heir to Barbarossa, his mother Constance of Sicily was heir to Roger II; they had been childless for nine years before producing the son who was destined to unite the two greatest heritages of the known world.

His father died when he was three years old, so the Germans perforce elected another Emperor, Otto IV, a Welf, though Philip of Swabia was to keep the cause of the Hohenstaufen alive in Germany for another fourteen years, warming the seat, as it were, for Frederick.

Constance now settled down to eliminate German influence in Sicily and to prepare her boy for rule in the country alone, but within a year she too was dead, and Frederick was left, the sport of fortune, technically the ward of the Pope Innocent III (though he was not to meet him until he was seventeen), more particularly receiving an eclectic and highly practical education from his observation of the various forces contending in his kingdom. Normans, Germans, Byzantine Greeks, Arabs and Italians all had their share in this cosmopolitan society, but no one had established exactly what the shares were.

In 1211, with Philip of Swabia cruelly murdered in Germany, and Otto IV prepared to invade Sicily, the situation looked desperate for the young King. However, a revolt in Germany called Otto home, and the Waibling (Ghibelline) princes elected Frederick as Emperor, deposing Otto. Pope Innocent gave his support to Frederick, as he thought that if the two emperors could keep each other busy fighting it out in Germany, they would have no thought for Italy, and Rome.

The journey north to claim his birthright was a romantic crusade to the young Frederick; he tells us that he set off 'as torn and ragged as a beggar boy', and he had to raise money in Genoa by issuing promissory notes marked 'Valid the day I become Emperor'. He had a hair-raising escape from the Milanese, flinging himself on a horse and swimming a river bare-backed, and he was forced to cross the Alps, with his pathetic army of 60 knights, at the most difficult part, because all the other passes were under Welf control.

Otto was bringing his army down to Constance to repulse the invasion of the 'boy from Apulia' as he was universally known, and the town was decked out to receive its Emperor. Frederick arrived just three hours before Otto, and forced his way in.

From this point on he had a wild success —after all he was the true heir, and with Barbarossa's red-gold hair he could not fail to win support. In 1214 Otto was defeated for him by Philip Augustus at the battle of Bouvines, and in 1215 Frederick was crowned at Aachen, personally driving in the last nails of the shrine to Charlemagne that his grandfather had begun. In 1220 he was crowned in Rome, and the dream was coming true.

But he had had to forfeit so much in order to achieve this success, giving the Pope control over the German Church in return for his recognition as Emperor, and confirming the baronage in the rights and territories they had taken already, in order to gain their support. In Germany the only force he could really rely on was the Teutonic Knights, whose developing power and settlement of Prussia he carefully fostered. In North Italy he managed to assert his authority a little more, though the rebelliousness of the Communes was something to live with, not fight against.

So now he turned to Sicily, to build there an undefeatable basis of power. Here was an absolute monarch, modelled severely on the Arab and Byzantine precedents so close at hand; the country was not governed through any feeble feudal structure, but by trained, salaried and responsible bureaucrats. State monopolies (like the silk industry run by the Jews for the crown) and customs brought in so

much money that Sicily was without doubt the wealthiest monarchy in Europe.

Frederick was to carry these trends to the uttermost, wringing from the country not only obedience, but also *carte blanche* for any project he had a mind to carry out. His methods of attaining military might are typical: to give himself a navy he simply forced any ship that put into a Sicilian port to give itself up to his service. For an army he used Muslims, who would not be affected by the excommunications that thundered round his head. They had been recruited simply: Frederick put down a Muslim rebellion in Sicily, and cleared a town on the mainland to receive them (converting the cathedral into a mosque, and inhibiting all Christians around from attempting to convert the new inhabitants). They remained as devoted to him as any janissaries.

An army and a navy were not enough: Frederick needed trained civil servants as well, so in 1224 he established the University of Naples—the first secular university in Europe. To make sure of its success he gave it enviable privileges (including cheap food and lodgings) and forbade any Sicilian from attending any other University. Those who were studying abroad had to come home at once and enrol at Naples.

The new Pope Honorius III, decided to go against previous policy, and help the Emperor, so long as he would fulfil two conditions: he must go on crusade, and he must help root out heresy. The latter presented no problem, for Frederick declared that any heretics in his kingdom were sinning as much against himself as against God, and firmly instructed his secular officials to help in their capture and punishment—except of course for the Muslims, Jews and Orthodox Greeks, who were such helpful adjuncts to the Empire. The crusade was a different matter—he was very busy at home, and it must wait; time and again he put it off, until he was forced by Honorius to set the date of his departure at August, 1227.

That same year, however, the amenable

Honorius died and was succeeded by a man who was to live and breathe hostility to the Empire, Gregory IX. He was a fanatic who possessed worldly wisdom and a wide experience; though he was 86 at the time of his elevation, he continued to be tremendously active until his death fourteen years later. In those years he had built up the Inquisition as a papal weapon, issued the Decretals (a code of all the additions made to the Canon Law in the previous two centuries), founded one university and practically re-founded another, and watched the growth of the friars of Dominic and Francis, whom he also canonised. Above all things, however, Gregory aimed to smash Frederick, whom he saw as encircling the Papacy, and threatening to take control in Rome; the Emperor was ostentatiously *Roman*, and the Pope knew there was no room for him there. So he became the demon, the Anti-christ, the worst man in the world—all the forces of papal propaganda swung into action.

It must have been annoying to see Frederick sail off on crusade promptly in August 1227, but the Pope's joy was great when he heard that two days later Frederick had come back again, forced to return by a terrible outbreak of plague on board ship that would inevitably have killed everyone if they had stayed at sea. Here was proof that the Emperor was not to be trusted, and an excuse to excommunicate him. The following year when Frederick set off once more, not only did Gregory remain obdurate about the excommunication, but smartly invaded Sicily in the absence of the King.

Yet for a while, all the luck was on the side of the Emperor: he took Cyprus on his way to the East, and on his arrival found he could gain what he came for without a fight: the Sultan of Egypt was in the middle of a quarrel with the Sultan of Damascus, so Frederick stepped in to give moral support to the Sultan of Egypt. He spoke fluent Arabic, and with his background he

was as much of an eastern potentate as the Sultan; they got on tremendously well,[1] and the Sultan granted the Emperor Jerusalem, Bethlehem and Nazareth. Frederick had been provident enough to marry the heiress to the throne of Jerusalem, so when he reached the Holy City he majestically crowned himself in the Church of the Holy Sepulchre.

He returned to Sicily in 1230, and the papal forces made a swift withdrawal from his territories. It must have been a galling time for them, for here was Frederick the Champion of Christendom, having won the holy places at practically no cost, and with little effort, and having quietly feathered his own nest considerably in the process. Salimbene says that it was Frederick's proud boast 'that he never reared a pig but he had its bacon.'

Riding around on his black horse 'Dragon', handsome, clean-shaven and with his grandfather's red hair, he made an impressive figure, tough and athletic. He took only one meal a day, and lots of exercise, but most astonishing of all, he bathed every day: his moorish bodyguard and his negro band, his chief officers of state, chief justices, jesters and rope-dancers all went with him. So did the rich treasury, and the royal zoo, with its famous collection of all kinds of birds, leopards, lions, panthers, bears, an elephant and a giraffe. Somewhere in the train would be the royal harem, guarded by its eunuchs. A noisy, bustling, immensely worldly cavalcade, enough to convince any pope that it was the rout of Satan.

Frederick astonished the world by displaying strange things, and by doing strange things: Nietzsche compared his intellectual curiosity to that of Leonardo da Vinci, and in many ways one must admit him to the ranks of Renaissance men. He spoke nine languages and could write seven of them; he was an accomplished poet, and passionately interested in science. His treatise on falconry shows the depth

[1] De Joinville owed his life when captured in Egypt to his relationship with the German Emperor 'Ferry' (Bohn ed., 1876, p. 441).

of his research and the intensity of his powers of observation. He encouraged scientists at his court to translate Aristotle and indulge in all kinds of research; no holds were barred, and many of the experiments were cruel, particularly those Frederick inspired, such as bringing up children in silence to see what language they would speak—naturally they all died before they could tell him. His cynicism and scepticism led him to take up a standpoint towards religion that was at times blasphemous—he would often make jokes such as, when passing a field of corn, 'What a lot of Gods are growing here!'

Knowing how badly Frederick was treated by the Church, one can perhaps have a certain sympathy; but to the papal party his behaviour was an ever present reminder that the enemy was devilish. This was an era of religious revival—the 'Great Halleluja movement' for peace and penance; friars preacher terrifying their audiences with fabulous tales of purgatory and hell; and Joachim of Flora scaring people to death with his calculations of when the world was going to end.

In 1241 Gregory summoned a general council to Rome to depose the Antichrist Frederick, but the latter smartly captured a boatload of prelates on their way there, and the council had to be put off. The Emperor now marched on Rome, but the centenarian Pope quietly died before he arrived.

For two years Frederick threatened, pleaded, bullied and wheedled the College of Cardinals to make them elect a Pope favourable to the Empire. They finally chose Innocent IV, who certainly had been on the imperial side before his elevation, but having taken stock of the situation, he decided to continue Gregory's policy. He convened a general council at Lyons in 1245 to order the deposition. Frederick now turned to move on Lyons, but was seriously delayed by the loss of Pavia, which was essential to him in order to preserve his lines of communication. Its loss came in a silly way: a small party of exiled

Guelfs had taken it while all the Ghibellines had been at a wedding-feast; but the results were disastrous for Frederick, who found the city impossible to reduce, and was caught off-guard before it in 1248 by a papalist army drawn from the Communes and defeated.

He died in 1250, and his heirs lasted only a little longer: his son Conrad survived him by four years, to be succeeded by his own illegitimate son Manfred. This one lasted only two years, being beaten by the papally-supported 'crusade' of Charles of Anjou. In 1268 Frederick's grandson Conradin, last of the Staufens, aged fifteen, crossed the Alps to claim his patrimony. When defeated he was tried, condemned and beheaded in the Naples market-place. The popes had won.

The best biography (if rather Wagnerian in tone) is by Ernst Kantorowicz: *Frederick II*, trs. Lorimer (Ungar, New York, 1957).

John of Gaunt

John, by the grace of God, King of Castile and Leon, Duke of Lancaster and Aquitaine, Earl of Derby, Lincoln and Leicester, Lord of Beaufort and Nogent, of Bergerac and Roche-sur-Yon, Seneschal of England and Constable of Chester was born in March 1340 at Ghent, and the English with a typical disregard for pronunciation called him John of Gaunt. He was the fourth son of Edward III and his beautiful Queen Philippa, and was brought up in the atmosphere of the early years of the Hundred Years' War when England was winning all on land and sea, and his elder brother the Black Prince was setting the pattern for the world to admire.

We know little of his early years, overshadowed as they were by greater personages. He appears in battles during his early adolescence, and in 1357 we find him meeting the poet Chaucer and becoming his patron. Two years later he married Blanche, the second daughter of Henry of Lancaster, after the king the most prominent and richest man in England. She was very beautiful, well worth the £20 ring he gave her at their marriage in Reading, and the rich rejoicings there. Afterwards they moved to London, where the city proclaimed a tournament: twenty-four knights appeared wearing the badge of the city, and won all their bouts; at the end of the day, when they took off their helms, all were astonished to see, instead of the mayor and aldermen, the king, his four sons and nineteen of the principal barons of England. Three years later, when the plague had carried off the old Duke of Lancaster and his eldest daughter, Gaunt came into a rich inheritance which would have made him a leader in English affairs even if he had not been the king's son.

Now began his long and tragic love affair with Spain. In Castile the new king, Pedro, had been struggling with the warlords who really ruled his land, and the more he failed, the harsher his methods became. His people called him Pedro the Justiciar, but the barons called him Pedro the Cruel, and he had also succeeded in making enemies of the Pope and the rulers of France. His half-brother Enrique of Trastamare gathered together the support of all Pedro's many enemies, and forced him to fly the kingdom; he went for help to the Black Prince in Bordeaux.

Edward was a staunch supporter of the principle of legitimate inheritance in monarchy, and viewed the cause in the spirit of knight-errantry; furthermore a Castilian alliance would be most useful, for they possessed a large and valuable fleet. So in 1367 Lancaster led the van of the Black Prince's army over the pass of Roncesvaux and on into Castile to restore the rightful king. Even though Enrique had the great French general Bertrand du Guesclin in charge of his forces, the English were irresistible, and soon the usurper was making his daring and romantic escape north into France.

Lancaster was deeply impressed with this victory, though he had not the political sense to see what harm it did the English cause. His brother lost his health in Spain,

and also lost the support of the Gascons because he had fruitlessly spent their taxes on this foreign war. Pedro paid nothing, and immediately the English left was routed once more by Enrique, who this time finished the job and had him murdered. Now Castile was a firm ally of France and their joint navies could easily outmatch the English. It had been a major disaster, but John of Gaunt remembered only the victory.

He had suffered a severe blow in the death of his wife, a victim of the plague. Chaucer describes her in his *Book of the Duchess,* and she was plainly a subject fit for his pen, beautiful to perfection, stately, kind and gentle, a creature designed to inspire great love, 'and every day her beauty newed'. She had the Duke so much enthralled that he found any company, however pleasant, as naked as a crown without jewels if she was not there; and when she died he was heart-broken:

> I have of sorwe so grete woon
> That joye ne gete I never noon,
> Now that I see my lady bright,
> Which I have loved with al my myght,
> Is fro me deed and is agoon.

We know from other sources that Chaucer was painting a fair picture of his patron's sorrow, for Lancaster attended the annual memorial service to her in St. Paul's whenever he was in England, and left instructions that he should be buried beside her, ignoring the claims of Constance of Castile and the love of his old age, Katherine Swynford.

Lancaster now went to Aquitaine to relieve the Black Prince, who was so seriously ill that he had to direct military operations from a litter. It was during the siege of Limoges that a curious incident occurred: Lancaster was present in the mine below the walls when it joined unexpectedly with a counter-mine, and a hand-to-hand battle ensued, Lancaster and his opponent talking all the time to find out each other's names, for they found themselves equally matched, and very much in the dark as to what to do about it.

In 1371 he married again, this time for politics rather than for love, taking as his bride Constance of Castile, heir of Pedro the Cruel. From now on he styled himself king, and it was ever in his mind to turn *de jure* into *de facto*. In 1373 he led a huge army to France, thinking to go on to Castile after winning back England's continental possessions; but he was defeated by the Fabian tactics of the French, who withdrew before him, taking everything with them, even to the sails of the windmills. In five months he marched from Calais to Bordeaux, losing half his men and gaining no booty.

He returned to England convinced that the bid for France had failed, and that the great necessity was peace. In 1375 he went to Bruges to begin the negotiations, which were long and hard, but he met there a most interesting man who would prove useful to him in time to come. His name was John Wyclif (*q.v.*).

The next year Lancaster had to face 'The Good Parliament', one of the strongest demonstrations of popular discontent short of revolution that England had experienced. The people were angry at the continued heavy taxation, disappointed at the poor results in the war with France, discontented at the exactions of the 'French' popes of Avignon and at the poor showing of the Church in general, and above all they were suspicious of the king's ministers and of the power of John of Gaunt. Edward III had long since given himself up to pleasure and left affairs of state to others, whilst he basked, old, ill and rather loose-witted, in the control of his mistress, Alice Perrers.

The Speaker of Parliament, Sir Peter de la Mare, spoke out bravely and forcefully, demanding a scrutiny of public accounts, the impeachment of the king's ministers and his mistress, and the appointment of a council to look after the affairs of the realm, and keep them firmly out of the hands of Lancaster. The death of the

Black Prince (a popular hero who was thought to support the party of reform) urged them on: plainly Lancaster would take the crown when his father died and the Black Prince's son Richard was due to succeed. Their thinking was really quite sound on the basis of previous experience, but it was unfair in this case. Lancaster had worshipped his brother, was on excellent terms with the princess Joan, and was to be Richard's most loyal subject; he was furious at the implications of the Good Parliament, and as soon as it was dissolved, he declared it to have been no parliament at all, and its acts null and void; he restored those whom it had impeached, and imprisoned Sir Peter de la Mare.

One of the great supporters of the reforming party had been William of Wykeham, Bishop of Winchester. He had risen from low estate to this eminence by favour of a grateful king, who much appreciated his efficiency in the royal service. Lancaster hated political bishops, and felt strongly that William was a traitor in daring to criticise the king who had raised him up; government was the business of the nobility, not that of low-born churchmen. Gaunt had William's temporalities confiscated, and had him banned from coming within twenty miles of the court; furthermore he called Wyclif to London to lead a propaganda campaign against the bishop.[1] Most probably Gaunt did not understand Wyclif's ideas, or their significance, and he certainly would not have supported his heresies; he merely knew Wyclif to be very strong in preaching down worldly priests, and decided to use him for this purpose.

By accepting this commission, Wyclif did himself a very good turn: he must have known that Lancaster was as conservative in his religious beliefs as any man alive; perhaps he also knew that he was as conventional in his belief in the feudal structure of society. Once Gaunt took on a servant in any other than a lowly capacity, he also took on himself responsibility for

[1] Some recent studies have cast doubt on this traditional view of Wyclif's work for Gaunt, though the main part of the account is incontestable.

protecting that servant. Thus when on 19th February 1377, Wyclif went to St. Paul's for trial as a heretic, he was accompanied by Lancaster, Percy the Marshal, and an impressive defence council engaged by the Duke. The cathedral was full to overflowing—Wyclif had been preaching for six months, and Bishop Courtenay of London was determined to silence him; this was a *cause célèbre*. Percy cleared a way for the ducal train with considerable violence, and the bishop protested—this was no way for one accused of heresy to appear at his trial. When the indictment was to be read Courtenay insisted that the 'prisoner' should stand, but Percy insisted that he should remain seated. A tremendous row ensued and Lancaster soon lost his temper, threatening to drag the bishop from his cathedral by his hair. Then came the inevitable riot, and Wyclif went free.

The citizens of London were seriously worried by this demonstration of baronial power, feeling that it was not only ecclesiastical authority that was being threatened, but also their own. A mob set off and sacked Percy's town house, and then went on to Lancaster's great palace of the Savoy. Luckily both were dining out, and when the news came, just as the oysters were being served, they left their dinner (the Duke barking his shins against the form) to go in the ducal barge at high speed to Kennington where the Princess Joan and Prince Richard lived. The mob were eventually calmed, but a warning had been given.

In June 1377 Edward III died, and Lancaster made every effort to ensure a peaceful succession for Richard, ostentatiously making peace with all his enemies, and withdrawing to his estates for a year. They needed his attention, and he was ready for a rest. The Duchy of Lancaster was a palatinate, which meant its ruler had quasi-regal status there; his income was enormous—in 1394 his receipts were £16,593 16s. 4¼d, he was followed by a perpetual retinue of 300, and his estates over the whole of England were protected by over thirty castles.

He would still be a great man in retirement.

In 1378, however, he was called on to repulse the French navy, which was harrying the southern coast, and had even come up the river to burn Gravesend. As usual the French quietly disappeared, and in order to come back with some victory, the Duke invested St. Malo, and would have succeeded but for the bungling of the Earl of Arundel.

He returned to find London seething once more: the Constable of the Tower had entered Westminster Abbey to retrieve a sanctuary man, had scattered the choirmonks in the middle of mass, struck down the sacristan, and murdered his prisoner on the steps of the altar. Courtenay refused to come to Windsor to discuss the matter, and Lancaster lost his temper once more and offered to drag him there 'in spite of the ribald knaves of London'. Unbearable tensions were building up, and soon would break.

In 1380 Lancaster went to establish peace on the northern border, convinced that the perpetual wars with Scotland were as harmful to England as were those with France. He may well have been making peace with a view to war—his war to win Castile, but he certainly showed himself an exceptionally able peace-maker and diplomatist, a strange thing in a man so hot-tempered and bred to war.

In May 1381 he set off north once more to renew the truce, and this journey certainly saved his life, for almost at once the Peasant's Revolt broke out, and the chief object of the revolutionaries was to get rid of Lancaster, whom they blamed for everything. As soon as they got to London they made straight for the Savoy and systematically destroyed everything there—indeed they punished looters with death, for the aim was to wipe out every trace of Lancaster, to preserve nothing. Crying loudly 'We will have no king called John' (for many of the peasants were barrack-room historians), they tore up his cloth of gold and his tapestries, ground his plate underfoot and his jewels to powder, smashed the furniture, and finally set fire to the ruined palace, inadvertantly burning thirty of their number who lay drunk in the cellars.

Lancaster kept his head: he concealed the news from the Scots until they had signed the truce, knowing that they would take this golden opportunity to invade if they could, then quickly turned south. He was infuriated to find that his former friend the Earl of Northumberland was barring his way, taking advantage of the situation to avenge his jealousy of Gaunt's interferences in border affairs. He was forced to take refuge with the Scots, who treated him nobly and honourably, civilised behaviour which he was to recall and repay at a later stage.

Having got a royal order to open the way south, he went to join the king, and forced Northumberland to make a public apology; but soon his mind was on other things, for the time seemed ripe for the invasion of Castile. Enrique had been succeeded by his son Juan, and Portugal seemed willing to support an invasion. Parliament maddeningly delayed matters, and the Duke was disgusted to see the money and energies of the country diverted into the ridiculous 'crusade' to Flanders organised by the political bishop of Norwich, Henry Despenser. He must have noted with interest, however, the amounts of money that could be raised for making war by selling indulgences to religious ladies.

In 1383 the King of Portugal died, and Juan of Castile claimed the crown; this infuriated the Portuguese, who had no love for the Castilians, and they elected John, half brother of the late king to succeed him. John now appealed for English support.

The Duke was desperate to be off, but there was no sign of a parliamentary grant, and there was much to do. The truce with Scotland had run out and the Scots had promptly invaded; Lancaster was instructed to go and wreak vengeance. Despite his anger at having to make war on the Scots when he wanted above all things to be elsewhere, he still remembered their

kindness, and allowed the citizens of Edinburgh to remove themselves and their possessions before he went in, and also managed to persuade his soldiers to restrain themselves from burning 'the Paris of the North'. He had also to make a further truce with France.

He returned to Parliament with a reputation of a peacemaker, and found the old bitterness against him dying fast. Richard was beginning to show his true nature, and in comparison, old John of Gaunt didn't seem such a villain any more. He successfully foiled two plots of Richard's favourite the Earl of Oxford to have him murdered, and he gained in popularity as the subjects of unsuccessful assassinations always do.

If the court party couldn't kill the Duke, they would have to join with the popular cry and let him go to Spain; he stood a fair chance, for John of Portugal had just soundly defeated the Castilian army. If he failed he would no longer be a power in the land, and if he succeeded, he would be a friendly power in another land.

So at last the dream was to come true, and taking a leaf from Despenser's book, Lancaster turned his invasion into a crusade: the Castilians supported Pope Clement, the English Pope Urban. So in February 1386 the indulgence-seekers began their profitable tour of England once more, proclaiming a holy war against the anti-pope.

The army Gaunt took was large—some 10,000 men, and when he landed at Coruna King Juan promised him 5,000 more, and in a rush of good feeling agreed to marry Gaunt's eldest daughter Philippa. It proved a good match, founding a magnificent dynasty in Portugal; their second son was to find fame as Henry the Navigator.

Galicia was conquered and held at tremendous cost to the Duke's fighting force, and when the invasion of Castile proper began in March 1387, his army was reduced to 1,200 men. Juan nobly swelled the army with double the numbers he had earlier promised and they pushed forward. Yet again, Lancaster was to be faced by the

Fabian tactics he had seen in France: the Castilians wouldn't fight, so the English drank the strong wines of the country and contracted dysentery and then, weakened, fell victims to plague. Soon, out of the 10,000 Englishmen who had set off, only 900 remained, and Lancaster had to withdraw to Portugal. There he treated with Juan, agreeing to his son's marriage to Catherine, Lancaster's daughter by Constance of Castile, and to vest in the issue of this marriage all the rights he and his wife claimed in Spain. He was proving a much better diplomat than a soldier, small consolation to one who saw himself as simply a soldier.

There was trouble in England, once more. His youngest brother, the Duke of Gloucester, had welded together all the elements of opposition to the court party, Warwick and Arundel, and even Lancaster's son Henry of Bolingbroke, Earl of Derby. They removed the king's ministers and forced him to make Gloucester regent, and held the Merciless Parliament to impeach the hated favourites. But by May 1389 Richard had recovered sufficiently to defy the Lords Appellant, and to recall his uncle Lancaster. He had been glad enough to see him go, but he welcomed him back with tremendous joy: he came with the stature of a European politician and peacemaker, the one remaining element of stability to which England could cling. Richard made the palatinate hereditary, and gave him the Duchy of Aquitaine.

In March 1392 Lancaster began four years of difficult negotiations with France to make a lasting peace: an arduous task, but the one remaining aim of his life. In the same period he had to clear the north of England of robber bands of returned soldiers who had taken the moral of the merry tales of Robin Hood with great gusto. He had to meet a serious challenge from Arundel, who probably still smarted from the St. Malo incident, and envied Gaunt's power. Finally he had to settle the confused problems of his new Duchy of Aquitaine, where he demonstrated his superlative skills in diplomacy.

Perhaps the most important event of these years of negotiation and action was the death in March 1394 of Constance of Castile. The marriage had never been anything but political, and for twenty years Lancaster had openly kept a mistress—Katherine Swynford, who had been the governess of his children by Blanche of Lancaster after her untimely death. She had borne him four children, who had taken the surname of Beaufort from one of Lancaster's lost lordships in France; one of them, Henry, was to become a cardinal, and chancellor of England. Katherine lived quietly with her children on her estates in Lincolnshire, and it must have come as a surprise to all when the doyen of the aristocracy married her and had the Pope and the King legitimate their children. He had always looked down on nobodies, and now he had married one, presumably the privilege of his place.

In 1396 came his triumph, when he arranged the meeting between Richard and Charles VI of France, and the former married the latter's daughter, and both agreed to a twenty-eight-year truce.

After such a triumph he deserved a peaceful old age, but he was to have no rest. Richard was now mad for revenge on the Appellants, dreaming of absolute rule, and even of becoming Holy Roman Emperor. He had Gloucester, Arundel and Warwick arrested, and exiled Arundel's brother the Archbishop of Canterbury. Arundel was executed, Warwick sentenced to perpetual imprisonment, and Gloucester died in prison at Calais, plainly murdered on Richard's orders.

Lancaster's supporters now clustered around his son, looking for a lead. Henry of Bolingbroke gave it: he accused the Duke of Norfolk, who had had charge of Gloucester during his imprisonment, of defaming the king, and challenged him to a duel—a trial by battle. All was set for the trial at Coventry on 16th September 1398, and Bolingbroke was beginning his charge, when Richard threw down his warder, and to the astonishment of all, banished both contestants. He fancied that by this act he would rid himself both of the tool he had used to murder his uncle, and the leading contestant against his absolute power in England.

The blow was too great for old Lancaster, and he made his long and complicated will, worrying not only about his earthly succession, but more particularly about his fate in the after-life. He managed one last trip to the border to make a final truce with the Scots, but in December he made his last stop at his castle in Leicester. The king visited him there and tried to cheer him up, but the only news that could do that would be the news of his son's pardon. In February 1399 he died.

He was a tall, spare man, reserved and proud. He was courageous in battle, and easily roused, but he was loyal to a degree and chivalrous in every sense of the word. He loved the tournament, and specialised in absolutely fair play, a quality rare in his day. He was a great patron, of poets, scholars, clergy, monks, and indeed of the poor. Perhaps rather blimpish, he was nevertheless the ideal English gentleman, and like all of his type he did not see where his own virtues lay: a soldier who was far and away at his best at a peace conference, a hot-tempered fighting man who restrained the tempers of others.

See the biography by S. Armitage-Smith: *John of Gaunt* (Constable, London, 1964; Baines and Noble, New York, 1964).

Genghiz Khan

In 1238 herrings from Yarmouth were sold dirt-cheap, for the Dutchmen and Scandinavians did not come over to fetch their usual large quota of imports. They stayed home to protect their families from the terrible menace of the Mongols—a menace from the other side of the world, and barely a generation old in its gestation. Some rumoured that these were the envoys of a strange Christian king of the far East,

Prester John, but those who had felt their unparalleled savagery can hardly have agreed with this view.

A century before this date the Mongols had been under the dominion of the Chinese, and even after their revolt in 1138 they had been disunited into factions fighting an internecine war. But about the year 1154, one Temujin was born, grandson of the Mongol Khan; he was to be known to the world as Genghiz Khan.

His father died when he was thirteen, and he immediately began to fight for his inheritance, supported by a small band of followers. Faction after faction fell under his rule—though it was no easy battle, he was once caught and tortured, but escaped to fight again. By the year 1206 he was supreme among the Mongols, with the treasured title of Khan.

These years of petty warfare made the man, as much as his natural background. He relied on the swiftness of the Mongol pony, and on horror: for his techniques were an elementary blitzkrieg—and not so elementary as all that, in his wars in China he killed eighteen million people. He was treacherous, merciless, but above all fast: an enemy already demoralised by his reputation was overwhelmed by his speed.

In the years between 1208 and 1214 he subdued northern China, and then turned to the mighty Empire of Qwarism, which stretched from Persia to China, from the Caspian to India. Though the Emperor was in a position to field an army of half a million, he had not the speed and tactical skill of the Mongols, and he was soon overwhelmed.

Terrible destruction followed the wake of the Mongol armies, and indeed this was a part of their warfare; but reconstruction was attempted, and Genghiz was as interested in the building of his own empire as he was in the plundering of others'. He organised good road and post systems, and encouraged good learning; he gave his blessing to the codification of laws, and saw that they were kept. Like his successor, Kublai Khan, whom Marco Polo was to admire and love, Genghiz was interested in religion, in an eclectic sort of way, unwilling himself to come down in favour of any particular one. In his realm, be it noted, clergy and scholars of all sorts were free from tax.

His interest in religion should not delude one, however: he was responsible for mass-destruction and murder on a scale unknown until our own century; he was licentious enough to require 500 wives and concubines; he was a drunkard—possibly the cause of his death in 1227, when he was about to conquer south China.

His sons and grandsons carried on the war against the world, and soon Europe felt their lash. Though attempts were made to ally the Mongols with the West against the Muslims, little came of the experiment, though Franciscan missionaries brought back thrilling accounts of their dangerous journeys east and north. Russia, Poland, Hungary and Silesia were engulfed, but in 1241 the death of Genghiz's successor called a halt to the advance in the West, whilst the heirs bickered over the inheritance. When the advance was renewed, it was against the Assassins and Muslims, only to be halted in 1260, by the Mamluks under Baybars.

There is a biography by René Grousset: *Conqueror of the World* (Oliver and Boyd, Edinburgh, 1967; Grossman, New York, 1966).

Gerard Groote

There was a long tradition of spirituality in the Netherlands and north Germany, in which the most retired mysticism managed to combine successfully with both a concern for the world of daily life and the speculations of university clerks. Its culmination in the *Devotio Moderna* of the late fourteenth and fifteenth centuries was the last great outburst of popular religion within the Church of the Middle Ages, and compares favourably with the movement that had produced the friars in the thirteenth century. Indeed, its most popular

product, Thomas à Kempis' *The Imitation of Christ* had a Franciscan title, and a Franciscan intensity about it. The conviction is so deep and burning that within a short while the book which begins as a manual of the Christian life becomes a direct dialogue with Christ himself. The keynotes of the writing are Light and Love, but the message is one of effort: 'If you look for rest in this life, how can you attain eternal rest? . . . For love of God cheerfully endure everything—labour, sorrow, temptation, provocation, anxiety, necessity, weakness, injury and insult; censure, humiliation, disgrace, contradiction and contempt . . . Do you imagine that you can always have spiritual joys at will? My Saints did not, but had many troubles, countless trials, and great desolation of soul . . . Wait for the Lord; fight manfully and with high courage. Do not despair, do not desert your post . . .' (Penguin Translation by Leo Sherley-Price, 3.35.)

This message owed much to the founder of the movement Thomas served—Gerard Groote. He was born in 1340, into a rich burghal family of Deventer, and was educated at Prague, Cologne and Paris, where he achieved the heights of knowledge. He was fascinated by science, particularly astronomy and magic (at that time very much within the purview of science), and was a noted bibliophile, spending on one occasion alone in the Paris bookshops a tankard full of gold. He borrowed countless books to read and copy, and supported copyists to work for him in his own house; he would have crowed with delight (for his speech was naturally extravagant) at the modern invention of speedy photocopying. So fond was he of his library, that he never went anywhere without it, carefully crated for protection and speedy access.

He could afford all this because he was rich, with his townhouse and country farm, and his two prebendal stalls in rich cathedrals. He dressed finely, and entertained extravagantly, enjoying good company. But all this had to go suddenly, when in a moment of personal crisis he was converted by a Carthusian to the belief that his hedonistic life was worthless, that only close attention to the things of the spirit can reap the final reward. Life was too short to pay attention to petty things, and soon the *bon viveur* was living on a diet of peas boiled up with a herring, for this was the least trouble in cooking.

He spent three years in the Charterhouse, thinking things out with that intensity and urgency that was to characterise his life and message. For not only had his life in the Church been 'useless', but the Church itself seemed 'senile' and rotten. Everyone was concerned with his own personal profit and promotion, and nothing could be had without a payment, little or great. So he went back into the world to preach a return to values, a one man crusade against the immorality and corruption of the clergy, against the frauds of bogus money-spinners, and the heresies of those who were their own Gods. Thousands came to him, people who had given up hope, but now saw the chance for a new way, but there were many, and they were influential, who hated him, for where he could not convert he started prosecutions in Church courts against immoral clergy, and he had studied both law and theology, and knew the ropes. The campaign grew in force, and finally the Bishop decided to muzzle him. He accepted the authority (for he believed throughout in the virtue of obedience to authority), but he was bitterly upset.

He had already given over his own house to a group of pious women who wished to live together in religion, but who, for various reasons, could not or did not wish to enter religion. There were no vows, and anyone could leave whenever they wished. Men wanted similar places, and Gerard set them up, aiming to give them the reformed Augustinian rule, influenced in this by the great thinker John Ruysbroeck. In fact Windesheim became an Augustinian house, but after his death of plague in Deventer (aged only 44) his followers established communities more in keeping with his individualistic pattern. They became the Brethren of the Common Life, devoted to the copying of texts, and the education of children: to them came Thomas à Kempis, Nicholas of Cusa, and Erasmus. Their fame spread wide, and houses opened all over the Netherlands and north Germany, devoted to a spirituality that gave a living daily example to the world, and was not susceptible of formal rules drawn from the distant past. Gerard would have been a little shocked, but Francis, the more daring, would have approved, as did Martin Luther, and other reformers, Catholic and Protestant, who drew upon their tradition.

There are two articles on Gerard and his movement in E. F. Jacob's *Essays in the Conciliar Epoch* (Manchester Univ. Press, 1943.)

Gerald the Welshman

Giraldus Cambrensis, Gerald the Welshman, was born *c.* 1146 in the castle of Manorbier, near Pembroke. He was the youngest of four sons born to William de Barri, one of the great Norman lords of South Wales, and Angharad, daughter of Nest. Nest the beautiful, daughter of Rhys ap Tewdwr, Prince of South Wales, had been the mistress of Henry I King of England before marrying Gerald of Windsor. From their union sprang the great family of Fitzgerald, the Geraldines, powerful in Wales, and to be even more powerful in Ireland in and after its conquest.

He could not have had a better family background, and yet it was to be his downfall in an altogether unexpected way. Whilst his elder brothers, especially Philip, whom he loved above all men, trained for war, the young Gerald was destined for the church, and his Fitzgerald uncle David, Bishop of St. David's, gave him his elementary education, and his passionate devotion to this the premier bishopric of Wales.

He studied at St. Peter's Abbey, Gloucester, and then at Paris, before returning to Wales to begin his career. He immediately showed himself a mighty worker for the rights of the Church, and struggled against corruption and malpractice wherever he found it. He showed no fear of the unruly people, the wicked barons or the corrupt clergy. Tall and strong, filled with the self-confidence of the nobly born, he turned his face, with its long shaggy eye-brows that made him immediately recognisable, against all forms of disorder. When the Bishop of St. Asaph came to claim a church that rightly belonged to the See of St. David's, Gerald stood out against him, and when the Bishop began to excommunicate him, he had the bells rung wildly, and calmly began to excommunicate the Bishop. Gerald won, and the King laughed when he heard the story, and soon Gerald was Archdeacon of Brecon, and ripe for promotion.

He longed openly for promotion—to the bishopric of St. David's—but two insuperable barriers stood in his way. The King would have no relative of a Welsh prince in this position (and Gerald was so openly Welsh he referred to English kings as tyrants), and on no account would he have any strong bishop there. The See of St. David's had a good claim to metropolitan status in Wales, and if this claim were made good, four dioceses would be withdrawn from the control of the Archbishop of Canterbury. Plainly Gerald was such a man as would push this claim to its limits.

So an English Benedictine was elected on the King's orders, and Gerald returned to Paris to study and teach canon and civil law. No doubt his grievance fermented in his mind, but when he returned he had dinner with the monks at Canterbury, and was shocked to find them ploughing through course after course of rich food and wine, and 'gesticulating with fingers, hands and arms, and whistling to one another in lieu of speaking, all extravagating in a manner more free and frivolous than was seemly.' So much for the monks of St. Benedict—but worse was to come. The Bishop of St. David's was an absentee,

tyrannically milking the diocese while he ran about England picking up benefices.

In a mood of fury he crossed the Midlands towards Wales, and fed his grudge well whilst staying the night with the Bishop of Worcester. There he met a Cistercian abbot called Serlo, who quite moved Gerald by commenting to the Bishop 'Think you that such youthful beauty could ever die?' Later on, he cemented the friendship by commenting in Gerald's hearing that he 'would await the stroke of death with greater confidence if he were a black mastiff than if he were a Black monk!' He had himself once been a Benedictine, fat and sleek, but a serious accident had occurred—his horse had run away with him through a narrow gateway, and he had been badly injured. The thoughts of death that this accident had brought on had turned him from a fat Benedictine to an austere and very thin Cistercian.

Gerald harboured his ill-feeling towards the Black monks till the end of his days, but for the moment he comforted his despair by taking service with the King. He proved a faithful and efficient royal clerk, and Henry II much appreciated his work, but the bar on his elevation still prevented all hopes of the one reward he desired. There was talk of a crusade, but Henry turned on his clerics angrily 'The clergy may well call us to arms and peril, since they themselves will receive no blows in the fray, nor shoulder any burdens that they can avoid.' So instead Gerald was sent with Prince John to the conquest of Ireland in 1184.

John much appreciated Gerald's service, as his father did, and offered him several Irish sees, but he refused them, wanting only one bishopric in the world. Instead he set to work composing his *Topography* and *History of the Conquest of Ireland*. These were to be the first volumes of a whole series describing the Celtic fringe according to a similar basic plan. The volumes on Scotland were never written, though he completed his works on Wales. As with Ireland, so in his *Description of Wales*, he ended with chapters on how the land may be conquered and governed; but for Wales he appended a special chapter 'In what manner this nation may resist and revolt'!

As he says 'Not wishing to hide the candle he had lit under a bushel', he held a three day reading of his *Topography of Ireland* in the university of Oxford, giving a notable feast each day, complimenting himself that thereby 'the ancient and authentic times of the poets were in some manner revived.' This must rank as one of the earliest of publishers' parties.

In 1188 the crusade that had been brewing so long seemed at last a possibility, and Gerald toured Wales with the Archbishop of Canterbury, preaching and appealing for adherents. He did not lose the opportunity of getting another book out of the experience, and wrote his *Itinerary through Wales* from the 'great notebooks' he wrote up on this journey, and very nearly lost on another.

He was so successful in his preaching of the crusade that when he next met Prince John, who was Earl of Pembroke, he was accused of deliberately denuding the province of fighting men so that his Welsh relatives could take it over without any defence being offered!

After the death of Henry II and the departure of Richard on Crusade, John, who seems to have favoured Gerald most of all, despite his occasional outbursts of bad temper, offered him the sees of Bangor and Llandaff, but he turned down both, for the usual reason, and turned his mind to study once more. Paris was now cut off by war, and so he went to Lincoln, where a Paris theologian, William de Monte, was running the finest school in England. This pattern of a return to university study whenever an interval offered the chance, regardless of age or academic excellence, is a pleasing aspect of medieval life from which we might learn.

His time in Lincoln gave him great pleasure, though he recalls how famine struck the area whilst he was there, and his study was besieged by beggars; he took down from their hanging-poles all his many gowns and hoods with their rich furs and sold them to feed the hungry. His writings abound with little reminiscences such as this one which gave them a homely touch of reality.

So relaxed had he become as a scholar, that it was almost with despair that he heard that the see of St. David's was vacant again, and plans were afoot to appoint a useless English monk. He wrote off to the worldly Archbishop of Canterbury, Hubert Walter, declaring that 'The Chapter . . . will never consent to the election of a monk . . . wholly ignorant of their native tongue and unable either to preach or hear confession save through an interpreter. For we seek a physician of our souls, not a conductor of funerals, nor do we wish to have a dumb dog or a tongueless shepherd set over us. Enough long since and more have we endured from the follies of pastors fresh from the cloister's shade . . .'

The Chapter was overtaken by an access of courage, and defying the Archbishop, they elected Gerald, and he set off at once for Rome to get his election confirmed, and to establish the metropolitan status of his see. He arrived late in 1199, and all seemed to go well, for he obtained the Pope's commission to investigate the matters.

He hurried back to England, but found that the Archbishop had been busy: by alternate threats and promises he had set the Chapter of St. David's by its ears, and it no longer stood four-square behind Gerald. However, he collected the necessary documentary evidences, and sped off back to Rome. There too the Archbishop had been at work, and his proctors, well supplied with money for bribes, were ready to denounce him, and promote Canterbury's candidate to the see.

Gerald spoke out vigorously against the English intriguers at the papal court, indeed against the English in general: '. . . for the English are the most worthless of people under heaven; for they have been subdued by the Normans and reduced by the law of war to perpetual slavery; and our own Merlin testifies thereto . . . The English in their own land are the slaves of the Normans . . . while in our land we have no cowherds, shepherds, cobblers, skinners, mechanics, cleansers of our sewers, save English only . . .' And he goes on in the same vein for some time!

He received yet another commission from the Pope, and returned once more to Wales, where, despite continual harrying from the Archbishop and his servants, he struggled to further his cause. He had even to sell his precious library, feeling 'as though his very bowels were being drawn out of him', to provide finance to keep on with the fight. He had some support: the Prince of Gwynedd said 'For as long as Wales shall stand, this man's noble deeds shall for all times be noised abroad . . .'; but even he realised the hopelessness of Gerald's fight, noting that 'neither a skilful dicer nor yet a valiant knight may always win what his heart desires.' But the support he had was minimal, and the Chapter of St. David's, terrorised out of their wits by the Archbishop, now turned against their elect, whom they saw as a bringer of trouble rather than a defender.

Once more Gerald appealed to Rome, and had to lurk about in many hiding places before he could get a ship to the Continent, for the Archbishop had ordered the ports closed against him. He amused the Pope with his tales of the bad grammar and worse theology of Hubert Walter, whose background before becoming Archbishop of Canterbury had been wholly financial and administrative. But though the Pope was amused by Gerald's wit and invective, and recognised the justice of his case, he was in no position to decide in his favour against the mighty Archbishop, representative of a church in which he took the deepest interest. So in his final judgement he allowed that neither Gerald nor the Archbishop's candidate had been duly elected, and ordered another election. Unabashed, Gerald pressed for a decision on his other suit—the metropolitan status of

his diocese, but all he got was another commission to investigate the claim, and he turned miserably for home.

The journey was a tiresome struggle, bedevilled by creditors, and at one point he was captured by a Burgundian knight. Archbishop Walter's proctor had been captured a short while before, and had described Gerald to his captor, warning him to lay hold of the first tall man with shaggy eyebrows to come from the south. However, Gerald managed to turn the tables on the proctor, pointing out to his captor that he was the most valued clerk of the Archbishop of Canterbury, and would fetch a much higher ransom than a poor archdeacon. So he was released, and, only pausing to laugh immoderately at his enemy's unlooked for plight, sped off to Rouen to gain the help of his friend King John.

The wrangles continued, and at last Gerald realised he would be defeated yet again, so he sprang his last trick. Suddenly, without warning, he agreed to the election of the least harmful candidate who had the backing of the Archbishop. His former enemies were amazed, and hurried to cement the peace, by giving Gerald the expenses he had incurred on his suits to Rome, and allowing him to resign his archdeaconry in favour of his nephew, son of his beloved elder brother.

We know little of his later years when, having given up the struggle of his life, he turned to writing full-time. In 1207 he went to Rome again, this time purely for the pleasure of a pilgrimage. When the Bishop of St. David's died, a Welshman (albeit insignificant) was at last elected, and in Canterbury the great Stephen Langton ruled—at last an archbishop Gerald could respect. He dedicated to him his books on *The Welsh Church* and the *Description of Wales*. He died in 1223.

Gerald was a prolific writer, often disorganised, more often partisan, sometimes over vain. At times he could command the highest eloquence and style, but he is at his best in transmitting stories with a racy charm that commands attention. He was the

Herodotus of medieval England, but he had that extra dose of wit and humour that make him an original. Above all he was Welsh, passionately so. He ends his *Description* with a piece of eloquent story-telling that has its power today. He tells how Henry II asked an old Welshman whether he thought the army he had brought into Wales would prove sufficient to conquer the land. The old man said that the army was strong enough *almost* to succeed:

'Nor do I think, that any other nation than this of Wales, or any other language, whatever may hereafter come to pass, shall, in the day of severe examination before the Supreme Judge, answer for this corner of the earth.'

The Autobiography of Giraldus Cambrensis has been pieced together from a number of his works by H. E. Butler (Fowler, London, 1937).

Gerbert of Aurillac

Dull times occasionally produce exceptional men, and in this category Gerbert (later Pope Sylvester II) is outstanding. He was born about 940, to poor parents, and entered the local monastery of Aurillac early in life. He must have chafed somewhat at the bonds of a provincial community where there was no room for his spirit of enquiry and restless energy to flower. When, in 967, the Count of Barcelona visited the monastery and noticed this young man, he must have realised his chance, for the Count arranged with the Abbot for Gerbert to go to study in Spain.

The Moors were to be, from Gerbert's time onwards, the subject of a strange love-hate fascination for the Latin West. As infidels, they were to be expelled—that was the Christian's plain duty; but before they were expelled or annihilated, the scholars of the West had to learn from them, for they were both the real and the intellectual heirs of ancient Greece. Many of the great scientific, mathematical and philosophical treatises of the Greeks only existed in

Arabic versions, and the great scholars of the Arab world had been studying and commenting upon them for many years. The Moors held the key to a treasure chest of knowledge.

Gerbert studied hard in Catalonia, most particularly the mathematics in which the Arabs excelled. The knowledge that he gained in those years, and his skill in mediating it (which was to grow in later years) made him the much desired companion of Popes and kings. In the year 970 he went to Rome on a mission for the Count of Barcelona, and so impressed all he met that he was sent off by the Pope (almost as a present) to the Emperor Otto I.

The Otto's were a highly sensitive and intelligent breed, who had a dream of the restoration of the Roman Empire in all its glory under their rule. They recognised and used intelligence wherever they found it, and plainly Gerbert was a great 'find'. He taught the sixteen-year old future Otto II, communicating to him the excitements of the frontiers of knowledge, and sharing his passionate dreams of Empire. Gerbert was to work hard and long for the Otto's at the dull and tiresome tasks of politics, with comparatively little reward except towards the end of his life, but he was never to lose their friendship, or weary in his devotion to them.

In 972 he went to Rheims, which was to remain his base for many years. The Archbishop, Adalbaro, had need of good teachers, and Gerbert spent the next few years perfecting his new course of study and the various new techniques he invented for it. He concentrated on secular knowledge, which up till his time had been taught in a dry-as-dust and highly theoretical manner. Gerbert gave everything a practical twist, and was as interested in the problems of communication of knowledge as he was in the material itself—though he was to contribute much that was new here too.

He made great use of Boethius' logical works, preparing the ground for the twelfth century Aristotelian revival. In mathematics he introduced the Arabic numerals, and the abacus. For students of rhetoric he made a huge chart explaining the subject, using a double column of 26 sheets of parchment; he also insisted that students of public speaking should have practical experience in the courts. In astronomy he made the students take actual observations, and invented a precursor of the telescope. Similarly in musical education, he demanded that students should use actual instruments, and himself invented a new technique for playing the organ. Students flocked to him, recognising his versatile genius and his passion for education, and even after they had left he would continue to teach them by correspondence course, as it were, explaining abstruse points in Boethius, and how to make mathematical, musical and astronomical instruments.

In 980 Otto II made him Abbot of Bobbio, but he proved too strict for the monks and local barons, and when his protector died three years later he had to flee their wrath. The heir to the Empire, Otto III, was only three years old, and a terrible power struggle followed. Gerbert rushed round Germany, working immensely hard to shore up support for his new young master. It was a hard task, but he won by sheer endurance. Even then there was to be no rest, for his next task was to aid the Empire by supporting Hugh Capet in his struggle against the decaying remnants of Charlemagne's heirs.

It was a hard time: Gerbert had to sit by and see the archbishopric of Rheims (in which he would have dearly loved to have succeeded his friend Adalbaro) given to the Carolingians by Capet in a gesture of reconciliation, and to watch the chaos that followed. When finally the archbishopric was given to him, and the Carolingian deposed, he had to suffer excommunication by the Pope, who favoured the enemy. By 997, when he could at last return to the side of Otto III he surely must have wondered whether his support for this family was well placed.

But Otto was a charming boy and an ideal pupil, who learned fast, and repayed his tuition with close affection. He would write to Gerbert when he was away 'Otto, most faithful of his pupils in steadfast perseverance, to Gerbert, master beloved above all others . . .' In 999 Otto arranged to have his tutor elected Pope Sylvester II: together they would create a Christian Empire in which splendour and justice would triumph in unity.

They had (if they had known it) but little time, and the facts of life, which they constantly ignored, stood against them. Sylvester immediately set to work, using all the diplomatic skill he had gained in the sad years in Germany and France to resolve squabbles and disputes and promote a genuine unity in Christendom. He concerned himself with the remotest parts—with the war in Spain against the Moors, with Russia and Hungary, and with Norway, where, at his insistence, the runic alphabet was dropped, and Roman practices introduced.

What this learned, versatile, energetic, and absolutely loyal man might have done for Christendom is a subject of wonder, but the facts remain tragic, that he died in 1003, one year after Otto.

See H. P. Lattin: *The Letters of Gerbert* (Columbia Univ. Press, New York, 1961).

Giotto

Giotto was born in 1266, some 14 miles from Florence to a family of moderate standing. His father was rich enough to own properties in town and country, and sent the boy to school. Later Giotto was to write a little undistinguished poetry. On the other hand a man thought to be his brother became a blacksmith, so his family cannot be called anything but ordinary.

Sometime after the year 1272 he entered the workshop of the great Florentine painter Cimabue. He probably also studied in Rome, spending some time examining antique sculpture. Sculpture and architecture were at that time well in advance of painting, which was still in the grip of the Byzantine tradition of flatness. The sculptor's aim was realism, roundness, and Giotto gained his notions of design from study and practice in this field. The new architects also showed him how to provide a stage for the action of his pictures, and he learned from them the importance of perspective. The results for painting were to be profound—Boccaccio tells us that Giotto's audience were so unused to his kind of painting that they took for real what he had painted, and his *trompe-l'œils* at Assisi and Padua still deceive the viewer.

His first major commission came when he was about 25, when he was asked to paint a crucifix for the Santa Novella Church in Florence. He was certainly earning enough by this time to get married and start a family, and he had attracted the notice of the papal court. Vasari tells the pleasant story of him drawing a perfect circle freehand as his masterpiece for the papal envoys. True or not, it was his uncanny skill and perfection of execution that so impressed people.

In 1296 he received the important commission to fresco the walls of the upper church at Assisi with scenes from the life of St. Francis. He worked with a large team of skilled assistants who came to him to learn their craft; amongst them were some of the most famous names in early fourteenth-century Italian painting, who were to build the Renaissance. Giotto himself probably did the designs, painted the important heads, and corrected the final work, but the rest was left to his team.

In 1298 he was called to Rome to work directly for the Pope. His most important work was a massive mosaic, dramatic and colourful, for the atrium of old St. Peter's. Since early times pilgrims had had a very upsetting tradition of kneeling to the East on entering the basilica to adore the sun. Now Giotto's mosaic of the storm-tossed boat on the Sea of Galilee would meet their eyes, and give the message of the Church in danger. St. Catherine was to kneel before this work towards the end of her life,

and inspired by its message, give herself in penance for the Church's sins.

Giotto executed a number of other commissions in Rome, including a fresco commemorating the proclamation of Jubilee by Boniface VIII in 1300. Later he returned to Florence, but was soon on his travels again, executing commissions in Rimini and Padua.

During the years 1304-5 he was engaged on the massive frescoes for the arena chapel at Padua. Enrico Scrovegni gave this chapel in payment for his father's usury to the strange order of the 'Joyful Knights', who were a kind of medieval rotary club, where rich men earned merit in good works, having previously made their fortunes by fair means or foul. The paintings show an incredible range of emotion, portrayed with loving attention to detail; highly dramatic events of tremendous import are held still for us to examine at our leisure. Painting is no longer simply a celebration by beautification—now a new, literary quality has entered, and a depth of meaning.

By 1311 Giotto was back in Florence, a rich man, owning land, and putting his money to work by hiring out looms. In 1317 he began his work on the Bardi chapel of Santa Croce, returning to his Franciscan subjects. Ten years later he had gained respectability for his craft, and he was able to enrol himself and his pupils into the guild of physicians and apothecaries.

During the years 1329 to 1333 he was employed by Robert of Anjou to paint his chapels and castles in Naples. The two seem to have got on very well together, and a number of examples of Giotto's wry humour come from this period. One day the king came to him and said, 'Giotto, if I were you I would rest a while, now it is so hot.' The painter grimly replied, 'And so I would, if I were you.'

In 1334 he was back in Florence once more, where he was made master of the works at the cathedral. 'The Florentine republic desires that an edifice shall be constructed so magnificent in its height and quality that it shall surpass anything of the kind produced in the time of their greatest power by the Greeks and Romans.' He designed and began to build the Campanile.

In 1335 he went off to Milan to work for the Visconti but, old and tired, he just managed to get home to die in 1337. People who came afterwards revered him as the restorer of the whole art of painting, and few reached the heights of beauty achieved by this squat and ugly little man who loved what he saw, but was too good humoured and realistic in his outlook to overestimate its importance.

There is a biographical and critical study by E. Battisti: *Giotto* (Skira, New York, 1960).

Owen Glyn Dŵr

Owen Glyn Dŵr, Owen of the Glen of Dee Water, was born about the year 1354, a moderate mountain squire heir to £200 p.a., rich enough to deserve a London education, and to take service in the king's armies, but never important enough to merit even knighthood. Yet, in the century when the great Welsh dynasties were gently dying out, their lands and powers transferred to English barons, he was the heir also to two of the four great princely families of Wales. History may not always be written in terms of individuals, but had Owen gone the way of acceptance that his relatives and forbears took, Welsh history would have been very different, and immeasurably less.

Owen's father died in 1370, and, probably under the protection of their neighbour the Earl of Arundel, he was sent to London for the fashionable finishing school-type education of the inns of court. He was to prove a great patron of Welsh bards in later life, so Shakespeare may have been right when he said that the young Glyn Dŵr took a great interest in poetry and music.

He went on to serve the crown as a soldier in Scotland, and possibly in Ireland.

Bravely wearing a scarlet flamingo feather as his crest, he showed his prowess by driving Scotsmen before him when he had only the butt of a broken lance left for a weapon.

Back home he married well, the daughter of a flourishing Anglo-Welsh judge, and prepared to settle down to rule his pleasant estates in peace, and enjoy bardic entertainments. He fathered six sons with surprising speed, and made many friends who would serve him well at a later stage.

Why, at the age of 50, he should suddenly organise a rebellion and claim the title Prince of Wales, is a baffling problem; but this is what he did in September 1400. He appears to have had no grounds for opposition to the new régime of Henry IV (though if you are going to organise a rebellion, the best time is at the start of a new dynasty with a shaky title), indeed most of his annoyance seems to have been directed against his neighbour, Reginald Grey of Ruthin. Grey was certainly promoting his own interests at court with his friend, the new King Henry IV, and promoting them to the exclusion of Owen's.

The English levies rushed to the spot, and within days the rebellion was crushed, presumably another 'spot of bother' in Wales, effectively dealt with. In fact the whole thing had only just begun, though it is quite possibly true that the Welsh saw as little of the future as the English at this stage. The one thing they did see was Owen, the leader at last, who by that subtle combination of separately unimportant qualities was raised above the level of the ordinary mortal. Welsh scholars left the universities to go and join him, Welsh labourers threw down their hoes and went as well. Their loyalty was absolute—an English chronicler notes with amazement that the Welsh prisoners would suffer death rather than give information.

Despite English expeditions to wreak vengeance in North and South Wales in 1401, Owen's cause grew fast; always avoiding an open fight with the enemy (and, knowing the climate and the countryside, this was easy to do), Owen steadily increased in stature as a nationalistic hero. He sent missions to Ireland and Scotland to raise support for the Celtic cause. Iolo Goch records the dangers of these missions, wishing, when in 1405 John Trevor set out on another journey to Scotland, that he could hide the good bishop in a nutshell, or cover him with the mantle of invisibility.

In 1402 a great comet shot through the skies, and the Welsh took this to be a sign of victory from above. They ambushed and captured Owen's enemy, the king's great friend, Reginald Grey of Ruthin, and only gave him up for the fantastic ransom of £6,666. They captured also Edmund Mortimer, but the king was not so anxious to ransom him, for his nephew, the great-grandson of Lionel Duke of Clarence, had a better claim to the throne than did Henry IV himself.

Owen may have had his moments of mysticism, but his basic quality was a sound common sense: he might have taken the capture of Grey as a chance to get his own back on his worst enemy—instead he made money out of it; now, with a seemingly unransomable prisoner (a great problem for a highly mobile guerilla force) he made political capital instead. He won Edmund over to his cause, and married him to his daughter Catherine. Now the rebellion was not just to win the throne of Wales, but that of England too.

An English attack on three fronts, and a sortie against Owen's home led by the young prince—the future Henry V—did little to dent Welsh morale, but in July 1403 a big chance was lost—the embittered former ally of the king, Hotspur, broke out in rebellion before his father Northumberland and Glyn Dŵr could reach him to give help, and was decisively beaten at Shrewsbury. Within Wales Owen went on capturing castles and consolidating his position, and he made a treaty with the French in mid-1404, on which he put many hopes. Unfortunately the first result was useless, a French fleet made an aimless

show of force, but exerted none before going home again.

However, Owen continued in his vein of success, though by now there was more show than reality. In February 1405 he made the Tripartite Indenture, which gave the south of England to Mortimer, the north to Northumberland, and Wales, with English land to the Severn and the borders of Staffordshire, to himself. This boastful treaty was followed by three crushing blows from the English, and the Welsh position was only saved in the August by the landing of 3,000 seasoned French troops.

They moved slowly into England and took up position in the ancient defence works on Woodbury Hill, near Worcester. Henry IV came with a large force, and the two armies faced each other filled with irresolution, until French morale cracked, and the whole force retreated into Wales.

The failure of the French, the gradual wiping out of the last few rebels who opposed the house of Lancaster in England, and the capture of James, heir to the Scots throne (q.v.), these were the terrible set-backs the Welsh rebellion had to face. From 1408 Owen was alone, and Henry could face him untrammelled by other worries.

Owen still showed the great confidence in his country that inspired the great rebellion, and in March 1406 he issued the Pennal manifesto on the future organisation of the Welsh Church. He had had strong support from churchmen, some great, some not. An amusing story about the battle of Pwll Melyn shows the less attractive side of the religious camp followers who surrounded him. Before the battle a friar had preached with great spirit, saying that all who fell would sup that night in heaven; when he saw that defeat was in the wind, he began to slip away, but was held up by some soldiers who pointed out to him that he was missing the chance of a heavenly banquet; he smartly informed them that this was one of his fast days, and was away like the wind.

Such ungrateful followers (and there were a few) did not deserve what Owen planned for them in his Pennal letter: St David's was to be a metropolitan see, holding primacy over the three Welsh bishoprics, and those of Exeter, Bath, Hereford, Worcester and Lichfield. Welsh speaking clergy alone were to serve in Welsh churches, and no ecclesiastical revenues should go to England. Two universities were to be set up in Wales, so that scholars need not travel abroad to gain an education.

It was a dream of greatness that was soon overshadowed by reality. Prince Henry was showing the first signs of his military genius, and was taking one by one Owen's remaining castles. His wife and children were captured, Mortimer and his greatest captains died in sieges or in battle; by 1410 he was a hunted mountaineer, a bandit with only his charisma left.

Yet he lived on, and was never caught. In 1412 he held to ransom Davy Gam Esq., whose death at Agincourt Shakespeare records with such fine pathos. Fragments of information kept coming in until 1416, when he was believed to have died, somewhere in Herefordshire. But the Welsh chroniclers do not record his death, but speak of him as 'vanishing'.

There is a biography by J. E. Lloyd (Oxford Univ. Press, London and New York, 1931).

Pope Gregory the Great

Pope Gregory the Great was one of the most notable products of the city of Rome in the middle ages. Born there about the year 540, he was heir to the two great traditions: his grandfather had been Pope, and his whole family was very closely attached to the Church; his ancestry was of the noblest, carrying with it the duty of serving the city.

He was well educated, although he was not taught Greek, and throughout his life despised the adoration of the literati for the pagan classics, and their addiction to rules

for fine writing: to him clarity was the sole aim. He was taught the law, for he seemed destined for the city government, and perhaps in these years of study he developed that tremendous passion for justice that was to be at the heart of his papal policy. He also developed his love of pictures and music, for he was no puritan; once again, he was to draw on these resources as Pope when he was establishing the beautiful ritual and music for the Church services. This was to play a large part in attracting the pagans to the Catholic faith, and it is probably Gregorian chant that symbolises the Middle Ages for many people today.

In 573 he was Prefect of the city of Rome, inheriting a substantial fortune from his parents, and owning the family palace on the Caelian Hill. But the very presence of riches and power seemed to crystalise for him and in him his family's traditional devotion to the Church, and in one of those sudden and exciting *bouleversements* of the mind devoted to art or religion, he gave up his high office and sold all he possessed. The substantial fortune was devoted to setting up monasteries in Sicily, and to feeding the poor; his own palace was converted into the monastery of St. Andrew, and within it he became a humble monk.

Legend has it that at some time in the next year or so he observed the English boys on sale in the market place, and made his pun about converting Angli into Angeli. This is unlikely for one who despised literary tricks, but he certainly developed a deep desire for the conversion of these people, and indeed seems to have set off himself on this mission. But the people of Rome would not lose so good a man, and he was recalled, to continue his meditation and Bible study in his monastic cell.

In 579 the Pope sent him to Constantinople to represent him there. His ignorance of the language must have hampered his mission somewhat, but he gained much wisdom from his observation of the workings of the Byzantine state, and from his conversations with heretics of every kind, whom he made it his especial duty to try to convert. He also found time to write his great commentary on the book of Job— the *Moralia*—one of the favourite books of the middle ages.

In 585 he returned once more to Rome, and continued there lecturing and writing on biblical subjects, and helping the citizens deal with the recurrent problem of plague. In 590 he was (much against his will) elected Pope, and few in the history of that office have been more suited to the task. His book on the duties of a bishop— the *Pastoral Care*—shows a deep insight into human nature and the problems of exercising authority, and was to remain a text-book for the medieval Church (being translated into Anglo-Saxon by Alfred the Great for the use of his own clergy). His fourteen books of letters directed to all parts of the known world, and covering myriad subjects, show his energy and devotion to duty. He who had thought to devote his life to quiet meditation had now to drag his mind down to the depths of estate management, and even lower, to diplomacy.

Rome, Ravenna, Genoa and Naples alone remained within the Empire, the 'unspeakable Lombards', as Gregory calls them, and the Franks having swept over the rest of Italy. Constantinople would send no aid to retake the lost territories, and yet continued to provoke the barbarians who surrounded them into a war that was slowly grinding the life out of the province. Gregory wrote from 'amongst the swords of the Lombards' to the Emperor pleading for peace, only to receive replies accusing him of little short of treachery.

Relations with the empire were in a sad state, though the Pope laboured to improve them. The Patriarch of Constantinople (on the principle that this was 'New Rome') claimed not only to share the see of Peter, but also to hold the title of *Universal Bishop*— a right Gregory could never allow him.

By gentle persistence (and with the aid of deaths—natural and unnatural—of his enemies in Constantinople) Gregory won his way to a general peace in Italy, and a wider recognition of his rights as Pope. In 603 he had the great joy of seeing the heir to the Iron Crown of Lombardy baptised a Catholic—the Catholic Queen having won over the Arian King.

Gregory's diplomacy was exercised in the name of peace, justice and orthodoxy. In the troubled world in which he lived the civil powers warred constantly for predominance, and the church was broken by numberless schisms: in this atmosphere no justice could be had, and the one true faith was merely a meaningless ideal. To Gregory the answer was clear—the much desired unification could only be achieved under the aegis of a central authority. Just as he recognised the civil authority of the Emperor, so he worked steadily towards a position where the primal see of Peter should be the central authority in spiritual matters.

Gradually he extended his claims, and, by demonstrating his concern, and showing impeccable standards of justice in confused issues, he won a large measure of respect for Rome in Istria, Dalmatia, Illyria, Gaul, Spain and Africa. But the chief area of his concern in many ways was England. This was the lost province, indeed almost nothing was known of it in Rome when the mission set off from the monastery of St. Andrews, under the leadership of Augustine in 595.

Rumours of what lay ahead soon spread dissension among the missionary-monks, and they sent Augustine back to Rome, hoping to be let off their unenviable task; but he soon returned to them with renewed authority, and letters to the rulers and bishops of Gaul to give all possible aid. Had they known it, the king of Kent, to whom their mission was directed, was as afraid of the monks as they were of him: although he was married to a nominal Christian, he met Augustine's party in the open air, fearing magic.

They soon convinced the King however, and it was not long before Augustine was sending back to Gregory the glad news of the royal baptism, closely followed by thousands of others. He also sent a list of questions on difficult subjects for the Pope's definitive advice. Gregory was naturally delighted and replied at once, sending also the authority for setting up the Christian dioceses of the new mission field. So speedily did he write, that on reflection he sent after the messenger to say that he had changed his mind on one point: the pagan temples were not to be destroyed, but, if well-built, they were to be purified and consecrated for Christian use; a very sensible suggestion, that shows Gregory's mind well.

The mission progressed slowly outside of the Kingdom of Kent. Augustine travelled to Aust, on the Severn, to hold conference with the Celtic bishops of Wales and the West Country. The differences between Rome and the Celtic Church were minimal—a question of different dates for Easter, and different ways of shaving the monk's tonsure; but the Welsh hated the Anglo-Saxons, and probably saw little reason for giving the benefits of eternal life to their deadly enemies. Furthermore they were suspicious of the pride of the man from Rome, who so despised provincials that he didn't even rise from his chair to greet them. A little good manners, and perhaps history would have changed remarkably.

Gregory was not to live to see his favoured mission progress over the whole land, for he died in 603, but he would have been glad to witness the scene, say, of the conversion of Northumbria, which Bede describes so well in Book II, cap. 13 of his *Ecclesiastical History*. The court was assembled to hear Paulinus, Augustine's colleague, and first the pagan high priest, Cofi, spoke. He told how he had devotedly served the old religion all his life—none better—and he had to admit he had had little benefit from it; perhaps a new faith would give real benefits. Then an aged councillor spoke in a parable: life, he said, is like the flight of a sparrow through a feasting-hall on a mid-winter's night; we

all know about the light and warmth of life, but we are ignorant of, and fear the dark and cold outside; if the new faith can cast rays of light outside the hall, let us accept it. Then Paulinus spoke, to a people already half-convinced. Cofi, the high priest demanded to be armed and given a horse, and he rode off that minute to his temple. Whilst a gaping crowd stood wondering at his madness, he flung his spear into the heart of the shrine, and then set fire to it.

These were the great days of conversion, and very much under the influence of a Pope who was forced by his office to sit at the centre of things, when he would have preferred by far to be present at such scenes as Paulinus was to witness.

There is no single good biography of Gregory: see F. H. Dudden's *Gregory the Great* (2 vols., Russell and Russell, New York, reprint 1967) and P. H. Batiffol's *Saint Gregory the Great* (Burns and Oates, London, 1929).

Gregory VII

In 1073 a noisy Roman mob grabbed hold of Cardinal Hildebrand, and elected him Pope Gregory VII on the very day of his predecessor's funeral. It was all very embarrassing for one who held the office in high esteem, but he recalled with affection that Gregory the Great had been equally popular with the citizenry, and hastily regularised the situation by a proper and highly formal election. It was a good job that he did not have foresight of his last view of the Roman people, howling for his blood.

He was by birth a Tuscan, about 50 years old at the time of his elevation, small, weak-voiced, but with that flashing imperious eye that was a mark to medieval man of sure authority. Known jocularly as 'Elijah', he had a high regard for the Old Testament, and more for St. Paul in the New. He had seen the papacy in its worst period of decline and subjection to secular control, and for thirty years he had served its cause in ever more important capacities. Having spent a few months in a monastery, he was garbed as a Cluniac monk, and like all monks he was deeply concerned with authority, blessed and cursed with the vision of the power conferred by God.

He was not learned, and he was a poor judge of character, but he had a vision, which he confided to paper early in his pontificate. In the *Dictatus Papae*, the thoughts of a Pope, he gave chapter headings for a treatise on the powers a proper papacy should have: 'He alone may use the insignia of Empire. The Pope is the only person whose feet are kissed by princes. He may depose Emperors. He may be judged by no-one. The Roman Church has never erred, nor ever, by witness of Scripture, shall err to all eternity.' These startling thoughts were, for him, merely a beginning.

At first the programme went well, for the as yet uncrowned Holy Roman Emperor, the charming Henry IV, had a full-scale revolt to deal with, and could not afford the time to take umbrage at the commanding tone of the new Pope. His bishops were less under protection, for they at once received peremptory instructions about the putting down of clerical marriage and concubinage, and the immediate abolition of simony—any kind of payment for any of the offices or services of the church. Delaying tactics were of no use—Gregory promptly sent out decrees ordering the laity to cease using churches served by priests who practised such evils. The bishops could only hope that he meant what he said about personally leading a Crusade to the East: perhaps that would get rid of him for ever.

But this was not to be the end of Hildebrandine reform: he now turned his attention to lay investiture. This seemingly harmless custom of the secular proprietor of the church giving to the bishop his pastoral staff and ring was an important element of feudal society by which the King and his barons organised their relationship with the Church in its secular

role as a substantial landowner. To the King who considered himself to be the true representative of Christ on earth, this was merely a common-sense relationship.

So Henry IV kicked against papal interference, and uttered defiance. He arranged for his bishops to renounce the authority of the Pope, and then, with grand panache, deposed him. Gregory was not put out, for he felt himself to have a far superior power, and in deposing Henry, and excommunicating him and his bishops, he knew that he was inflicting a greater penalty by far. The episcopate and the princes came to heel with remarkable speed, and in October 1076 it was agreed that the Pope should sit in judgement on the Emperor early in the following year. The threat of hell-fire had its power.

Yet cunning was to forestall the intended triumph of the Pope, for, in the worst winter known, crossing the most dangerous Alpine pass, Henry came to Gregory at Canossa, and stood before the castle gates, barefoot and in penitential robes for three days, pleading for forgiveness. No spiritual ruler could ignore such signs of penitence, whatever the political situation, but Gregory must have realised how political an act Henry's stand was.

Probably even Gregory was not deceived, and he quickly arranged for support in another direction—the only one, from the South. Here ruled the Normans, under Robert Guiscard, a notorious marauder, and thief of papal lordships. At first he gave little support, for when Henry invaded in 1081 and 1082, Robert was busy invading Greece.

In 1083 Henry burst into Rome and, whilst Gregory was immured in Castel Sant' Angelo, had his own nominee crowned Pope, who promptly crowned him Emperor. At last the Guiscard advanced, and Henry fled before him, but Rome was not at all welcoming to the barbarian hoard, and a tremendous sack ensued. The populace was enraged, and when the time came for the Normans to withdraw, Rome was too dangerous for its Pope. Gregory went with the Normans. His last year was spent in the extraordinary air of Salerno, and he died, in 1085 with the words 'I have loved righteousness and hated iniquity; therefore I die in exile' on his lips.

Gregory VII is not a man one may like, but he had worked immensely hard for an idea. Without his aid William the Bastard might not have become William the Conqueror (q.v.); Poland, Hungary, Russia and Byzantium all felt his pull, as well as Norway and Sweden. All he wanted was that people should give him their kingdoms as vassal states, and he should nobly return it to them in fee, that was all. It was, in fact, little enough, but it meant a lot to him— the real sign of Christ's kingdom on earth, no little sign, but so difficult of achievement, for feudal kings, above all people, knew the power of the vassal's tie.

There is a life by A. J. Macdonald: *Hildebrand: A Life of Gregory VII* (Methuen, London, 1932).

Robert Grosseteste

Robert Grosseteste was born about the year 1168 to a poor Suffolk family. It would be interesting to know how poor, for other members of the family went into the church—his sister became a nun, for example. Certainly he was known to be of humble origins: the Earl of Gloucester was amazed at the courtesy of one from such a background when dining with Grosseteste, who sharply reprimanded a servant for dishing him up with the largest fish.

Whatever his background, Grosseteste was so outstanding in mind and character he could overcome it. People were always tremendously impressed with him, and he probably had little difficulty in finding a patron to pay for his schooling (possibly at Lincoln) and then on to Oxford.

His first major appointment was in the household of the Bishop of Hereford, where his skills in law and medicine were noted especially.

He probably spent a further period at Oxford before going on to spend some time in Paris doing his higher degree in theology. After Paris, about the year 1214, he returned to Oxford, where he acted as its first chancellor, holding the office for about a decade.

His early lectures show his interest in music (which was to be an abiding passion), astronomy and linguistics. He had discovered Aristotle, and showed a remarkable skill in interpreting him, being inspired with a deep love of exactitude, which was later to lead him further into linguistics and into the field of mathematics.

He grew astonishingly quickly, for his mind was able to make gigantic intuitive leaps, at the same time as being absolutely disciplined. He saw everything in sharp perspective, but he was also able to see implications and areas of possible development with the same clarity. This strange combination made him both recognisably important, and also an extremely uncomfortable companion. Increasingly he became critical of the directions in which scholarship was growing, catering for students who required education in order to gain promotion in church and state rather than to make them more proficient in God's service. So, more and more he stressed the preaching office, and saw in the newly arrived friars of both orders a pattern for his own and others' lives. Towards the end of the second decade of the thirteenth century he became reader to the Franciscans at Oxford, and himself gave up all his benefices save one, his prebend at Lincoln.

He gave himself consistently to study, extended old fields, and entered new. He learned Greek, and at least began to study Hebrew. With the aid of collaborators such as his great friend Adam Marsh—a Franciscan of powerful scholarship— and John of Basingstoke who had gone to Greece to study the language at the feet of the Archbishop of Athens, he prepared all the necessary technical aids to translation, sent to Greece for manuscripts, and employed Greek scholars. He translated some fifteen works, some as large and important as Aristotle's *Ethics*. He was an immensely methodical worker, and, again with the aid of Adam Marsh, prepared a detailed subject index to his library of some hundred volumes.

At the same time as he translated, studied and wrote on theology and philosophy and preached widely, he found time to study science and carry out experiments, especially in the field of optics. The impact of Aristotle's scientific work on Europe was as marked as that of his philosophy, and he found a notable interpreter in Grosseteste. This work of interpretation was badly needed, for not only were the ideas of the ancient Greeks immensely revolutionary to the medieval mind, but the method of their introduction was chaotic in the extreme. As new pieces were discovered in no sort of order, and without any authentication, they not only needed translation, but also the very closest interpretation. It is as if various volumes of an encyclopaedia are washed ashore on a savage island, volume twenty first, next a piece of volume one, with probably an odd novel following, and so on. The natives have a real problem, and it will be seen that the mind of the man who can interpret for them the underlying philosophy is of no mean order.

Of course, Grosseteste was in a much better position than that of an ignorant native with no other resources on which to draw; but his careful exposition of Aristotle's philosophy of science, with its highly advanced notions of studying species in order to find out about individuals, of building theoretical models, and of experimenting in order to determine truth, was an immense intellectual feat.

Add to all this scholastic effort his appointment in 1235, when he was well on into his sixties, as Bishop of Lincoln, the largest diocese in the land, and we still have not plumbed the depths of his power to work productively. He at once set to work—again with the aid of Franciscans

and Dominicans—to reform the morals of both clergy and laity in his diocese.

He was a serious minded man, filled with devotion for the salvation of souls, and he would admit of no opposition. He thoroughly visited his diocese (a novelty in the Church, this), and had a tremendous row with his own dean and chapter who stoutly objected to his authority. He would stand for no irreverence—he banned the Feast of Fools in the cathedral—and he laboured mightily to ensure that each church was served by a resident priest who was sufficiently learned to conduct the services and preach. Monasteries, great lords, the King and the Pope themselves might try to get their friends, relatives or servants instituted to benefices, but if they were inadequate, or had made no provision for a resident curate, Grosseteste would have none of them. His great wrath was roused when, as on one occasion, a monastery presented to him for institution a scarlet-gowned and beringed fop who was not only illiterate but also untonsured. Such people were guilty of attempted murder of their proposed parishioners' eternal souls, and he made quite sure they understood what he thought of them.

He made few friends this way, but he was fearless. King John was enraged when he forbade clergy from serving as royal justices, and instigated inquisitions into lay morality, but Grosseteste was unmoved. He gave Simon de Montfort and other barons staunch support in their fight for justice in the land, and his spiritual backing meant much to these men—particularly Simon—when their confidence ran low and hope seemed ever more dim.

The Pope himself was not exempt from Grosseteste's searching criticism. This is not to say that he was in any sense against the Pope, or against the King: he was simply for justice. When he travelled to the papal court at Lyons in 1245 and 1250 to lash with his tongues the wrongs of the church, he felt himself to be paying the deepest respect to the papal office, in that he wanted for it and from it nothing but the best. To carry out papal commands he knew to be wrong had no virtue of obedience—it was simply dishonouring an institution from which should emanate no wrong commands.

He died in 1253, having acheived much in the world of scholarship, and later generations in the fourteenth and fifteenth centuries would respect and remember him for that alone; but to Wycliff and other English reformers he was to stand out as the unshakeable rock of justice, who had seen the right way and followed it, ignoring all other petty influences.

See *Robert Grosseteste, Scholar and Bishop*, ed. D. A. Callus, (Oxford Univ. Press, London, 1955).

Harold Godwinson

Harold Godwinson was King of England for nine months, and we have little personal information about him; but all the romances cannot build a more exciting tale than the few facts we have about his life.

He was born about 1022, second son to Godwin Earl of Wessex and Gytha, sister-in-law to Canute. Godwin, though an Anglo-Saxon, had been Canute's favourite counsellor and had risen to his position as premier earl of England with a speed born of ruthlessness and ability. His family was large, and he plainly intended to pass on to them all his powers: his eldest daughter Edith he married to Edward the Confessor, and his sons Harold, Tostig, Gyrth and Leofwine all rose to the rank of earl. The black sheep of the family, Godwin's eldest son Swein, lost all his hopes by seducing an abbess and murdering his cousin; he was packed off to the Holy Land on pilgrimage, and died on the way back at Constantinople.

Harold was already carrying out the duties of an earl by the time he was 21, and no doubt looked forward to untroubled promotion as a result of his high birth; but all was not well between King Edward and Godwin, and trouble was boiling up. Edward had been brought up in Normandy, and tended to favour his boyhood

friends, rewarding them with high positions in both church and state; furthermore, he knew that Godwin had been largely responsible for the sad death of Edward's brother, and could never bring himself to view such a man with any more than the necessary favour. In 1051 there was trouble between Godwin and the Norman 'fifth columnists' in Dover, and, after a great struggle, the whole family went into an expedient temporary exile for a year, to regroup their forces.

In 1052 Godwin and his family returned, and quickly demonstrated to the king that their place in the English power structure could not be ignored. Godwin only lived out the year in his new won power, for the next Easter he died dramatically in the presence of the king, having unwisely called down on himself the vengeance of Heaven if he had had any part in the death of the Confessor's brother. He promptly had a stroke.

Harold now took up the leadership of England's most powerful family, and soon he and his three brothers who were earls had practically the whole country under their control. There is no doubt that he took his duties with the utmost seriousness, and he showed no desire for the throne, negotiating in person the return of the heir-apparent, Edward's nephew, from his exile in Hungary (where Canute's murderer could not reach him). He was far too busy pushing back the onslaughts of the Welsh in Hereford and Monmouthshire to have thoughts of the succession. With dogged thoroughness he wasted the lands of South Wales until the Welsh, driven to despair, murdered their king and brought his head to Harold as proof that there was no spirit of rebellion left. The king's widow, Ealdgyth, was daughter to the Earl of Mercia, and Harold was to make a politic marriage with her in 1066 to win the family's support, and widow her once more.

In 1064 Harold put to sea from Bosham, near Chichester, probably on a diplomatic mission. On landing in Ponthieu he was arrested by the local count, and sent a prisoner to William, Duke of Normandy, who treated him with considerable respect, taking him on an expedition against Brittany, and giving him arms, a sign, in an age when signs were respected, that he was making Harold his man. Long before, in 1051, Edward the Confessor had seemed to promise William the crown, and now the Duke was making sure of the loyalty of the leading citizen of the country he was to claim. Harold's ready response, and his seeming willingness in taking an oath over sacred relics to act as William's representative at the English court, may seem strange; but he probably acted out of politeness— we know he was a man fond of using oaths, but not a great respecter of them— and the situation of two years hence cannot have had any reality to one who was not clairvoyant. England seemed moderately secure, no great changes were in view, and the practical possibility of a continental duke of little background or importance successfully claiming the throne of England must have seemed remote.

Yet on his return the tragedy began to work itself out, and it cannot have been long before Harold regretted ever having made that oath. The Northumbrians had taken a good opportunity to depose his hated brother Tostig from the earldom, and though Edward, who was fond of him, hoped for a restoration, Harold did nothing to help. Tostig retired in a huff to Flanders, breathing fire, and determined on revenge; his friend the king of Scots would support him against the treacherous Northumbrians and the unfaithful rulers of England. The Welsh were restive again, and from Norway Harold Hardrada was threatening; suddenly from all directions England was in danger, when early in Janury 1066 Edward the Confessor died.

It is highly possible that Edward nominated Harold as the next king on his death-bed, but whether he did or no, Harold was elected and crowned the following day; the nobility of England well knew in that fatal year that they would need a great war-leader for king if England was to

remain under English rule, and Harold alone would do. He quickly set about gaining the full support of every important leader in church and state, and organising as best he could for war. The Anglo-Saxons were doughty fighters, even though the methods they used were conservative, but the problem was—where and when to place the army? The invaders would bring picked men, who would be fresh, but they would choose the time and the place; if two invasions coincided in time, but not in place, tragedy would ensue.

First of all came Tostig, Harold's brother, ravaging his way up the eastern coast to Scotland and his ally-king. Then in September came Harold Hardrada, with three hundred ships, crammed with Viking troops, swooping down, as they had done for years, on the Yorkshire coast. Harold was in the south, where he had been awaiting the Norman invasion for months, for it was delayed by opposing winds. He had had to withdraw his fleet from the Channel station, as it was running out of provisions, and many of his soldiers had returned home for the harvest. Nevertheless he rushed north and met the combined armies of Tostig and Hardrada at Stamfordbridge on 25 September. Such was the slaughter, in which both the invading chieftains died, that when Harold, having made peace, saw off the remaining Norwegians, they only needed 24 of their 300 ships.

Two days after the battle, the wind had changed, and William crossed over and landed his troops in England with no opposition. 250 miles divided the two armies, and Harold cannot have heard news of the landing before the evening of 1st October. Within eleven days he had got his army to London, and remained there for only three days more to give time for the troops he had sent for to rush in to join his army. Had he stayed longer he could have taken an infinitely superior force which would have defeated William, but he had just had one of the most tremendous victories in English history, and was probably convinced of the superiority of his troops. Furthermore it was his own earl-dom William was ravaging, and the more time the enemy had to establish himself, the worse the problem would grow.

On the night of Friday 14th October, Harold was encamped on rising ground some ten miles out of Hastings, and about nine o'clock the next morning William's force reached the hill facing this position from the south. Neither side numbered more than about 7,000 men, but their tactics differed greatly. The Normans were using cavalry and archers, whilst the Anglo-Saxons were massed together behind a wall of shields, ready to hurl missiles at the enemy and, when they got too close, to hew them down with massive two-handed axes.

At first things went very badly for the Normans for, although their arrows worried the English, they could never get close in to fight in any other way. Then, elated by what must have seemed another great victory, the English began to pursue the retreating enemy down the slopes, only to find that on foot they were no match for cavalry, and were themselves hewn down by sword. The Normans now began deliberately to tease the English out, and gradually the shield-wall thinned. At the highest point, beside the standard, Harold's brothers, Gyrth and Leofwine, were already dead, and he survived alone to see the shield-wall break. As dusk drew on he was struck down, not by an arrow, but by a Norman sword, as the Bayeux Tapestry clearly shows. A few of the English made a last stand in the wooded country that lay behind the battle-field, and in the orgy of slaughter, many Norman knights fell to their deaths in a hidden ravine.

When they found Harold's body it was stripped, and not recognisable from the face at all. Only marks on the body proved it to be his. Gytha came offering to buy her son's corpse for its weight in gold, but William refused, giving the job of burial to one of his knights.

Harold was a keen sportsman, and a considerable soldier; he was filled with courage as were few who were called to be king, and he could act with great political skill and inspire considerable loyalty. What he achieved is overshadowed by his successor, but is quite enough to provoke the question 'What might have been . . . ?'

For a biography see H. R. Loyn's pamphlet *Harold, Son of Godwin*, published by the Hastings and Bexhill branch of the Historical Association in 1966.

Sir John Hawkwood

Sir John Hawkwood said to two friars who had greeted him in normal fashion with 'God give you peace', 'God take away your alms'; for as they lived by charity, he lived by war, and to him it was as genuine a vocation as theirs.

He was the son of a moderately well-off Essex tanner, but we know little of these early days in England. He first springs to our attention in France in 1359, as leader of a troop of freelances called the White Company. There were a thousand lances, and to each lance went a heavy-armed knight, a squire and a page. The lances were so heavy they needed two to manoeuvre, and they were only used in defence, receiving a charge with an impregnable hedgehog effect. Other weapons were used in close fighting, and there was a large body of infantry in support armed with yew bows so large they had to be planted in the ground to operate them.

The White Company was usually the master of any situation, but in this year they were running after an enemy they could not engage. There was plague in the rich lands of France, so they moved rapidly into Italy to see what pickings there were there for well organised marauders.

Sometimes they plundered and spread terror; at others they used the protection racket; but in a nation so incredibly divided into infinitesimal and mutually hostile parts, the craft of the mercenary brought the best pay of all. Hawkwood's first spell, serving Pisa against Florence, brought the White Company 25,000 florins a month. Anyone who could bid higher bought loyalty for a time. In 1368 he served for Milan against Pisa, but within another four years he was fighting for the Pope (no longer the White Company, but now as the Holy Company) against the Milanese. In 1375, just for a change, they went back to being freelances and levied 220,000 florins' worth of protection from the Tuscan cities in the course of one Summer.

It was not all unscrupulous though: Hawkwood left the papal side when a cardinal he was serving ordered the complete massacre of an enemy city; he worked hard to avenge the murder of his father-in-law Bernabo Visconti, and from 1380 he loyally served the interests of one city, Florence (though he did take on a number of small jobs for other cities when financially pressed).

He was undoubtedly a fine general who was widely respected for his cunning and verve. Once, when the Milanese thought they had him surrounded they sent him a trap containing a live fox. Hawkwood let the fox go, sent the empty trap back, and led his army out of the encirclement with little difficulty.

He spent his last years in his large Florentine town-house, or on his country estate, and when he died he was given a magnificent funeral in the Duomo. His wife and children had large pensions and endowments. One of his descendants was to return to Italy—the poet Shelley.

Henry I

Henry I was born in the year 1068—a factor he himself regarded as highly significant, for he was the only son of the Conqueror born after the conquest of England, and to Henry this meant he was heir to the throne. He was not an attractive proposition: he was dissolute to a degree, producing at least a score of bastards; but far worse he was prone to sadistic cruelty— on one occasion, for example, personally punishing a rebellious burgher by throwing him from the walls of his town.

At the death of William the Conqueror, Henry was left no lands, merely 5,000 pounds of silver. With these he bought lands from his elder brother Robert Curthose, Duke of Normandy, only to see them taken back again a few years later by Robert, in unholy alliance with his brother William Rufus (q.v.).

Henry could do little to avenge such treatment, but in England he found numerous barons who were tired of the exactions and ambitions of their king. He formed alliances with some of these, notably with the important De Clare family. He, and some of the De Clares were with William Rufus on his last hunting expedition, and it is thought that the king's death was the result of Henry's plotting.

Certainly he moved fast to take advantage of it; leaving Rufus's body unattended in the woods, he swooped down on Winchester to take control of the treasury. Two days later he was in Westminster, being crowned by the Bishop of London. His speed is understandable when one realises that his elder brother, Robert, was returning from the crusade, and claimed (with good reason) to be the true heir.

Henry showed great good sense in his first actions as King. He arrested Ranulph Flambard, William's tax-gatherer, and recalled Anselm (q.v.), the exiled Archbishop. Furthermore he issued a Charter of Liberties which promised speedy redress of grievances, and a return to the good government of the Conqueror. Putting aside (for the moment) his many mistresses, he married the sister of the King of Scots, who was descended from the royal line of Wessex; and lest the Norman barons should think him too pro-English in this action, he changed her name from Edith to Matilda. No one could claim that he did not aim to please.

In 1101 Robert Curthose invaded, but Henry met him at Alton, and persuaded him to go away again by promising him an annuity of £2,000. He had no intention of keeping up the payments, but the problem was temporarily solved.

He now felt strong enough to move against dissident barons who might give trouble in the future. Chief amongst these was the vicious Robert of Bellême, Earl of Shrewsbury, whom Henry had known for many years as a dangerous troublemaker. He set up a number of charges against him in the king's court, making it plain that if he appeared for trial he would be convicted and imprisoned. Thus Robert and his colleagues were forced into rebellion at a time not of their own choosing, were easily defeated and sent scuttling back to Normandy.

In Normandy Robert Curthose began to wreak his wrath on all connected with his brother, thus giving Henry an excellent chance to retaliate with charges of misgovernment and invade. He made two expeditions in 1104–5, before the great expedition of 1106 on which Robert was defeated at the hour-long battle of Tinchebrai, on the anniversary of Hastings. No-one had expected such an easy victory, but Henry took advantage of the state of shock resulting from the battle to annex Normandy. Robert was imprisoned (in some comfort, be it said); he lived on for 28 more years, ending up in Cardiff castle whiling away the long hours learning Welsh. His son William Clito remained a free agent, to plague Henry for most of the rest of his reign.

In England the struggle with Anselm (q.v.) over the homage of bishops ran its course until the settlement of 1107. In matters of secular government life was more simple: Henry had found a brilliant administrator, Roger of Salisbury, to act as Justiciar for him. Roger had an inventive mind, a keen grasp of affairs, and the ability to single out young men of promise. He quickly built up a highly efficient team of administrators, and established new routines and forms of organisation within which they could work. To him we owe the Exchequer and its recording system of the Pipe Rolls, the circuits of royal justiciars

spreading the king's peace, and the attempts at codification of law. Henry's good relationships with his barons, and with the burgeoning new towns owed much to skilful administration. Certainly he was able to gain a larger and more reliable revenue this way than by the crude extortion his brother had used.

In 1120 came the tragedy of the White Ship. The court was returning to England, and the finest ship in the land was filled with its young men, including Henry's son and heir William. Riotously drunk, they tried to go faster and faster, when suddenly the ship foundered. All hands (except a butcher of Rouen) were lost, and England was without an heir.

Henry's only legitimate child was Matilda, but she was married to the Emperor Henry V of Germany, and so could not succeed. But in 1125 her husband died, and Henry brought her home and forced the barons to swear fealty to her—though they did not like the prospect of a woman ruler. Henry then married her to Geoffrey of Anjou, the Normans' traditional enemy, and the barons were less happy—especially when the newly-weds had a terrible row, and Geoffrey ordered her out of his lands. In 1131 Henry, absolutely determined, forced the barons to swear fealty once more, and the fact that they did so is testimony to his controlling power. Matilda and Geoffrey were reunited, and in 1133 she produced a son whom she named for his grandfather. If only Henry could live on until his grandson was old enough to rule, all would be well.

But in 1135, against doctor's orders, he ate a hearty meal of lampreys, got acute indigestion, which turned into fever, and died. He was buried at his abbey in Reading —some said in a silver coffin, for which there was an unsuccessful search at the Dissolution.

Henry II

Henry II was born at Le Mans in 1133. He was the eldest son of the Empress Matilda, daughter of Henry I, by her second marriage to Geoffrey the Fair of Anjou. His parents' marriage was tempestuous, and both parties were glad when politics brought a separation, with Matilda going to England to fight King Stephen (q.v.), and Geoffrey to Normandy to win a heritage for young Henry.

He first came to England at the age of nine when his mother made her dramatic escape from Oxford (where she was besieged by Stephen) across the ice and snow, dressed all in white, to welcome him at Wallingford. His next visit, when he was fourteen, showed his character: he recruited a small army of mercenaries to cross over and fight Stephen in England, but failed so miserably in the execution of his plans that he ended up borrowing money from Stephen to get back home. A third expedition, two years later, was almost as great a failure. Henry was not a soldier, his were skills of administration and diplomacy; warfare bored, and sometimes frightened him. For the meanwhile he now concentrated on Normandy, of which his father had made him joint ruler. In 1151, the year of his father's death, he went to Paris to do homage to Louis VII for his duchy. There he met Queen Eleanor, and she fell in love with him. She was bored by Louis, whom she called 'more monk than man', and she was extremely highly sexed. Her liaisons scandalised Europe, and indeed Asia, where it was suggested that she took Saladin for her lover, though this was quite untrue. Henry's father was said to have been her lover too, but now she set about getting a divorce to marry the young duke with such high prospects.

Henry was by no means averse. To steal a king's wife does a great deal for the ego of a young duke; he was as lusty as she, and late in their lives he was still ardently wenching with 'the fair Rosamund' Clifford, and less salubrious girls with names like 'Bellebelle'; finally, she would bring with her the rich Duchy of Aquitaine, which she held in her own right. With this territory added to those he hoped to in-

herit and win, his boundaries would be Scotland in the north, and the Pyrenees in the south.

Henry was, apart from his prospects, a 'catch' for any woman. He was intelligent, had learned Latin and could read and possibly write; immensely strong and vigorous, a sportsman and hard rider who loved travel; emotional and passionate, prone to tears and incredible rages; carelessly but richly dressed, worried enough in later life to conceal his baldness by careful arrangement of his hair, and very concerned not to grow fat.

But now he was in the prime of youth, and in 1153 when he landed with a large force in Bristol, the world was ready to be won. He quickly gained control of the West Country and moved up to Wallingford for a crucial battle with Stephen. This was avoided, however, because in the preparations for the battle Henry fell from his horse three times, a bad omen. Henry himself was not in the least superstitious— he was the reverse, a cheerful blasphemer— but he disliked battles and when his anxious advisers urged him to heed the omen, he willingly agreed to parley privately with Stephen. The conference was a strange occasion: there were only two of them there, at the narrowest point of the Thames, with Henry on one bank and Stephen on the other. None the less they seem to have come to an agreement to take negotiations further.

That summer Stephen's son died mysteriously, and Eleanor bore Henry an heir (about the same time as an English whore Hikenai produced his faithful bastard Geoffrey). The omens clearly showed what was soon confirmed between the two—that when Stephen died, Henry should rule in his place. A year later Stephen did die, and in December 1154 Henry and Eleanor were crowned in London.

Henry was only 21, but he soon showed his worth, destroying unlicensed castles, and dispersing the foreign mercenaries. He gave even-handed justice, showing himself firm, but not unduly harsh. A country racked by civil war sighed with relief. Only two major difficulties appeared: first Henry's failure in his two Welsh campaigns in 1157 and 1165, when guerilla tactics utterly defeated and on the first occasion nearly killed him; second was the reversal of his friendship for Becket when he changed from being Chancellor to Archbishop of Canterbury in 1162. The whole story of Thomas Becket is dealt with in detail earlier in this book.

The quarrel with Becket was linked with the King's determination to continue his grandfather's reform of the administration of justice in the country. He was anxious for a uniform pattern, operated by royal justices, to control the corrupt, ill-administered and unequal local systems operated by barons and churchmen. At Clarendon in 1166 and Northampton in 1176 he got his council's agreement to a series of measures which established circuits of royal justices dealing with the widest range of criminal activities. The method of operation was novel too, relying on a sworn jury of inquest of twelve men. Though not like a modern jury, in that they were witnesses rather than assessors, the assize juries were the ancestors of the modern English legal system.

Henry travelled constantly, and much of the time in his Continental territories, for there were constant rebellions to deal with, usually inspired or encouraged by Louis of France. Henry was determined to keep the integrity of his empire, and to pass it on as a unity. To do this was no small task, but in 1169 Henry held a conference with the King of France which he hoped would achieve his objectives: he himself again did homage for Normandy, his eldest son Henry did homage for Anjou, Maine and Brittany, and Richard for Aquitaine. The next year he had young Henry crowned in his own lifetime. If anything could preserve the succession, surely this would? Yet in fact it brought all the troubles in the world onto Henry's head, as will be seen, for he

had given his sons paper domains, and had no intention that they should rule *his* empire. Yet a man with a title does not rest until he has that title's power.

Late in 1171 Henry had a pleasant interlude in Ireland—escaping from the world's condemnation for the murder of Becket. He spent Christmas at Dublin in a palace built for him out of wattles by the cunning Irish.

Meanwhile Eleanor had been intriguing with her sons, urging them to revolt and demand their rights. Early in 1173 they trooped off to the French court, and with Louis joined in an attack on Normandy. Henry clapped Eleanor into prison and went off to meet the new threat. Whilst he was busy meeting this, England was invaded from Flanders and Scotland, and many barons who fancied a return to the warlord days of Stephen broke into revolt.

Plainly it was St. Thomas's revenge, and there was no hope of dealing with the situation without expiation. In July 1174 Henry returned to England, and went in pilgrim's dress to Canterbury. Through the town he walked barefoot, leaving a trail of blood on the flinty stones, and went to keep his vigil of a day and a night by the tomb, not even coming out to relieve himself. As he knelt, the assembled bishops and abbots and all the monks of Christchurch came to scourge him—each giving him three strokes, but some with bitterness in their heart laying on with five.

It was worth it though, for the very morning his vigil ended Henry was brought the news that the King of Scotland had been captured. He moved quickly northwards, receiving rebels' submissions all the time. He met up with Geoffrey who had fought valiantly for him, and commented 'My other sons have proved themselves bastards, this one alone is my true and legitimate son.'

Returning to France he quickly came to an agreement with Louis and his three rebel sons, giving each a substantial income, though still no share of power.

Richard set to work reducing the Duchy

of Aquitaine to order, and quickly proved himself an able general who performed tremendous feats, such as capturing a fully manned and provisioned castle with three walls and moats to defend it. But the people were less easy to subdue—they loved war for its own sake as their poet-leader Bertrand de Born shows well in his works:

'. . . I love to see amidst the meadows tents and pavilions spread; and it gives me great joy to see drawn up on the field knights and horses in battle array; and it delights me when the scouts scatter people and herds in their path; and my heart is filled with gladness when I see strong castles besieged, and the stockades broken and overwhelmed, and the warriors on the bank, girt about by fosses, with a line of strong stakes, interlaced . . . Maces, swords, helms of different hues, shields that will be riven and shattered as soon as the fight begins; and many vassals struck down together; and the horses of the dead and wounded, roving at random. And when battle is joined let all men of good lineage think of nought but the breaking of heads and arms: I tell you I find no such savour in food or in wine or in sleep as in hearing the shout "On! On!" from both sides, and the neighing of steeds that have lost their riders, and the cries of "Help! Help!"; and in seeing men great and small go down on the grass beyond the fosses; in seeing at last the dead, with the pennoned stumps of lances still in their sides.'

(qu. Marc Bloch, *Feudal Society* (Routledge and Kegan Paul, London, 1961) p. 293.)

These robust knights were actively encouraged by the young King Henry. He was handsome, charming and beloved of all, but also feckless and thoughtless—far keener on tournaments and frivolity than the serious business of government. Then in the middle of his new rebellion he caught dysentery and shortly died. His devoted followers were thunderstruck—one young lad actually pined to death—and the rebellion fizzled out.

The young king was dead, but Henry, wary of previous errors, was not going to rush into making a new one. He called his favourite youngest son John to his side and ordered Richard to give his duchy into his brother's hands. Richard—his mother's favourite—had made Aquitaine his home and worked hard to establish his control there; he refused to give his mother's land to anyone, unless it were back to Eleanor herself.

Henry packed John off to Ireland (which he speedily turned against himself) whilst he arranged to get Eleanor out of her prison and bring her to Aquitaine to receive back the duchy. Meanwhile the new King of France, Philip, was planning to renew the attack on English territories, and all three, Henry, Richard and Philip, were *supposed* to be planning a joint crusade.

In 1188 Henry, already ill with the absessed anal fistula that was to cause him such an agonising death, refused pointblank to recognise Richard as his heir. The crazy project for substituting John was at the root of it all, though Henry may have deluded himself into thinking he was playing his usual canny hand.

But diplomacy was giving way to the Greekest of tragedies. In June 1189 Philip and Richard advanced on Henry at his birthplace in Le Mans, and he was forced to withdraw with a small company of knights, showering curses on God. Instead of going to the safety of Normandy, he rode hard, his usual long distance, deep into Anjou. This worsened his physical condition and, in high fever, he made no effort to call up forces to his aid. Forced to meet Philip and Richard, he was so ill he had to be held on his horse whilst he deliriously mumbled his abject agreement to their every condition for peace.

Back in bed after his last conference he was brought the news that John, for whom he had suffered all this, had joined the rebels' side. Two sons—both rebels—were dead, two sons—both rebels—lived, and it was his bastard Geoffrey who now tended him in his last sickness. There was not even a bishop in his suite to give him the last rites. Over and again he cried out in agony 'Shame! shame on a vanquished king!'

After his death the servants plundered him, leaving him in a shirt and drawers. When the marshall came to arrange the burial he had to scratch around for garments in which to dress the body. A bit of threadbare gold edging from a cloak was put around Henry's head to represent his sovereignty.

And yet Henry had forseen it all. According to Gerald of Wales he had long before ordered a fresco for one of his rooms at Winchester: the picture showed an eagle being pecked by three eaglets, and a fourth perched on his head, ready to peck out his eyes when the time should come.

See J. T. Appleby's *Henry II—The Vanquished King* (Bell, London, 1962).

Henry III

Henry III was born in 1207 and succeeded his father John on the throne of England in 1216. It was a ravaged inheritance, the scene of civil war and anarchy, and much of east and south eastern England was under the control of the French Dauphin Louis. But Henry had two great protectors—his liege lord the Pope, and the aged William Marshal (*q.v.*).

The Marshal, by a combination of military skill and diplomatic ability, saw off the Dauphin by September 1217, but less than two years later he was dead, and a triumvirate ruled in his place: the papal legate Pandulf; the Poitevin Bishop of Winchester Peter des Roches; and the Justiciar Hubert de Burgh. The legate departed in 1221; two years later Henry came of age and, rejecting Peter, chose Hubert to be his chief counsellor.

Trouble soon came, as Hubert attempted to re-assert royal authority. Barons, who had kept their castles undisturbed and exercised their powers without supervision, were now called to account to the haughty justiciar, and the party of Peter des Roches did not fail to underline the annoyances involved. The years 1223–4 were taken up with quelling rebellions.

Meanwhile the situation abroad was even more disturbing: the French king Philip Augustus (*q.v.*) was eating up English lands in Gascony, and Henry's mother Isabella made a bad situation worse by her marriage with Count Hugh of Lusignan. It was only in 1230 that a badly prepared English force set out for France and, after much squabbling, all it was able to do was make a demonstration march through Gascony.

Hubert had already had one dismal failure in Wales in 1228, and his arrogant attempts to build up a personal base in the Marches provoked a Welsh raid in 1231 which did more to harm his good name. Hubert was thrust out of power, to be replaced by Peter des Roches' Poitevins. But by 1234 they had upset the baronage of England (who had never taken kindly to foreigners other than Normans), and Richard Marshal combined with Edmund of Abingdon, Archbishop of Canterbury (*q.v.*) to force the King to replace them.

Henry now began his period of personal rule, and the world was to see what sort of King he would make. He was a simple, direct man, trustful on first impression, but bearing a life-long grudge when people let him down. At times lavish and life-loving, he could show another side of his nature, that wicked Angevin temper and streak of vindictive cruelty. He had a very refined taste, and enjoyed building and restoration work more than anything else. Surrounded by barons who had been proved in the hardest schools of war, the King had the spirit of an interior decorator; the nation could have borne the expense of his artistic tastes, could have forgiven the eccentricity of it all, but Henry showed time and again that he was timorous as well as artistic. He feared thunderstorms, and battle was beyond him.

The Crown had some 60 castles in England, and these were in a bad state after the troubles of John's reign and the minority. Henry travelled about tirelessly rebuilding them and making them more comfortable, spending at least ten per cent of his income on building works. He personally instructed his architects in great detail, and could not wait for them to finish—it must be ready for his return 'even if a thousand workmen are required every day' and the job must be 'properly done, beautiful and fine.' In addition he built or restored twenty royal houses, decorating them sumptuously. The painted chamber at Westminster was 80ft. long, 26ft. wide, and 31ft. high. The walls were all wainscotted (at Winchester even the pantry and cellar were wainscotted) and painted with pictures and proverbs. The subjects of the pictures varied according to the royal moods—in May 1250 the Queen borrowed a book about the crusades, and a year later the walls at Clarendon showed Richard the Lionheart duelling with Saladin. Wherever there were no pictures, there was the King's favourite decor—green curtains spangled with gold stars. The floors were tiled, the windows glazed (and barred after 1238 when an attempted assassination scared Henry out of his wits—he even had the vent of the royal privy into the Thames barred over) and fireplaces provided the ultimate in luxury. Special rooms sprouted everywhere, including the room where the royal head was washed.

If his private comfort bulked large in Henry's mind, his public display of piety came a close second: these were neatly combined in the royal bedroom where a window was fitted to look into the chapel. His greatest project was the rebuilding of Westminster Abbey, on which he spent nearly £50,000—the equivalent of £4,000,000 today. He had been so thrilled with St. Louis' *Sainte Chapelle* that he had wanted to put it on a cart and roll it back to England. That was impossible, so he had to build his own. He finished it in 1269, and proudly put up the inscription 'As the rose is the flower of all flowers, so this is the house of houses.'

For a while Henry had reason for pride: he married Eleanor, daughter of the Count of Savoy, and sister of the Queen of France, the finest match in Europe; his sister Isabella was married to the Emperor Frederick II, and his son Edward to Eleanor of Castille. He persuaded the Germans to elect his brother, Richard of Cornwall, King of the Romans.

On the other hand, his foreign policy was leading him into dangers. In 1242 he foolishly allowed himself to be led into supporting his mother's ambitions in Poitou, and the enmity with France was to continue needlessly until the settlement of 1259. Louis IX (*q.v.*) had no desire to be his enemy—in 1254 all England was amazed at the French King's generous gift of an elephant, which the historian Matthew Paris went to draw in the Tower of London.

In 1246 Henry's mother died (to almost universal relief) and he generously invited his four Lusignan half-brothers to live out their orphanage under his roof. He gave them large incomes, but they took more, milking the land as hard as they could in the last moments before bankruptcy. The English hated them for their avarice, pride and foreign-ness.

In ecclesiastical affairs Henry's hands were hopelessly tied—the Pope had always been his chief prop, and the King could not afford to lose his aid. There was a strong movement for reform, but the papacy's desperate need for money to prosecute its war against the Hohenstaufen made reform a secondary consideration, and indeed frequently blocked it. But Henry may justly be criticised for his foolishness in accepting the papal offer of the crown of Sicily for his son Edmund in 1250. The payment was to meet the astronomical debts of the Pope, and Richard of Cornwall had already wisely turned down this bad bargain, commenting that he had been offered the moon, if he could reach it.

Henry's need for money dominated most of his domestic policy. During the period of his personal government he obtained what he needed by getting legalists and professional civil servants to manipulate the complex chaos of the feudal government he had inherited. Government became a secret and centralised affair, excluding the barons, great and small. There are many comparisons here with the tyranny of Charles I.

In 1258 came the explosion: Parliament refused a grant unless Henry should exile his grasping half-brothers, and allow a commission of enquiry. A committee was set up to control the appointment of Crown officials, examine and reform local government, and supervise the affairs of the realm in general.

This was a revolt, but it had many obscure roots. One cannot assess how deeply felt were the demands for just and equal government voiced by Simon de Montfort (*q.v.*), but certainly there were other elements in the baronial party which were reactionary rather than revolutionary, wanting to return to baronial government for its own sake. On this issue the reformers split, Gloucester leading the conservatives, and de Montfort the radicals. Henry saw his chance, and deftly using the ever valuable support of the Pope, shook off the Committee's control.

Now came war, and the stunning defeat of the royal party at Lewes in 1264. From this point onwards Henry was very much a broken man, though prone to bouts of vicious anger. The initiative was passed to his son, the Lord Edward, who defeated de Montfort at Evesham, where Henry was rescued, scratched and shouting 'Do not hurt me.'

Henry longed for revenge, and disinherited the rebels, who fled to hide-outs in the fens to continue the war. The papal legate Ottobono persuaded the King to go so far, in the *Dictum de Kenilworth* of 1266, as to allow the rebels to buy back their estates. Still not satisfied, the disinherited, under Gloucester's leadership, took London, and Richard of Cornwall negotiated an easier peace. In 1267 the Statute of Marlborough embodied much of what de Montfort had fought for, and the long years of trouble were over.

Henry had at least survived, and his last years were happy in that he finished building his patron saint's Abbey of Westminster. The wheel of fortune that decorated so many of his palaces' walls had come round, and all the rage and terror were done with. Henry died in 1272.

Henry IV

Henry IV was born at Bolingbroke, in Lincolnshire, in 1367, the very day his father, John of Gaunt, and the Black Prince were winning the last of England's three great victories in the first phase of the Hundred Years' War at Nájera. He was well educated, being able to write in both English and French, and understanding Latin; he enjoyed disputing with scholars, and always gave careful attention to paperwork. Extremely pious, he never missed the chance to visit a shrine. A great jouster, he could also relax pleasantly—he loved music and always had his bandsmen by him.

He quickly took his place in the political set-up of his day, and in 1387, in the absence of his father, joined the opposition to Richard II; but when his father returned to England he forced his son to withdraw. He spent the years 1390–2 campaigning in Prussia with the Teutonic Knights. After a brief respite at home he rejoined them, but finding not all to his liking, set out for the Holy Land, making an impressive and expensive progress through Europe to mark his return.

No doubt he thought Richard had forgotten his early peccadillo, and in every way he was encouraged to believe this, being granted the Dukedom of Hereford, brought to him by his marriage with Mary Bohun. In 1398 he sneakily reported to Parliament that Norfolk had cast doubt on the trustworthiness of the King, and Norfolk promptly called him liar and traitor. The Court of Chivalry decreed that the pair should meet at Coventry in September to fight it out.

In the months of preparation Henry built up massive popularity, especially in

London, and all were amazed when, the joust about to start, King Richard decreed that it should not go on, that Norfolk was exiled for life, and Hereford for 10 years. Henry grudgingly obeyed, for Richard suggested shortening the term to six years, offering a pension of £2,000 a year in the meanwhile, and guaranteed his patrimony should Gaunt die during his absence.

Gaunt did die in February 1399, and the King confiscated his estates and converted Hereford's banishment to a life-sentence. Enjoying the joke, Richard departed for Ireland.

Henry landed at Ravenspur (where Edward IV was to land some seventy years later to finally settle with Henry's grandson) with a few friends and a small force; people flocked to his support, hating Richard for his exactions and misgovernment. By the time they reached Bristol they numbered thousands. Henry declared he had only come to regain his duchy, but the tremendous welcome, combined with Richard's plight, deserted in Wales on landing from Ireland, was too tempting. Richard was taken and carried to London, the fiction of an amicable reunion being spoiled by his desperate attempt to escape through a window at Lichfield.

On 29 September 1399 Richard resigned the throne, and Henry was acknowledged as King. He can have had little notion of what he faced. The people were glad enough to say good-bye to Richard (though there was a rebellion in his favour the next year—which hurried on his death —and numerous plots and rumours of survival) but they were less anxious to welcome a strong ruler.

In foreign affairs the reign began badly, with Henry moving against the Scots and failing miserably—a failure that was underlined two years later then the Percies roundly defeated the Scots at Homildon Hill. In September 1400 Owen Glyn Dŵr raised revolt in Wales, and was to be an active menace for a number of years to come. The seas were not kept (Henry did little but encourage the English to indulge in piracy, which got them well hated by everyone) and the English coasts lay open to French attacks. In 1403 they burnt Plymouth, and in 1405 they marched with Owen deep into Worcestershire.

Domestic affairs went equally badly. In 1403 the Percies (the Earl of Northumberland and his son Hotspur) raised revolt, dissatisfied with the results of Homildon Hill, and only the King's speed caught Hotspur at Shrewsbury and defeated him before he could link up with Owen, or with the forces of his father. Henry's poor standing in the land may be judged by the fact that after this rebellion the Lords refused to attaint Northumberland of treason.

In 1405 came the 'tripartite indenture' by which Northumberland, Glyn Dŵr and the Earl of March plotted to divide the land between them. The learned Archbishop of York, Richard Scrope, raised the standard of revolt in the north, fearing that the anti-clerical ideas of the commons were gaining ground under Henry. He was taken by a ruse, and the King in a rage ordered his execution; everyone was deeply shocked—the royal action seemed to confirm the Archbishop's fears. Scrope died a hero, being led to execution riding bareback a 'collier's sorry mare', chanting psalms, encouraging Mowbray his colleague in rebellion, and joking with the King's doctor about the final cure. Scrope's tomb became a place of pilgrimage— Henry had made him a martyr.

The King was now prostrated by his first bout of illness, an illness that was to lay him low time and again in this latter part of his life. His contemporaries called it leprosy, and there are signs of epilepsy, but more and more it began to look like nervous collapse. Henry became deeply concerned with his health, believing each bout of sickness to be a manifestation of divine wrath; yet in between times he remained burly and handsome, with his thick brown beard and his regular teeth, all of which he kept sound in his head until his death.

Henry was to have other battles—with his parliaments and his councillors. Parliament was worried about the massive expenditure, and constantly held up grants by attempting to impose controls on the Crown. One of the leaders in this work was the speaker, Thomas Chaucer, son of the poet, and cousin to the Beauforts. These, led by Henry Beaufort, Bishop of Winchester, were the children of John of Gaunt by Katherine Swynford; formally legitimised (though excluded from succession to the throne) they found no real place in society. As half-brothers of the King they should be high in rank, but there was always that ceiling above them.

In 1409 they allied themselves to the Prince of Wales, released from campaigning against Owen, and eager for new fields of battle. They managed to get Arundel to resign the Chancelorship, and Beaufort took his place. A large scale enquiry into government finance revealed huge deficits, but nonetheless they managed in 1411 to send an English expedition to the aid of Burgundy.

All this was done during the illness of the King, but he was sufficiently recovered by October 1411 to return to take charge. An autocrat by nature, he was furious at what had happened, and promptly brought back Arundel to replace Beaufort. Arundel had spent the slack time moving mightily against the Lollards, and the King had given him every support, keen as he was for orthodoxy. To show everyone he was truly master, the King now sent an expedition to help the Armagnacs, sworn enemies of Burgundy.

It was an expensive gesture, redolent of a senile king. The Prince was touring his territories raising troops, ostensibly for the French expedition, but others said a coup was planned by Henry Beaufort to replace the King by the Prince. Late in 1412 the Prince brought his troops to London, but in an emotional reunion with his father a peace was made. There was not long to wait. Henry died in 1413.

Henry V

The materials for the history of Henry V form a rich patina that shines gloriously, but hides all that lies beneath. He remains for us little more of a personality than the gilded image he had set upon his own tomb. Yet there must have been something there beneath the gilt, for he achieved much in a short life, and was the idol of his people, and of a succeeding age when Tudor historians and dramatists searched for a worthy forebear of their crown.

He was born at Monmouth in 1387, with no expectation at all of royal estate. He learnt grammar and harping, but spent most of the time in sport. Richard II was very fond of him, and kept him at court in high favour when his father Henry of Bolingbroke was exiled.

But on Henry's return and usurpation of the crown, his son was to have even greater estate. Now Prince of Wales, he was forced to take his duties seriously and learn the art of war from Hotspur in order to meet the rebellion of Owen Glyn Dŵr. In this long war Henry, although young for a commander, learnt much about guerilla tactics, the value of the long-bow, and especially about siege warfare. He was a passionate engineer—supervising the batteries of guns, and the miners who sapped walls, and above all playing with the great siege engines. Towards the end of his life he had a special machine made for the attack on Meaux, but the town fell before it could be used. Henry insisted that it should be tried out for him, just to prove that it would have worked.

From 1408 onwards Henry was brought into the political arena: his father was subject to crippling illnesses which meant that his son had to act as regent for him; but as soon as the King recovered he would insist on taking over power once more. The two were divided on the issue of foreign policy. France was in a dreadful state, with Charles VI continually lapsing into bouts of madness; during these periods there were two contestants for power—the Duke of Normandy and his party, and the Duke of Orleans and his followers (who were known as Armagnacs). Henry IV favoured the Armagnacs, whilst the Prince was pro-Burgundian, and in 1411, whilst the Prince was regent, he authorised a highly successful English expedition in support of Burgundy. His father was furious, and on recovering excluded his son from his Council for the rest of his reign.

There were rumours that the Prince was planning to take the crown, but if he was, he was forestalled by his father's death in 1413. His first actions showed him to be both serious-minded and pious, and he wisely moved to placate some of the enemies his father had made. Early in 1414 he successfully scotched a rebellion of the heretical Lollards led by his own companion-in-arms Sir John Oldcastle, and amply demonstrated to the Church his willingness to extirpate heresy.

All his thoughts lay in France, which his great-grandfather Edward III had claimed. Henry, an acute legalist, made much of the claim, but it was rather more of a religious conviction based on desire for glory that drove him to France. God should be the judge of his claim, rewarding him with victory. Henry V was in much the same state of mind as Henry VIII was to be when he wanted a divorce from Catherine of Aragon.

He pawned his jewels and raised loans, and ordered 1,500 ships. Vast stores of provisions and armour were collected, and 15,000 horses. 2,500 men-at-arms (each with squire and page) and 8,000 archers were arrayed, with perhaps twice that number of non-combatants (including 15 minstrels who went as a sop to Henry's passion for music, amongst whom was doubtless the author of the *Agincourt Song*).

Before this vast armada sailed, Henry uncovered a plot against his life. Richard Earl of Cambridge, son of one of Edward III's younger sons, had cunningly joined together all the interests that stood against, or had been harmed by the House of Lancaster. But Henry V had been very kind to some of his father's enemies, and now he had his reward, for the Earl of March revealed the plot, and in a dramatic Council at Porchester Castle Henry forced the assassins to confess. They were tried and executed,[1] and on 11th August the fleet finally sailed.

For five weeks the expeditionary force was halted in the fever marshes round Harfleur, and when the town finally fell, Henry had lost a third of his men. The garrison was sent off to collect their ransom money, and Henry foolishly compacted with them to meet in Calais in November. So, instead of consolidating his position, Henry was forced to lead his bedraggled men a 200-mile journey through rough and hostile country. The fords of the Somme were well guarded, and the English had to wearily cast about for a place to cross, and by this time the French, armed to the teeth, and outnumbering the English four to one, were ready to fight at Agincourt.

Henry tried to treat with them to save his army, but the French happily refused. The King now voiced his famous conviction that 'This people is God's people' and that, small and tired though his army was, it would win. On 25th October the French cavalry attacked over recently ploughed land that was soaked with rain; they faced English bowmen sheltered behind a sharp hedge of stakes, men who could send five arrows a minute, arrows that could pierce an oyster-shell at 250 yards. The French who reached their objective, struggling through mud in heavy armour, were too tired to resist the English club-men, and carnage ensued. Henry, fearing an attack from the rear, ordered the killing of all non-noble prisoners (the nobility would fetch a ransom), and 7,000 Frenchmen died, to 500 Englishmen. Only two English nobles perished—one was the excessively fat Duke of York, who died in the press of asphyxiation, or of a heart attack.

Henry returned to England in triumph:

[1] Cambridge's grandson, Edward IV, was to depose Henry's son.

the barons of the Cinque Ports carried him through the waves ashore, and a crowd of 20,000 met him at Blackheath. The Mayor of London presented him with two bowls, each containing £500. An observer noted that never once did Henry smile, insisting that all glory was due to God. He was now a fanatic for France. And indeed for more: his favourite reading matter concerned the exploits of Crusaders, and now Henry welcomed to England the Emperor Sigismund, who was planning to unite Europe, end the papal schism, and lead a crusade against the Turks. Sigismund was a veritable little League of Nations, and whom better could he approach than the son of a crusader who had just shown himself the outstanding military leader of Europe? Henry was beguiled, but still he did not smile, for he wanted France first, and Sigismund must help.

In 1417 came fresh preparations for war and all were mulcted to pay for it—even the geese: every goose in England, bar the breeders, was to contribute six wing feathers for arrow-flights. Careful preparations for the clearance and keeping of the Channel were made, and late in July Henry set off.

He attacked Caen, whose walls were seven feet thick, but his guns, firing stones two feet wide, soon dealt with the defences. The town fell in a fortnight, but not quickly enough for the demanding nature of the King, who authorised looting and butchery. Falaise took longer, but all Normandy now knew of the King's power and tactical ability. St. Vincent Ferrer visited his camp to denounce him, but after a long private meeting with the King, saw the justice of his cause, even if he saw him only as another Attila, scourge of God. Henry showed himself a reasonable master to the conquered Normans, allowing them to continue their own customs, and cutting the hated salt-tax in half.

By late July 1418 Henry was before Rouen, second largest and strongest city in the land. Its walls stretched five miles, punctuated by 60 towers; it was well stocked with food and arms, and crowded with refugees. Henry drew a circle round the town, establishing large camps connected by deep entrenchments, and blocking the Seine from traffic. As the town grew short of food, they expelled 12,000 refugees into the ditch; Henry refused to let them through his lines, and both sides watched them starve. Negotiations wrangled on, but in late January 1419 Henry entered the capital of his duchy. He now had a real base, with its attendant territories, no longer just a bridgehead. He was ready to negotiate.

He was lucky in that he had a choice of two sides, for the Queen had thrown in her lot with the Burgundians, giving them control of Paris, whilst the Dauphin was established in the Armagnac base at Poitiers. Months of haggling ensued, in which the Burgundians offered the beautiful Princess Katherine (tricked out for the occasion at the expense of 3,000 florins) as a suitable prize. Henry wanted much more, and his exorbitant demands slowly forced the Duke of Burgundy into attempting an alliance with his rival the Dauphin. But when the two leaders of the bitterly hostile factions met on the bridge at Montereau in September 1419, the Armagnacs could not resist such a chance, and hacked down John the Fearless with an axe.

The new Duke of Burgundy, Philip the Good, was set on vengeance at whatever cost, and immediately treated with the English. Henry should marry Katherine, and he and his heirs should rule France as a separate nation on the death of Charles VI. The terms were ratified at the Treaty of Troyes in May 1420, and in the following January Henry brought his bride to England. The welcome was rapturous, and the royal pair went on an elaborate progress round the country, visiting shrines to pray, and collecting money for the war.

In March Henry's brother Clarence led a foray into Dauphinist territory, and was defeated at Baugé; the spell was broken— the English were not invincible. By June Henry was back in France once more, reducing enemy castles that threatened his hold on Paris. His temper was hard—he had always had a trace of savagery, and now it came out. At Meaux the defenders had brought an ass on to the battlements and flogged it to make it bray, shouting to the English to come and rescue their king. A joke in poor taste, but Henry showed by his brutal replies when the town capitulated that he would not be mocked.

After an interval at Paris, he heard of a Dauphinist attack on Burgundy, and was preparing to go to meet this when he fell feverish. He was carried in a litter as far as Corbeil, but then had to give up. He was taken back to Vincennes, where he made careful arrangements for the government of his lands in the minority of his nine-month-old son. He spoke sadly of his desire to rebuild the walls of Jerusalem— were he not dying so young he might well have achieved his aims. Towards the end he was heard to mutter 'Thou liest, thou liest! My portion is with the Lord Jesus Christ.' One hopes so. He died, 31 August 1422.

After an impressive journey home, his body was given to an even more impressive tomb, a monument to English pretensions, and perhaps it is fair to say, to English xenophobia. For in an age when kings and politicians had less idea of geography than a schoolboy today, and less notion of the political state of the world than the average newspaper reader, the English people had a firm belief that they could master others as 'God's people' and the impression was to die hard. The lilies of France were not removed from the English flag until 1803.

There is a biography by H. F. Hutchison, *Henry V* (Eyre and Spottiswoode, London, 1967).

Henry VI

Henry VI was the son of a great king— Henry V—and inherited from him two crowns, and great responsibilities; but he was also grandson, on his mother's side, of a mad king—Charles VI of France—and the second heritage was to vitiate the first.

Henry came to the throne on his father's death in 1422 when he was but nine months old. Apart from making strict provisions for the straitness of his education, his guardians took little notice of him for some years, not even bothering with a coronation until 1429. His uncle Bedford was too busy trying to stem the tide of resurgent France, and his uncle Gloucester was too busy fighting it out with Beaufort for supremacy in England. Debts were mounting up—in 1433 they totalled £168,000—and the war in France continued to soak up money. On Bedford's death in 1435 there was no really able member of the royal house left to direct military operations.

In 1437 Henry's minority ended. At first he took a keen interest in affairs, and in many ways was an attractive king. He was generous, truthful, deeply pious, and in no way devious. His black dress, with round-toed shoes and townsman's gown was an outward symbol of his sincere humility and simplicity. He was shy and retiring, a puritan who was shocked by the nude bathers at Bath, and disturbed by any feminine display. Too much work tended to bring on crises of nervous exhaustion, fore-runners of the autistic state of his later periods of imbecility. He was happy when left alone to his devotions, and to his religious and educational foundations, such as those at Eton and King's, Cambridge.

The immensely rich Cardinal Beaufort, who had been his father's tutor and with whom Henry got on very well, was glad to remove the burden of government from the King's shoulders. Beaufort was experienced in both domestic and international affairs, and a skilled administrator. His followers were handpicked for their proven ability.

In 1443 when Beaufort retired, he was succeeded by his second-in-command, William de la Pole, Duke of Suffolk. He realised the terrible drag of war on the losing side, and negotiated a two-year truce, and a marriage for the King to a French princess, Margaret of Anjou, daughter of the King of Sicily. Henry was so scared of women that when Margaret landed, he dressed up as his own messenger, so that he could get a good look at her without any embarrassment. The sixteen-year-old girl was not unnaturally annoyed, but Henry plainly liked what he saw, and became for the rest of his life the abject creature of this intrepid and courageous lady. So thrilled was he by marriage that he offered to give back Maine to her father. The English were appalled, and darkly muttered that Suffolk must have negotiated this as a secret clause in the marriage-treaty.

Suffolk was well hated in the country. He was a grasping and avaricious man, and did not know how to court popularity. Instead, he now moved to defeat his two greatest rivals. The King's uncle Gloucester (whose wife had already been imprisoned on a charge of witchcraft some years previously) was impeached at Bury St. Edmunds, and within five days of his imprisonment his death was announced. Though a noted patron of the arts and scholarship (to him Oxford owes its university library, still centred around 'Duke Humphrey's') he was not a pleasant person, nor a good politician. His death, however, turned him into the mythological 'Good Duke Humphrey', and fed fuel to the fires of hatred for Suffolk.

On Gloucester's death, Richard Duke of York, nephew of the Duke of York who had been killed at Agincourt, emerged both as probable heir presumptive to the crown and, next to the King, the largest land-owner in England. Suffolk could not tolerate such power and, accusing him of misdirection of the war in France, arranged for his appointment as the Royal Lieutenant in Ireland, a virtual banishment.

The country was in a bad state, with disorder and feuding, piracy and open robbery, and no justice to correct it all. The royal finances were in a worse state—the debt now stood at £372,000. New taxation was urgently required, but its imposition would set off an explosion.

In 1450 the King was forced to banish Suffolk to save him from the wrath of the Commons, but his ship was caught at sea by a marauding band seeking vengeance, and he was roughly executed with six strokes of a rusty sword. Adam Moleynes, the King's secretary, was murdered in Portsmouth dockyard by angry sailors demanding pay. In the country, bands of unemployed soldiers wandered around looting and wrecking, led by men with such names as 'the Queen of the Fair' and 'Captain Bluebeard'.

Finally the rebels got a real leader, Jack Cade, who instilled military discipline into his men, and was able to scatter the royal forces and enter London, where they tried and executed James Fiennes, the Treasurer. The rebels dispersed after a week on promise of pardon. They had made their point. In the chronicler Gregory's graphic phrase, they were 'as high as pigs' feet'.

York now returned from Ireland—just too late to take full advantage of the rebellion many thought he had fomented. Finding little real advantage for his cause, and much desire for a settlement, he turned on the rebels, punishing them fiercely, and so earned for himself and his cause the hatred of a large sector of the population he needed if he were to win through.

The nation seemed to be recovering when, in mid 1453, the King lapsed into his first bout of imbecility, recognising no one, and communicating nothing. York leapt at the chance and quickly established himself as Protector—assumedly with an eventual claim to the succession; but two months after the beginning of the King's illness, Margaret bore him a son, and York's hopes of the crown were dashed. At Christmas 1454 the King recovered, and York was forced to give up the protectorship. He withdrew to his estates in the north, to gather an army.

In May of the following year the Yorkists defeated the Lancastrians at the first battle of St. Albans, and the King was captured and many of his leading supporters killed. In the autumn Henry relapsed once more into madness, but by Christmas he was well again, and the Queen managed to get him to Coventry, centre of Lancastrian support, to build up an army. The Yorkists also made elaborate preparations for a new trial of strength, but when the two armies met at Ludlow in 1459, the Yorkist forces were routed.

In the following year Warwick, Salisbury and Edward Earl of March landed in Kent and prepared a fresh challenge. At Northampton the Lancastrian army was defeated and the King captured. The new-fangled guns had got wet in the rain, and would not work for him.

The Duke of York now returned from Ireland once more, and entering Parliament he boldly claimed the throne, as true heir, before King Henry, of Richard II; but the lords demurred, and would only go so far as to recognise him as heir to Henry, for there was another Lancastrian force undefeated in the north led by the indomitable Margaret of Anjou, now ready to fight like a fury for the rights of her child. York moved up to Wakefield to meet her, and was defeated and killed, his head displayed upon the castle gates wearing a freakish crown of paper and straw.

Margaret moved south in February 1461, defeating Warwick at the second battle of St. Albans. Her army of wild Scots and Welsh was a fearful sight, and Henry, with his horror of bloodshed, persuaded Margaret to withdraw it from London, lest it ravage the town.

Edward Earl of March, now the Yorkist leader after his father's death, saw his chance, and marched on London from the West Country. He was 'elected' king in Henry's place there, and immediately led his troops in pursuit of the Lancastrian forces, catching and defeating them at Towton. Henry and Margaret with their son fled to the north.

Margaret and the Prince of Wales sought refuge in Scotland, but soon left for the Continent, where they moved round begging for support to regain the throne; the Queen, who had once been the height of fashion, was now so poor she looked like a peasant woman, but she did not give in. Henry, who had never reached Scotland, was captured in 1465 wandering aimlessly in Lancashire, and brought to London with his feet tied to the stirrups of his horse. He was kept in the Tower, unwashed and badly dressed—perhaps not knowing where or what he was.

The chances of restoration were dim, and when they came, even Margaret did not recognise them. Warwick, realising that he had lost, and would never regain control over Edward IV, was now prepared, in alliance with Louis XI of France, to put Henry back on the throne. For a long time Margaret could not bring herself to ally with the man who had caused the family's downfall, but she finally agreed, and in October 1470 Warwick swooped down on England, and Edward, taken by surprise, had to escape to the continent. Henry was washed and dressed, and brought out from the Tower.

But the country was not behind the move, and those leaders who thought that only baronial opinion mattered still were out of date. When Edward IV returned in March 1471 he had little trouble in sweeping away the resistance. At Barnet Warwick was killed, and Prince Edward at Tewkesbury. On 21st May he entered London, and that night, between eleven and twelve o'clock, Henry was murdered in the Tower.

St. Hugh of Lincoln

St. Hugh of Lincoln was born in 1140, youngest son of a Burgundian knight. He was only eight when his mother died, so his father, who then retired to a monastery, took him with him. As a young man he became increasingly interested in the stricter vocation of the Carthusian order, and finally defected to the Chartreuse. When he was 39 he was called to England to take charge of Witham Abbey, the first Carthusian house in England, and a part of Henry II's penance for Becket's murder. Hugh got on well with the King, whom he closely resembled—indeed it was rumoured that he was Henry's natural brother.

After 7 years at Witham, Hugh was made Bishop of Lincoln, a huge diocese that had suffered years of neglect. Typically, he set off in humble clothing, carrying his few necessities on the back of his saddle, embarrassing his lordly escort considerably. He found the cathedral almost in ruins, and immediately began to rebuild, frequently taking a hand with the hod. He wore out teams of attendants each day, and said of himself, 'I am sharper and more biting than pepper, and often I flare up over trifles', yet he seems to have inspired almost universal affection. He was passionately fond of young children, and there are several accounts of the great and terrifying saint reduced to drooling by particularly pleasant babies. He had a strange power over birds: at Witham he had a tame finch, and at Stow he had a tame swan, which was a fearsome beast to all but Hugh; with him it was like a lap-dog, following him around, eating from his hand, and when he was seated pushing up his sleeves to rest its head on his chest. But primarily Hugh was concerned with people—the needy, the oppressed and the sick. Above all he enjoyed the burial service, which he considered to be the crown of life and the most joyful sacrament a priest could perform—he would keep royalty waiting for dinner because he had found a corpse by the wayside and insisted on burying it. This concern for people brought him into conflict with authority in large measure, but he never showed fear nor did he govern his tongue. Once when Henry II, by no means a patient man, was bitterly angry with him and refusing to speak, he joked about the King's descent from the daughter of a tanner; he shook Richard until he forced him to give him the kiss of peace, and called John a liar to his face. In fact he was frequently legally wrong in these disputes with the crown, and it is remarkable that he was able to persuade such men that it is more important to be morally in the right.

His close contacts with the court never changed his way of life, and twice a year he went back to Witham for a month to live as an ordinary monk, deliberately choosing the job of the community's dishwasher. Towards the end of his life he made a pilgrimage back to the Chartreuse, stopping at every shrine he could take in, for he collected relics as a boy collects stamps: he had been known to use his teeth to gnaw pieces from holy bones to swell his collection. When he got back to England he was too ill to reach Lincoln to die by his cathedral, but he had reports from his architects, and died happy in the knowledge of progress. When the cortège reached Lincoln late in November 1200, King John, the King of Scotland, the Prince of Galloway, archbishops and bishops, earls and barons, abbots and priors were waiting there to see it up the steep hill to burial. Then came the miracles, and in 1220 canonisation. In 1280 Hugh's choir was finished, and a company richer and more royal than that which saw his burial came to witness the translation of his body.

The medieval life of St. Hugh by Adam of Eynsham is one of the finest of medieval biographies; it is edited and translated by Decima Douie and Hugh Farmer in Nelson's Medieval Texts. The best modern biography is by R. M. Woolley: *St. Hugh of Lincoln* (Society for Promoting Christian Knowledge, London, 1927; Macmillan, New York, 1927).

John Hus

John Hus was born in Bohemia in 1371. At that time Prague was the seat of the Holy Roman Empire, and a great cosmopolitan centre. It was also the great cultural centre of eastern Central Europe, and to its university came Hus at the age of nineteen or so, ambitious, pleasure-loving, and a devotee of chess. He did well in his studies, progressing quickly through the ranks until by 1401 the poor scholar had been changed into the Dean of the Arts Faculty.

At the university Hus came in contact with the strong movement for moral reform that had developed in Prague during the previous half-century; the leaders were keenly critical of the sadly corrupt state of the Church, and of the exactions and interference of the Pope. They proposed to remedy the situation by preaching, and the Bethlehem chapel was set up, a foundation where there would be two sermons in Czech every Sunday and Holy Day. In 1402 Hus became preacher at the Bethlehem chapel, and was immediately popular. His sermons had the common touch—'Hodek, the baker, or Hůda, the vegetable woman' were quoted as freely as St. Augustine. He also introduced the novelty of congregational hymn singing as part of the service, and wrote hymns in Czech himself for the people to sing.

Hus's popularity was not restricted to the common people—the rich merchants and the courtiers favoured him as well as the university men, and the Queen herself made him her chaplain.

At university Hus had learnt Wyclifite philosophy, and had used it in preparing his own lectures; but in the first year of the new century Czech scholars began to bring back from England copies of Wyclif's theological works—Jerome of Prague brought a batch late in 1401 and Nicholas Faulfiš and his colleague brought a more up to date collection in 1407. Hus and the other Czech masters at the university found these works extremely interesting, confirming many of their own opinions, and laying a groundwork of suspicion about other matters as well. The dominant German faction at the university condemned the works, however.

Hus's attacks on corruption in the Church grew more and more bitter, so that in 1408 the synod of Prague tried to silence him. He further fell out with the Archbishop over policy towards the Council of Pisa. The Council, trying to end the schism, had urged complete neutrality on all parties until it should come to a conclusion, but the Archbishop, and the Ger-

mans at the university strongly supported Pope Gregory XII. Hus led the Czechs in support of the Council of Pisa, and now he resolved to follow Wyclif's advice and bring the state in to correct the Church's faults. King Wenceslas supported Pisa too, so Hus and Jerome of Prague joined with him, and the King resolved the situation by giving each Czech member of the university three votes to the German's one. Hus was promptly elected rector (autumn 1409).

The Archbishop, not to be beaten, excommunicated Hus, and organised a huge burning of Wyclifite literature, but the King made him compensate the owners of the destroyed books, and made Hus write to the Pope disavowing Wyclif's teaching in 1411.

Whilst Hus had royal support he was safe, but in 1412 came the crucial situation which parted the ways. The Pope, eager to prosecute a crusade against his enemy Ladislas of Naples, sent salesmen into Bohemia to sell indulgences. Hus was deeply shocked at this, and at the conduct of the salesmen, and preached powerfully against the whole proceedings; but the the state could not afford a break with the papacy, and so three young protesters were picked up and beheaded. Hus organised a huge funeral procession to the Bethlehem chapel, where the martyrs were to be buried. Prague was brought under an interdict by the Archbishop.

Not wanting the people to suffer because of him, Hus moved out of the city to stay with friends and write: he wrote mostly in Czech, using a flowing conversational style, and his works did much to establish the use of the vernacular in his homeland. But they did more—they circulated his views widely in writing, and gave his enemies the chance to set up a substantial heresy charge.

In 1414 Sigismund, King of the Romans (and heir to Bohemia) organised the Council of Constance, and invited Hus to come and put his case before a general council of the Church, offering a safe-conduct both ways. Hus went, hoping to affect the outcome, but his enemies had been hard at work, and he was arrested on a charge of heresy. Sigismund protested, but the cardinals told him that they were not bound by his safe-conducts, and threatened to break up the Council if he made too much fuss.

He was kept in squalid conditions which caused him to become very ill. In April 1415 Jerome arrived, attempted and failed to get a safe-conduct and was caught and imprisoned on the same charge. In June the Council heard Hus, but he refused to recant unless they could prove to him from the Bible that what he had said was wrong. On July 6 he was unfrocked, and handed over to Sigismund for execution. He sang as the flames rose round him.

Jerome recanted, but later demanded to be heard again before the Council: he abjured his recantation, and said his greatest sin had been to deny that good and holy man John Hus. He was burnt at the same stake in May 1416.

The Bohemian Reformation movement that sprang from these two martyrs was to shake Europe, and later to inspire Martin Luther to do the same.

There is a biography by Matthew Spinka: *John Hus: A Biography* (Princeton Univ. Press, New Jersey, 1968).

Pope Innocent III

Pope Innocent III was born about 1160 as Lothario of Segni, son of Count Trasimund and his noble Roman wife. He studied in Rome, and then went on to the university of Paris. Whilst there he met Stephen Langton, and crossed the Channel to visit the shrine of St. Thomas Becket. From Paris he went on to Bologna to study canon law. His family connections assured him of easy promotion in the Church, and at the age of 29 he was made cardinal deacon. However the enemy Orsini faction was in control at the time, and he was forced to endure a period of inactivity during which he wrote three books.

On the death of Celestine III in 1198 he was elected to the papacy as a non-party candidate. Not yet made a priest, he had to receive both priest's and bishop's orders before he could be consecrated Pope. This was by no means unusual, and the new Pope had a high ideal: his office was to him the highest in this world, and he was determined that all should be made to see this. His legal training and administrative skill made it possible for him to reorganise the secretariat to deal with a vastly increased amount of business, and today 4,800 letters from his pontificate still survive to prove his efficiency and claim of omnicompetence.

In Italy he set to work to reduce the rebellious city of Rome to obedience (a hard task, not really achieved until 1208), and he regained control of the papal states. The death of Constance of Sicily in the year of his election left Innocent guardian of the heir Frederick II. The Germans tried hard to gain control, especially Markward of Anweiler, but Innocent fought him vigorously.

The infancy of Frederick II left a major gap in Germany too, and his uncle Philip went to protect Hohenstaufen interests there. Now came a dual election in the Empire, source of incredible confusion: the majority cast for Philip, who was crowned with the proper regalia, but a minority voted for Otto of Brunswick (nephew of Richard and John of England) who was crowned in the proper place—Aachen. In this stalemate Innocent claimed the right to choose the Emperor, and gave the crown to Otto in 1201; but Philip was the more powerful until his murder in 1208. Then the electors unanimously confirmed Otto, who came to Rome for his coronation.

Unfortunately he moved on to claim the Kingdom of Sicily, trying to capture Frederick, whose right to the Empire might militate against his own. Innocent could not tolerate such an attack on a papal fief, and excommunicated Otto, calling on Philip Augustus to act against him. In 1211 he declared Otto deposed, and the electors chose Frederick, who went north to win his crown. Otto returned to Germany too, but after his defeat at the hands of Philip Augustus at Bouvines in 1214, his power waned, until his death four years later from an overdose of medicine.

Innocent claimed he had the right to raise up and depose kings, and practised this wherever possible—in Serbia and Bulgaria, Hungary and Armenia. He received the Kingdom of Aragon as a papal fief from Pedro, and after a long tussle with John, did the same with England. He was equally firm in his dealings with Philip Augustus, insisting that he take back his spurned wife Ingeborg, though he was willing to legitimise the children of his illicit marriage with Agnes of Meran.

Not all his concerns were secular, by any means. One of his major worries lay in the advance of heresy in the south of France, where a rich culture received the new heretical doctrines of Catharism with pleasure because they allowed the Count of Toulouse and his subjects to spurn and disregard a corrupt Church. Innocent tried first the methods of preaching to convert these Albigensians, but the work of St. Dominic and others progressed slowly. In 1207 the papal legate was assassinated, presumably with the connivance of the Count, so Innocent authorised the use of force, and in 1209 began the crusade under the leadership of Simon de Montfort. There was terrible destruction and a war verging on genocide, but finally the Albigensians were to be wiped out.

A similar pattern emerged in the East. Innocent was devoted to the idea of the restoration of the Holy Places and, torn by internecine strife as Europe was, he manged to organise the fourth crusade. When the crusaders came to negotiate for their transport with the aged and blind Doge of Venice, Enrico Dandolo, they found a master bargainer. Not sufficiently wealthy to afford his charges, they were forced to retake Zara for the Venetians from the King of Hungary as a part-payment for their transport east. Innocent was furious,

for worse was to come: the Emperor Philip persuaded the crusaders to divert their aim to Constantinople, to restore his father-in-law, Isaac Angelus, and the Venetians were glad to agree, lusting after the control of the entrepôt of the East, which had previously been used exclusively by the Pisans and Genoese.

In 1203 Byzantium was taken, and the Emperor Isaac restored; but soon the Greeks and Latins quarrelled, as they always had done, and in the following year the crusaders took complete control, amid dreadful scenes of lust, avarice and destruction. The imperial tombs were burst open to search for jewels, and a whore was seated on the patriarchal throne in Santa Sophia. The horses that now decorate St. Mark's in Venice were a part of the weighty loot. The Empire was hacked up between the crusaders, and their leader Baldwin of Flanders elected Emperor. Innocent, disturbed, and longing for the relief of the Holy Land, was for a while quiet, but then, thinking that the schism between East and West had been at last ended 'miraculously' he gave forth his praise for this stinking triumph. He tried to convert it into a victory of the church, but the instruments were fouled.

The climax of his career came in 1215 when the fourth Lateran Council was convened, and 412 bishops pressed in with 800 abbots (one bishop died in the crush) to hear his words. Always proud of his voice, he chanted the 'Come Holy Ghost' and began the Council with a sermon. He longed for the purification and reformation of the Church, and most of the canons of the Council were directed to this end. They were well-designed legislation and were to have a remarkably good effect throughout Europe. His other hope was for a proper Crusade, and to this he gave a substantial part of his own fortune, and offered to go in person.

To this Council came Dominic, to ask permission to set up his new order of friars. Innocent readily gave ear to all plans for reformation: he had already gently regularised the *Humiliati* of Milan, and received the strange visitations of Francis. Though a great potentate who thought much on power, he could well recognise simple faith, and the needs of simple people. He had written with his own hand the privilege for Francis's Poor Clares, and though he thought poverty too high an aspiration (and he was right) he wished the new movements nothing but good, and gave them powerful support.

But he was worn out, and in the middle of negotiations for the shipping for his crusade, he died, in July 1216. Like William the Conqueror, his dead body was stripped of its rich vestments by greedy servants, and he had achieved his own poverty.

There is a biography by L. E. Binns: *Innocent III* (Methuen, London, 1931).

James I, King of Scots

James I, King of Scots, was born in 1394 to Robert III and Annabella, the reigning king and queen. The time was not propitious, for his father was too ill to rule in person, and his elder brother, the Duke of Rothesay was a disgrace to the family, and brought great harm to his country by his evil life. The government was in the hands of Robert's brother, the Duke of Albany, and it was not long before Albany and Douglas arrested Rothesay, and carried him through the pouring rain to Falkland castle, where he either died of the resulting fever, or was starved to death. A chronicler comments somewhat unfairly 'hee eete his owne fingres. . . . the which was against goddes lawe and manes lawe.' The episode was dramatically portrayed by Scott in the *Fair Maid of Perth*.

Albany was probably wise to 'restrain' Rothesay, but he was ambitious, and the King had now only one son left; so he decided to send James secretly to the court of France, an old friend to Scotland, where he could be brought up in safety, and educated in refinement. So in February, 1406, the boy was taken to the Bass Rock,

there to await a Dantziger ship with its load of merchandise to take him on to France.

James recalled in his poem *The Kingis Quair* how he got up early, and was rushed on board ship to catch the wind, whilst all those who must stay behind shouted 'fare well' and 'St. John protect you.' But the winds were too high, and 'Upon the waves weltering to and fro' the ship was forced nearer and nearer inshore, until some Yarmouth pirates were able to capture them, and bring the rich prize to the King.

Henry IV was delighted, and laughingly told the boy that he knew French well enough to teach him in England. After taking the throne from Richard II Henry had had trouble in Wales, in the north of England, and with France and Scotland, and now Providence had placed in his hands the key to parts at the least of all these situations.

He was placed in the Tower, where he found already resident Albany's son Murdoch, and Owen Glyn Dŵr's son Gruffydd. Their conditions varied: once, when quartered in Nottingham to avoid a London plague, James was taken to a tournament by Henry, along with his own children. However, back in the Tower again, Murdoch had to complain that his mattress was rotting and falling to pieces, and the sheets hadn't been changed in two years!

It was the lack of liberty that hurt most though, and James shows in his poem how hardly he took it. He asks himself what he has done to deserve this loss of liberty,

'Since everyone has thereof sufficiency
That I behold, and I a creature
Put from all this—hard is my luck.
The bird, the beast, the fish also in the sea,
They live in freedom each one in his kind;
And I a man, and lacketh liberty;'

Harder still to see the kindly but feckless Murdoch released to go back to Scotland to establish the Albany dynasty in his place, while he was left to be used as a pawn. A substantial number of Scotsmen had gone to France to serve against the English, so now Henry V brought their King over, still a prisoner but treated with hypocritical pretence as an ally, so that all Scotsmen who did not immediately lay down their arms could be treated as rebels, and hung when caught.

At the end of his reign, Henry V began negotiations for the return of James, for he was desperate for money, and a good ransom could be charged. When Henry died, the negotiations were continued by the council of the infant King Henry VI, and the Beaufort party were determined to profit from the business by marrying James to their niece, the lady Joan. Strangely enough, politics coincided with love at first sight, and we have the King's description of the event.

The Kingis Quair, a rather self-conscious imitation of Chaucer, describes how miserable James was, and the delirious change that he underwent on sight of Joan Beaufort. He tells us how the long nights were a misery to him, a man of action who had been forced to do nothing for eighteen years, whilst his country descended ever deeper into the mire of chaos. So he would rise early, to see how the sun

'with the tickling of his heat and light,
The tender flowers opened them and spread;'
He went, this special morning, just as usual, to his window to see the world go by, for even though he could not take part in its joys 'to look it did me good.' He was at Windsor, and beneath his tower prison was a garden, neatly fenced in, with herb plots at each corner, with Junipers growing in the middle, and many trees and winding alleys hedged in by hawthorns; and on the trees sat singing nightingales. They hopped about so sprightly and looked so fresh and chipper that James grew broody once more and began to ask himself what they had to sing about.

Then he saw her, coming into the garden with two women attendants,

'The fairest or the freshest young flower
That ever I saw, methought, before that hour.'
The blood all rushed to his heart,
And in my head I drew right hastily,

And at once I lent it forth again,
to see whether she was real.

She was real, beautiful, and magnificently dressed in an attractively loose garment
that for rudeness to speak thereof I dread. She was smothered in jewels—pearls, emeralds, rubies and 'quaking spangles bright as gold.' and she sportingly wore a chaplet of red, white and blue plumes. She was in fact dressed to kill, the Beauforts were very rich, and very determined; but James was as impressed with the woman as he was with her jewels.

They were married in February 1424 in what is now Southwark cathedral, and, the ransom having been arranged, progressed north to their kingdom.

James now began to prove, in these few years that were left to him, what energy and ability had been pent up in those long years of imprisonment. Murdoch had proved a most incapable successor to his father, and the restless barons had had a fine time, completly unchecked by law and order. Now James waded into the situation, arresting malefactors and bringing them to justice, declaring his aim to 'make the key keep the castle and the bracken bush the cow.' He made many good laws, and saw that they were kept—the alehouses in his reign closed promptly at 9 o'clock. He encouraged the movement for church reform, and (interestingly enough, like Owen Glyn Dŵr) tried to introduce the English system of Parliaments into his country.

The barons hated him, and longed for their old ways, so that when James' dim old uncle, the Earl of Atholl, plotted to take the throne in 1437, he received support. The court was at Perth, and had found the castle unready to receive the King, so he was lodging for a while in the house of the Blackfriars. That February evening he was sitting loosely dressed before the fire, talking with the queen and the court ladies, when they heard the noise of the assassin's gang. Catherine Douglas rushed to bolt the door, but, finding that the great bolt had been removed, pushed her arm through the staples and let it be mangled while the paving-stones were lifted and the King dropped through to the sewer vault below.

At first the intruders were deceived, and would have gone, but a sound from below made them lift the paving stones once more. The queen tried to stop them, but was wounded in the attempt, and the highlanders dropped down. James had no weapons, but fought manfully with his bare hands. When his body was recovered, there were sixteen wounds in the breast alone.

Joachim of Flora

Joachim of Flora was born about 1132 in Calabria to a moderately wealthy Norman family. Here, in the Norman kingdom of the two Sicilies, so recently established, East met West in a peculiarly fruitful situation. Under the vigorous administration of Normans, Greeks and Arabs combined to establish for a while a civilisation which welded together the best elements of North, South and East. Yet there was tension, which gave that liveliness and spirit to the life of the Sicilies; tension that also inspired enquiry, self-examination, and at times brooding foreboding.

At the age of fifteen, Joachim had completed his education, and entered the royal administration. He was not happy here, and longed to go East on pilgrimage to explore the roots of the strange world in which he lived. His father indulged him, and financed a great party of friends and servants to make him a princely retinue.

Arrived in Constantinople, he suffered a traumatic shock, for the city was in the grip of plague, and people were dying all around in agonies. Joachim the dreamy visionary was awakened to a real apocalypse. He dismissed all his company save one friend, shaved his head, put on rough clothing, and moved on to Palestine. They fell in with a band of Saracens even poorer than themselves, and joined together, en-

joying the chance of sharing a genuine poverty. In Palestine Joachim retired to a hermitage to meditate, and when he came out of the wilderness, he too wept over the cities of the plain, doomed to destruction amidst horror such as he had seen so recently by reason of their sin.

He returned home and lived a vagrant life, not revealing his identity until his friend got into trouble for picking a fig in an orchard and needed the protection of a great name. His father had given him up for dead, and now sent him to regularise his life in a Cistercian monastery as a lay brother. He was happy to be their porter, and gained a considerable reputation as a lay preacher of power: the ordinary folk understood his simple language and homely bearing, and he knew them far better than the educated clerics.

When he came to take his vows, however, he had to give up this life, and turn his mind to the interpretation of the Scriptures. As his meditation progressed he grew more and more retired: on his election as abbot in 1178 he successfully appealed to the Pope for demotion, for the cares of the world would interfere with his real vocation, and administration was for him a waste of time.

No doubt the Pope agreed because he anticipated great things from Joachim: so holy a man (and none in all Italy had such a reputation as he did) so deeply given to contemplation, must produce writings which the Church would treasure. No one realised until long after his death that what he did produce was a time-bomb that was to rock the Church.

Joachim had had his apocalyptic vision, and it remained with him, increasing in intensity until his death. All knew that before the triumph of Christ in this world, Antichrist would come, with chaos in his wings, and the struggle between light and darkness—Armageddon would be more terrible than anyone could tell.

Joachim concentrated his mind on this, the third and last age of the world. The first age, that of the Father had been from Creation until the birth of Christ, and

Joachim calculated that this had lasted 1260 years. The second age, that of the Son was then almost over, and in 1260 would begin the last age of the world—that of the Holy Spirit.

Who will stand in this last day—who will carry the burden of the struggle with Antichrist? Joachim's answer was plain—it would be the monks.

In 1202, Joachim died, loved and respected throughout Italy. He left behind him a number of rather obscure writings, and a great tradition. This was to be taken up by the heirs of St. Francis, the spiritual Franciscans who wished to keep his rule, and rejected the worldly changes imposed upon them by authority. In Joachim they found *their* authority: the enemy, the worldly Church, was Antichrist, and they, who wished genuinely to follow Francis in the imitation of Christ, were the true monks of God. This path led them to a tragic end, being repressed by the Church, with all its instruments of terror, as heretics.

There is a biography by Henry Bett: *Joachim of Flora* (Methuen, London, 1931). See also Marjorie Reeves, *The Influence of Prophecy in The Later Middle Ages* (Oxford Univ. Press, London, 1970).

Joan of Arc

Joan of Arc was born about the year 1412 in Domrémy, in the Duchy of Lorraine. She was brought up to ordinary peasant occupations—sewing and spinning, hoeing and shepherding. She was extremely pious, going often to mass and confession (which her neighbours attended but once a year) and for this she was teased by the boys. She did take part in simple country festivals—dancing and singing at the local fairies' tree, close to the magic well, but such elementary superstition was harmless. So close was she to the Church that she would scold the churchwarden if he forgot to ring for compline, and she missed it by his negligence.

At the age of thirteen she began to hear voices—angels and saints who were to speak with her regularly for the rest of her life, directing her every act. She was shy of speaking about these revelations, though we know from her that they spoke with very fine accents, no trace of dialect, and gave her wise advice. She was to go to the castle of Vaucouleurs, which Robert de Baudricourt kept for the Dauphin, and get him to send her to the Dauphin. She would then beat back the English, and lead her prince to his coronation at Rheims.

Large claims for a small girl, and no wonder de Baudricourt told her uncle (who had brought her to the castle in 1428) to take her home and cuff her soundly into better sense. The situation was too bad to indulge in nonsense. The Treaty of Troyes had acknowledged Henry V's claims to the French crown, and by its terms the Dauphin had no rights, and Henry VI was true king of both countries. The power of Burgundy backed English domination, and the Dauphin cowered behind the Loire. In October 1428 the English came in force to take the bridgehead of Orleans that would give them access to the Dauphin, and allow them to defeat him at their leisure.

Early in 1429 Joan was back in Vaucouleurs, where her fiery persuasions now brought the citizens to her side—one recalled how she was as anxious to get to the Dauphin as a pregnant woman is for the birth. They brought her sensible men's clothes to replace her red dress, some arms and a horse. After all, a prophecy had said that a maid from Lorraine would right French wrongs. The Duke of Lorraine called her to see him, and gave her his safe-conduct. Even de Baudricourt was at last won over (having set a priest to see whether she was devil-inspired first) and gave her a sword and an escort of eight men to go to her prince.

The journey to Chinon took eleven days, through hostile territory. Joan was fearless, and some of her escort, who had set out with every intention of raping her on the way, became devoted admirers. She was a woman of great appeal (a problem for her to the end of her life), and the Duke of Alençon recalled later how, on campaign, he had frequently seen her prepare for bed and admired the beauty of her breasts. But he felt no desire, for the Maid, beautiful as she was, inspired in her followers a high devotion to her cause, that sublimated their feelings for her as a woman.

She arrived at Chinon on 23 February 1429 and saw the Dauphin, who sent her off to Poitiers to be examined by his clerks and wise men. She gaily told them 'Me, I neither know A nor B' and they reported that, though simple and uneducated, she was doctrinally sound. It was worth a try, for the Dauphin's cause looked as black as could be, so he gave her arms, and she set about framing her force. Her rules were hard: all soldiers to go to confession, no swearing (even the Duke of Alençon was reproved for this) or looting, and no camp-followers. She showed all the pity of a woman for French and English dead and wounded alike. Yet it was plain from the start that, simpleton and pious as she was, she was a masterly soldier: she carried her lance well, performed all the soldierly tasks to perfection, and was a fine planner and organiser; she showed particular skill in the disposition of artillery. But above all it was her dash and courage and her power to inspire those who followed with those same qualities that marked her out. She just would not wait—once at Orleans she woke in the middle of the night, leapt into her armour so fast that she was on horseback before her squire was ready, and he had to hand her lance to her through the first floor window as she dashed off to take the first bastion. She was truly an inspired soldier.

Joan entered Orleans on 29 April, and soon inspired the defendants to action; but before she led them to the attack on the English bastions, she made an elaborate circuit of the defences, calling out to the English to go home, for she had no desire to hurt them. Not unnaturally the 'God-dams' called back rather rudely, and Joan was deeply upset. She was easily wounded

by abuse, and the foul-mouthed d'Estivet was to be her biggest burden in the period of her trial.

When the assault on the greatest bastion came Joan was there first with the scaling-ladder, but she was wounded by an arrow in the chest and, a little girl once more, she was carried to the dressing station for anointment with olive oil and lard, weeping and afraid. But on 8 May the English raised the siege, and all was joy— every citizen turned out for a massive torchlight parade of victory.

She now persuaded the Dauphin that they must fight their way through to Rheims for his coronation: ordinary oil had cured her wounds, but at Rheims lay the holy oil that would turn the Dauphin into a king by divine right. In high spirits she sent a small token present to the widow of Bertrand du Guesclin, who had rescued France's fortunes in the last century, just as she was doing now. She was convinced all would fly before the justice of the cause —'were they hung from the clouds we should beat them.' But she had no silly notions about herself; to a nervous Franciscan who came to treat with her from beleaguered Troyes, carefully making the sign of the cross and splashing holy water, she said, 'Approach boldly, I shall not fly away.' When people brought her things to touch, she laughed at the thought of it.

On 17 July the Dauphin was crowned, and Joan gave way to floods of tears. Having mastered her womanly emotions, she now begged him to make for Paris, which lay an easy target before him. But the Dauphin was tired, tired of battles, and probably tired of Joan. Whilst the military faction at court were pushing on with the war, Charles VII, the Victorious as he liked to call himself, was busy trying to come to humiliatingly poor terms with Burgundy. Whilst Joan was fighting on the outskirts of Paris (where she was wounded in the thigh), the King plotted, and soon withdrew his forces, disbanding them on 21 September. Alençon was sent home, whilst Joan was kept at court, idle and depressed.

The King ennobled her family (which she did not desire—all she had ever asked was that her town should be freed from taxation), and felt that he had done quite enough.

In April 1430 Henry VI arrived in France for his coronation, and the Duke of Burgundy showed off his true colours by laying siege to Compiègne. Joan secretly made off to aid the garrison; in a sortie she found herself cut off from retreat, and was forced to surrender to the Burgundians. There was great rejoicing in the English and Burgundian camps, and Charles VII and his advisers did not show themselves to be very upset.

Joan made two attempts at escape, the second one by leaping from a high tower, where she sustained injuries. She was being badly treated, she knew her fate, and she was bitterly upset by the news from Compiègne.

The English purchased Joan from the Burgundians, and she was moved to Rouen in December 1430, where a show trial was to be staged at English expense. Pierre Cauchon, Bishop of Beauvais, a scholar and diplomat devoted to the English cause, was to mastermind the whole proceeding: Joan was to be proved a witch and a heretic, and burnt. The court was skilfully packed and, before its proceedings began, inconvenient evidence in Joan's favour was carefully suppressed.

Throughout the five months in interrogation Joan showed a remarkable spirit. Her peasant guile and common sense combined with her humour and self-control to defeat the elaborate ruses to break her. Battered with questions from all sides, she kept her head: 'Fine lords, ask one at a time . . .'; when asked whether angels appeared to her naked, she smartly enquired whether her judges were accusing God of parsimony; when the notary was caught out suppressing parts of the evidence, she told him to beware not to do it again, or she would pull his ears.

But as the time wore on the pressure told on the maid, kept in chains in an English dungeon, with no recourse to the comforts of the Church, and threatened with the bestial assaults of her keepers, and their foul insults—the court thought the latter terribly funny, and nicknamed d'Estivet 'Benedicite' the well-spoken. Also the English, particularly the Earls of Warwick and Stafford, were losing patience.

On 24 May Joan was brought to the place of justice, with the open threat of death hammered home by a cunning preacher. All was confusion—the large and noisy crowd preventing proper proceedings. Joan tried to appeal to the Pope, but was refused. Then she was presented with a form of abjuration, which she must sign or burn. She only half understood its implications, believing that all she was promising was to resume female dress. When the English insisted she sign with a cross, she obeyed with a laugh. For she could well write her name, and when she had had a command in the French army she had only put a cross to those letters that were meant to deceive—her friends would then know not to believe their contents. It was a great joke.

But no joke when she found she was back in chains for life in an English prison, with the guards pressing round to abuse her, and no access to the Church. No joke when she realised what the abjuration really meant—a declaration that all she had done was the work of the Devil. She very deliberately resumed male dress, and now Cauchon had her—she was a relapsed heretic, her only fate possible the fire.

On 30 May 800 guards attended her to the market place, after she had at last had the privilege of confession and received the holy sacrament. After a long sermon she began to make her last prayers, but was rudely hustled to the stake at once. An Englishman made a cross of sticks, which she thrust in her dress so that she should see it as she burnt. The flames rose up and she cried loudly six times 'Jesus.' Many wept—even Englishmen; but the force of law was present, and the fire was raked back from her charred body to show clearly she was dead and had not escaped. Then it was built up once more, and finally the ashes were scattered in the Seine. Cauchon and his cronies received their reward, and letters of protection from the English king, lest anyone should try to do them harm for what they had done.

In 1449 Charles VII at last took Rouen, where all the trial records were, and early the following year an enquiry was mounted into the legality of the condemnation. In 1455 the Pope gave his gracious permission to Joan's mother (now a pensioner kept by a grateful city of Orleans) and her two brothers to demand a process of rehabilitation. The immensely thorough enquiry lasted a year, and all who were still alive who had contact with the maid were examined. In 1456 her condemnation was reversed. In 1920 she was canonised.

See the admirable documentary biography by Régine Pernoud: *Joan of Arc* (Macdonald, London, 1964; Stein and Day, New York, 1966).

John of England

Matthew Paris wrote, 'Foul as it is, hell itself is defiled by the presence of King John', and this pretty well sums up John's reputation—until 1944, that is. For in that year Professor Galbraith demonstrated, in a lecture, to an astonished world that the chief chronicle source for the reign of John was utterly unreliable. Since then bad King John has been getting better and better, until now he is nearly well again, and a leading scholar in the field has seriously warned us that the twentieth century could well create its own John myth.

A man who can create so many myths (or rather have them created about him) is clearly outstanding in some way, but the myths hide the truth. Plainly the chroniclers who invented stories about him after his death can tell us little, and we should not take too much notice of people who condemned John for carrying out his father's (and his brother's officials') policies and administrative routines, nor indeed those who condemned him because of the bitter troubles that happened in the succeeding reign, troubles which were by no means entirely of John's making. Recent historians have turned to the administrative records of his reign, and found there a very different picture; but still the lingering doubts remain—were these records the results of John's skill and application or of those of his able staff?

John was a paunchy little man, five feet five inches tall, with erect head, staring eyes, flaring nostrils and thick lips set in a cruel pout, as his splendid monument at Worcester shows. He had the tempestuous nature of all his family, and a driving demoniac energy: Professor Barlow says that 'he prowled around his kingdom', which is an evocative phrase, but it would be truer to say that he raced around it. He was fastidious about his person—taking more baths than several other medieval kings put together, and owning the ultimate in luxury (for that time), a dressing-gown. He loved good food and drink, and gambled a great deal (though he usually lost—the results of his typical impatience and carelessness are recorded on his expense rolls); above all things he loved women. Some say his 'elopement' was the cause of his loss of Normandy. He was generous to the poor (for instance, he remitted to them the penalties of the forest law), and to his servants; at the least he went through the motions of being a Christian king. He was extortionate, though if one considers the terrific increase in his outgoings (a mercenary soldier cost him 200 per cent more in wages than he would have done in Henry II's day) one can understand some of his actions in this field. He was deeply concerned about justice, took care to attend to court business, and listened to supplicants with sympathy; he had also an urgent desire for peace in the land, saying that his peace was to be observed 'even if we have granted it to a dog.' But for all that, he had two totally unredeemable vices: he was suspicious, and enjoyed a cloak-and-dagger atmosphere; and he was not trusted—simply he did not inspire trust in his subjects. Dr. Warren says of him with some justice that if he had lived in the twentieth century he would have adored to run a secret police.

He was born at Oxford on Christmas Eve 1167. He was oblated for a monk at the abbey of Fontevrault at the age of one year, but was back at court by the time he was six—plainly he had no vocation, but he probably picked up at this early stage his fastidiousness and his passion for books: his library followed him wherever he went. He was his father's favourite, but he turned against the old man when his chance came, as he did against Richard (who had been very generous to his brother) when the latter was in captivity in 1193. The episode was a miserable failure, but it possibly sowed the seeds of distrust for John in England, where they began to sprout luxuriantly in 1199 when Richard died and John came to the throne.

Immediately the challenge came: Philip Augustus, the wily King of France, was backing John's nephew Prince Arthur (son of John's elder brother Geoffrey) as a contender for the throne, and England's French possessions fell prey to civil war. John found grave difficulty in dealing with the situation, for a number of reasons, but in 1202 he made the remarkable coup of capturing Arthur by force-marching his troops eighty miles in forty-eight hours; but then his prosecution of the war became listless, and he lost much sympathy by his brutal murder of Arthur whilst in a drunken rage. By 1204 Normandy was lost.

The loss of Normandy seemed to wake John up, and he now deployed his every energy in building up the coastal defences of Britain, now faced with an enemy the other side of the Channel, instead of just more of her own territory. The navy was built up, and the army, and John poured a quarter of his annual revenue into defence. But he could not persuade the baronage to

support him in a counterstroke to regain Normandy: the barons of the north country had never owned land in Normandy, and did not see why they should pay to regain southerners' castles for them. These 'Northerners' as they called themselves, were a hive of discontent, and more was to be heard from them. Meanwhile John sailed angrily about in the Channel, cursing ineffectually.

Other troubles were to come first, however. In 1205 the Archbishop of Canterbury, Hubert Walter, died, and John assumed that he would have the choice of the new archbishop. However Pope Innocent III was no man to support secular control over church appointments, and supported the right of the monks of Canterbury to select their own archbishop. For two years the storms blew between England and Rome, then Stephen Langton was appointed. Meanwhile John had driven the monks into exile and appropriated the revenues of the archdiocese. He had fallen out also with his half-brother, Geoffrey Archbishop of York, over tax-collection, and he too fled abroad while John collected his revenues. Four bishops joined in his flight—tension was growing to snapping point. In 1208 the Pope put an Interdict on England (which in effect meant the clergy went on strike, or, in certain cases and areas, worked to rule). John began negotiations with Innocent, but, finding that he demanded unconditional surrender, stopped them and took over all ecclesiastical properties and incomes. He did leave the clergy sufficient to live, though barely; but he still gained a large increment to his usual finances. In November 1209 the Pope took the final step of excommunicating the King, which, in that it made him an outlaw in Christendom, did far more damage than the Interdict.

John used his enlarged treasury to restore order in Scotland, Ireland and Wales, and to rebuild the old alliance with Otto IV of Germany and the Count of Flanders against Philip Augustus. He planned a two-pronged attack on France, to take place in 1212. But that year turned out an unlucky one for John, for the barons again refused to serve abroad, and the army he had was needed to put down a revolt in Wales; the Pope was threatening to demote him, and Philip Augustus was planning a massive invasion of England. John had to give in in one direction, for the pressure was much too great: he chose the Pope, and wisely so. He agreed to return to the *status quo* in the matter of church property and establishment, and to pay compensation; he further resigned his kingdom into the hands of the Pope, to receive it back in return for his homage and an annual tribute of 1,000 marks (a mark being two-thirds of a pound).

He had won a notable ally in Innocent III, who supported him faithfully throughout his troubles. Then his fleet, his own creation, had the good luck to find the French fleet at anchor and unprotected, destroyed it, and so made a French invasion impossible. On the crest of a wave, John determined to put his two-pronged invasion plan into action, but once more the northern barons refused to play, and he set off to punish them. Stephen Langton had arrived on the scene by now, and managed to persuade John not to provoke the barons further.

In 1214 he finally managed to put his long cherished plan into action, but the two attacks were not properly co-ordinated; Otto was defeated at Bouvines, and John was deserted by his Poitevin knights.

In 1215 John faced a baronage in turmoil: they could point to the failure of his expensive schemes, he ascribed his failure to their total lack of support. The situation could not be more tense. John's nervousness can be seen in his taking of the cross, a blatant attempt to reinforce his alliance with the papacy. In April the Northerners met at Stamford; they were by now a mixture of northerners and southerners—the name was now merely a nickname—but by and large they were the younger element in the kingdom, roughnecks out for a spree. They moved south and were let into London by a faction (just as Wat Tyler's followers were to be on a later occasion), and received the expected encouragement from Philip Augustus in the form of siege engines brought over by one Eustace, a renegade monk turned pirate.

John offered arbitration, but the barons turned it down, and while he put his faith in an appeal to Rome, Stephen Langton, in co-operation with William Marshal and other more stable and sensible barons, were working on the Northerners' demands to incorporate them into a general charter, which would not only govern feudal relationships, but would also lay down a more general pattern of legality in government. On 15 June John fixed his seal to the draft of Magna Carta, and on 19 June attested copies were sent to all parts of the kingdom.

The King did his part thoroughly (though for how long he would have continued is another matter), but the barons continued to distrust him. They remained in arms, organising tournaments as their excuse, saying that the prize would be 'a bear a certain lady would send.' This was civil war, and John took to it with a fiendish glee. He reduced the north and the east, and was about to mop up the remainder of the opposition in London when Philip Augustus' son Louis landed in force to help the barons (May 1216). John had been riding hard for months, and was sick with dysentery after a bout of over-eating; whilst crossing the Wash, the whole of his baggage-train was lost. At Neward Castle on 18 October, he died, desiring to be buried near his patron saint Wulfstan in Worcester Cathedral.

He was by no means a good man, and his energies could well have been put to a better use, but in a different situation he might well have made a great king. His constant failure was discipline, over himself first, and others second. John reminds me of nothing so much as the type of person who is brilliant in many ways, and has many gifts, but leaves after two terms 'not suited to teaching in this type of school.'

There is an excellent biography by W. L. Warren: *King John* (Eyre and Spottiswoode, London, 1961; Norton, New York, 1961).

John of Salisbury

John of Salisbury (whose real name was Little) was born at Old Sarum between the years 1115 and 1120. He was proud of his birthplace, and fond of his family: his brother Richard shared a part of his exile and one of the first acts of his return to England was to rush home to see his aged mother.

He was sent to the parish priest to learn his psalter at an early age, but the schoolmaster was a bad choice: he practised crystal-gazing, divination, and the raising of spirits, and used his scholars as magician's assistants. John did not have the touch, and was soon excluded from the seances.

About 1136 he went to France to begin twelve years of university study; his first teacher was Abelard, but he was to have many others, for these were the days of real student power, when the searcher for knowledge transferred himself at will from master to master as he grew dissatisfied with one, or heard of a better. John supported himself by coaching rich pupils, and so gained many well-endowed friends, most notably Peter of Celle, a relation of the counts of Champagne.

In 1148 he joined the papal court, and gained considerable experience of its ways, besides valuable contacts. In 1154, wishing to return to England he used a reference given him by St. Bernard to gain the post of secretary to Theobald, Archbishop of Canterbury.

He was sent on three trips to the papal court in the next four years, for his close friendship with Adrian IV made him the ideal envoy. On his first trip he persuaded the English Pope to invest the English King with Ireland, and was immensely proud of this dramatic coup; but Henry II was not as grateful as he might have been— he distrusted the cosmopolitan scholar whose influence owed nothing to himself. As far as Henry was concerned, it was other people who should be grateful to *him*, and John was made well aware of the cloud of royal displeasure.

So he turned to writing his two substantial treatises—the *Polycratus* and the *Metalogicon*. They were written expressly for a close personal friend he had met in the household of Archbishop Theobald— Thomas Becket, now Chancellor of England. The fact that Becket had the King's ear was certainly very much in John of Salisbury's mind, but he was honourable enough to back up his patron when conditions had radically altered.

John's writings are humane and witty, very English in their distrust of extremes and indeed in their blatant patriotism. He was scholarly, as one might expect, and he had mopped up all the classical learning and literature that was then available. He had an eye for humour—fond of Plautus and Petronius, of whom he possessed a fuller text than we have today. He knew the Fathers well, and was immersed in the Scriptures. Patently, he had a deep respect for law, both canon and civil. But philosophy was for him the greatest joy, and his anger knows no bounds when he thinks of the dry pedantic logic-choppers of Paris who prostitute a noble art.

He is above all frank—he denounces nonsense about omens and portents, witchcraft and astrology with gusto. Where he finds evil and corruption, he opens it up, even if it be at the centre of Christendom, at the papal court; but he does it with a gentle mocking wit, worthy of his beloved Petronius. The banquet he attended at Canossa, for example, from nine a.m. to twelve p.m., with delicacies from as far apart as Babylon to Barbary, or his classic description of the canvasser for ecclesiastical preferment, who has a biblical defence against invalidation: if he is of low birth, so was St. Peter; if under age so were

Jeremiah and St. John the Baptist, when first set apart for their ministry . . . if unlearned, so were the Apostles; if married, so were the bishops St. Paul said were to be chosen . . . if he is of a slow tongue like Moses, an Aaron can be found to speak for him . . . St. Peter's assault on the high priest's servant will serve as an excuse for violence . . . the tax-gathering of St. Matthew for entanglement in public affairs. If he is accused of gluttony and wine-bibbing, so was Our Lord, etc. etc.

In 1161 Becket was made archbishop, and John was one of the party sent to fetch the pallium for him from the Pope. He was also engaged to write the life of Anselm, on whom Thomas was to model his archepiscopate, and whom he hoped to get canonised.

As the quarrel with Henry II grew worse, so did the position of Becket's friends. In 1164 John and his brother Richard were forced into exile, John going eventually to stay with his old friend Peter of Celle, now abbot of Rheims. He occupied himself with the writing of his *Historia Pontificalis*, memoirs of his experiences at the papal court. Money for expenses was raised by writing letters for others—John was the finest letter-writer of his day—and soliciting gifts from rich friends and former students.

John worked hard in Becket's cause, but it was clear to him that the situation could only be resolved by a sensible diplomatic reconciliation. Becket's behaviour was outrageous, and although John remained consistently loyal, he flung all the weight of his charming persuasiveness into the scale of moderation.

For a while he could do much in restraining his headstrong master, but once they were returned to England there was nothing he could do to prevent the fatal course. On that last day of Becket's life, when the knights had gone from the refectory to arm themselves, and the Archbishop had followed them shouting angrily to the door, John once more reproved him. To stir up the wrath of wicked men was

folly, he said, and told Thomas firmly that he was the only man in the room who wished for death.

After the murder John worked devotedly for the canonization of his master, and for the restoration of good order in the Church. In 1176 Louis VII of France, an old friend, invited him to become bishop of Chartres, and he went there, to work as hard as ever, fearless and humane. He died in 1180, leaving twenty-four of his books to the cathedral library, a part only of a great library. He had had many books, but even more friends, and to those who still read him the quality of mind and heart that attracted them is very plain.

There is a biography by C. C. J. Webb: *John of Salisbury* (Methuen, London, 1932).

John Scotus Erigena

John Scotus Erigena was born in Ireland in the first years of the ninth century. We know nothing of his early years, but by 847 he had reached eminence in France as head of the palace school of Charles the Bald. These two seem to have got on very well together, though their backgrounds were wildly different: one night at dinner Charles, finding John's Irish table manners hard to bear, said, 'How far is a Scot from a sot?' (for at that time, annoyingly enough, the inhabitants of Ireland were called Scots). John quickly replied, 'The length of a table,' a joke even a court jester would have feared to make.

France was at this time beginning to show some national feeling, and had adopted as patron saint St. Denis, who was (incorrectly) associated with Dionysius the Areopagite, converted by St. Paul in Athens, who was (incorrectly) supposed to have written a number of Neoplatonic treatises. The Popes had happily compounded this chain of error by sending copies of these Greek works to be stored in the royal abbey of St. Denis near Paris. Unfortunately, until the arrival of John, nobody could read them, so he set to work to prepare a translation.

John was a competent Greek scholar—a matter for wonder in that age, but the Irish schools had preserved some of the best of the learning of the ancient world; he was also a man of startling intellectual capacity, and a mind not suited to accept the trammels of convention. When asked by Hincmar of Rheims to denounce the heresies of the Saxon Gottschalk, he produced, in 851, a thunderclap of a book *On Predestination* which denied the real existence of evil, and declared that God does not desire the death of any soul. The Church was astonished, and condemned the book for heresy in 855, trying to laugh the whole thing off by calling it 'Scot's porridge.'

John appeared to take no notice, and joined in the controversy over the Eucharist raised by the teachings of Paschasius Radbertus. He calmly declared that the Host was merely a memorial of God's true body. The Pope was naturally alarmed: not only was the man producing dangerous ideas, but in promoting the works of Dionysius he was extolling everything Greek; at this time the western Church was in high controversy with the Byzantines.

Whilst Charles the Bald lived, his friend John was safe from persecution, and he went on to produce his great work of a quarter of a million words *On the Division of Nature*.

However, in 877 Charles died, and John took advantage of an invitation from King Alfred to go to England to teach at Malmesbury. Some years later, or so the chronicler William of Malmesbury would have us believe, his pupils stabbed him to death with their iron pens, 'because he tried to make them think.' A fitting end to a stormy career.

See H. Bett: *Johannes Scotus Erigena* (Cambridge Univ. Press, 1925; Russell, New York, 1925 reprint 1964).

Julian the Apostate

Edward Gibbon wrote of Julian the Apostate that he 'deserved the empire of the world'; he was certainly one of the most attractive characters to rule the Roman Empire. He was born in 332, son of the younger brother of the Emperor Constantine. Spared because of his extreme youth the massacres that were a common part of the struggle for power after the death of his uncle, Julian was none the less an orphan by the age of five, and grew up in an atmosphere of hatred and mistrust.

His teacher was a Gothic eunuch who had a passionate love for the great classics of Greek literature, and Julian made an ideal pupil, for he had a fine intellect and a sensitive nature. He was impressionable, emotional and enthusiastic, whilst being capable of turning his talents and energies to new tasks with thoroughness and devotion. He was compounded of two significant parts: by nature he was puritanical, ascetic and hard-working, yet he also longed to restore and respect all the beautiful and moving elements of a civilisation that was doomed.

He toured Asia Minor in search of scholars who would teach him Greek philosophy, and the mysteries of the old Gods. This was not easy, for Christianity was triumphant over paganism, and with official support was settling to the task of uprooting it for ever. However Julian managed to find what he wanted in the Greek communities of Asia Minor and at the University of Athens. He attended secret spiritualistic seances, and was inducted into Mithraic rights—standing in a covered pit whilst a bull was slaughtered above him so that he could bathe in its blood. At the age of twenty he had completely rejected Christianity, though he would not be able to do this publicly for some years to come.

During this period of study Julian was repeatedly interned by the suspicious Emperor Constantius, although he showed himself loyal. In 355, when very serious trouble threatened the security of Gaul, Constantius decided to test Julian's fidelity and worth by sending him there as his commander, and making him his heir. The results were truly amazing, for the dreamy philosophical youth now showed himself to be a commander of genius: within two years he had restored the province to peace, re-established the frontier of the Rhine, and gone far towards rebuilding the defences along that frontier. He even found time to attack the immense problems of corruption in the administration, and to set up an equitable taxation scheme.

Success was a dangerous thing for a general or for any member of the royal family in the Byzantine Empire. The eunuchs continually whispered suspicion into the ears of the Emperor, and plotted Julian's downfall. At one time they would say that he was plotting to declare himself Emperor, at another they more subtly suggested that he had had such a brilliant success that the Rhine would need no more attention for years—so why not withdraw his troops? They were needed desperately at the other end of the Empire to face the Persian threat.

But Julian's troops would not go—at least not without their general, and they concentrated round him in his headquarters in Paris, and despite his declared opposition, acclaimed him as Emperor. He could not but accede to their demand, took this opportunity of announcing that, as his uncle had fought under the sign of the cross to establish Christianity, he would have the support of the old Gods in his battle to re-establish paganism.

Julian recognised Constantius as the 'elder Augustus', and deferred to him in many respects, but such a position was untenable, and in 361 the two Emperors moved their armies to a confrontation. Luckily for Julian, Constantius died *en route*, so that he succeeded to the universal rule without a battle. He set to work at once: the temples were opened, and public sacrifices were resumed; the Christians were not persecuted, but the privileges that had been showered upon them since the time of Constantine were withdrawn. He crusaded for a new view of paganism, as morally better, founded on more ancient precedent and more beautiful than the Christian religion. He wrote constantly, and debated endlessly. Seeing the Jews to have suffered for their religion as much as paganism had suffered from Christianity, he gave them favours, and planned to rebuild the Temple in Jerusalem. It was to be the last bit of official support the race and creed had in sixteen hundred years.

The administration was thoroughly purged of sycophants and trouble-mongers, and corruption was pounced upon wherever it was found. Morality, good sense and philosophy were to replace all that in the new pagan empire.

To prove to the world that his system was right, and that the favour of the Gods really meant something, Julian set out to invade Persia in 363. His army stretched out ten miles behind him, and, feeling a new Alexander, he struck straight for the capital, Ctesiphon. The Persians scorched the earth, and constantly harried the Romans, but they moved on. Then, in a little skirmish, Julian was struck through the body with a lance, and shortly after died, aged 32.

The invasion collapsed, and with it Julian's great dream. Christianity triumphed more effectively than ever before, and heaped revilement on the name of Julian. But his successor carried his body back, to be buried in Tarsus, whence came the Christian who resembled him most.

See Gore Vidal's brilliant and faithful fictional reconstruction: *Julian* (Heinemann, London, 1964; Little, Brown and Co., Boston, 1964).

Justinian

The reign of Justinian is distinguished for the historian by possessing two official sources, both from the hand of Procopius, and contradicting each other in every respect: the one is base flattery of the worst order, the other, the *Secret History*, written for only the most private circulation, is the most vindictive indictment of foulness ever written. Justinian was a most interesting example of the split-personality: of peasant birth, his manners were those of a sultan; ascetic and hard-working, a puritan of sorts, he loved to distraction and elevated to his own dignity a music-hall star and prostitute; served by a succession of great men whose loyalty was only outshone by their genius, he nevertheless was subject to paranoic suspicion.

Born about 478 in Macedonia, Justinian came to Byzantium in the service of his illiterate uncle Justin, commander-in-chief of the Guard. In a troubled succession Justin was elevated to the Empire in the year 518, and he urgently required the services of his educated and hard-working nephew. In effect, Justinian ruled in his name, and had sufficient power not to want to supplant him; he was, after all, enjoying a fine training for his chosen task in life, and in 527, on Justin's death, he became one of the most truly worthy successors the Empire had known.

The early years were hard. Justinian worked devotedly to heal the schism in the Church (for he loved the intricacies of theology as well as recognising the political importance of religion), but despite grand gestures, like closing the pagan university of Athens, he was to achieve little in this complex field.

His marriage with Theodora cannot have helped matters. She was beautiful, intelligent and witty, but she was also the daughter of the circus bear-leader, and had led a life full of licence, vice and crime. As Empress she was undeniably brave, and often gave good counsel, but she was abominably haughty, and vicious to her enemies. Her party affiliation in Constantinople—which was divided into the circus crowds supporting either the Blues or the Greens—encouraged a dangerous rivalry in the city that was soon to lead to riot.

For extortion, not government, ruled the roost, and barely one-third of the taxes levied reached the imperial coffers, quite apart from the 'extras' that lined the pockets of Justinian's ministers Tribonian and John of Capadocia. Justinian had inherited a treasure of 320,000 pounds of gold, but

that had all gone, and the screw ground down even harder on the poor of the city. In 532 they rose in revolt—the Nika riot—and for three days the mob ruled Constantinople, whilst the Emperor, losing heart, prepared his getaway. But Theodora refused to go: 'Those who have worn the crown should not survive its fall. I will never live to see the day when I shall no longer be saluted as Empress . . . As for me, I stay . . . The purple is a good winding sheet.' Justinian could not go without her, so his general Belisarius was sent with his mercenaries against the Hippodrome mob, and soon its arena was flooding with the blood of 40,000 revolutionaries.

Justinian was a surprisingly resilient character, and soon he was busy rebuilding the burnt-out ruins, forgetting the empty treasury. The incredible beauty of Hagia Sophia that rose in the next few years at his command was to cost him as much as he had inherited. He loved building—it was to be one of the great passions of his life.

Another was order, and one thing that desperately needed ordering was the law of Rome. A vast accumulation of legislation and commentary, so huge in extent that no one man could read it, and so disorganised and antiquated that no one could apply it, the laws which should have been the central organising principle of the state lay helpless. In 528 Justinian set up a commission of ten to produce a new code, removing obsolete legislation, and standardising the remainder. In 530 he gave his minister Tribonian the task of organising another commission to produce an amalgam of all that was best in the many commentaries. In three years of unremitting labour, the commission reduced the literature from 3,000,000 lines to 150,000, producing the *Pandects*, or *Digest*. No one henceforward was to be allowed to write commentaries upon this. At the same time a course-book for law students, the *Institutes*, was issued. The new legislation that Justinian produced at this time, and later, the *Novellae*, were to complete the

Corpus Juris Civilis, undoubtedly Justinian's greatest and most constructive contribution to his own Empire, and indeed to the world in times to come.

His Empire was dear to his heart, but much of it was ruled over by barbarian Goths and Vandals who, apart from their crime of being neither Greek nor Roman, were actively persecuting the orthodox Church, or putting forward an heretical interpretation of the Christian faith. So a great reconquest was planned, in much the same spirit as the later Crusades against the Muslims in Spain and the Near East.

The ever present Persian menace was dampened down by a number of forays and campaigns, and in 532 Justinian and Chrosoes, King of Persia, signed an 'eternal peace' (it was to last barely eight years), leaving Belisarius to move his highly mobile cavalry, the cataphracts, against the Vandals in North Africa. Belisarius was a wonderful general, as fine a soldier as Robert Graves describes in his faithful reconstruction. But until Totila came upon the scene, his opponents were a very unworthy lot. Belisarius had no need to bother about them, for his real opponents lay at home—the whispering suspicion of the eunuchs, the envy and fear of his monarchs, and, worst of all, the lascivious nature of his wife, in whom he foolishly trusted. As Sampson's strength ebbed away with the cutting of his hair, so Belisarius was to fade from a world conqueror to a powerless and weak-willed man on discovery of his wife's treachery and baseness. But with Gibbon we must say, 'the name of Belisarius can never die', for, in an age when the road to greatness lay through dishonour, he kept faith with the unworthy, and remained true to standards few could comprehend.

He swept through Africa with ease, and by 536 was busy liberating southern Italy. He was delayed in Rome by Witigis, who brought 150,000 men to invest him there, but was facing no serious problems to the liberation of the whole of Italy, when Justinian interfered. Disturbed by Belisarius's success, and fearing that he would declare himself Emperor of the West, he sent his eunuch Narses with an army to work against Belisarius and keep a close eye on him.

Though Belisarius deserved the Emperor's absolute trust, one can see why Justinian worried. The Goths were shortly to negotiate with Belisarius and offer to have him as their king in place of Witigis. Narses was an excellent choice for a general to replace Belisarius: a tiny, effeminate creature, who had spent his early years serving in the women's quarters, he had a strange passion for warfare. He read all the books on the subject, and studied the campaigns of Belisarius with a scholar's eye, and he was to show later on that he could turn all these studies to account when given a completely independent command.

Before he could complete the subjugation of the Goths, Belisarius was needed on the eastern frontier. The Slavs invaded constantly, on two occasions reaching the walls of Constantinople itself, and the 'eternal peace' was breaking down on the Persian frontier. Belisarius must have hated leaving a job unfinished, and Italy was left denuded of troops for Narses had been recalled as well as himself. This gave the Goths a breathing space, and they at last found the great leader they needed.

Totila was a brilliant general, a man of great courage and appeal, and he knew how to rule. He very soon had the native population on his side, and by 543 he had so far undone Belisarius's work in Italy as to be entering Naples. In the following year Belisarius was ordered back, but with no money, and hardly any troops, Justinian's optimism coming to the fore again. He re-took Rome, but could do little more than sit there and remain on the defensive. In 548 he demanded to be recalled, and went to Byzantium to face his family difficulties, and the revilements of his ungrateful sovereigns, who confiscated every bit of his personal property.

Meanwhile Totila swept on, until there were but four Byzantine cities left in Italy.

He even began raiding across the Adriatic —not only was he retaking Justinian's winnings, but now he was threatening his original capital. Narses, with the ear of the Emperor, got the necessary troops and money and moved into Italy. He defeated Totila, who died in the action, and repelled a massive Frankish invasion. By 555 Italy was at peace once more, and in the Empire.

An expedition against Spain was also mounted, and though only the south-eastern part was taken, this was to remain Byzantine for 70 years. Elsewhere barbarian kings rushed to acknowledge Justinian's overlordship, for he played the diplomatic game with great skill: bribing one barbarian to attack another; loading favours on yet another in return for troops; and using his impressive ceremonial resources to persuade ignorant and unsophisticated rulers that he was truly lord of all.

But it all cost incalculable sums, and within the Empire the horrors of war had destroyed agriculture, depopulated the towns, and inhibited trade. The soldiers were quickly followed by tax-gatherers, and no-one could tell which were the worst. Attempts were made at re-organisation and restoration: probably the first industrial espionage agents carried silk-worm eggs from China to Byzantium in a hollow walking stick. Building went on everywhere, for it was Justinan's passion: new aqueducts brought water, and round the borders of the restored empire a vast chain of castles grew. Yet this cost money too, and by degrees, all possibility of a recovery of the economy of a potentially rich area died out.

Justinian was a tireless worker—he often made do with one hour's sleep a night. Gibbon compares him well with Philip II who also thought he could support a doomed empire by fanatical attention to detail, trying to take the weight of the whole administration on his own Olympian shoulders. He was, above all, an optimist—he had to be, to believe that what he did, and even more, what he was trying to do, was possible. He died in 565, as a contemporary tells us 'after having filled the whole world with noise and troubles...'

There is a biography by P. N. Ure: *Justinian* (Penguin, Harmondsworth, 1951). Penguin have also published Procopius' *Secret History* (trs. G. A. Williamson, Penguin, Harmondsworth, 1966), and Robert Graves' historical novel *Count Belisarius* (Penguin, Harmondsworth, 1968).

Stephen Langton

We know little of the early years of Stephen Langton. He was probably born in Lincolnshire, but our first real knowledge of him is as a student and later as a teacher at the university of Paris, where he was to remain until 1206. He studied under the great Peter Lombard, and became a fine biblical scholar, and a skilled lecturer and preacher.

His surviving works show something of his character in this period. He was gentle and kindly, though he had a sharp sense of humour; above all he had great moral courage, and a strong love for his homeland. His lectures often contain little English anecdotes—on one occasion he quotes an anti-Latinist who thought the cry of 'Wassail' a hundred times more cheerful than 'esto hilaris'. Perhaps his nicest aside is a comment on Samuel's going to Bethlehem for the anointing of David on the pretext that he wants to make sacrifice, Langton says, 'This was not Samuel's primary object in coming; it is an unusual way of speaking. Your reply to the question, "why do you come to the schools?" would not be: "I come to sit down and look at the walls"; and yet that is what you do.' (Beryl Smalley, *The Study of the Bible in the Middle Ages*, 2nd edn., (Oxford Univ. Press, London), 1952, pp. 200, 118 and 207.)

In 1206 Pope Innocent III summoned Langton to a cardinalate at Rome. The see of Canterbury was vacant, and King John (*q.v.*) was pushing hard to get the election of his own nominee against the wishes of the monks. So instead, with papal support, they elected Langton. Plainly he was entering on a difficult heritage, but he cannot have known how difficult it was to prove. John was implacable, and the Pope proclaimed the Interdict in March 1208.

Langton was to spend another five years kicking his heels in Rome, but at no stage do we find him impatient or angry. In January 1213 the Pope pronounced sentence of deposition on John, and at last he began to give way. By July Langton was back in his homeland again, bringing absolution for the King.

He plunged straight into the whirlpool of politics, giving a firm moral lead to those who wanted a settlement. He was committed in any case, for he had to get back the church property John had confiscated in the period of the Interdict, he had to oppose royal interference in canonical elections, and last, but by no means least, he had to moderate the dangerous papal control over the ecclesiastical and secular affairs of England that had resulted from John's over-hasty donation of his kingdom to the Pope. A certain amount of control from Rome was accepted by every Christian, but it was too far away for rigid control to be exercised; a certain degree of independence was necessary for the health of the Church, and vital for that of the state.

Langton placed before the angry but ignorant barons the coronation charter of liberties of Henry I as an example of the sort of settlement they required. He moderated the more dangerous demands, and pointed to the necessity of a settlement that was universal, and not just in favour of the barons themselves. Some of the hotheads were not amenable to control, but by and large the barons listened to the wise counsel of Langton and William Marshal (*q.v.*). On the other hand, Langton went to considerable trouble to moderate John's wrath, and point out to him the value of some kind of settlement.

Yet after Magna Carta had been sealed there were still tremendous problems. Some of the barons felt it was not enough, and prepared for war, and John was not used to denying himself the pleasure of revenge. He wrote to the Pope describing the Charter he had sealed in rather invidious terms, and suggesting that he had been bullied into sealing it. The Pope, as overlord of the kingdom, was furious at such goings-on behind his back, and immediately sent excommunications thundering against all who had worked against his honest vassal (now as a crusader-to-be even more in the Pope's favour).

Langton refused to excommunicate the people he had been working with for the past two years, and to ditch the hard-won settlement before it had had a chance to work. He was suspended by the Pope and ordered to come to Rome to explain himself, and there he was detained until 1218, when both Innocent III and John were dead, and he was allowed to return home. He now had to aid those who were guiding the steps of the young King Henry III, and in 1222 he held the great Church Council at Oseney where he promulgated his 'Constitutions' for the Church in England, establishing a new tone and higher standards in the ministrations of bishops and clergy.

In 1223 he had to take a part in the struggle against those 'wild men' who felt that the good government instituted by the Great Charter was a lot of inhibiting nonsense. In particular a leading baron, Fawks de Breauté seemed to feel that, because he served the crown on occasions, he should not be under the restraints of the law. He had married a wife against her will, and Langton protected her from him, and pressed the many other charges that stood against him. He finally succeeded in getting the reissue of the Great Charter in 1225 by making the grant of clerical taxation for the war in Poitou conditional upon this.

He died in 1228 at Slindon, in Sussex. He had worked for good order in his country without ceasing, and had brought gentle commonsense to work in a situation ripe for civil war; he had not lost his temper.

There is a biography by F. M. Powicke: *Stephen Langton* (Merlin Press, London, 1964; Barnes and Noble, New York, 1927).

Louis IX (St. Louis)

Louis IX was twelve years old when in 1226 he came to rule the kingdom his grandfather Philip Augustus (*q.v.*) had so enlarged and well established. He had been carefully brought up by his pious and domineering mother Blanche of Castille, and was to bend to her will to the day of her death in 1252. This was a strange relationship, for Louis worshipped his mother, and she was a sound political adviser, but he feared her as well, and she was capable of hurting him. She hated his Queen, the vivacious Margaret of Provence, and did all in her power to keep them apart: Joinville relates how once at Pontoise the King was lodged in apartments over those of the Queen, and slipped down to sleep with her; but first he ordered the servants to beat the dogs so that they should howl him a warning if they saw the Queen Mother approaching, so that he could escape back to his own room before she should arrive (Bohn edn., *Chronicles of the Crusades*, 1848, p. 504.)

The barons of France hated the rule of Blanche of Castille, and called her 'the she-wolf' (though to be fair this was a name commonly given to medieval Queens.) In 1226 they rebelled, but had few leaders and were easily divided. Typical among them was Thibaut of Champagne, who veered from rebellion towards writing poems of courtly love to Blanche, and only retired from the fray after Louis' more energetic brother Robert of Artois had poured ordure over him at court.

In 1241 there was further trouble, in Poitou. Isabella, Queen mother of England had married her old love, Hugh de Lusignan, but she longed for her former high estate, and when Louis made Hugh swear fealty to his brother Alphonse of Poitiers she flew into a rage, and declared her intention to deprive Hugh of his conjugal rights if he did not rebel. Henry III (who had already had a fiasco in France when he joined in the previous rebellion of 1230) came with a small force, and Aragon and Toulouse joined in. Toulouse had been deeply scarred by the Albigensian crusade, and the terrors of the inquisition that followed, and had good cause for rebellion. But Henry fled on sight of the French royal army, and Isabella, after a shot at getting her way by poisoning, retired to plague the nuns of Fontevrault with her company. The rebellion died down, and an active policy of re-settlement quietened Toulouse.

Louis' kingdom was calm again, indeed it had never seriously been threatened, for the heritage of strict control from Philip Augustus remained firm. The King could now get on with the business of saving the souls of his people. For Louis his kingdom was like his family: each night at bed time he would instruct his own children in moral tales from history, and hear their prayers, and he tried to treat the nation so. He organised sermons with one hand and public charity with the other; he built great churches and abbeys, notably the crowning glory of the *Sainte Chapelle*, which Henry III envied so greatly. Blasphemy was punished severely, as was heresy: Louis welcomed the Inquisition, and did not flinch when hundreds went to the flames—he was purging the land of sin.

Publicly he set a fine example of scrupulous honesty, and a total lack of covetousness; his people and his neighbours learnt to trust him absolutely; his currency was so good it drove out bad, and so the nation throve. In matters of justice he was open to all, wherever he was, and absolutely even-handed—his brothers, the barons, even churchmen had to submit to the rule of law. He suppressed blood feuds and trial by battle, and, lest injustices should flourish in corners of the land that were inaccessible to him, he sent round yearly a group of Franciscans to enquire into abuses. The people loved him for the peace, order and justice he gave, and when the shepherds of north-east France heard of his captivity in 1251, they set out in a rabble, intent on rescuing their lord, not realising how long and hard the way would be.

At last the King was able to go on Crusade, leaving his kingdom safe in the hands of his respected mother. Joinville describes well that moment of setting out, with the captains yelling to the stevedores, 'Is your work done? Are we ready?' and the ships moving out of the specially built harbour town of Aigues Mortes, with all the clergy standing in the castles singing 'Come Holy Ghost'. They were soon very sick, and seeing things, so they all processed three times round the mast (Joinville being supported under the arms) and hoped for the best.

They made a base in Cyprus, and in May 1249 the expedition set off for Egypt. It was terribly ill co-ordinated, and lacked all planning or advance information; after the initial joy of capturing Damietta, they had a six months wait for re-inforcements and for the flooding Nile to subside. Idleness provoked indiscipline, and even the puritan King had to wink at the fact that his own attendants were running brothels within a stone's throw of his tent.

In December they began at last the march on Cairo, but Robert of Artois foolishly involved the army in the battle of Mansūrah, which quickly turned into a terrible rout. In full retreat the army fell into chaos, which sickness and the harrying tactics of the Saracens made into very hell, described movingly by de Joinville who experienced it all. Captured by the exultant Saracens, the King and his army were brutally treated, with many of the soldiers murdered out of hand. Louis was threatened with torture to try to make him give up some of the Latins' Syrian castles as the price of his release. When he refused the Patriarch of Jerusalem was tortured before him, with ropes pulled tighter and tighter round his wrists.

In the end Louis agreed to give up Damietta and pay a massive ransom for himself and his army and, as the remnants of his force filtered up into Palestine and freedom, they were subjected to jeers: 'You have landed in Egypt thinking to take possession of it. You have imagined that it was only peopled with cowards! you who are a drum filled with wind.' (op. cit. p. 554).

Louis spent the next four years in Palestine, restoring fortifications and miserably wondering whether to go or stay. Believing the rumours that the Mongols would join in a pincer movement to destroy the Mohammedans, he sent the Franciscan William of Rubrucque into Tartary, but received back an insulting reply.

In 1254 Louis returned to Europe, and found a fresh cause, and indeed a nobler one; for the next decade he acted as a universal peacemaker. With incredible difficulties he forged a lasting peace with England in the Treaty of Paris of 1259, but he had to pay dearly for Henry's agreement. He had already settled Flanders in 1256, and the claims of Aragon on Provence had been renounced in return for a substantial renunciation of claims by the French in 1258. Wherever there was discord in Europe, Louis was called in, because people recognised that he would act with justice and honesty, and entirely without self-interest. In 1264 he was asked to arbitrate between the English barons and their King, and gave his decision in the Mise of Amiens.

In that same year his brother Charles of Anjou, a man of cold ambition and absolute single-mindedness, had persuaded the King to allow him to accept the crown of Sicily, for Sicily would make an excellent crusader base. Louis was now desperately ill: he had suffered all his life from erysipelas, had contracted malaria, and the resultant pernicious anaemia, and had further reduced his resistance by continued hard penances. His judgement was no longer very sound. When Charles, having established his dominion in Sicily, called on him to attack Tunis, saying that the Emir was favourable to Christianity and could easily be persuaded to provide a base for operations against Egypt, Louis went, though he had to be held on his horse. The fevers of Tunis killed most of his men, and killed him in 1270.

Louis had believed passionately in his divine mission, and this had given him the strength of will to do so much, to endure such trouble. It gave an air of authority to this tall willowy ascetic, which people in that time instinctively recognised. His humble devotion to duty, his absolute honesty made him trusted by all. His piety and plain hatred of sin made him a saint (he was canonised in 1297), but a saint with a difference, for successful kingship was rarely associated with sainthood. To many he seemed regal and distant, a mother-dominated puritan, not a real man, but to de Joinville he showed himself a loving friend—even playful. One day at Acre, when all were depressed, and Joinville seemed out of favour with all, he sat at a window, his hand through the grating to feel the cool air, wondering what to do if the King gave up the Crusade; the King came up and covered his eyes with his hands, and after springing him from his mood in this way, calmly comforted him. (op. cit. p. 465.)

De Joinville's magnificent record of the crusade is also available in Everyman and Penguin editions.

Ramon Lull

Ramon Lull was born on Majorca about the year 1232. The island had only very recently been conquered by Aragon from the Moors; Ramon's father had been one of the leading men in the conquest, and had been rewarded with considerable estates. He must also have had influence, for at 14 years of age his son was made a courtier companion to the two princes of Aragon, Peter, who was ten, and James who was four.

Ramon enjoyed court life, and eagerly learnt the chivalrous manners and troubadour songs; he also learnt to forget morals and enjoy himself. Though he married when he was 25 and had a son and daughter by his wife, he was compulsively unfaithful.

When he was well into this kind of life, at the age of 30, he had a revelation that was to completely change his course. He was writing a vernacular love song—he had the tune, and now he was fitting the words to it; looking up from his paper, he had a vision of Christ on the cross. Deeply shocked, he fled to his bed to hide there. A week later he took up his pen where he had left off, and the same thing happened. Three times more he tried to finish the song, with the same inevitable results. In fear of damnation he went to confession, and set about re-moulding his life.

He was utterly unprepared for the religious life—a spiritual illiterate, with the profound desire of the converted to do something, to make a genuine contribution. He made careful provision for his wife and children, leaving practically nothing for himself, and set out on a great tour of the pilgrim-shrines of southern Europe—tasting poverty and self-denial for the first time.

Back in Spain, about the year 1264, he visited the great Dominican leader Raymond of Pennaforte. He was already thinking of devoting his life to the conversion of the Moors, amongst whom he had been brought up, and dreamed of holy martyrdom; but Raymond showed him that his effort would be useless at the moment—a missionary who knows no theology has little to offer, and when he has no languages he cannot even offer that little. So Ramon went home to Palma to study Latin, theology and philosophy, and Arabic.

At first Arabic sounded to him 'like the voices and languages of beasts', but he soon overcame his problem by purchasing a Moorish slave, who worked with him for nine years, before ending the partnership with the attempted assassination of his master. Ramon was not an easy man to work with, and it is interesting that many years later in Cyprus he was again the subject of an attempted assassination.

His powers were now great—towards the end of his period of instruction he wrote a million-word treatise in Arabic, which also shows a fine command of theology and philosophy. For the rest of his life he barely ever stopped writing, and nearly always at very great length. His English biographer mentions over two hundred and sixty works attributed to him —many immensely lengthy, and written in a diversity of languages. For he believed in the power of words, and in the power of logical argument, and his belief was passionate. Westerners needed to know about the Moslems and other non-Christian peoples if they were to be roused to the effort of converting them; he shows a fine understanding and sympathy for these people. Language-centres must be set up to train missionaries. Studies must be devoted to the finding of logical arguments which would convince the 'Gentiles' that Christianity was the one true faith. This was his message and he wrote it, time and time again, the only change in his ideas being the slow realisation that an element of force—a new Crusade beginning in Spain and forging through North Africa back to Palestine—was after all necessary, as well as the persuasive tongue of the Lullian missionary. Wherever there was a Pope, king, university, religious order, or town council even, that would give an ear to his message, he would travel there to preach. His journeys were as lengthy as his writings.

In 1274 he spent a period as a hermit on Mount Randa in Majorca, to gain the inspiration to write his great 'Art' (by which he meant 'Method') of converting the unbeliever. This book, which he believed to be absolutely fool-proof, was to be the basis of all his teaching in later life.

In 1275 he rejoined Prince James, who was perhaps his closest friend, at Montpellier. Whilst there the King died, and divided his lands between Peter and James— the latter becoming King of Majorca.

James immediately set up a college at Miramar for teaching oriental languages and the 'Art' to Franciscan friars preparing for the mission field.

Once the college was established, Ramon set out on a tour of Europe, trying to persuade others to set up similar institutions.

In 1282 he was back with King James, and wrote (amongst many other things) his two most famous works—the semi-autobiographical romance *Blanquerna*, and the *Book of the Lover and the Beloved*, a poetic evocation of the love a man might offer to God. In these he showed his mastery of style, and allowed some of his earliest influences as a courtly poet to come to the surface in the fanatical poor preacher with a long white beard. The welding of these two characters makes him an outstanding character in the literary history of late medieval Europe.

Rome, Paris university, Montpellier— his travels in these years that follow are amazing: one wonders how he found time to whirl round Europe so fast, never mind the endless writing, lecturing, and attendance at the courts of the mighty, waiting hours for an interview to put his case to the same procession of frosty negative faces.

In 1290 he prepared to turn his back on all this, and go at last on mission to Tunis. But at Genoa, with the boat ready to sail, he had a breakdown. Wearied with the constant refusal of support, very much alone, he was possessed by fear—suppose he proved a failure after all his talk? He let the boat sail without him and fell violently ill, horror-struck to find what he had done.

It is impossible to psychoanalyse at this distance, but some of the roots of Ramon's nervous collapse seem clear. He had placed great reliance in the Dominican order: his own son had been christened after the saint, and his Spanish nationalism made him look on Dominic with special fervour; his first spiritual director after his conversion had been a Dominican. Yet they had rejected him and scorned his 'Art' and ideas, even though he had attended three of their chapters-general to speak on missionary work. The people who had fostered him most were the Franciscans— the rival order.

His illness was in some senses a crisis of identities, but much more a search for a parent—and a foster-parent at that. As he grew more sick his talk was all of joining one or the other orders of friars. Then, suddenly hearing of a boat in the harbour bound for Tunis, he insisted on being put aboard, and as the vessel stood out to sea his illness fell away from him—he was an individual once more.

The visit was short and sharp: he preached openly, saying that if anyone could disprove his arguments he would become a Moslem. He was arrested and put on a ship for Genoa, but returned on shore almost immediately to preach. A riot ensued, and Ramon now realised he was doing no good, so he slipped back on board once more and returned to Italy.

His experiences had lent more urgency to his message and in 1294 he addressed the Pope once more. He pointed out that the Mongol Empire was three times the size of Christendom, and if the Mongols were converted to any other religion than Christianity, disaster would surely ensue.

There was no reply, and Ramon wandered around looking for support with an increasing sense of disillusion. He at last joined the Franciscans, the third order of laymen, which must have helped him somewhat. Naples, Montpellier, Paris, Barcelona, Majorca, Cyprus all saw him in the next few years, and in each place he wrote—philosophy, astronomy, mathematics, polemical works, allegory and poetry all flowed from his pen—but to little effect.

So in 1305 he decided on the ultimate, and wrote his *Last Book*: 'I can do no more than I have already done. I find none who will lend me in any way effective help. So I set down my arguments in final form and order, once and for all, that, on the Day of Judgement I may stand guiltless and unafraid before the company of Heaven— nay before God himself.'

He could not help himself, though, for however deep his disillusion went, his spirit still urged him on, to see the Pope, to visit the university of Paris once more. At Paris he attended a class given by the new young star of the philosophical world Duns Scotus (*q.v.*), who thought at first the students were playing a trick on him when he saw this poor old man with his long white beard amongst them.

He now set off for Barbary once more— this time to Bugia, one hundred miles east of Algiers. He managed to debate with learned Moslems before the Kadi, but proved too good to be allowed to go on. After a lengthy and at times very uncomfortable imprisonment and two near lynchings, he was banished with the threat of execution if he should ever return. On the way home he was shipwrecked.

All this at 75 years of age must have told on his constitution, but he continued as before, writing and appealing to great men for aid, and collecting large sums of money for a projected crusade. In 1309 he was back in Paris again, lecturing to vast crowds, and vigorously opposing Averroism, a doctrine that elevated philosophy to the level of theology, and one that had caused Thomas Aquinas and many others considerable trouble.

In 1311 he attended the General Council of the Church at Vienna, and wrote there of what he seemed to others—a fantastic hopeless dreamer. Nevertheless, he at last won his way—it was decided at Vienna to set up five oriental language institutes and to tithe for six years to finance a new Crusade.

The old man returned to Majorca filled with enthusiasm—in the course of the next two years he wrote forty books and pamphlets, and campaigned to get the support of secular lords in Spain and Sicily for his movement.

Then he returned to Barbary, and in Tunis had some spectacular successes— mainly because he carried letters recommendatory from the King of Aragon, whose trade the Moors valued. But then, flinging caution to the winds, he returned to Bugia and preached openly there. The Moors stoned him, and some Genoese sailors rescued the body—dead or very nearly so—to carry back to Ramon's home in Palma.

When the Turkish invasion shook Europe in the next century, people remembered the message of Ramon Lull, and the people who had put him off with 'In God's good time'.

There is a biography by E. Allison Peers: *Ramon Lull: A Biography, with Bibliography* (B. Franklin, New York, 1969).

Macbeth

In the ninth century the Scots of Argyle under the leadership of Kenneth MacAlpin took advantage of the Viking invasions to overrun the Picts of central and northern Scotland. In the next two centuries the Kingdom of Scotland pushed down into Strathclyde and Cumbria, leaving only two remote states intractable beyond the Grampians—Caithness of the Norsemen, and Moray, home of the nationalist Celts of that time.

Now Macbeth was son to the sub-King of Moray, and his mother was a sister of King Malcolm II of Scotland. When he married the widow Gruoch (who brought with her a son called Lulach the Fatuous, who was to carry on resistance for a while after his step-father's death), his claim for the throne was complete, for Gruoch, by the traditions of the house of MacAlpin, should have been Malcolm II's heir, instead of his grandson Duncan who came to the throne in 1034.

Macbeth served Duncan as a general for six uneasy years before killing him somewhere in Moray in 1040, and taking the throne. He had considerable support, for his claim was sound, and he represented the old Celtic element of Scotland, rather than the Argyle Scots who favoured an alliance with Saxon England. Malcolm Canmore, Duncan's son, fled to the English court after his father's murder, and married first a Norse woman, and then Margaret, great-niece to Edward the Confessor.

Macbeth ruled wisely, and in 1050 took time off to go on pilgrimage to Rome, perhaps to make amends for his crime. It did no good however, for in 1054 he was defeated by Siward, Danish Earl of Northumbria, who installed Malcolm on the throne. Three years later Malcolm defeated Macbeth at Lumphanan in Aberdeenshire, but had the good grace to bury him on Iona, traditional resting-place of kings.

For a discussion of Shakespeare's sources, see R. J. Adam, 'The real Macbeth,' *History Today*, vol. vii, no. 6, June, 1957, pp. 381–387.

William Marshal

The office of Marshal to the king was a hereditary perquisite of a middling Wiltshire family. The duties were various, but mainly they consisted of acting as second-in-command to the constable of the royal household, maintaining order in the palace and guarding it, looking after the stables, keeping the rolls of those who performed their military service, and checking the accounts of various household and state departments.

From this family came William Marshal, whose biography was written by his squire John of Earley[1] so providing us with one of the deepest and most fascinating insights into the life of a great baron of the late twelfth and early thirteenth centuries.

His father, John Marshal, whom the *Gesta Stephani* rather unkindly describes as 'a limb of hell and the root of all evil' was a man who loved warfare, and played the dangerous game of politics with great success.[2] At first he supported Stephen (*q.v.*)

[1] An unknown poet composed the biography, but depended for his materials on the reminiscences of the squire who was in continuous service with William from 1188 to his death in 1219.
[2] At a late stage in his career he was instrumental in Henry II's showdown with Thomas Becket at the council of Northampton.

but, when he began to realise the failings of the King and the potentialities of Matilda's party, he changed sides. Almost immediately he proved by a consummate act of bravery and hardihood, that he was worth having: escorting Matilda to safety in his castle of Ludgershall, John found that the party was going dangerously slowly because Matilda was riding side-saddle, so he persuaded her to ride astride, and stopped behind to delay the pursuers at Wherwell. His force was soon overpowered by the numbers of the enemy, and John took refuge with one of his knights in the Abbey. The opposing party promptly set fire to the church, and John and his knight had to take cover in the tower (John threatening to kill his knight if he made any move to surrender.) As the lead of the roof began to melt and drop on the two soldiers, putting out one of John's eyes, the enemy moved off, convinced that they were dead. They escaped, in a terrible state, but triumphant, to John's castle.

He plainly expected his children to be as tough as himself, as an incident of the year 1152, when William was about six, will show. King Stephen went to besiege Newbury Castle, which Matilda had given John to defend; the castellan, realising that provisions and the garrison were both too low to stand a long siege, asked for a truce to inform his master. This was normal practice, for if the castellan were not at once relieved, he could then surrender without being held to have let his master down. Now John had not sufficient troops to relieve the castle, so he asked Stephen to extend the truce whilst he, in turn, informed his mistress, and agreed to give William as a hostage, promising not to provision and garrison the castle during

the truce. This he promptly did, and when he received word from Stephen that the child would be hung if he did not at once surrender the castle, he cheerfully replied that he had hammer and anvils to forge a better child than William.

The child was taken out for execution, but at the last moment Stephen relented with that soft heart that was his undoing, and though his officers presented such enticing plans as catapulting William over the castle walls with a siege engine, he would not give in. Later on he grew attached to the child, and one day when William was playing an elementary form of conkers with the King (using plantains), the child saw a servant of his mother, the lady Sibile (sister of the Earl of Salisbury), peeping in to check up on his safety. He cried out a greeting, and the servant had to run for his life. The child did not know what dangers he was running, but it was a good and early training for his future career.

When he was thirteen William was sent to serve in the retinue of his father's cousin, the chamberlain of Normandy. This was his apprenticeship in knighthood, and was to last eight years. As a squire he would learn by experience all the skills of a knight, and the elaborate code of honour that went with it. After he had been knighted in 1167, he began to go round the tournaments to make his name, and earn a living by the spoils. He was eager for the fray, so eager in fact that in his earliest tournaments he concentrated too much on the fighting, and forgot to take the plunder. He had to be warned by elder and wiser knights of the dangerous folly of such quixotic behaviour—a good warhorse captured from an unseated opponent could fetch £40.[1] Even so, his heart was

---

[1] The cost of a warhorse in the early fourteenth century has been noted as roughly equivalent to the cost of a light tank in 1939 (N. Denholm-Young *History and Heraldry* (Oxford Univ. Press 1965) p. 20). Albertus Magnus has a splendid description of a war horse:

'They rejoice in the music of war and are roused by the clash of arms. They leap and break their way through the host by biting and kicking. Sometimes they love their lords so dearly that if they lose them they starve and pine even to death. Sometimes, in grief, they shed tears.'

(*Lib. xxii de animalibus*, tract. ii, cap. 42, qu. H. Johnstone, *Edward of Carnarvon* (Manchester Univ. Press, 1946) p. 76).

really set upon fame, and he recalled in old age the pride he experienced as a youngster when, having retired to the refuge (a hut regarded as neutral territory in a tournament) to fix his helmet, which an unlucky blow had turned on his head, he overheard two knights outside commenting on how well he was fighting.

He was, however, only the second son of a middling baron, and he could not live off honour; so it must have been wonderful news for him when in 1170 he heard of his appointment as captain of the guard and military tutor to King Henry II's heir, the fifteen-year-old Henry, already crowned in his father's lifetime in (as it turned out) a fruitless attempt to ensure the succession. In 1173 it fell to his lot to make the young King a knight.

Henry seems to have had a good sense of humour, for in 1176 when the two were cantering back into town after a tournament, William managed to bag another knight, and led him reined behind, with the King following. A low-hanging water spout swept the knight off his horse, but Henry kept what he had seen to himself, and the laugh was definitely on William when they got home to find he was leading a horse, but no knight to ransom.

Tournaments were so frequent at that time that a real enthusiast could attend one a fortnight, and William and the King must have attained a record number of attendances. This was the equivalent of hunting to the nineteenth century country gentleman, though much more rugged. In ten months William and a colleague captured one hundred and three knights, and risked death on each occasion: one memory William kept of these days was having to receive the prize as hero of the day kneeling with his head on an anvil whilst a smith tried to prize off his battered helm. Another memory he retained was arriving too early for a fight, and dancing with the ladies who had come to watch—in full armour!

Then came trouble—William's enemies began to spread rumours that he was the lover of Henry's wife, and seeing that the suspicion could not fail to mar their relationship, William cut out on his own. He was immediately inundated with tempting offers from great lords who wanted to engage his services—three times he was offered £500 a year and more, but he turned them down and went instead on pilgrimage to Cologne.

He was soon recalled to service with the young King in 1183, but it was only to see him die of a fever. At the last William promised that he would carry out Henry's vow to go on crusade, and having buried his master, he carried out his promise.

He came home in 1187 to take his place as an esteemed servant of the King, and to marry the second richest heiress in England, who brought him the Earldom of Pembroke, and extensive lands in England, Wales and Ireland. He served Henry II in his final bitter years and once, when he was covering the king's retreat, he put the fear of God into Prince Richard who was leading the pursuit. The Lionheart cried out, 'By the legs of God, Marshal, do not kill me', and William killed his horse for him instead.

Such conduct was dangerous, but when Richard came to the throne he showed the Marshal that he respected him for it, and when he went on crusade he made William one of the four associate justiciars appointed to help William de Longchamp, who had the care of the kingdom. This was excellent training in administration and justice, which was to stand William in good stead later when he had to bear responsibilities far greater that those with which a simple soldier can deal.

It also gave him lessons in how to deal with the immensely difficult Prince John, who, fearing (with some justice) that Richard intended to leave the kingdom to his nephew Arthur of Brittany, had to consolidate his position whilst his brother was away. When he heard that Richard had been captured on his way home and was being held to an incredibly stiff ransom, John's ambitions became boundless, and the Marshal had, added to his normal duties, the double problem of keeping the prince in check and raising a vast sum of money.

Richard returned to find in William a wise counsellor now as well as an incomparable soldier, and he used him well; but in 1199 he died, and William worked with skill and energy for the smooth accession of John. This King was to bring him worse problems than ever he had known.

For the next seven years William had to watch John losing Normandy to the Marshal's old friend Philip Augustus, knowing there was nothing to be done about it. Instead of knightly virtues, treachery was now the order of the day, and when he taxed the French King with using traitors, he had only this for reply: '. . . it is now a matter of business. They are like torches that one throws into the latrine when one is done with them.'

Attempting to rescue something out of the chaos of the loss of Normandy, William undertook the negotiations with France to make peace, and find a formula by which the English barons might retain their lands in France. What he found instead was the implacable suspicion of John who, fearing that William was going over to the French side, confiscated all his castles and official positions, and took his two eldest sons as hostages.

So William spent the next five years in Ireland, looking after his vast estates and interests there far away from John, but unfortunately, in an area in which John took an especial interest. Every move William made was countered by the royal officials, and active hostilities soon commenced. However, William had the better and more faithful knights and, despite the royal offensives, he tended to win, so in 1208 a truce was made.

Soon afterwards William received on his lands William de Briouse, whom John regarded as a bitter enemy, and so the quarrel flared up again. Finally the sixty-six-year-old knight had to come to court and offer to fight an ordeal by battle to prove his faith. No one dared to take up the challenge, though a winning contestant would have rocketed into favour with the King.

But by the year 1212 John was in serious trouble, and was to learn where his true friends lay. William swung the baronage of Ireland into support for the crown, helped to organise the vital *rapprochement* with the Pope, and prepared to gather the King's friends together and put his castles in order in readiness for the inevitable struggle. A great moderating force was Stephen Langton, the Archbishop of Canterbury, who was to be associated with William throughout the struggle, persuading John to accede to those demands of the barons which he had helped to formulate.

In 1216 William was back in the saddle as commander-in-chief of the royal forces opposing the barons and their ally the Dauphin and his French troops. All was well between the Marshal and the King who had so badly misjudged him, and now John tried to make amends. But the years of suspicion and discord still told: when he gave William the castle of Dunamase, he was upset that his justiciar failed to hand it over—he had forgotten an arrangement he had made secretly with the justiciar that William was to have nothing, whatever documents he produced, without a secret handshake (holding each other's thumbs) being given.

Now as John lay dying in Newark Castle, with half his kingdom in enemy hands, and a nine-year old child as his successor, he realised the worth of the man he had hounded so long, and urged all present to commit the kingdom into the care of the Marshal after his death.

William was an old man, the treasury was empty, discord reigned, and the position seemed hopeless—he wept and begged to be excused; but John of Earley, his squire, pointed out what honour there was to be won, and changed his mind for him in a flash. 'It goes so straight to my heart that if all should abandon the King except me do you know what I would do? I would carry him on my shoulders, now here, now there, from isle to isle, from land to land, and I would never fail him, even if I were forced to beg my bread.'

Filled with a sense of the glory of his task, the regent now raided the rich stores of jewels and clothing accumulated by the royal house 'against a rainy day' to pay the soldiers he so desperately needed. He sent out showers of letters of protection to the enemy barons, tempting them to change sides. Gradually he built up his powers for the decisive blow, at Lincoln in May 1217.

There William led the charge, with the wily Bishop of Winchester who found a way in, and fought up and down the streets of Lincoln with many a shout of 'Ça! Dieu aide au Maréchal!' Finally they reached the open space in front of the cathedral where William personally captured the French commander and received three massive blows which left permanent dents in his helmet. The worthy Dame Nicola, who had kept the castle for so long for the King against enormous odds, was at last relieved, and the war was almost won.

The Marshal sped down to Dover to intercept the convoy of reinforcements coming from France, and then set about making peace. He was generous—perhaps over-generous—to French and English alike, there was no victimisation, and little recrimination. The speediest route back to peace was chosen, for England had suffered enormous damage from the civil war.

This was perhaps the worst time for William—the period of reconstruction. He knew well how to fight, but the sheer boredom and worry of administration of this kind must have borne heavily on the old man. Disputes and claims had to be settled so that both sides were satisfied, and no one would have a pretext for re-starting rebellion. Above all money was needed to oil the wheels and restore the losses of war, and the best way to make rebels is to overtax them. He even had to ban tournaments, which would obviously lead to dangerous positions being taken up once more. He must have wondered what he had come to

—the greatest fighter in Europe, and the one who loved a fight better than anything. Instead he spent his time setting up judicial commissions and trying desperately to balance the budget.

He continued hard at work until the end of February, 1219, when he was taken ill and confined to his bed in the Tower. Doctors came and went but could do nothing, and quickly all his family and his knights and retainers gathered round him for the end. He asked to be taken up river to his manor of Caversham near Reading to die, and there, he and his household went, in mid-March, followed by the young King Henry III, the papal legate, and all the highest officers of state.

He urged the King 'to be a gentleman', and told him that if he should follow the example of some evil ancestor, he hoped he would die young. He worried long and hard over who should be his successor, and found no-one who could unite all under his rule, so wisely chose the papal legate. He made his will, and worried for a moment at the lack of provision for his young son Anselm, but, remembering his own career, felt that he could make his own way. 'May God give him prowess and skill'. He remembered an unmarried daughter and made provision for her 'until God takes care of her.' He had always been a religious man, founder of monasteries, crusader, and honest knight. He called for silken cloths he had thoughtfully brought back from the Holy Land thirty years before, and gave instruction that he should be covered with them at his funeral.

He wanted to be buried as a Knight Templar, and when the master of the order came to clothe him, he said to his wife 'Belle amie, you are going to kiss me, but it will be for the last time.' Happy now that all the arrangments had been made, William could rest a little, and wait comfortably for death. He talked gently with his knights—one of them was worried that the clerks said no one could be saved who did not give back everything he had taken. William set his mind at rest—he had taken

500 knights in his lifetime, and could never restore the booty, so if he were damned there was nothing he could do about it. 'The clerks are too hard on us. They shave us too closely.' When his clerk suggested that all the rich robes in his wardrobe could be sold to win his salvation, he said 'You have not the heart of a gentleman, and I have had too much of your advice. Pentecost is at hand, and my knights ought to have their new robes. This will be the last time that I can supply them . . . .' He was a religious man—true—but he could not abide nonsense and knew his own duty.

In his last days he was very gentle to his family. One day he said to John of Earley that he had an overwhelming desire to sing, and when John urged him to do so, as it might improve his appetite, he told him it would do no such thing, people would just assume he was delirious. So they called in his daughters to sing for him, and when one sang weakly, overcome with emotion, he showed her how she should project her voice and sing with grace.

On 14 May, William suddenly called to John of Earley to open all the doors and windows and call everyone in, for death was upon him. There was such a press that the abbots of Nutley and Reading, come to absolve the Marshal and give him plenary indulgence, were barely noticed, except by the dying man, who called them to him, made confession, prayed, and then died with his eyes fixed upon the cross.

The cortège moved slowly up to London for the great state funeral, and there William's old friend Stephen Langton spoke his eulogy over the grave: 'Behold all that remains of the best knight that ever lived. You will all come to this. Each man dies on his day. We have here our mirror, you and I. Let each man say his paternoster that God may receive this Christian into His Glory and place him among His faithful vassals, as he so well deserves.'

There is a biography by Sidney Painter: *William Marshal: Knight-Errant, Baron, and Regent of England* (Johns Hopkins, Baltimore, 1933). A translated version of the medieval life has been made by Jessie Crosland: *William the Marshal* (Peter Owen, London, 1962).

Simon de Montfort

Simon de Montfort was the third son of Simon III of Montfort, the great leader of the Albigensian Crusade against the heretics in Toulouse. He was born about 1208, and was just entering his 'teens when his father was killed, crushed by a stone flung from a mangonel.

The fate of the younger son in medieval society was not a happy one, but the Montforts were very conscious of family ties and Simon's eldest brother Amaury made a generous gesture. Through his father he was heir to high position and estate in France, and through his mother he was heir to the Earldom of Leicester in England: John had followed his usual practice and given the Montfort rights and estates in his realm to the Earl of Chester; if Simon could get them back, Amaury would forgo his own claim.

It took two years of negotiation before Simon could regain from the Earl of Chester his title and a part at least of his estates, in 1231. The King, Henry III, liked him—he was young, fiery, a good soldier, but above all French. Henry preferred cultured foreigners to the philistine English who always tried to restrain him; anyway impoverished foreigners looked on him with gratitude, which was better than English barons who assumed they had a native right to everything, and failed to see the King as the bounteous liege lord of all.

Simon had reason to be grateful, but what he got in terms of income was certainly insufficient to support him as a great baron. Throughout his life he was dogged by debt, a constant reminder of his first status, whilst never gaining his full legal rights. In many ways his career can be seen as a search for sufficiency for himself and his large family—but the sufficiency was seen in royal proportions.

Early in 1238 Henry gave him his youngest sister, Eleanor, in marriage. She was the widow of William Marshal's son, and so a substantial heiress quite apart from being the King's sister: but she too was never to get her legal rights, and, if anything she was to be as litigious and demanding as he was. Though their marriage was to be tempestuous—both Simon and Eleanor were quick to flare up —they remained devoted to each other, sharing each other's labours and interests in a remarkable manner.

But the marriage had been a speedy affair—almost, so it seemed to the suspicious, a shot-gun wedding; and no one had been consulted or informed about it beforehand: in typical fashion Henry had decided on the whole thing without reference to anyone but Simon and Eleanor, and then had seen the whole thing carried out at once. People were naturally suspicious and annoyed, so Simon wisely went off to Rome until the noise had died down.

But whilst Simon was away, Henry had been thinking things over. The man was altogether too powerful, and impecunious to boot; there's no smoke without fire, and perhaps Simon had seduced Eleanor. So, in mid 1239, at the churching of the queen, Henry broke out into a violent and ribald denunciation of the Earl and Countess of Leicester. He would not be calmed, so they left the court and went over to France, Simon later going on crusade to Palestine.

In 1242 he returned to France to find Henry involved in his utterly stupid invasion of Poitou, instigated by that virago his mother Isabella, who had married the count of Poitou, and then decided that her royal eminence was not sufficiently honoured there. Simon joined the King in the fighting, but found the whole expedition so badly planned and misdirected that he told Henry to his face that he ought to be locked up.

Despite this, the King now realised he needed Simon's military support, and brought him back into favour in England. The next few years were pleasant—Simon

not only had the King's goodwill, but his debts were dealt with and he was given the magnificent residence of Kenilworth, a pair to his wife's great castle at Odiham. He cultivated friends at this time, and especially friends in the Church, for, despite his military training and career, he was a serious-minded man, and recognised virtue and worth. Bishop Grosseteste was an especial friend, and Simon sent him two of his sons to be educated, remedying some of the defects he felt in himself; later in his career he was able to dictate his will to his son Henry.

Other friends were in the two orders of friars, and these were to give him great support at the time of his rule in England. Amongst them Adam Marsh was to be a continual (and often critical) close counsellor, confessor and friend to the whole family. Typical of one of his letters to the earl is this: '. . . In the middle of all the cares weighing upon you I do not want to read you a lecture and so weary your ears that have to listen to so much business . . . Work, I beg you, to gain the salutary comfort of the divine words, and meditate often upon the Holy Scriptures. It is, I think, very necessary for you to study . . . Chapters 29, 30 and 31 of the book of Job, and everything in that same book that relates to your position, with the gentler dissertation of St. Jerome.'

He needed the book of Job when that letter arrived, during his stormy governorship of Gascony, which began in 1248. Claimed by a number of rulers who were ever ready to pounce on this rich territory, it was tied to England by its wine trade, though internal government was in the hands of factitious nobles and burghers, whose feuds tore the country in shreds.

Simon determined on settling the country and used iron methods in achieving his ends; the disorderly barons trailed to Westminster with inflated tales of woe, and as always, Henry listened. The Earl was achieving good order in the land, but surely, in doing so he was going too far and abrogating royal rule. Did he perhaps want the land for himself? Anyway, by 1252 Henry was already regretting his commission, and wanted to give Gascony to his eldest son, Edward. There was the usual scene, with Henry wildly denouncing the Earl, all decorum lost, and, so hot did they become that Simon and Henry had to be parted to prevent them from coming to blows.

Yet, within the year Gascony was in such high disorder that the King had to recall the Earl to settle things there for him. Simon could not forget the insults of that last council, and Henry would not forget the shame of having to rely on his hated brother-in-law once more, but for a while there was peace between them. The truth came out for a moment one day in 1258 when the King, overtaken by a thunderstorm whilst picnicking on his barge on the Thames took refuge in the house de Montfort was then using. The Earl twitted him with his fear of thunder, but the King flashed back in a rage that he may fear the elements, but his worst fear of all was of Earl Simon.

The Earl was now employed as a diplomatist, first going to Scotland, and then, during the years 1257–9 to France to negotiate the peace of Paris. Simon was influential with the French King, St. Louis, and used this and other levers to delay the signing of the peace until Henry should give to himself and his wife their full rights.

The position in England was fast deteriorating, however. Henry had foolishly engaged himself in a bid to make his son Edmund King of Sicily, a policy that brought no results, but shockingly depleted the treasury. He had also brought over to England his numerous Poitevin stepbrothers and sisters, children of his mother's second marriage. He loved them —but nobody else did, for they were a rapacious band, sweeping off rich heiresses and heirs, high positions in church and state, and salting away their immense fortunes in foreign banks.

The barons and the citizens of London were enraged, and in 1258 a baronial council was set up (including Simon) to monitor royal government and institute reforms based on a statement of aims called the Provisions of Oxford. They got rid of the Poitevins (who made a passing attempt at poisoning the whole baronial council) and appointed new officials—particularly at the local level of castellans and sheriffs.

The scheme foundered on personal rivalry between the Earl of Leicester and the Earl of Gloucester: Gloucester saw himself as the natural leader of the English barons, regarding de Montfort as one of the aliens against whom he fought. English xenophobia was boundless, and there is no doubt that this baronial crisis was in some senses representative of this hateful passion. The barons' treatment of aliens was markedly vicious, and in each outbreak the Jews were the first to suffer.

Early in 1261 Henry took over personal rule once more having persuaded the Pope to absolve him from his oath to the Provisions. He replaced all the baronial council's nominees, and for a time ruled supreme, whilst the quarrel between Simon and Gloucester protected him.

But in 1263 the Earl returned from France at the urgent solicitation of the barons, declaring that, as a crusader he was 'as gladly willing to die fighting among bad Christians, for the freedom of the land and Holy Church as among pagans.'

Simon quickly gained the upper hand, but his followers were young men, easily swayed, and on the royalist side the vigorous and cunning Prince Edward was coming into his own as a leader who could win men to his father's cause. At each defection the Earl raged against the faithlessness of the English, and that he and his sons would fight alone, if need be, for the 'just cause'.

Arbitration was tried—the case to be brought before the French King at Amiens in January 1264. Simon broke his leg on the way, and had to send proctors, but the decision was foredoomed—Louis would not decide against a brother king: Henry, he declared, had full rights to govern unrestrained, though he should ensure that ancient rights and charters were kept.

There were now only two courses open to Simon—it was either complete subjection to the King, or war against him. The barons chose war under de Montfort's leadership. After a series of inconclusive forays involving more trickery than generalship, Simon caught the whole royalist force by surprise at Lewes on the 14th May. Knowing that many people still believed him incapacitated by his broken leg, he mounted his standard over his wheel-chair, and tied in it two captured royalists to draw the brunt of his attack. Edward broke one section of the baronial line, but indulged in a wild pursuit of those who had taken flight, and only returned to the battle when it had been lost, his father taken prisoner, and his timid uncle Richard of Cornwall, King of the Romans, prisoner also, having been extracted with some difficulty and much ribald humour from a windmill in which he had taken refuge.

Simon now made the arrangements for government: he, his friend the Bishop of Chichester and the new young Earl of Gloucester were constituted electors of nine councillors for the king. In effect this was a polite fiction for a de Montfort protectorate. Gloucester was carefully excluded from any real power, and all key positions were entrusted to Simon's family and friends. He had learned to distrust the English during his first period as a leader of the barons, and now he had come into his own, though the eminence proved lonely.

In January 1265 a parliament was called, where the Church was well represented, but of the barons only de Montfort's friends came; in addition, and for the first time came some representatives of boroughs and knights of the shire. The barons had tried to call a meeting of knights at St. Albans in 1261 but the King had outwitted them. Though much has been made of this 'first true English parliament' there is no suggestion that it was convened on democratic lines; rather is it that the baronial

party had support from the citizens of London and other towns, and from those who appreciated the more just local government of the sheriffs and castellans appointed by the baronial council in contrast to the injustice of the king's nominees. Stubbs caught a touch of Simon's character when he called him a 'buccaneering old Gladstone'.

Young Gloucester now began to kick against Simon's overweening power, just as his father had done, and all too late de Montfort moved to placate him. But Gloucester had had time to consolidate his position in the west, and whilst Simon was at Hereford, trailing his royal prisoners wherever he went, he managed to liberate Prince Edward. A previous armed sally to get him out of Wallingford Castle had failed when its castellan had promised to deliver him by mangonel if the rescuers did not desist; now a more subtle scheme was tried. A fine horse was sent as a present, and Edward was allowed out of the city with a mounted guard to exercise and try his present out. He tried each of the guard's horses first 'for comparison'—in fact to tire them—and then mounted his own steed and swept off, easily outdistancing all pursuit.

Gloucester now effectively pinned Simon's army behind the Severn, breaking all the bridges, and destroying transports. De Montfort's son, another Simon, was slowly bringing a relief force up from the south but, resting at Kenilworth, they carelessly relaxed the guard, and Prince Edward fell on them at dawn and destroyed the force.

Simon the elder knew nothing of his son's defeat, and had at last found a crossing point for his army, which was now resting at Evesham. Prince Edward carefully prepared the attack, which took place on 4th August. All entries were to be blocked, so that de Montfort was completely surrounded. The leading divisions were to raise standards captured at Kenilworth, so that the enemy should be deluded into thinking they were the advance-guard of young Simon's relief force. When the Earl had a chance to appreciate the position he quickly realised how good Edward's tactics were—they had been learned from himself. The situation was untenable—it was flight or death. Simon chose to fight.

The slaughter began: early on the King was found and removed to safety, but Simon fought to the last, on foot when his mount was killed. When he finally went down they cut off his head and mounted it upon a lance for the victory parade. The body was horribly mutilated.

Revenge ran riot—there was no quarter or mercy. All who had taken part in the baronial rising to the end were dispossessed. They fled to the fen country, where, under the name of the Disinherited, they kept up the struggle—now for survival—for another two years. Henry foreswore all he had promised, and Eleanor and her children counted themselves lucky to escape to the Continent.

The great story ended in squalor: Simon and Guy de Montfort, fighting in Italy for Charles of Anjou, caught the son of Richard of Cornwall in church in Viterbo in 1271. They foully murdered him, a pointless revenge for a father who would never have countenanced such an act.

Eleanor died in France in 1275, still loaded with debts, but having been kindly treated by her nephew Edward. Her youngest daughter, another Eleanor, did achieve a crown—she married Llewelyn, Prince of Wales. But their daughter died, in 1337, amongst the Gilbertine nuns at Sempringham, and with her ended the line. The name lived on, however, for to the English Simon de Montfort was a saint and martyr, a stately parallel for Thomas Becket. In the first thirteen years after his death, over two hundred miracles were recorded as being the result of his saintly intervention.

See M. W. Labarge: *Simon de Montfort* (Eyre and Spottiswoode, London, 1962). See also the useful survey of the biographical literature provided by Clive Knowles in the Historical Association pamphlet g.60, 1965.

Muhammad

Muhammad, the Prophet of God was born about 570, a member of the Hashimite clan, which formed a part of the tribe which controlled Mecca. His father died shortly before his birth, and his mother when he was six years old. After that his grandfather, and then his uncle brought him up. The care and protection offered by the clan at this time meant that family loss such as Muhammad experienced was not so serious as otherwise it might have been. At a later stage in his life the clan loyalty was to protect him once more, when his enemies might well have done away with him.

Mecca at this time was a rich and powerful city. It contained the great shrine of the Ka'aba, which housed a black meteorite, and numerous idols, besides being the centre of worship of Allah and three assistant goddesses. The town grew rich in other ways as well, for it was the starting point of the trade with Syria, and through it filtered most of Arabia's imports. As a centre of idolatry and wealth it stood in sharp contrast to the poverty and purity of the desert arabs.

Muhammad appears to have engaged in trade until the age of forty. When he was twenty four he had gained the favour of a rich widow (who was herself forty years of age)—Khadija. He first directed her business interests and then married her. She was to have a deep influence on his life in many ways: a cousin of her's was a Christian, and on his journeys to Syria Muhammad had the chance of talking with other Christians, monks and hermits.

We cannot tell why he suddenly left Mecca to go to a cave and meditate at the age of forty, after a successful business career and a happy marriage, but even if we knew the facts, Muhammad's nature would still not reveal itself easily. In his cave he was visited by one whom later he identified as the Archangel Gabriel, and received the first of those heavenly dictations that were swept together in high disorder after his death to make up the *Koran*.

He came down into Mecca to preach his doctrine—the unity of the Godhead, and a life after death that contained reward and punishment for the actions of this life. Basically it was a religion of Jehova, and much akin to Judaism and Christianity, though the doctrine of the Trinity was firmly rejected. He called it Islam—abandonment—both of paganism for the one true God, and of oneself in the will and purposes of that God.

The hard-headed Meccans were not pleased at this rejection of their shrine, nor did they view the bid for power of one so humble as being at all decorous; but they did him no harm, for he was under clan protection, and so they confined themselves to sneering laughter. Muhammad offered a compromise—he had a sudden revelation that the three goddesses could stay in the shrine with Allah, but the Meccans showed no interest, so he promptly retracted this revelation, suggesting that it had been an inspiration of Satan. It is, however, interesting to note that when he finally triumphed and cleared the Ka'aba of its idols, he allowed the black stone to stay, and countenanced the extravagant devotion to it that had been practised for so many years.

In 622 the inhabitants of Medina, some 200 miles north of Mecca, agreed to harbour Muhammad and his followers, and to protect them with arms. Muhammad showed himself a fine diplomat in making this agreement, and was to keep his promise that, whatever happened, henceforth Medina would be his domicile. So came the Hijira—the secession from Mecca but Muhammad barely escaped with his life, for the inhabitants wisely viewed this move with disfavour. He had to hide in a cave, where a friendly spider webbed over the mouth to deceive pursuers, giving a rather different message from that given by its later colleague to Robert Bruce.

In Medina was a large community of Arabs who had become Jews, and Muhammad plainly hoped to work hand in hand with them—for in every basic way his message was the same as theirs. But they proved obdurate, and so he was forced to develop his doctrine in isolation, emphasising now the Arabist, rather more than the universalist basis of his message. Judaist elements were uprooted from his doctrine—prayers must now be said facing Mecca, no longer towards Jerusalem.

The Jews' rejection of his ideas undoubtedly soured Muhammad, and turned him more towards the ideas of military domination which had been present in his mind since his treaty with Medina was made. The Jews were to suffer first—they were exiled, community by community, until only one group remained, and their six hundred men were slaughtered, and their women and children enslaved.

The Muslims now began to raid the Meccans' caravans to support themselves—an old Arab custom—and the Meccans retaliated with raids on Medina. Muhammad did not fight, but he went with his soldiers to pray them on (on one occasion becoming so excited as to throw a handful of sand at the enemy!). In 627, when the Meccans invaded in force, he seems to have directed the defence of Medina personally, building a large entrenchment before the town.

He was now no longer merely a prophet, he was also a ruler of a state, and much involved in law-making. Each of his dicta were religiously collected, and gradually a philosophy grew up to clothe the bare bones of the doctrine originally enunciated. Of necessity it was not thought-out, being produced piecemeal, each new problem demanding a fresh answer, and so enlarging the scope and definition of his movement. The essential tenet of the Jihad, the holy war against the pagans, undoubtedly grew with the enmity of the Meccans, for although Muhammad proclaimed a universal God, he had no doubt that He was the God of Mecca, and should be worshipped there. How could this be, when His house was cluttered with pagan idols, and anyway His true believers could not go there?

So in 628 Muhammad's strong desire to worship in Mecca overcame his bellicose nature and, to the surprise and annoyance of his followers, he negotiated a truce with the Meccans to allow pilgrimage to the Ka'aba.

This was, in effect, only an interlude, for the Meccans' resistance was now fast crumbling, and within a year Muhammad led his troops to take the city with barely a blow struck in its defence. Power was falling into his hands fast, and soon the whole western part of Arabia was his. Armies set out to extend the empire of the faith, and Muhammad considerably wrote to the King of Persia and the Emperor of Byzantium inviting them to become Muslims.

His last years were more merciful, less strident, and he learned to win supporters by more politic means than force. His increasing indulgence, with some twelve wives, and a passion for perfume, may have been at the root of this change. Certainly he became more intensely concerned with religious matters at the same time, so one cannot portray him as a hedonist. Unlike some of the saints of the Christian faith, he did not concentrate his teachings exclusively on the pains of hell, but spoke with feeling, as a man who had enjoyed the pleasures of this world, of the rewards of the next.

He died in 632, and within twenty years of his death the Empire of the Faith contained the whole of Arabia, Palestine, Syria, Persia and Egypt, and to the north the armies faced the Caspian, to the east, India, whilst to the west they moved across North Africa, to threaten Christian Europe through Spain.

See F. Gabrieli: *Muhammad and the Conquests of Islam* (Weidenfeld and Nicholson, London 1968; McGraw-Hill, New York, 1968) and Sir John Glubb: *The Life and Times of Muhammad* (Hodder and Stoughton, London, 1970; Stein and Day, New York, 1970). One should not neglect Carlyle's impassioned portrait in *Sartor Resartus; Heroes and Hero Worship* (Every-man, London; Dutton, New York); though often wrong-headed and repulsive, it has great power. Carlyle made that desperate bid to leap into real history through the flames of emotion and imagination. He often falls short and lies an easy target for the unemotional and unimaginative.

Nicholas of Cusa

Nicholas of Cusa was born in 1401, son of a moderately well-to-do boatman on the Moselle. His father, like most rising businessmen, would have liked to see his son follow him, but was enraged to find him studious and disinclined to the barge traffic. The situation grew worse the older the boy grew, and on one occasion his father knocked him clear overboard with a blow from his oar. So Nicholas ran away, to seek the protection of the local count, to whose family he remained devoted for the rest of his life.

The Count sent him to the Deventer school of the Brethren of the Common Life, the school which had educated Thomas à Kempis, and was to educate Erasmus. Here Nicholas flourished in scholarship and became subject to the influences of tolerance and mystical devotion that were to remain with him for the rest of his life. In 1416 he went to the university of Heidelberg, but the following year moved to Padua, where he concentrated on canon law, but also learnt his love of mathematics. His attachment to classical studies stems from this period. In 1429 he was to make the great discovery of twelve plays of Plautus, and later, on a mission to Constantinople, he spent considerable time in the search for Greek manuscripts. Some 270 of his books remain in the library at Cues, a substantial part of the enviable collection of Renaissance texts and theological works he built up in a lifetime of book hunting.

He graduated Doctor of Canon Law in 1423, and spent some time in Rome, where he heard St. Bernardino of Sienna preaching in the streets. Returning to Germany he was soon able to find patrons who recognised his worth, the most notable being the Cardinal Orsini, who took him as his secretary to the Council of Basle. The Church was in a sad state at this time: antipopes threatening each other with excommunication, the papacy in exile from Rome, and the whole Church fearful of the threat of the Bohemian heresy. The Council had been convened as a last desperate measure to set all to rights by common consent: in some sense, Christendom had agreed to try to start again, but, unfortunately, without giving much thought to the means by which they could function. Lacking any real notion of the concept of democratic organisation, medieval institutions constantly turned to look for one central authority, and when that was absent, a collapse into chaos was very near at hand.

Nicholas eagerly took up the idea of the Council—to resolve disputes and provide good order (what he called 'harmony') by the common consent of representatives of all parties. As intellectuals greeted the League of Nations after the First World War, so the learned men of the fifteenth century grew excited about the possibilities of the General Council. Nicholas set to work to write a book on the subject, which thrilled with his passion for that unity which comes from a genuine recognition and acceptance of the difference of the constituent parts. It seemed plain to him that the Council was not only the answer to the problems of the Church, but would be a very good idea for the State as well—should not the Empire have its Council too?

Whilst he was busy writing his glowing defence of the new system, however, the system was proving in practice how difficult it was to work. Extremists seemed able to dominate in an institution designed to promote a middle of the road tolerance, and in the voting disorder reigned. Fraudulent manipulation of the Council's decisions often hampered the possibility of any action being taken. The early 1430's were

years of despair for many, and among them Nicholas was well to the fore.

The election of Eugenius IV as Pope turned him in his tracks: here was a man of action, who could make decisions, and whose deepest concern was that of Church unity. By 1436 Nicholas was a firm supporter of the Pope, even though Eugenius was absolute in his hostility to the Council of Basle. Nicholas was now his chief agent in the promotion of Church unity, and spent long hours in negotiations with the Bohemian heretics. In 1437 he went off to Constantinople to bring back the Emperor, the Patriarch, the Primate of Russia and representatives of all the other eastern patriarchs to Florence to negotiate an end to the schism between Rome and Byzantium. When he got back, he rushed off to Germany to persuade the various prelates and princes to support the Pope's Council of Florence, as against the Church's Council at Basle.

In 1447 Eugenius died, and the following year the Council of Basle was dissolved, and the anti-pope resigned—it seemed that unity had triumphed in the person of Eugenius' successor, Nicholas V. No one had worked harder for this than Nicholas of Cusa, and he was made a cardinal Prince-Bishop of Brixen, and legate for Germany and Bohemia. He straightway began an arduous tour of Germany and the Low Countries, reforming the morals of monks and clergy, and stamping out superstitious practices and fraudulent miracles wherever he found them.

In 1452 he at last entered his new diocese of Brixen, but found there a grim heritage. The Church was in dire need of radical reform, but was dominated by the local aristocracy, who were ready to put up a united front against all change. This party was led by the violent and determined Archduke Sigismund of the Tyrol, and for twelve sordid tiresome years the disputes raged on, breaking out in the end into open warfare, with the Archduke leading a force of 3,000 infantry and 500 horse against the reforming Bishop.

These sad last years would have soured a lesser mind, as Nicholas began to realise that Church reform was faced with almost impossible odds, and could never be achieved by the light of reason alone. In fact they were the years in which his best writing was achieved. He had always been eclectic in his studies—as a geographer he had made the first map of Central Europe; he had composed a dialogue of statistics, which Leonardo was to read with profit; he had anticipated Copernicus in his theories of the earth's movement; he had written numerous mathematical works, including a book on Calendar reform, and had studied Arabic mathematics; perhaps this last interest promoted his work against Muhammadanism, which shows a careful and tolerant reading of the Koran. But now his mind turned back to his earliest years and he wrote his great work of mystical devotion, *On the Vision of God*, which was to take the practical stand of a man of the world, mid way between the dry academicism of the schools, and the emotional anti-intellectualism of the recluse.

He died in 1464. He provided in his will for scholarships at his old school in Deventer, and endowed in his home town a hospital for thirty-three men over fifty years old. His library went there, and with it his heart, which is buried beneath the chapel floor.

See H. Bett's *Nicholas of Cusa* (Methuen, London, 1932).

William Ockham

William Ockham was born, probably in the Surrey village which bears his name, about the year 1288. He joined the Franciscan order, and went to Oxford to study about 1308. His particular speciality was logic, which he applied with the coldest clarity to the study of philosophy. He is well known for his principle of economy (though it had in fact been previously enunciated)—Ockham's Razor: Entities are not to be multiplied without necessity.

The clarity of mind which was able to reduce arguments to their basic constituents, and to criticise these, soon gained for him a European reputation. Whilst he was lecturing in Oxford in 1317 he received the first copies of lectures being delivered on the same subjects in Paris, and his own lectures were eagerly read and replied to there. With such a reputation, and such logical ability, he could not avoid accusations of heresy from the less able, and in 1324 he was called to Avignon to answer various charges before the Pope.

At Avignon he met the General of his order, Michael of Cesena, who was embroiled with the papacy over the question of evangelical poverty. This crucial belief in the real poverty of Christ and his disciples, and its example for the Church, had split the order even in St. Francis's own lifetime, and now Pope John XXII was preparing to denounce it. Ockham became deeply concerned in the imbroglio on the Minister-General's side: all his training told him that the doctrine was true, and his experiences at Avignon disgusted him—this Babylon of corruption could not be right.

In 1328 Cesena and Ockham fled from Avignon to join the anti-papal German Emperor Lewis of Bavaria, who had already recruited to his side the great political thinkers Marsiglio of Padua and John of Jandun. Ockham took up residence at Munich, and mounted lengthy and convincing attacks on the papal position, during which he accused Pope John of seventy errors and seven heresies. He showed that the papacy had claimed too much power, and had badly misused it, that giving to one man—whatever his claims—plenitude of power in this world was nonsensical.

Towards the end of his life (about 1348) he became reconciled with his order and with the Pope, whilst refusing to retract from the logical positions he had established. His influence on the reformers who followed him—particularly those who looked to the General Council as an answer to the Church's problems—was profound.

Otto III

Out of the chaos that resulted in Germany from the break-up of the Carolingian Empire, one dynasty rose to the heights of power—the dukes of Saxony, whose business-like approach to government, and energetic campaigns against the threatening Slavs and Magyars won them the respect of the other ducal houses. Otto II won international recognition by marrying in 972 the Byzantine Princess Theophano.

He died in 983, leaving the three-year old Otto III the problems of his estate. His capable mother and her protégés ruled for him, and weathered the dangerous storm of a Slav uprising. He grew up in very Byzantine surroundings, an intellectual who knew Greek, was very pious, and had high ideals for the restoration, or as he called it the 'renovation' of the Roman empire.

He began to rule in person when he was fourteen, and must have seemed to the barbarous Saxons a very strange duke—delicately handsome, supercilious, a writer of poetry in foreign languages, and one who plainly felt his natural home to be in Italy. He went there in 996, to rescue the Pope from the control of the Crescentii who ruled Rome.

Back in Germany, Otto decided upon a settlement of the Eastern Question of his day, and introduced a completely new policy. Now that the states to the east of Germany were Christian he recognised them as federal states of his Empire. No longer were they a place for the Saxons to ravage and milk on the pretext of crusade.

In 998 he was forced to return to Rome, where Crescentius had been making trouble again. He treated the rebels severely—after all they had had one chance. This time he remained in Rome, setting up a court modelled clearly on Imperial Byzantine traditions—he even appointed a grand admiral for a non-existent fleet! He made his friend, the immensely learned Gerbert (q.v.), Pope, and bathed in the romantic luxury of believing that all things were well because he had followed the right pattern.

But his German subjects could not happily see their Emperor permanently settled in Rome, and objected strongly to his 'soft' policy towards the Slavs. He was forced to pay a number of visits home to put things to rights. On one of these, in the year 1000, he indulged his romantic nature by opening the tomb of Charlemagne. One of his companions gave a description to a chronicler: 'We entered in unto Charles. He was not lying down, as is the manner with the bodies of other dead men, but sat on a certain chair as though he lived. He was crowned with a golden crown, and held a sceptre in his hands, the same being covered with gloves, through which the nails had grown and pierced. And above him was a tabernacle compact of brass and marble. Now when we were come in unto the tomb, we brake and made straightway an opening in it. And when we entered into it, we perceived a vehement savour. So we did worship forthwith to him with bended thighs and knees; and straightway Otto the Emperor clad him with white raiment, and pared his nails and made good all that was lacking about him. But none of his members had corrupted and fallen away, except a little piece at the end of his nose, which he caused at once to be restored with gold; and he took from his mouth one tooth, and built the tabernacle again and departed.' (*Cambridge Medieval History*, vol. iii, p. 214. Tycho Brahe had a false nose made of gold and silver, so perhaps this incident is not quite as odd as it seems.) Charlemagne was to remain undisturbed until Frederick Barbarossa felt the same urge as Otto.

Then came more trouble from Italy, where the independent feeling of the towns that led to the great communal movement, combined with annoyance at having German governors getting all the best jobs, was even breeding revolt in Otto's beloved Rome. He was deeply hurt, and said to the rebels, 'Are you not my Romans? For you I have left my country and my kindred. For love of you I have abandoned my Saxons, and all the Germans, my own blood . . . I have adopted you as sons, I have preferred you to all. . . . And now you have cast out your father. You have encompassed my servants with a cruel death, you have closed your gates against me.' (op. cit., p. 214.)

All his oratory failed, and in January 1002 he fell victim to the Roman fever that was already decimating his army. His bride from Byzantium arrived too late, so the imperial crown went to his cousin, Henry II, an unromantic man whose chief passion was his own chastity, and who had no interest in Italy.

The Germans' strange love for Italy, that was to lead them time and again to tragedy in the middle ages and the sixteenth century, persisted through the times of Goethe, and still persists today, when tourists have replaced the soldiers. The true beginning of this long passion was the romantic young king who died of it.

See B. H. Hill (ed.): The Rise of the First Reich: *Germany in the Tenth Century* (John Wiley, New York, 1969).

St. Patrick

The evidences for the life of St. Patrick are scanty and confused, indeed some would claim that there were two St. Patricks. Scarcity of material alone has prevented the writing of two biographies.

Patrick was born, towards the end of the fourth century, probably in the west country. His father had a substantial country estate, and was a town councillor. Both his father and grandfather held ecclesiastical titles, but his home was not at all godly: the ecclesiastical titles were part of a common tax avoidance scheme. As a young man Patrick learned little of religion, or anything else; in later life he was constantly embarrassed by his own ignorance.

When he was about sixteen years of age a massive Irish slave raid took place, and he was caught, along with many others and taken across the sea. In Ireland he had the lonely job of tending cattle, and he grew into the habit of constant prayer, discovering God out of the depths of his solitude and despair. Then came a series of dream messages urging him to go to the sea side, where he would find a ship to carry him home.

He had to journey some two hundred miles to find one, and he may have had some assistance here, for there were a few Christians in the south of Ireland at least before his return. The master of the ship was a pagan, probably half-raider, half-trader, and there was some trouble making the arrangements. The master wanted Patrick to seal the pact by sucking his nipples, after the pagan fashion, but he would only give a Christian oath.

After three days at sea, they reached land, but in a desolate part of Scotland or Wales, for they wandered lost and ever more hungry for twenty-eight days, with the crew regarding Patrick as a Jonah on land. He was challenged to prove his faith, so he prayed, and soon a herd of swine appeared, and the sailors broke their fast.

Patrick was now twenty-two, ignorant, but sure that he must return as a missionary to Ireland as soon as he had had some training. Later tradition would have him go to Gaul to study at the most advanced centres of learning, but he probably really spent some time at an English monastery, soaking himself in the Latin Bible, which he came to know as thoroughly as he was ignorant of more sophisticated learning.

Although his friends urged him not to go back (and some enemies brought up careless sins of his youth as evidence of unsuitability), Patrick was determined to return to Ireland to be its bishop. He got considerable financial support from home, and made a base in Armagh, where he quickly set up his school for the children of noblemen and others who would become his priests, monks and nuns. He was much patronised by the Irish chieftains, and had some trouble with rich ladies who insisted on throwing expensive gifts for him onto his altars. When the local kingdom fell in the tribal warfare endemic at this time,

Patrick joined the party of refugees, and died with them in exile, *c.* 460, probably being buried at Downpatrick.

In the course of a few years Patrick had gone far towards establishing Christianity as a real force in Ireland, most particularly in the north. He was a fearless man, who fought paganism with the conviction of one who expects the end of the world very soon. Proud in his aristocratic birth, he treated with kings as an equal, at one stage excommunicating a British sub-king for his barbaric raiding techniques. His simple nature went out to the Irish who had done him so much harm in that traumatic moment of capture, yet who responded so warmly to his preaching.

See R. P. C. Hanson's *St. Patrick, His Origins and Career* (Oxford Univ. Press, London and New York, 1968).

Philip Augustus

Philip 'Augustus', the conqueror and founder of the French nation was born in 1165. He hated extravagance and wasteful display, was not physically courageous, and used cunning rather than prowess to achieve his ends. Yet his achievements were large, and though he may seem unattractive to us, his people remembered him with rueful pride.

He was crowned king during the last desperate illness of his father in 1180.[1] Louis VII had suffered endless insults at the hands of Henry II of England (who had amongst other things stolen his wife) and he passed on to his son a land that was barely a kingdom at all: the Angevin Emperor was overlord of more than half of the country, and the French royal domains were tiny, about six per cent of modern France. Philip was truly King of Paris and Orleans.

He quickly married Isabella of Hainault, a good match that gained him substantial rights in Flemish territories to the northeast. He made careful arrangements to make sure of his reversions there, and moved wisely to secure his interests against Philip of Alsace. By 1185 Amiens was his, and more was sure to come.

His main problem lay with the enormous Angevin Empire of Henry II, but he realised from the start that it was not unshakeable: made up of a diversity of lordships, each with different customs and allegiances, the Empire could be broken if tackled piecemeal. The obvious first target was Aquitaine, a land filled with rebellion, and only kept down by the persistent endeavours of a military genius, Prince Richard, who was to be the key to the situation for Philip.

Henry II had committed himself to marrying Richard to Philip's sister Alice as the price of the Norman Vexin, a crucial territory for the defence of Normandy. Richard had other ideas, for he was passionately devoted to Berengaria of Navarre. Henry did not press him—some said because he himself had designs on Alice. Here was a cause of war for Philip.

He moved with masterly cunning, and gradually won Richard away from his father, revealing to him Henry's plot to put his favourite John on the throne in his place. Together Richard and Philip made war on the aged King, and brought him to his knees: Richard's succession was assured, and Philip had won large territories in central France.

They now went off happily on Crusade to meet the threat of Saladin. But the happiness was soon dispelled: Richard the vassal, who owed his throne to Philip's care, was now the natural leader, strong, martial, generous and extravagant. Philip the suzerain, with his one eye and weak physique, parsimonious outlook and timorous nature, took a poor second place. The whole thing was set off at Messina, when Richard announced that he would not marry Alice, and called Berengaria to his side.

Philip (taking advantage of Richard's

[1] When Philip himself had been seriously ill, his father had taken the unprecedented step of going on pilgrimage to the shrine of Thomas Becket, whom he had supported in his exile.

captivity) quickly returned from the crusade, fomented discord in Aquitaine, and took the Vexin. He allied with the King of Denmark, in preparation for a future attack on England, and sealed the pact with marriage to the King's sister Ingeborg; but when she arrived he took a tremendous dislike to her (far worse than Henry VIII's towards Anne of Cleves) and tried to put her away. For twenty years he treated her dreadfully, marrying another and defying an interdict to avoid Ingeborg's company; but in 1213 he was to recover from his profound aversion, and he lived with her for the rest of his life.

In 1194 Richard returned to find most of the Norman frontier fortresses in Philip's hands, and he spent the next few years in winning them and the Vexin back again, building impregnable castles like Château Gaillard to keep them safe. But in 1199 he died, and in the following year Philip made a treaty with his old ally in villainy John (*q.v.*), which gave him most of what he had gained before. John desperately needed his help, for not only had the aged Queen Eleanor repossessed herself of Aquitaine, but Maine, Anjou and Touraine had declared for Arthur of Brittany, his elder brother Geoffrey's son. Philip, at last acting as a real suzerain, declared in John's favour.

Meanwhile he watched the situation develop. John had stolen the fiancée of the son of the lord of la Marche, Hugh de Lusignan (Isabella was to return to him after John's death), and war broke out between the English King and the Poitevin leaders as a result. In 1202 the Poitevins appealed John before his liege lord Philip to answer for his crimes, and he refused to appear. Philip promptly declared him a contumacious vassal, and confiscated his lands, giving Anjou, Maine and Touraine to Arthur.

John stirred himself to catch Arthur and kill him, but he was rapidly putting himself on the losing side. Arthur's new territories went over to Philip, who was by now pressing on into Normandy. He completed his conquest by 1204, and even dreamed of invading England, but found himself too busy securing his flanks in Brittany and Flanders. In 1206 John invaded in the south, but when Philip brought his army close, both sides thought it wise not to fight, and a truce was declared.

Diplomacy now took the place of war. John looked to his alliance with his nephew the Emperor-elect Otto, and to the friends his money bought him in the Low Countries. Philip was also busy supporting the cause of the Pope's candidate for the Empire, Frederick of Sicily, and building up his resources.

In 1213 the King of France had a massive fleet ready to attack England when he was stopped at the last minute by John's sudden and complete submission to the Pope. Philip turned to the conquest of Flanders when a surprise attack by the English destroyed his fleet, and he was forced to withdraw a little.

The next year John invaded in the south whilst Otto and his allies pushed in through Flanders, but Philip was well ready for both. He defeated Otto at Bouvines, and turned south to face John, who was forced to make a five year truce and withdraw.

Philip was happy to let his conquest of the north remain his life's work, and turned to more practical affairs of consolidation and building up of resources. Until the year of his death he was to turn a deaf ear to the Pope's appeals for aid in the Crusade against the heretics of Toulouse, and he was not very happy to see his son go off to the invasion of England in 1216. England, despite all dreams, would never again be conquered from France, and Gascony and Provence (as foreign to Parisians as England was at that time) would await other conquering hands.

Philip died in 1216.

Galla Placidia

A visit to the mausoleum of Galla Placidia in Ravenna is quite enough in itself to inspire one with a desire to know more of this remarkable woman. Daughter to

Theodosius the Great, and half-sister to Honorius, the Emperor under whom Britain was finally lost to Rome, she lived to see the great empire of the known world become the battleground of marauding barbarians, and the court that had ruled that empire sheltering disconsolately in the last territory it could call its own—Ravenna, an island of security surrounded by a waste of marshland and the sea.

She first storms onto the stage of history in 408 when Alaric the Goth was laying siege to Rome. The Senate consulted her as to the reliability of her cousin Serena, widow of Stilicho, the Vandal general who had served her father, and she advised that the woman be strangled for conniving with the enemy. Though a very devout Catholic, she lived in a world of treachery and sudden death, and witnessed many such scenes—and worse, for the most usual form of execution then was clubbing to death.

When Alaric sacked Rome, he carried off Placidia as a part of his booty but accorded her imperial honours. He died soon afterwards, and his brother-in-law Ataulf became king. Ataulf carried on for a short time Alaric's policy of attempting to convert the Roman Empire into a Gothic one, but rapidly became convinced of the superiority of a Roman structure. In 412 he offered to join with Honorius and to give up Placidia in return for supplies, but neither co-operation nor supplies came, and in 414 he married Placidia. This was by no means a forced marriage, and the description we have of the ceremony shows an interesting union of Roman and barbaric ideas: they dressed in the Roman manner, and the proper wedding hymns were sung, but the bridegroom's gift to the bride was fifty handsome youths dressed in silk, each carrying two platters, the one piled high with gold, the other with precious stones— the booty from the sack of Rome. Ataulf declared 'I hope to be handed down to posterity as the initiator of a Roman restoration.' (Olympiodorus fragment 24, and Orosius, vii, 42.)

We cannot tell what might have resulted from such a co-operation, but it was foiled by Honorius, who was deeply shocked by his sister's marriage with a barbarian and also was strongly influenced by the advice of his leading general Constantius, who longed to marry Placidia himself.

In 415 Placidia bore Ataulf a son, and called him Theodosius, after her father. But the child died, and almost as soon as they had buried their hope for the future in his silver coffin in Barcelona, Ataulf was murdered. His immediate successor treated her as a common prisoner, driving her before his horse on foot for twelve miles. Luckily for her this man only lasted a week, and his successor handed her over to Constantius in return for 600,000 measures of corn, as her husband had instructed on his death-bed.

In 417 she was married, much against her will, to Constantius. She soon settled down, bearing him a son and a daughter, and exercising her powerful influence on Honorius to raise her husband's status. Honorius was not keen on human beings— he loved poultry best of all but his sister he adored, and scandal ensued from their constant kissing. In 421 Placidia was elevated to the rank of Augusta, and her husband as Augustus became joint ruler of the Western Empire with Honorius.

Shortly afterwards Constantius died, and tensions began to arise between the brother and sister. She still hankered after an arrangement with the Goths, and a 'barbarian' party built up round her to oppose the 'Roman' party of Honorius. Difficulties came to a head as to who should succeed to the post once held by Constantius of *magister militum*, Generalissimo of the Roman troops. Placidia favoured Boniface, a fine man with a great military skill, but Honorius appointed another. Boniface fled to Africa to build up an independent position for himself there (where he got to know Augustine very well) and Placidia and her children were exiled to Constantinople where her nephew Theodosius II ruled.

In 423 Honorius died, and an obscure civil servant called John was pushed in as Emperor of the West. The proper heir was Placidia's son Valentinian III, who was only four years old and Theodosius decided to back his claim with troops. In 425 the child was clothed with the imperial robes in Ravenna. This was a great triumph for Placidia, but she had to contend for power with one of the most able men this century produced—Aëtius, a Roman general who led a Hunnish army, 60,000 strong. In 432 Placidia recalled Boniface from Africa to help oust Aëtius; he beat him, but shortly afterwards died, and Aëtius romped back to supreme power the next year, a control he exercised without interruption or challenge until his murder in 454.

These last years must have been sad ones for Placidia, who was not a woman to submit easily to such control, and had been more used to the bustle and plotting of power. However, the year of her death, 450, was to prove an exciting one for her, and one which showed that her daughter had much the same spirit. Honoria had fallen in love with her butler who had been put to death for his impudence, whilst she was deprived of her royal rank, and a steady marriage was arranged for her. So she sent to Attila begging him to come and avenge her, and sending a ring, promising her hand. Attila immediately made ready to invade Rome and fetch her, and everyone advised Valentinian to give his sister to the Hun in order to buy him off; but, at the insistent prayers of his mother, he refused. Two years later Attila was still demanding his royal bride, but this time there was no jointure between noble Roman and barbarian king.

Marco Polo

Marco Polo was about fifteen when his father Nicolo and his uncle Maffeo returned home to Venice from Tartary in 1269. They had left shortly before his birth, and had had incredible adventures in which they had endured great suffering but had gained riches in gold, gems and knowledge. For Europe longed to know more of the Mongols who had nearly overwhelmed the West a generation before: was this great power that straddled Asia still a menace and if so, of what kind? Was it true, as it was rumoured, that they were ruled by a Christian king called Prester John, with whom the West could ally to wipe out Mohammedanism? All that Europe knew was contained in the reports of a few Franciscan missionaries and emissaries who had never actually penetrated China.

Nicolo and Maffeo came back with messages for the Pope from the Ilkhan himself—Kublai, lord of the East. He had been delighted with his Western visitors and had treated them most courteously: he had showed great interest in the Christian religion and Western science, and had asked the Polo's to bring back with them oil from the lamp in the Holy Sepulchre, and a hundred learned preachers and teachers. He gave them a golden passport weighing twenty-four ounces as the key to all his domains.

Late in 1271 Nicolo and Maffeo and Marco set off back, bearing the holy oil and letters from the Pope, and accompanied by two Dominican friars. However, the latter soon took fright, leaving the three Polo's to go on alone on their 9,000 mile journey that was, in the course of three and a half years to lead them across territory which Western eyes would not see again until the mid-nineteenth century.

Kublai was pleased to see them back, and plainly took to Marco. The liking was certainly reciprocal, and he devotes the second book of his great work to celebrating the power, wisdom, tolerance and good government of the Ilkhan. Marco served him as a diplomat, moving all over the Empire and reporting back to Kublai on the state of his domains. He was pleased with the detail of the reports, something native emissaries seemed unable to supply him with; in a sense Marco Polo became the eyes through which an inevitably static ruler saw his Empire. Mongolia, North and South China, Burma, Viet Nam, Malaya, the East Indies and South India were all seen and reported upon. Luckily Marco filed his notes and draft reports and brought them back with him to form the basis of his memoirs. Though at times credulous, he was no fool—pointing out that the stuffed 'pygmies' from India were in fact monkeys. Where he was in a position to observe, he reports with great fidelity, and his book has been used as a guide by explorers in this century as well as in the last. But he was not primarily a geographer or natural scientist: his is the merchant's eye, and his account is superb when retailing the riches of Eastern ports or the wealth of the Khan's palaces.

In 1292 the Polo's were entrusted with a new mission, that of escorting to Persia a Mongol princess who was destined for its Queen. It was a difficult journey, lasting two years, and whilst they were resting in Persia the party heard of the death of Kublai. It was useless to return for there was always chaos after the death of a Khan, and his favourites would be the first to suffer. So instead they pressed on to Venice, arriving in 1295.

Marco was soon himself one of the sights of Venice, surrounded by exotic riches and curios and constantly trying to explain to visitors the vastness of his experience. The word 'millions' was ever in his mouth, and soon he became for one and all, in affectionate half-belief, 'Marco millions'. Perhaps his Tartar slave, Peter, could haltingly explain that his master spoke the truth—at any rate Marco was grateful enough for his services to free him in his will.

Three years after his return, Marco commanded a galley in one of Venice's many fights against Genoa. He was captured, and spent the next year in prison, with a Pisan called Rusticiano. Rusticiano was a hack writer who specialised in Arthurian legend —not a particularly suitable recipient of Marco's memoirs, but nonetheless he sent to Venice for his files, and the two set about getting the splendid story into book form.

After his release Marco returned to Venice to look after his flourishing business. We hear little of him, but we know he married and had three daughters, so he probably remained quietly at home. He died in 1324. On his deathbed people urged him to correct his book and cut out the imaginary element: he roused himself angrily, and said he had not told the half of what he had seen.

Though many people viewed his writings as in the same class as those of Mandeville, others used them. Missionaries and merchants followed his footsteps until in the mid fourteenth century the Turks brought down an Iron curtain across the route. Later Christopher Columbus studied the route, and dreamed of a by-pass.

It is well worthwhile getting hold of the best edition of Marco Polo's *Travels*, that of Sir Henry Yule (Hakluyt Society, 1903). It contains detailed notes on the places he visited. A valuable sketch of Marco is given by Eileen Power in her *Medieval People* (Methuen, London, 1963; Barnes and Noble, New York).

Richard I

Richard I of England was born at Oxford in 1157, the third son of Henry II and Eleanor of Aquitaine. He was his mother's favourite, as may be seen in the medieval preacher's story telling how the Queen came back from mass one day to find that one of her ladies had suckled the child to quieten him; she at once forced the child to disgorge the alien milk (J. A. Herbert, *Cat. of Romances in B.M.*, 1910, iii, 163). At the age of thirteen he was made Duke of his mother's Duchy of Aquitaine, and this was to be his home for most of his life.

It was a rough place, with rebellious barons and envious neighbours, which combination produced almost continual war, a state which ideally suited the young man. His capture of the 'impregnable' fortress of Taillebourg in 1179, well-defended and provisioned as it was, showed the world the quality of his military genius.

His family did not help, his brothers Henry and Geoffrey eagerly supported his Gascon rebels, and his father was continually against him, for Henry II favoured his youngest son John, and feared the restlessness and soldierly qualities of Richard. Slowly but surely Richard was forced into the arms of Philip Augustus to preserve his right to the succession; together they forced the aged King Henry, Lear-like, to his knees, excusing themselves with the thought that they were clearing the way for a Crusade, which they had sworn to undertake together two years earlier in 1187.

When Richard came to England as King in 1189 he was an attractive personality. In the prime of life, vigorous, efficient; his prowess as a soldier was unchallenged; he was handsome and romantic, a man of the South, surrounded by troubadours. And he was generous—William Marshal who had stuck by Henry II through everything, and had in the process deeply insulted Richard, was given the richest bride in England. Richard's bastard brother Geoffrey who had been equally faithful to the old King, was given the archbishopric of York. John was given a veritable kingdom within the Kingdom—a domain of six counties for his absolute rule—apart from his other appanages. The prisons were opened and all those who had suffered under Henry's vicious forest laws were freed.

Richard swept through the administrative machine like a whirlwind, making speedy judgements and arrangements that seemed at first glance very impressive. His fund-raising tactics were astonishing—he turned everything into money, offices, privileges, rights and exemptions were all sold (some of the earliest town charters were purchased in this strange time) and Richard gaily said 'I would sell London if I could find a buyer.' The money rolled in, and plans for the crusade went on apace. Crusading fever and the desire for finance combined to produce a massive and horrible persecution of the Jews, who had lived in peace in England until then; but even this was a popular move.

When Richard set off on Crusade he left England under the care of three justiciars, one of whom quickly died. The Justiciar of the South, William Longchamp was an unpopular appointment: men said he was the grandson of a runaway serf, and he was squat and ugly, abominably proud and supercilious. His first action was to remove the Northern Justiciar from power and take over complete control of the kingdom.

This gave Prince John an ideal chance to lead an ever-growing opposition. He had been well treated by his brother, but rumour told him that Richard intended to make Arthur, son of Geoffrey (fourth son of Henry II, and not to be confused with Geoffrey, Archbishop of York) his heir. In June 1191 Walter of Coutances arrived from King Richard, charged with the delicate task of resolving this situation. At first he moved warily, but when Longchamp foolishly tried to prevent the Archbishop of York from entering the country, John and his party called him to account, and he fled to the Tower. Walter was now forced to agree to the deposition of Longchamp, and to see John's star wax brightly in the land. John intrigued merrily with the French, but his mother firmly prevented him from going too far.

Meanwhile the crusade had gone slowly forward. Richard had been held up for some time in Sicily, where his brother-in-law William II had just died, and Tancred of Lecce had taken the crown, to prevent it falling into the hands of Henry VI of Germany. Richard had to see to the safety of his sister Joan, and get her dowry back, all in the middle of a revolution. More delay was caused by his final renunciation of his betrothal to Alice, Philip Augustus' sister (to whom Richard had been engaged since the age of three!), and the announcement of his forthcoming marriage with his true love Berengaria of Navarre.

In April 1191 the expedition at last set off, pausing only to take Cyprus from its

Greek tyrant, and supply itself with stores. Richard also married Berengaria here. On 8 June he reached Acre, which had been under siege by the Latins (themselves besieged by Saladin) for nearly two years. In a matter of a month Richard's skill, fresh troops, provisions and engines of war made it possible for the town to be taken. Philip Augustus went home, unable to contend with such brilliance, and realising that much could be won in Richard's absence.

In August the march on Jerusalem began, but the hot sun and the constant raiding of the Saracens made the going hard, and the crusaders, never notable for their ability to get on with one another, began to squabble. However, in September the road to Jaffa was opened by the battle of Arsuf where Richard showed his genius and bravery in open war—he was as good at this as he was at besieging, and the Saracens took careful note. The troops plodded on towards Jerusalem, but it was too late in the year, and the weather broke, forcing them back when only twelve miles from their target. Richard, who had excellent relations with Saladin (*q.v.*) and his family, now tried negotiations, offering his unwilling sister Joan as a pawn. But the talks did not bear fruit, and after one more abortive attack that brought the crusaders within sight of Jerusalem, Richard was forced to make a truce for three years, and leave. It was October 1192, and the news from home was very bad.

Richard was not destined to get home in a hurry, for he was ship-wrecked on the Istrian coast, and arrested by Duke Leopold of Austria, whom he had unwisely insulted at the siege of Acre. In February 1193 Leopold handed over his prisoner to Henry VI, and the Emperor had good reason to rejoice, for Richard was an important ally of his two chief enemies, Tancred of Lecce in the south and Henry the Lion in the north.

Philip Augustus rejoiced as well, eagerly offering to buy Richard from the Emperor, and busily eating up his Norman

territories the while. John was happy to agree, for Philip was prepared to put him on the English throne, and had a fleet ready for invasion.

But Richard's devoted mother (now well on into her seventies) had the situation well in hand, and set the defence machine to work. Soon Hubert Walter (who was to serve as Richard's chief minister for the rest of his reign) arrived in England with the news that the Emperor and the King were at one in their enmity to France, and all was well, bar a little matter of £100,000 ransom. Philip Augustus warned John 'Look to yourself, the devil is loose', for he knew that, staggering as the sum was, England could and would pay.

Richard returned to England in March 1194, to find a complacent, if impoverished land; only two castles stood out against him, Tickhill and Nottingham, and the King aided at the reduction of the latter in disguise. His enemies feared him as much as the Saracens, who quietened their children by saying 'King Richard is coming'; at his landing John's friend the castellan of Mount St. Michael died of fright.

In May he set off for the Continent to win back what Philip had taken from him. He was not to return to England—indeed during his ten year's reign he spent scarce six months here. But English money had to pay for the French wars, and during the next two years Richard spent some £700,000 of it. Philip slowly withdrew before him, and he built his lovely castle Château Gaillard to protect the resumed lands. It was the finest achievement of medieval castle-building, and Richard's greatest joy.

He died before finishing his plans for the reduction of France. In April 1199 he was busy punishing a minor baron who had not given up some treasure trove (as he thought), when an arrow pierced his arm, and the wound mortified. John came into his own.

There is a biography by Kate Norgate: *Richard the Lion Heart* (Russell, New York, 1924, reprint 1969).

Richard II

Richard II was born in 1367 at Bordeaux. His father was the Black Prince, son of Edward III, his mother the beautiful and popular 'Fair Maid of Kent'. He had a lot to live up to as a little boy, pale, blonde and feminine in appearance, stammering and blushing readily.

In June 1377 his grandfather Edward III died, a year after the Black Prince, and Richard came to the throne with a splendid and impressive coronation organised by his uncle Gaunt (*q.v.*). But Gaunt was hated in the land, the crown was deeply in debt, and the French war was going badly. More money was desperately needed, but the people were tired of paying for no results.

In 1381 came the crisis of the Peasants' Revolt. There were outbreaks all over the country, but the major force, led by highwayman Wat Tyler and his hedge-priest John Ball (*q.v.*), came to London and encamped at Blackheath, demanding the execution of 'traitors' such as Lancaster, the abolition of villeinage, and no more taxation. Richard alone kept his head (Gaunt was away in the north) and drew the rebels to a meeting at Mile End, where he promised to examine their grievances fairly, and issued pardons to all who had taken part. But while he was busy here, Wat Tyler had raided the Tower and dragged out the King's ministers to execution.

Richard was undaunted, and called for another meeting at Smithfield, where Wat Tyler prepared an ultimatum. Backed by serried ranks of bowmen he ambled over to the royal party on an old nag, and insolently swilled his mouth out with beer to show his power. Suddenly one of the King's party recognised him for a highwayman, and blurted this out; Tyler lunged towards him, and the Mayor of London, Walworth, struck him a fatal blow. He managed to turn his horse back to his men, moaning with his last breath, 'Treachery'; his followers bent their bows. At this point the king spurred forward saying 'What Sirs? will you shoot your King? I will be your leader, follow me.' He led them away from the body and spent an hour talking with them whilst the mayor raised a posse and surrounded them. He whispered to the King that now was the time for revenge, but Richard would have none of it, and ranked them up in bands to march home.

The extraordinary bravery and self-possession showed by this fourteen-year-old boy in Clerkenwell Fields is one of the great stories of English history, and should have been the prelude to a great and noble reign, instead of a disaster. But his action afterwards, countenancing severe repression, and the withdrawal of his grants shows him in a truer light; to one peasant who reminded the King that he had granted all freedom he moodily replied, 'Villeins you are, and villeins you shall remain'. Richard enjoyed the exercise of power for its own sake.

He was not to have power yet, and after the episode of the revolt he was back in tutelage again; Gaunt, the King's ministers, Parliament even—all seemed to have more power than the King. A growing number of courtiers, led by Robert de Vere, Earl of Oxford, fanned the King's impatience and petulence, fomenting discord between him and his uncles. Richard spent wildly (though the crown itself had to be pawned), giving expensive presents to his friends, and dressing to suit his state. His marriage to Anne of Bohemia (daughter of Emperor Charles IV (*q.v.*) in 1382 made a focal point for his court life, for he loved her to distraction, and when she died twelve years later at Sheen, he razed that palace to the ground in his anguish.

In 1386 John of Gaunt at last got his way and set out on the Castilian expedition, leaving Richard to rule unfettered. He straightway made it plain that his rule would be personal, taking no account of parliament or the aristocracy, and only those at court would share his mind and benefits.

The lords would not stand for this, and Richard's uncle Gloucester, Gaunt's son Derby, the Earls of Arundel, Warwick and

Nottingham combined with the Bishops led by Wykeham and Courtenay to make an opposition. Richard tried hard to shrug them off, but on being reminded of the unhappy fate of Edward II gave way, and submitted his government to a regulatory council.

Early in 1387 he moved into the midlands to try to raise troops to oppose the 'Five lords' but found little support, and indeed the five raised many more. Realising that Richard would have to be completely subdued, they 'appealed' (accused of treason) Richard's most notable courtiers. In the 'Merciless' Parliament that met in February 1388 the Appellants' wishes were carried out in full: Tressilian and Brembre were executed, as was Richard's tutor Simon Burley—he was thought to have given the King his divine right notions; the rest were banished. Parliament voted an *ex gratia* payment of £20,000 to the Appellants.

In May 1389 Richard announced dramatically that he was to resume power, but he was careful to continue in the lines laid down for him by the Merciless Parliament. Wykeham was Chancellor, and though Gloucester and Arundel were dropped, they returned to the government within a few months. Nottingham and Derby were won over. None of the banished friends were recalled. In November Gaunt returned, to Richard's evident joy, and universal peace seemed possible.

A more important peace was made by Gaunt in 1390 between England and France—the expensive and troublesome wars were over. Six years later Richard was to confirm his pro-French policy in his marriage to the seven year old daughter of the King of France. Meanwhile he spent the year 1394-5 in Ireland, establishing his rule there, and meditating on the possibilities of using Irish troops in England when the time should come. He was preparing with infinite care, subtlety and vindictiveness for his revenge. All over England friendships were made and sealed with the badge of the White Hart—

Richard's personal sign—so that troops could be ready when needed, a veritable private army.

In July 1397 Richard arrested Gloucester, Arundel and Warwick, and a parliament carefully managed by his servant Bushy was prepared to attaint them. It met in an open-sided building (possibly Westminster Hall, then in process of reconstruction) and archers bearing the white hart badge were clearly to be seen all round. Arundel was condemned to execution, Warwick to banishment, and Gloucester—well it was announced that he had died in captivity in Calais. Even Richard didn't want a public execution of his own uncle. Archbishop Arundel was exiled. Richard's statement of his prerogatives as King was accepted, and he was granted the customs on wool for life.

Having granted all that a king could desire, the parliament dispersed with a sigh of relief; but in December Norfolk, chatting to Gaunt's son Henry, recently made Duke of Hereford, suggested that Richard would go further, and have his revenge on anyone who took part in the rule of the Appellants. Hereford meanly repeated this statement in Parliament, and Norfolk called him a liar and a traitor. It was decided that they should fight it out at Coventry in September 1398.

Richard allowed the proceedings to go forward, but he was disturbed by the doubts any tyrant is heir to: what to do if Norfolk won, for then God would have shown him to be right. Conversely, if Hereford won, his immense popularity amongst the troublesome Londoners would make him a serious foe. So, at the last minute Richard called off the trial by combat, and banished both parties—Norfolk for life, and Hereford for a comfortable ten years.

It was a childish solution, but Richard was to add worse acts. In February 1399 Gaunt died, and Richard, greedy for money, converted his son's banishment to life, and confiscated the Lancaster inheritance. He promptly took his army over to Ireland to settle disorder there, leaving room for far worse disorder at home.

Hereford landed in July, with a small force of some fifteen men-at-arms, and a few friends: he had, he said, come to claim his inheritance. People flocked to his cause in thousands, and soon all England lay at his feet. Richard quickly ordered his troops back to North Wales, whilst he himself landed in the south, hoping to raise more troops there. He found no support, and by the time he had got up to North Wales his army had melted away.

Hereford was still strongly asserting that he had only come for his Duchy, and deceived Richard into coming to Flint Castle to treat with him. There he was made a prisoner, and transported to London—attempting to escape through a window at Lichfield on the way. On 29 September, having been refused a chance to appear before Parliament, Richard read his abdication speech.

He was hurried north to imprisonment in Pontefract, disguised as a forester. He probably began there a hunger strike against his bad conditions, but after a rebellion in his favour there is little doubt that he was murdered on Henry's instructions, in January 1400. He was buried at the favourite residence of Edward II—the King he had sought to have canonised.

There is a biography by A. Steel: *Richard II* (Cambridge Univ. Press, 1941).

Richard III

The historiography of Richard III is almost as interesting as its subject: viciously denigrated by Tudor historians and dramatists, he has in this century been elevated almost to sainthood by such remote personalities as a promoter of polar exploration and a detective-story writer. Perhaps the famous portrait (copies of which are at Windsor and the National Gallery) is at the root of it all: no vicious Crouchback here, but a worried nervous frown on the face of a puritan, the frown that was seen on his face as he rode to Bosworth field. His hands are ever active—in the picture pulling on and off a ring, in the chronicles playing with his dagger, pulling it half from its sheath and pushing it home again. And above all that look of serious-minded devotion—strange in a villain.

He was born in 1452, the eleventh child of Richard Duke of York, and before he was seven he was embroiled in the Wars of the Roses, a captive of King Henry VI. But in 1461 his elder brother took the crown as Edward IV, and Richard was made Duke of Gloucester and Admiral of the Sea—a resounding title for a nine year old.

Whilst his brother Clarence shared in Warwick's treachery, Richard stuck by Edward, going into exile with him, returning, and fighting by his side at Barnet and Tewkesbury. His devotion went futher, for he was clearly implicated in the murder of Henry VI, and may well have organised the whole thing. He was richly rewarded, and Clarence was filled with jealousy, trying to hide his bride Anne Neville from him by dressing her as a kitchen maid. Clarence had married her elder sister, and did not want to share the inheritance. In 1478 he was murdered in the Tower, and although Richard was not directly connected with this act, later rumours added two onto two.

During Edward's last years Richard ruled the North with a firm and even hand, and although he fell out with the King over the national disgrace at the treaty-making with France at Picquigny, and plainly disliked the royal councillors headed by Hastings, the accord was still strong, and strengthened by Richard's successful invasion of Scotland. When Edward died in April 1483 he left clear instructions that Gloucester was to be Protector for his thirteen year old son.

At this stage Richard clearly had no idea of taking the throne, but he faced a difficult situation: the Queen's family, the Woodvilles and Greys were numerous, and plainly wanted to take control; the nobility, headed by Buckingham, hated these upstarts, and would not tolerate their rule;

Edward's councillors, led by Hastings disliked both the Queen's party and the Protector.

Richard caught up with Rivers and Grey, who were leading the young Edward V to London, and, finding them in arms, joined Buckingham in their arrest. He now took over the protection of the realm and its heir (as was his right), but the Queen promptly took sanctuary with her other son Richard of York, and her daughters. For a while Richard let the situation ride, whilst he consolidated and thought out his position, but the stronger he grew the more fearful Hastings grew, and soon he was negotiating with the Queen to form an opposition to the Protector. Suddenly making up his mind, Richard had Hastings executed, and sent off word that the arrested Rivers, Grey and Vaughan should also be executed. The Queen was persuaded to give up Richard of York, and the two princes were now in the Tower. The coronation was postponed.

Nervous and excitable, Richard now felt himself forced to take the throne: Edward V would never tolerate for long an uncle who had dealt so hardly with his mother's family. The preachers informed the citizens of the strange news that not only were the princes in the Tower bastards, but Edward IV had been illegitimate too. Buckingham was sent to the Guildhall to bring over the eminent of London, and when Parliament was convened, he swayed it to ask Richard to take the throne. Richard pretended to be surprised, but quickly accepted after a conventional demur.

On 6 July he was crowned, and set out on an energetic progress round England, promising justice, splendour and wealth during his reign. His magnificence would outshine his brother's, but he would be as open to petitioners as ever Edward had been; he would be a kindly ruler to the Church, the poor, and to the tradesmen; the terrific burden of taxation would be reduced and made more equitable; above all there would be morality in the land—he made Jane Shore do public penance, and

sent round to the bishops urging them to tighten up their control.

But strange news was leaking from the Tower—the princes were dead—murdered at Richard's command, some said. The old nobility who had supported him began to shift restlessly—even Buckingham. It had all been done so quickly, and people felt tricked and aggrieved. Messages went over to Brittany to Henry Tudor, now leader of the Lancastrian party (though with a highly dubious claim to the throne), that if he came rebels in England would support him. Richard managed to scotch this October rebellion, and execute Buckingham, but the writing was on the wall.

During the early part of the ensuing year Richard made careful preparations to meet the invasion, but again foul rumours struck at his cause. In March the Queen (whom he had thought of renouncing) died, and folk thought that he planned to marry his eldest niece, daughter of Edward IV, to improve his claim. He vehemently denied the talk, but the mud now clung thickly.

Henry Tudor landed in Wales, much to everyone's surprise, neatly avoiding all the traps set for him. Richard moved down to Leicester to face him, leading the largest army England had ever seen. On 21 August he led his force out to Market Bosworth field, mounted on a white charger, and wearing the crown; his army was large—but elements of it were not trustworthy. After the initial shock of battle the King decided on a death-or-glory bid, and aimed straight for Henry Tudor. He killed his standard-bearer, but at this crucial moment Stanley defected, and joined the enemy. Richard was overwhelmed and killed.

Stripped of his fine clothes and armour, Richard's body was unceremoniously taken into Leicester, where it was exposed to the public for two days. Later Henry erected a suitable tomb over his grave in the Greyfriars, but at the dissolution it was destroyed, and the body thrown into the river. The fortunes of York were finally down.

There is a biography by Paul Murray Kendall: *Richard the Third* (Allen and Unwin, London, 1955; Norton, New York, 1956).

Saladin

Up and down England travellers are welcomed at the sign of 'The Saracen's Head', but few amongst the quiet drinkers will be thinking of the bitter feud raging now in the Near East. Yet, eight centuries ago, Christian soldiers, crying 'God and the Holy Sepulchre aid us', fought in just as bitter a war for the honour and glory of winning a Saracen's head; and one was never enough—the murderous slicing would go on until it decided who should have exclusive right to a land two nations claimed. For the Muslims knew that Jerusalem was Muhammad's holy place, where all the faithful would gather on the last day; and the Christians knew equally that here was the centre of the world, holy city of Christ's death and resurrection. For the moment the Jews, scattered as by a mighty wind to every part of the known worlds of both East and West, did not get a look in.

In this struggle the noblest of the Muslim leaders was Yussuf Salah-ed-din—Saladin to Western ears. He came from a family of Kurds, and was born in 1138 in a fortress overlooking the Tigris, where his father commanded and watched the main chance. The turbulent Kurds knew the meaning of loyalty, certainly, but success was their main motto, allied with self-reliance: Saladin's father changed sides at least four times before devoting himself to the service of the great leader Nur-ed-din. A sound politician, he realised that it was not worth while defending with your life the interests of anyone less than great.

Saladin grew up in Damascus in comfort, a shy and quiet youth, far more interested in theology than anything else. Then in 1164, his uncle Shirkuh, Nur's commander-in-chief, took him on a raiding party into Egypt. There the heretical Shiite Caliph ruled over the wealthiest country in the East, and gave tacit (and often financial) support to the Crusader states. To punish heresy, reap a rich harvest, and have the Christians in the jaws of the Muslim pincers—here was an attractive proposition indeed for the Syrians.

In two expeditions Saladin showed considerable promise as a soldier, but he did not enjoy campaigning. When in 1168 a final invasion was planned, he tried hard to be left out, to stay home and discuss theology. Unwillingly, then, he went, and saw his uncle acclaimed as vizier in Egypt, a popular deliverer from the oppression of earlier governments, and from the threat of Latin conquest.

However, early in the following year Shirkuh died from over-eating, and Saladin found himself vizier in succession. Now he began to feel his religious mission to govern and reconquer Muslim lands. He called his father and brothers to Egypt to help him (he was throughout his life a strong family man) and set about establishing his rule. He replaced the Caliph's ministers with his own nominees, put down rebellions of the Caliph's Sudani troops and deported them back home, and courted popularity. This was to be his secret of success—he knew that impressive ceremonial did not breed loyalty—it was the love a people had for its sovereign that won him power. He was generous—for being of a puritanical nature he needed little treasure for his personal use; he was approachable, and loved justice; he was merciful—the plight of widows and orphans brought tears to his eyes, and no suppliant went away empty-handed. But chivalry was not the whole answer—there was an element of sound political cunning there too: when in 1171 the heretical Caliph died he collected his relatives together—men in one place, women in another. They were allowed every comfort for the term of their lives, except that of sexual intercourse. Gently and nobly, he ensured that there should be no chance of a revived Fatimid caliphate.

Nur watched anxiously the successes of his protégé—successes no one could have forecast from the shy boy who disliked war. Saladin warily avoided any meeting with Nur, lest he should end his rise to power in the traditional Eastern manner; but in 1174 Nur died, and the position was radically altered.

Now Syria looked in a desperate state—Nur's heir was an eleven-year-old, and the emirs would plainly partition a minor's empire. In Jerusalem there was a child ruler too—a thirteen-year-old who had leprosy. The chance had come. Saladin picked seven hundred of his best horsemen and rushed direct across the desert (through Christian territory) to win the supremacy.

He had to face enemies on every hand—Syrian and Mesopotamian emirs, Christians, and the dreaded Assassins. These last were emissaries of the Old Man of the Mountains, a religious despot who practised murder as a fine art. His drug-addicted followers (hence their name—Hashishins) were sent out to murder those their leader felt to be blots on the face of his earth, and were promised fresh supplies on their successful return to the mountainous paradise. They were highly motivated, and therefore highly skilled assassins, and so they found their way into Saladin's tent, despite all precautions. He escaped with his life, but after another experience he decided that the Old Man was one enemy with whom it was best to treat.

Other enemies were more easy to defeat on the open field of battle (though over confidence led Saladin into a major defeat by the Franks in 1177—a rare event). By 1182 he had no enemies left in the Muslim territories, leaving him free to concentrate on the Franks.

It was to be a strange war, bringing out the fine military, but also the fine personal qualities of Saladin. Though it was a bitter fight, the strange qualities of chivalry intervened: once, when Saladin was invading the capital of a bitter enemy,

Reginald of Châtilon (whom he was to execute personally) he found a wedding was in progress. The Christians retired to the citadel, but Reginald politely sent out wine and meat for Saladin to share in the wedding feast, and the Saracen leader ordered his bowmen and artillery to avoid the tower in which the newly-weds were forced to spend their honeymoon.

In 1187 Saladin caught the whole force of the Franks at Hittin. Keeping them from water until they were crazy with thirst he finally moved in to demolish the army and capture the King of Jerusalem with the flower of his colleagues, and the True Cross, which they bore with them.

After this Palestine crumbled before him until (apart from a few castles) only Tyre and Jerusalem stood out against him. Tyre indeed would have surrendered, had not Conrad of Montferrat arrived in the nick of time and put spirit into the defenders. So Saladin turned to Jerusalem. He did not wish to take the holy city by storm, so he generously offered a pact to the inhabitants: he would leave them alone for a year, and if by then they should see no sign of rescue, they must cede the city to him, and he would escort them and their possessions to the nearest Christian territory. Though there were only three knights in the city, and it was crowded with refugees, Jerusalem turned down the offer and determined on resistance. Such foolishness had its own reward, for Saladin soon broke in, and the inhabitants had to pay ransom to be allowed to remove themselves. Saladin and his followers showed admirable restraint, and released thousands of poor folk who could not pay. Indeed, in response to the prayers of the wives and children of Christian knights already in his prisons, he released many a husband and father who would fight again. Their solemn promises to him were worthless, for the Christians believed that it was a sin to keep an oath made to a Saracen.

Whilst Saladin was showing such unwise generosity in Jerusalem, Conrad of Montferrat was working like a demon improving the defences of Tyre, and when the Saracen army came back before that city it was indeed impregnable. The tired armies of the faithful went home, happy in the belief that, in conquering all save one, they had done enough.

But the Archbishop of Tyre had sped to Europe in a ship with black sails to tell the incredible news, and the response was magnificent. Frederick Barbarossa set off, aged seventy, with a huge army of Germans, though he was never to see Palestine. France made preparations on a grand scale. England tithed the 'Saladin Tax' and Prince Richard swore to free Jerusalem. All Europe was in ferment.

In Palestine, the King of Jerusalem, whom Saladin had unwisely released on parole, recruited an army from the remains of the defeated garrisons and set out to besiege Acre. He had learned a lot from the Saracens in the period of his imprisonment: he now knew that they would not attack entrenchments. So, despite hunger and discomfort and defeat in the field, his siege army dug furiously. A Saracen city was surrounded by a Christian army, which was itself surrounded by a Saracen force. It was a bad time: the story was told of two friends who plodded miles to spend their last coin on thirteen beans; when they got home they found that one was bad, so all the way back they went, to change it.

Richard of England and Philip Augustus of France arrived in 1191. They brought elaborate siege engines, with nicknames like 'Kill-Greek' and 'The Bad Neighbour', and despite the enemy's cunning use of Greek fire, they made progress. Saladin's reinforcements were coming, but just as they arrived, the garrison of Acre surrendered.

Richard appreciated Saladin's soldierly chivalry but lacked his merciful nature: feeling that negotiations were not going fast enough, he butchered the Acre garrison. The Saracens' heads had begun to fall.

Saladin was sick, and his army was tired; Richard's brilliant tactics and the heavy armour of his soldiers made victory seem impossible. In 1191, when the Christians began moving down the coast in the move on Jerusalem, Saladin flung all he had at Richard at Arsuf, and nearly defeated him. But the mad charge of the close-packed knights, encased in steel, scattered his Bedouin, and stalemate was reached.

Diplomats crossed constantly between the camps, and chief of the Saracen emissaries was El Adil, Saladin's brother. Richard grew very fond of him, referring to him (to the horror of the Christians) as 'my brother'. He even suggested to Saladin that his sister should marry El Adil, and they rule Palestine as a Christian-Muslim state.

Richard was anxious for peace, for the news from home of the activities of his brother John was very bad indeed. Saladin was ever more sure he could not defeat Richard, and was equally anxious for peace. They became very close, in a strange sort of way: at Jaffa, Saladin, seeing Richard unhorsed at the height of the combat, sent him a fresh mount; later, hearing he was down with fever, he sent him fruit and mountain snow.

So a peace was made. The Christians could have the coastal cities they held, and Muslims and Christians should be allowed free access to each other's territories. Richard boarded his ship for England in October 1192, and sent Saladin a last message: when the truce was up, in three years time, he would return and take Jerusalem; Saladin replied at once—if he had to lose his lands, there was no one to whom he would rather lose them.

Acre was a good name for what the might of Europe had been able to wrest from Saladin. His last victory was to have lost so little. Yet perhaps his last victory was really more typical—that *he* kept the truce—pilgrims to Jerusalem were safely and honourably escorted.

At Damascus he took a little rest with his beloved family—and it was large—he left seventeen sons and one daughter. But his rest was brief. Four months after Richard had departed, he took a bout of yellow fever, and on 4 March 1193 he died, genuinely lamented by all. When they opened the treasury they found there was not enough to bury him—he had given it all away. The money for his funeral had to be borrowed. As the Christian legend ran, his empire now stretched no further than his winding sheet.

See S. Lane-Poole: *Saladin and the Fall of the Kingdom of Jerusalem* (Putnam, New York, 1898) and F. Gabrieli (ed.): *Arab Historians of the Crusades* (Routledge and Kegan Paul, London, 1969).

Stephen

Stephen, future king of England, was born about the year 1096. His mother was Adela, daughter of William the Conqueror, and heir to all his strength of will and temper. His father was Stephen Count of Blois and Chartres, a boastful character who had made himself the laughing-stock of Europe by running away from the siege of Antioch after having been made commander-in-chief there.

Adela's two favoured sons, Stephen and Henry, were both to find their fortunes in England. Henry, a Cluniac monk, quickly accumulated Glastonbury, the richest abbey, and Winchester, the second richest diocese in England, and set out on his career of financial wizardry and ecclesiastical statesmanship. A man of rare power, vision and taste, he was infinitely more attuned to great responsibilities than his brother.

Stephen had a ready charm, and his gay and seemingly open nature made him a great success at court. His uncle Henry I loaded favours on him: he was given estates in England of some half a million acres, and made a favourable marriage to the rich heiress of the Count of Boulogne. Matilda was to be both a loyal and an able wife.

In 1136 Henry died, and though he had made all his barons swear fealty to his daughter Matilda before his death, Stephen now moved speedily to get himself accepted as King in England. His brother swayed the Church to his side, the Londoners were bought with a substantial grant of privileges, and the Norman barons were persuaded that a woman ruler of well-known arrogance and intractability, married to the leader of the Normans' traditional enemies, the Angevins, would be no good prospect for England.

Stephen's dash and promises carried him through for a while, but quickly enough people discovered his faults: he was tricky, changeable, often stupidly weak; he simply could not be relied upon, nor could he trust others. In 1139 Matilda landed, and her bastard brother Robert of Gloucester opened the West to her. During the next eight years she was to win defectors from Stephen's bad government.

In 1141, at Lincoln, Stephen's barons deserted him in battle, and he fell prisoner to Matilda. But she proved as unhappy a mistress as Stephen had been master, and many people were glad when Robert of Gloucester was captured by Stephen's Queen at the rout of Winchester, and Matilda was forced to release Stephen to get him back.

Many barons favoured this dual situation in which they could bargain for their services, and live as war-lords. Castles sprung up all over the land, and in many parts a dreadful anarchy reigned, so that many people openly declared that Christ and his Saints were asleep, and the Devil ruled.

Matilda's son Henry had twice invaded and been repulsed in 1147 and 1149, but when he came again in 1153 he was backed by a tremendous accumulation of continental power. The death of Stephen's son Eustace prompted him to negotiate with the young Duke, and he was encouraged in this by the urgings of the Church and of the Norman barons who wished to regain their continental estates now under Henry's control. So Matilda's son was made heir, and for a further year Stephen ruled, in peace at last, until his death in October 1154. He was buried in his abbey of Faversham.

There is a biography by R. H. C. Davis: *King Stephen* (Longmans, Harlow, 1967; Univ. of California Press, 1967).

Stilicho

One of the chief troubles that beset the Roman Empire at the end of the fourth century was its paucity of great men who could deal with the enormous number of problems which faced it. Perhaps the most surprising element in this situation is the fact that the one great protector of Rome during the period of maximum pressure from the barbarian hordes was himself a barbarian—Stilicho, the Vandal.

Born *c.* 360, Stilicho made rapid advances in the favour of the Emperor Theodosius the Great, even to the extent of being given the hand of his niece Serena. In 385 we find him entrusted with a vital embassy to Persia; seven years later he is in command of the army in Thrace, and in 394 he is second-in-command of the entire forces of Rome in the fight against Argobast the Frank.

The following year Theodosius died, and the Empire was divided for ever, his eldest son taking the East, and young Honorius, aged eleven, ruling in the West with Stilicho as his guardian and regent.

He immediately made an impression on the barbarian world by journeying the length of the Rhine, receiving homage from the Teuton chieftains for his young prince. The same year (395) he first ran across Alaric the Goth, whilst leading the army of the East back across Greece; before he was able to give battle the army was removed from his control, to be taken to face a more serious threat further east, but the two barbarian generals had plainly got each other's measure.

Back in Italy Stilicho continued to administer the Empire, showing skill in his handling of its official machinery, as well as concern for even its most far flung elements. For example, between 395 and 398 he had in hand a programme for the restoration of the defences of Britain, a lost cause if ever there was one.

In 397 he led an army into Greece to deal with Alaric, but again was unable to do a thing, having to turn back to deal with Gildo's revolt in North Africa. To keep Alaric quiet he laid plans with him for an invasion of eastern Illyria, the territory to be shared between the Goths and the Romans (though he may himself have had dreams of an independent kingdom there). At home he increased his control over the Emperor by marrying him to his daughter Maria. His skill as a statesman was shown by his methods in dealing with the North African revolt: he replaced the corn that would be lost from Africa by organising shipments from Gaul, and gave to the brother of the revolt's leader a small army. This brother had had his children murdered by Gildo, so was well motivated as a general, and knew the terrain and the people very well: a natural success ensued.

In 401 Alaric determined to try out Stilicho on his own ground, and invaded Italy; they found themselves equally matched, so the Goths withdrew with a definite promise that the expedition to Illyria would take place. In 405, when Stilicho was ready to go, a combined invasion of Italy by the Ostrogoths and Vandals, along with a putsch in Britain and Gaul by the self-styled Emperor Constantine detained him. In 408 Alaric, upset at having had no aid from Stilicho, swept into Italy again, and had to be bought off at an exceedingly high price.

At this point the Emperor of the East died, and Honorius, knowing of Stilicho's plans for joint control of eastern provinces with the barbarians, became deeply disturbed, and wished to go to Constantinople himself to see to matters there. Stilicho strongly advised him to stay in Italy, which he felt would be lost without the presence of the Emperor, and offered to go himself. One of Honorius' servants, Olympius, now began to foment the rumour that Stilicho was planning a complete barbarian take-over of the Eastern Empire, which would leave the West entirely alone in a barbarian sea. The

Roman troops revolted, and Honorius was persuaded to do away with Stilicho. A letter was sent to Ravenna, where Stilicho was in sanctuary, ordering his honourable detention, for his own protection. When he submitted to this arrest, a second letter was read, ordering his execution. Stilicho could well have appealed to the Teutonic troops he had with him to rescue him, but chose not to foment a racial war himself, and submitted to the sword.

Olympius arrested all his henchmen and put them to the torture to wring from them the admission that Stilicho had planned treachery. No admission came, so the Roman soldiers were given the word to dispossess and slaughter barbarians wherever they were to be found. This was the end of barbarian co-operation with Rome in this era: they fled to join with Alaric, and the great sack of Rome became an inevitability.

Theodoric the Ostrogoth

Theodoric the Ostrogoth, the greatest of all the barbarian leaders, appears in the *Nibelungenlied* as Dietrich of Bern; he and Etzel close the action, weeping: 'The King's high festival had ended in sorrow.' The barbarian attempt at recreation of the Empire failed in tears also, though our respect for Theodoric's achievement remains undiminished.

Theodoric's father was a paid warden on the northern frontier of the Empire of the East, but the child was deposited in Constantinople as a hostage where he was brought up in the Roman tradition, being a great favourite of the Emperor Leo. He imbibed a great respect for the culture of Rome, though his education drew the line at reading and writing—to the end of his life he signed documents by tracing through a golden stencil.

When his father died he had to struggle with a contender for the leadership— another Theodoric, nicknamed Strabo 'the Squinter'. The struggle was long and complex, but finally our Theodoric won,

having gained the support of the Emperor Zeno, who adopted him, and in 486 accorded him the rare privilege of a triumph, and an equestrian statue in one of the squares of Constantinople.

The end of the struggle meant, however, that there was a huge force of Ostrogoths in Dacia with nothing particular to do, so Zeno wisely gave Theodoric his permission to invade Italy to try to clear it of barbarian control, and oust the resident ruler Odovacar. The invasion began in 488, but it took five years (and considerable help from the Church, which represented the only stability in the area) before Theodoric could enter Ravenna, having compacted with Odovacar to rule jointly. This treaty was kept for ten days, and then Theodoric treacherously stabbed his co-ruler, remarking coolly 'There certainly wasn't a bone in this wretched fellow.'

This bad beginning was by no means a precedent for Theodoric's rule. His government was Roman through and through—in constitution, practice and in the background of its officials. He published Roman laws, appointed consuls, and gave respect to the Senate. His reputation for justice and wisdom was very well deserved. His court became a centre of Roman culture which encouraged an artistic and literary renaissance, where men like Cassiodorus, Boethius and Venantius Fortunatus flourished. He ordered the repair of damaged aqueducts, theatres, drains, monuments, walls and basilicae, sending out directions to gather up with care broken pieces of marble for re-use. Ravenna is his monument, but Rome also owed him a new lease of life.

His foreign policy was remarkably successful, first marrying his sisters and daughters to foreign potentates, then taking over rule in neighbouring areas. When he died he was acknowledged overlord of the old Western Empire, with the exception of Africa, Britain and two-thirds of Gaul.

Like all his nation, Theodoric was an Arian: this, the second greatest heresy of the early church, proclaimed that the Son of God could not be eternal nor (therefore) equal to the Father, so that He was neither truly man nor truly God, but something in between. Theodoric found no difficulty during the major part of his reign in dealing with a Catholic Church, settling its many disputes (as the chief officer of state) and promoting its interests. However, in 523 the Emperor Justin proscribed Arianism throughout the Empire and thereby placed Theodoric in an extremely difficult position. The Church was now strongly against him, and his Roman officials also became increasingly resentful of an heretical ruler. He stamped out opposition with a bitterness unknown since he first came to Italy, putting Boethius and others to death with every refinement of cruelty. He sent the Pope off to Constantinople to get the edict rescinded, and when he returned empty-handed, Theodoric was overtaken by rage. In 526 he made a decree ordering the expulsion of all Catholics on the seventh Kalends of September next. That very day he died.

Arianism had never proved a problem to Theodoric until the edict came, and then perhaps the whole thing took on a new aspect. Theodoric had worked hard to recreate Rome, and had been brilliantly successful, but he had had little or no recognition from the city which had nurtured him, and whose standards he longed to emulate. Now instead came the gross and final insult which showed him before all branded as a barbarian, one who has no real part in the in-group that is eternal Rome. So he became again a barbarian, acting as he had when murdering Odovacar. His daughter tried to carry on his rule after his death, but her quarrelsome relations strangled her for writing to Byzantium: barbarianism had come again, in a matter of years Italy fell to pieces once more, a prey this time to the Lombardic invaders.

Warwick the King-maker

'Just now, although matters in England have undergone several fluctuations, yet in the end my lord of Warwick has come off the best . . .' (Report of the Milanese ambassador, qu. J. R. Lander, *The Wars of the Roses*, Barrie and Rockliff, London 1965, p. 125).

Richard Neville, later Earl of Warwick, Warwick the Kingmaker, was born in 1428, son to the Earl of Salisbury. His father had achieved his earldom by marriage, and as warden of the West March (Cumberland and Westmorland) had learned his fighting and political skills in one of the hardest schools there was.

His son, however, was to outclass him. In 1449 he married the heiress to the Warwick earldom, and so became a nephew by marriage of Richard Duke of York. York claimed to be descended from Edward III by the more legitimate elder line, and was to push this claim so hard against the weak and feckless Henry VI that the country fell prey to civil war—the Wars of the Roses.

At the first battle of St. Albans, Warwick showed his fighting skills by taking the royal army in the rear, creeping through the citizens' back gardens. York rewarded him by seeing that he got the captaincy of Calais, and there he trained himself for sea warfare, and showed himself just as skilled on water. In 1459, when a party of Yorkists had to decamp rather suddenly to the Continent, Warwick was the only one who could handle the boat (Lander, *op. cit.* p. 99). He won the support of the sailing fraternity of Kentishmen by his seamanship, and this was to be one of his chief areas of support for the rest of his life.

When Richard was killed at Wakefield in December 1460, and his head impaled on the main gate of York wearing a paper crown, Warwick was left as the mainstay of the Yorkist movement, fighting for the recognition of Richard's son Edward of March. Within four months Warwick had Edward accepted as King, having persuaded the barons that he was the inevitable answer to the problems raised by the rule of Henry. The hapless king was now in the hands of his wife Margaret, whose army of Northern pillagers was feared by all.

For three years Warwick held sway as he had intended, and Edward showed no signs of objection to his tutelage. In the north the Earl used cannon and complicated modern engines of war to stamp out Lancastrian resistance, and in the south he used his consummate political skills to build up the Yorkist cause amongst Church and people. The new administration had to prove itself and popularity was essential.

Warwick was no *preux chevalier:* he was an exponent of modern technology on the battlefield—indeed it let him down at the second battle of St. Albans, so heavily had he invested in it. There he had machines for shooting double-flighted arrows with heavy iron heads, machines for shooting wild-fire arrows, nets with caltraps to spike horses' feet, and great movable shields for the archers, that could be pushed over to present rows of spikes if a retreat proved necessary. But the enemy came from another direction than was expected, and all this equipment could not be moved in time.

Nonetheless, he was usually successful in his battles on land and sea, and he was an equally shrewd political tactician. He knew the power of popularity, and he knew the complicated arts of diplomacy. His failure lay in aiming too high—as the chronicler of Croyland said, he had 'A mind too conscious of a daring deed.' (qu. Lander, *op. cit.*, p. 162.)

Such a character could not help but impress the new King of France, the wily Louis XI. He tried to persuade Warwick to work for peace between the two countries, recognising that the Earl was not only the most powerful, but also one of the most sensible men in England. Peace would be a godsend to two tired countries, and would withdraw from the Lancastrians their last hope of foreign aid. Rumour had it that Louis wanted peace in order to be able to concentrate on crushing his own restless nobility, and was willing to make Warwick Duke of Normandy if he would come over to organise the campaign.

Warwick was as attracted to Louis as

Louis was to him, and fell in with his plans. Feeling confident of his powers he went ahead in planning a marriage between Edward and Louis' sister-in-law, and rejoiced in the sense of power that secret diplomacy brings. But Edward was beginning to flex his muscles as a politician, and the direction of his thinking was opposed to that of the Earl. He secretly married Elizabeth Woodville, who had a whole tribe of power-hungry relatives, and when all was revealed the balance of power in English politics was not only altered, but infinitely complicated.

Warwick was furious, and Louis, seeing that Edward was developing a policy of co-operation with France's enemy Burgundy (and strangely enough, it had been Warwick who had initiated the tradition of Yorkist—Burgundian alliance when he had been Captain of Calais) offered to support Warwick if he moved against the king he had set up.

But the Earl was not so precipitate, even though the king committed himself to the Burgundian alliance and forced Warwick to accompany his sister Margaret on her bridal journey to Charles Duke of Burgundy, and even when Edward removed his brother George Neville, Archbishop of York from the chancellorship. Instead he waited, trying to gain popular support in the North, his home country, and in Kent. When Edward looked like making war on France, Warwick carefully diverted the effort into an attack on the Hanseatic towns.

The support he looked for was never quite enough. Twice, in 1469 and 1470 he tried to replace Edward with his brother (and Warwick's son-in-law) George Duke of Clarence, but both attempts failed, and the two conspirators had to escape to France.

There Louis persuaded Warwick that there was nothing for it but a restoration (or 'readeption') of Henry VI, and arranged a marriage between Henry's son Edward and Warwick's daughter Anne. Margaret looked on the project with high disfavour, but saw in it her only chance, so agreed. In September 1470 the French put Warwick's invasion force ashore in Devon, whilst his brother John Marquess of Montagu made a lightning sweep from the north to capture Edward. The King escaped to Burgundy with only a few hundred followers, and it looked as though Warwick had made a clean sweep of the board.

It was not as easy as that: simple enough to put Henry back in London, but not so simple to settle the disputes between Lancastrians and Yorkists that immediately flared up once more over the whole country. Plainly Edward would soon be back in force, and public opinion lay with him, for the Burgundian alliance had brought rich profits in trade, profits that could not so easily be gained in France. Warwick argued and cajoled, not daring to do anything that would increase the opposition; but he was committed to Louis to mount an invasion of Burgundy, where he was promised the lordships of Holland and Zeeland if he could win them.

He was forestalled: in March 1471 Edward landed in Yorkshire, and the little support Warwick had built up for himself melted quickly away. Even his brother George, Archbishop of York, cravenly sued for pardon, and turned Henry over to Edward as the price. Warwick's army miserably trudged after Edward, and the heart went out of them when Louis announced that he had changed his mind and had made truce with Burgundy.

On Easter Sunday, 14 April, the two armies met on the field of Barnet in a dense fog, and Warwick and his brother John were killed in the rout. Edward had come into his own.

There is a biography by Paul Murray Kendall: *Warwick the Kingmaker* (Allen and Unwin, London, 1957).

Richard Whittington

The true story of Richard Whittington, unfortunately bears no resemblance to the fairy tale pantomine, but he has the advantage (unlike Robin Hood) of having actually existed. He was the third son of a rich Gloucestershire knight, and his mother was daughter of the sheriff of the same county.

He went to London to become a mercer where he quickly found success, for he was barely out of his teens when, in 1379 he gave five marks (66/8d) to the city loan. By 1393 he was an alderman, and in favour at court, for in 1397, when a Lord Mayor died in mid-term, Richard II appointed him to see out the time. He was elected mayor for the following year as well, and guided the city's fortunes through the tricky period of Richard's tyranny.

He was on equally good terms with Richard's supplanter, and with Henry V. The reason is not hard to seek: he was very rich, and ever ready to lend large sums (which he had sufficient business acumen to recoup —no mean skill in this period). On one occasion he loaned the crown the massive sum of £6,400. It is no wonder that he was elected mayor again in 1406 and 1419. He was a strict and business-like administrator.

He died in 1423, and his wife Alice (whose name reappears in the legend) had predeceased him. There were no children— not even a cat was left, for this entered the legend out of confusing a portrait of the sixteenth-century grammarian Robert Whittington, which contained a cat, with our fifteenth-century mayor.

So there was a lot of money which all went to city charities, and this is why Whittington was remembered with such powerful affection. He brought water to Cripplegate and a library to Greyfriars; he rebuilt Newgate gaol and St. Bartholomew's Hospital; and he restored and enlarged the Guildhall, and gave substantial buildings to the city. To his own parish church he gave a hospital to shelter the aged and a college of five priests to sing for his soul, for those of Richard II and Thomas of Woodstock and all their families. With such bequests he worthily entered legend.

See C. M. Barron: 'Richard Whittington: The man behind the myth', in A. J.

Hollaender and W. Kellaway (eds.) *Studies in London History* (London 1969, pp. 197–250); and J. M. Imray: *The Charity Of Richard Whittington* (London, 1968).

St. Wilfrid of York

If it were possible to imagine a Martin Luther who struggled to establish and defend the supremacy of the Roman Church in all its magnificence, then one has a clear picture of the character of St. Wilfrid of York.

Born in 634, to noble parents in Northumbria, Wilfrid carried the aristocratic vision with him throughout his life. When, at the age of fourteen, he decided to enter the church, he demanded from his father a rich and impressive retinue, and went to Aidan (*q.v.*) at Lindisfarne under the patronage of the Queen. For four years he endured the rough and humble life at Lindisfarne for the sake of a man he recognised for a saint, but when Aidan died in 652, the pull of a more sophisticated church exercised its attraction. Wilfrid had never taken vows as a monk of the Celtic Church, and now he was quite free to make his pilgrimage to Rome.

Accompanied by Benedict Biscop, a man of exactly the same background and inclinations as Wilfrid, he journeyd to Rome, soaking up the pomp and splendour, and recognising the historic necessity for the triumph of tradition. On the way out he had made a particular friend of the Archbishop of Lyons, and when he returned he gave double proof of his friendship: not only did he stay three years with the Archbishop, but also when his friend fell victim to the complicated politics of the Merovingian state, Wilfrid amply demonstrated his willingness to follow him to execution. Throughout his life we find evidence of his attractiveness as a person, but here, almost at its beginning we see to what extent he was willing to repay the friendship so many people offered him.

When Wilfrid got back to England, Northumbria was in her prime, and he was offered the abbacy of Ripon. This young man, scarcely twenty eight years old, now flung all his energies into the promotion of the cause of Rome, and plainly the conflict that had been brewing in the North since Paulinus had first visited this area was ripe for explosion. The Calendar was the root of much of the trouble—whilst the Celtic King Oswy was busy celebrating Easter, his Catholic Queen Eanfled was barely into Holy Week, and both professed Christianity. So, in 664 Oswy convened a synod in Hild's famous abbey at Whitby to decide between the two branches of the faith. Wilfrid spoke for Rome, and gave so strong a discourse, with such powerful arguments that the King decided it was unsafe to risk continuing in the Celtic persuasion. He chose Rome, whose St. Peter kept the keys of Heaven, and promoted Wilfrid as bishop of his province.

Wilfrid was now put into some difficulty, for he had to receive consecration that was properly canonical, and after the true sumptuous Roman fashion: England could not provide it, so he was forced once more to visit Gaul. There twelve bishops carried him to the altar in a golden chair, and made him a bishop in the midst of beautifully singing choirs. In love with civilisation, he forgot why ever he had come, and remained for two years, enjoying the rich and formal services, the correctitude of it all.

Yet while he stayed in Gaul, York was relapsing back into the old ways, and in his place Chad was made bishop, a humble, simple man, a close follower of Aidan, a disciple of Lindisfarne. When Wilfrid returned he could do no more than retire to his abbey at Ripon, and concentrate on that. He brought clever stonemasons and glaziers, chanters to train the choir, books for the library, and the rich discipline of the Benedictine rule to govern the monks. The aestheticism of Ripon would stand out against the asceticism of Lindisfarne.

In 669, Theodore of Tarsus arrived in Britain, and the new Archbishop of Canterbury was not only a leading scholar, but also a man filled with reforming zeal and administrative ability, an interesting combination. He straightaway began a tour of inspection of the English Church, and found much to censure, including the presence of Chad in the bishopric of York. Chad had received a totally invalid Celtic consecration. However, he had never wanted to be a bishop at all, and willingly agreed to step down. Theodore personally reconsecrated him as bishop of Mercia, lifting him onto the horse with his own hands when he complained that it would more befit his calling to walk humbly unattended to Lichfield.

Wilfrid now came into his own, but he found his cathedral at York a poor Saxon building, damp and unglazed, the roof full of leaks, and neither order nor respect anywhere. He soon set things to rights, for to him the words 'house of God' had a very real meaning. He was busy rebuilding the monastery church at Ripon, and building his abbey at Hexham, whose Church was to be the unrivalled architectural triumph of the century, this side of the Alps. Three stories high, and very long, the church was built of polished stone, the roof supported by a forest of delicate columns, the walls covered with reliefs and paintings. His altars were worthy manifestations of his mystical and ritualistic faith, and nothing was too good for the word of God—the Gospel Book at Ripon was written in letters of gold on purple parchment, with brilliant illuminations, and its golden cover was set with many fine jewels.

He was to have only four years in which to express his sense of the magnificence of his religion before his dogmatic and controversial nature landed him in the troubles that were to follow him for the rest of his life, and shake the Church in England to its roots. In 673 Archbishop Theodore enunciated the common-sense principle that the number of bishops should increase as the Church expanded, and Wilfrid refused to accept this. He felt convinced that he could manage his huge diocese alone, but, perhaps more important, he felt

this to be a bureaucratic measure that took no account of tradition: it was the Celts who had a surplus of bishops, and thereby had reduced the importance and significance of the office; Catholic bishops were part of a tradition that was intimately connected with Rome, not with Canterbury.

Typically, Wilfrid entered this dispute without any care to build up support at home—he was never an effective politician. He had for years gone against the wishes of King Egfrid in encouraging his chaste wife Ethelthryd to return to her heart's love—her nunnery on the isle of Ely. When Wilfrid and Ethelthryd won, and the King took a new wife, she turned against the Bishop of York, ever complaining against his power, his interfering ways, and his showy estate, which rivalled that of the court. She complained of him to Theodore, who, realising that Wilfrid would have no support at court, promptly appointed three new bishops for Northumbria. Now Wilfrid had never been made Archbishop of York, so that, although one of the bishops was intended to act as his suffragan, he would exercise no control over the other two. In effect, two thirds of his diocese was taken from him without his consent, and the new bishops were given abbeys he had built himself to be their centres of administration.

In 678 he decided to take his case to Rome, but again he met difficulties of his own making. He had consistently supported the Austrasian Franks against the aggressive tendencies of the Neustrians (mainly because he had personal knowledge of the Austrasian king in exile), and it was through Neustria, or westerly Gaul, that it was most usual to go on any journey to Rome. The Neustrians were well prepared, and almost killed an English bishop travelling through their territories because he was called Winfrid, but they luckily discovered their spelling error in time.

In fact Wilfrid took another route, landing in Frisia. Here he found an ideal mission field, and though his mission to

Rome was of great personal importance, he never lost the larger view to which he was committed. Luckily that year the shoals of fish were large, and the fishermen commensurately appreciative. When their king, Aldgils, received a secret message from the Neustrians offering him a good price for a captive Wilfrid, he ordered a feast to be made, without saying a word. In the middle of the feast he publicly announced the message, and promptly burnt it, saying what he felt about the Neustrians. No greater testimony could have been made to the attractiveness of the great Bishop, whose character appealed even in the darkest wastes of paganism—and he was to have a similar experience later on in his journey at the court of Lombardy.

In 679 Wilfrid reached Rome, and achieved complete success—he had to be consulted before changes could be made in his diocese, and he must have a hand in the making of such changes. He returned home in triumph to present the papal decision to the royal court, and met with the rebuff of a lifetime. Egfrid accused him of having gained the decision by bribery, deprived him of all his possessions, and ordered him to be chained in gaol. The Queen darted forward and snatched from him the little case of holy relics he always carried with him, and he was carried off to the darkest dungeons of Northumbria. He spent nine months in this condition, so impressing his keepers with his patience and holiness that he had to be moved from one to another. Then the Queen developed terrifying pains, and the King released him in a panic of superstitious feeling, and he wandered off into exile.

Mercia would not have him, neither Wessex, and so he ended in the wild and dangerous Kingdom of Sussex. Here, in a land cut off from the more civilised parts of England, paganism still ruled supreme, and once more Wilfrid was a humble missionary. He found a land reduced to misery by hunger—the harvests had failed, and the starving peasants went in crowds

to the high sea cliffs and, hand in hand, they flung themselves on the rocks below. Wilfrid remembered his time in Frisia, and taught them how to fish. They survived, and soon the rain came, and the corn at last began to grow again; suddenly he was a hero, and the King granted him Selsey (where he immediately freed the serfs) and crowds came to seek baptism.

Among the crowds came Caedwalla, a claimant for the throne of Wessex, and political power once more exercised its sway over Wilfrid. He put all his energies behind the rebel, managing to forget that he was a ruthless murderer, maddened by the desire to rule. In 685 Caedwalla achieved his aim, and the following year called Wilfrid to Wessex. He went and failed to denounce the man who planned to exterminate the Jutish population of the Isle of Wight and replace them with good Wessex stock, the man who killed the King of Sussex who had given Wilfrid refuge. There are some things about every great man that one fails to understand, and this is one.

Yet fate decided that he should not live out his life as the servant of this man: in the year that Caedwalla won Wessex, Egfrid of Northumbria had been killed in battle, to be succeeded by the learned Aldfrid, and Archbishop Theodore had decided that the time was ripe for reconciliation. In 686 Wilfrid returned to York as Bishop, and in the following two years the incumbents of the sees that had been carved from his moved or died, and he was given charge of them.

Perhaps he thought, or had been persuaded to think that the *status quo* had been re-established, but in the next two years bishops were appointed to the sees of Hexham and Lindisfarne, without Wilfrid's consent. The King seemed increasingly to favour the more Celtic elements, and to take umbrage at Wilfrid's arrant Romanism: in 690 Wilfrid was once more in exile in Mercia.

Thirteen years later a great council was convened in Yorkshire to resolve the impossible situation: Wilfrid was offered publicly a safe-conduct to attend, but secretly plans were laid to entrap him. Whatever was done, whatever arguments were presented, he firmly denied the power of the Archbishop of Canterbury, asserting that those who went against the Pope's decision were disobedient. In a fury, the authorities stripped him of every last thing, down to 'the least tiny part of one cottage'.

The English Church was rocked to its depths with a sense of shock which no reversal to paganism could achieve. Hurriedly, Wilfrid was re-granted his monastery of Ripon, on the condition that he would never again exercise his function as a bishop. This he refused to agree to. King Aldfrid was all for torturing him, but the Archbishop had to remind him that Wilfrid had come to the conference under safe-conduct. They ordered that his followers should be treated as pagans, dishes they had used being ritually scoured before Christians could eat from them, food they had blessed being thrown away as was food that had been used in pagan sacrifice. Aldhelm wrote a letter, begging Christians to consider what they were doing to the man who had done so much for them. Stalemate was once more achieved.

Wilfrid turned once more to appeal to Rome. The journey that had once been a glad voyage to the fount of all must now have seemed the ultimate in torture. He was old, ill-used, and very tired. He went, once again, via Friesland, and was delighted to observe the progress of the mission there under Archbishop Willibrord. He arrived in Rome in 704, and after four months got the Papal decision in his favour for a second time: the Archbishop of Canterbury was to re-convene his council and set all to rights.

The journey home was worse than the journey out. Just before reaching Paris, Wilfrid fell into a coma which lasted four days: but he was absolutely determined to get the papal decision accepted in England. The council re-convened in 706 and fol-

lowing the papal instruction, gave back to Wilfrid his two abbeys of Ripon and Hexham, and the bishopric of Hexham. It was enough to call a victory, and the tired old man acknowledged his satisfaction. In 709, whilst on a journey into Mercia, Wilfrid died, secure in the knowledge that the Church for which he had fought was not only vindicated, but also established.

For a biography, see E. S. Duckett: *Anglo-Saxon Saints and Scholars* (Shoe String Press, Connecticut, reprint 1967).

William the Conqueror

Robert, heir to the rough and ungracious Duchy of Normandy, saw Herleva, daughter of a rich tanner of Falaise, at a dance and fell in love with her. Like other royal heirs, he could not marry her for a variety of petty reasons that in sum said no, and so, as his concubine, she bore him Adelaide and William, bastards both, but the latter to turn his unsightly title into that of William the Conqueror.

He was born about 1028, and cannot have seen much of his father, who succeeded to the Duchy at much the same time. He lived with his mother, who was married off for respectability to the Vicomte Herlwin. She soon produced for him brothers Odo and Robert, who were to reach dizzy heights with William, and though Odo was to fall, Robert Count of Mortain was at William's death-bed.

In 1035 William's father went on pilgrimage to the Holy Land, but died on the return journey, leaving an eight-year-old Duke to rule the most notoriously unruly land in Europe. William spent his boyhood and adolescence in a maelstrom of feuding marauders; his two guardians, his steward and his tutor all met violent deaths. Only his very lack of importance protected William the Bastard.

In 1042 he received knighthood and began the long toil of controlling his duchy, a process the Normans found highly objectionable, for in 1046 they broke out in revolt. William had to ask for the aid of the King of France, and at Val-des-dunes they beat the rebels—William's first victory.

He now began to establish his borders. To the south west he began the long fight with Anjou for the buffer territory of Maine. The north east was to be protected by a less military process—marriage. His sister, showing rare devotion, married three marcher lords in succession: as one was killed in battle she married the next. William himself married Matilda, daughter of Baldwin of Flanders. Though this was a diplomatic marriage, William remained faithful, for he had strong views on adultery. Matilda produced many children, and acted as her husband's lieutenant when he was away from Normandy.

Flanders was a good ally for anyone interested in the sea-crossing to England, and even at this stage, 1051, William was very interested in this desirable prize. The King of England, Edward the Confessor, son of William's great-aunt, had been brought up in Normandy (a refuge to which he undoubtedly owed his life), and preferred the company of continentals to that of Englishmen. He may have suggested to William that he was a possible heir, for Edward was childless, and such a promise was easy to give when it bought the friendship of one so powerful. Edward's line had ruled Wessex for five hundred years, and the ending of a dynasty was a subject that powerfully exercised the mind.

The next decade was taken up with the struggle for Maine, and this was the time when William learned his craft and built a reputation. Occasionally the devil he had in him broke to the surface to shock the world: in the siege of Alençon the defenders spread the wall with skins soaked in vinegar, for they knew the Normans' childish passion for fire, and some ribald wits pointed to them and shouted 'The tanner!' When he caught them William cut off their hands and feet: he was no gentleman in war.

In 1064 Harold Godwinson was caught and honourably entertained. One of William's daughters fell madly in love with him. He accompanied the Duke on a badly organised and ineffective raid on Brittany and, despising the Normans on the basis of this one experience (he was after all the leading man of a highly sophisticated nation temporarily in the grip of a barbarian people), gladly gave his oath to serve William's cause in England. The idea was of course laughable, and Harold's experience in Wales (which was in much the same relationship as Brittany was to Normandy) showed him that he was a far better general than William.

But the Duke took a great deal more account of the oath of vassalage than did the English prince, and when Harold accepted the death-bed nomination of Edward and the Witan's confirmation, he was genuinely shocked: Maine had become his by the promise of the last Count, why should not England? He was so filled with righteous indignation that when he finally landed in England he wore round his neck the relics on which Harold had sworn the oath.

The great expedition was planned. Diplomacy won the support of many—the most important being the Pope, who, persuaded by Cardinal Hildebrand (later Gregory VII) that William, if he won the land, would hold England as a vassal of the Papacy, sent him a personally blessed banner. A massive fleet was prepared, for this was to be a cavalry invasion, one of the first in Northern Europe, and troops came from Brittany, France and Flanders for the gold on offer. The Normans (mostly sons and heirs rather than established barons) came attracted by the high promise of reward. The spirit that had won the Dane-law in England and the two Sicilies, that had sent Vikings to America was again at work.

Kept in port for a month by contrary winds, and forced at the last minute to change all the invasion plans, the force that finally sailed on 27 September must have been rather low-spirited. They landed at Pevensey, whilst Harold was away in the North with his army, and found themselves hemmed in by the great forest of Andredsweald, which hampered progress, and prevented news from filtering through. For a fortnight they aimlessly plundered and built castles, only gradually becoming aware of the splendid victory Harold had won at Stamford Bridge.

Finally they learned of the English advance, and William ordered his troops on to meet him. Harold held a good position, and the first wave of Normans were easily repulsed from the shield wall, the Bretons scuttling for safety. The rain of English missiles was deadly, and William must have wondered whether the new cavalry tactics were worth the trouble, for he was unhorsed three times, and rumours of his death were so rife he had to show himself bareheaded.

Later attacks did better by drawing the English down into the valley of slaughter, and the archers began to take their toll. The carnage on both sides grew heavy and William mentally promised an abbey on the site of the battle to sing for the souls of the dead.

The victory was his, but at a great price —his first move on London was repulsed and he turned off up the Thames valley to await the English decision. They had the choice of capitulation to an army in the field, or of accepting the leadership of a more direct heir, the young grandson of Edmund Ironside, but he had no troops and had, after all, been brought up in Hungary. They accepted William, and on Christmas Day he was crowned in the new Westminster Abbey.

He gave to his followers the earldoms of those who had died behind the shield wall, and dashed back to Normandy to enjoy the praises of the world. The churches who had prayed him on got their reward (but not the churches of the cowardly Bretons) and the Pope got Harold's banner.

For nine months he spent an easy life at home, whilst his followers fought to win the domains he had given them.

Resistance was strong—in Herefordshire a character called Eadric the Wild ran a guerilla war against the invading Richard fitzScob, and this was the general pattern.

The years 1068–71 were to be spent subduing revolts and building castles. Exeter was broken, then Mercia. Northumbria now threatened, for Edgar the Aetheling had allied with Malcolm Canmore King of Scots. Harold's sons invaded the West Country. There seemed no end to it, and William was forced to bribe the jaded Normans to stay and fight.

In 1069 the Danes invaded, and William spent the winter ravaging the North. This ruthless destruction of a territory equivalent in size to his own duchy was an object lesson to the English, and one which they took; but it can also be seen in another light: that barbaric temper, often controlled, but appearing madly when opposition of a personal kind was met—the Bastard would have his way, come what may.

The last flare came in the Isle of Ely, where a thegn of Peterborough had retired with the abbey treasure to keep it out of Norman hands. Hereward the Wake had a great fortress, protected by secret paths across the marsh, and to him came Bishop Aethelwine of Durham and Morkere earl of Northumbria. For a time the Danes came too, but William bribed them to go away, and in 1071 took Ely, the last stronghold. Hereward escaped, and disappearing into the fenland mists entered the realm of legend, full circle from Beowulf.

A foray into Scotland reduced Malcolm Canmore to obedience, and now at last William's land was secure; but plainly the *ad hoc* policies of the first years were not enough to keep it so. England must be wholly given over to Norman rule. The King himself took the lion's share of the land—about one fifth; the church had about one quarter, and the lay vassals were given the rest. There were only some three hundred of these lay 'tenants-in-chief', and of these only about one hundred were important barons, the rest being royal servants. Of course the tenants-in-chief themselves had vassals and servants who had to be given estates by their immediate lords, but even so, in 1070, for every Norman landholder there were some three hundred English folk.

The Normans were strangers in a strange land—somewhat like young Englishmen in nineteenth century India, though the Normans, instead of bringing new knowledge and higher standards, came to find them. They were boorish, and often bestial, but they had inquiring minds, and were an imitative people.

It is in this background that we must set the making of Domesday Book. Made at incredible speed, in the course of a few months, this massive survey of the resources and landownership of the country is a triumph of administrative skill. It told the rulers of England a great deal, and it warned the ruled that they had entered a new age. William died before the whole of the operation was completed, and it tells us much of his character and of his son's, that after his death nothing more was done to it.

The barons and the administrative officers were essential to William's government, but without the Church it could not have carried on. The Church provided the only literate members of the community, and this meant more than just clerks: moral support (in the truest sense) meant a great deal to William, and with it came wise counsel and the feeling of continuity in a life constantly threatened by violent death.

The King had an able ally in Lanfranc of Pavia, whom he made Archbishop of Canterbury. A strange choice, for Lanfranc was a mild mannered schoolmaster, sixty years of age, and a committed monk not in the least interested in worldly promotion; he had, moreover, had a nasty brush with William twenty years earlier when he had opposed the latter's marriage. Yet the two worked together well in Normanizing and up-dating the English Church.

It was often a rough business: the foreigners had neither understanding nor sympathy for English traditions, and cheerfully moved the sites of cathedrals from quiet villages to populous towns, knocked down old buildings and built new, behaving with the reckless abandon of earlier castle builders. The powers of bishops were drastically enlarged, and they were given courts entirely separate from the state, which took note of moral offences. The Hildebrandine offence against simony and clerical marriage and concubinage was actively pursued, though William judiciously avoided the Pope's larger claims—only one man was to rule in England.

As the years wore on, William grew stouter and more bald. He had his troubles, though most of them were family ones. His half-brother Odo, not content with his bishopric and charge of Kent, plotted a mad-cap scheme to win the papacy and had to be restrained. His children were not a happy lot—the daughters pious, the sons the opposite: the eldest Robert (Curthose—'Shortboots') was a feckless troublemaker (though plainly his mother's favourite); Rufus was a cynic and Henry cruel.

In 1087 William was fighting on his French border, and the day proving long and taxing, he fell heavily on the iron pommel of his saddle. He was carried to rest, but plainly his stomach injury was serious, and he ordered a careful inventory of all his possessions so that he could make his will. The mind of the maker of Domesday Book was at work. Perhaps also he thought of the pious expedition he had recently sent off to bring back his father's body from its lonely tomb in far-off Nicea.

His death was shabby, too. As soon as he expired everyone rushed off to protect their estates from the chaos they knew would follow the death of a great king, and the servants stripped the room of its valuables, and left the half-naked corpse untended in squalor. Even at the funeral at Caen a Norman appeared and claimed that the land of the abbey had been stolen from him by William, and stood by, arms akimbo, until a collection had been taken up from the mourners to raise the price of a grave plot.

There is a biography by Frank Barlow: *William I and the Norman Conquest* (English Univ. Press, London, 1965; Verry, Lawrence Inc., Connecticut, 1966).

William Rufus

William Rufus has had an extraordinarily bad press: contemporary chroniclers hated him as anti-clerical, and Victorian historians denounced him from the dark suspicion they had that he was a homosexual. Yet he continues to arouse our interest, if not our sympathy, and the mystery of his death will continue to invite interpretation.

He was born in 1056, and was the Conqueror's favourite son. Short, stout and red-haired, he was much given to hunting, and cared little for higher pursuits, though he had been tutored as a child by the excellent schoolmaster Lanfranc, Archbishop of Canterbury.

At the Conqueror's death his possessions were divided according to his wishes: Normandy went to his eldest, feckless, happy-go-lucky Robert Curthose; England to Rufus; and to Henry five thousand pounds of silver. Lanfranc ensured that William took over rule in England without much difficulty, but the problems that lay in the future were already evident. Many Norman barons owned estates in Normandy as well as in England, and did not want two separate rulers. Odo of Bayeux, recently released from prison, and his brother Robert Count of Mortain, speedily built up a rebellion against William and in favour of Robert as lord of all.

Robert Curthose did little to help them, and the majority of people in England came down on the side of William, so the rebellion was soon crushed. Rufus had not yet shown his worst side—he seems to have behaved himself whilst Lanfranc lived. But in 1189 the Archbishop died, and now the King set out on a career of unrestrained license and extortion. He blasphemed wildly, and was only amused by the shocked looks of the churchmen; his cynical and satirical sense of humour was not well suited to the age or to his station.

In fund-raising he had the skilled assistance of Ranulph Flambard, who wrung money out of every corner of the land by fair means and foul. Bishoprics remained unfilled so that the revenues filtered off into the royal coffers, and taxes new and old were raised. On one classic occasion Flambard called out the militia (some 20,000 strong) as if to go on active service, and then collected the ten shillings each they had brought as subsistence money before sending them home again.

The money was needed for the conquest of Normandy—a project close to William's heart. Robert was a feeble ruler (in nature and in action very similar to his nephew Stephen) and the Duchy was fast degenerating into anarchy. In 1090 Rufus took the eastern parts of Normandy with relative ease, but finding stiffer resistence in the centre, promptly desisted. The following year he joined Robert in an attack on their brother Henry, who had purchased territories from Robert in the western parts of the Duchy which Robert now wanted back again. Naturally Rufus gained a considerable share of the evil winnings of this project.

At home he extended the English boundary in the north by annexing Cumberland and Westmoreland in 1092, and two years later made further progress in this area by putting a pro-English King on the Scots' throne. Norman extension into Wales also continued during his reign, though it was largely brought to a halt by a stiffening of Welsh resistance in 1094.

William Rufus had many troubles with the Church, most of which he brought upon his own head, for in 1093, when very ill and in fear of death, he agreed to the elevation of Anselm as Archbishop of Canterbury. William could be very religious when ill, but on recovering he lost all that, and his relations with Anselm were a continuing struggle until the Archbishop retired from the fray into exile in 1097.

In 1096 however, a dream had come true. Robert Curthose, anxious to go on crusade but lacking the necessary finance, had agreed to mortgage his duchy to William. The King took over, very vigorously began to restore it to order, and attempted to regain the border counties of Maine and the French Vexin. He even proposed (at the cost of yet more taxation) to accept Poitou as a similar mortgage for the Duke of Aquitaine.

His continental plans were cut short on 2 August, 1100, when Walter Tirel shot him whilst they were hunting together near Winchester. The body was left for some peasants to fetch in for a speedy burial in the Cathedral, whilst Tirel fled abroad, and Henry took over the land. No one can tell for sure what actually happened—though the official story was that this was a regrettable hunting accident. Probably it was a plot between Henry (who stood to lose everything if Robert Curthose returned whilst William ruled) and the powerful family of de Clare. England had been taxed enough—they would try a new son of the Conqueror.

The detailed record of the reign is to be found in E. A. Freeman's *The Reign of William Rufus and the Accession of Henry I* (2 vols., Oxford Univ. Press, London and New York, 1882).

John Tiptoft, Earl of Worcester

John Tiptoft, Earl of Worcester was one of a generation of scholar-statesmen of the fifteenth century who turned out to be more ruthless than the uneducated barons to whom they succeeded. He came of a distinguished family, indeed his father had been a close friend of Henry IV, Speaker of the House of Commons, and later Lord Treasurer.

He was born about 1427 in Cambridgeshire, and educated at home. In 1440 he went to Oxford and spent three years at University College in what was for then a palatial suite of three rooms, attended by a personal chaplain. His father had extensive estates, and his mother was a substantial heiress, so in 1449 he was able to marry well —to the sister of Warwick the Kingmaker. He was made Earl of Worcester, and in 1442 took over his father's old position of Lord Treasurer.

He remained for some years in this eminent position, but life became increasingly difficult as the dispute between Lancaster and York aggravated for he had strong connections on both sides. In 1458 he resolved this difficulty by going on a diplomatic mission to the Pope, and then on pilgrimage to the Holy Land, with a 'small' retinue of some twenty-seven persons.

The ship ran into difficulties, meeting a violent storm, and the master was put to the last resort in his book of seamanship. He scribbled on bits of paper the names of all the saints he could remember, stuffed them into a hat and passed this round the passengers. Each one selected a piece, read the name of the saint, and threw it into the sea, mentally promising a mass for the said saint if ever they should reach land.

The storm abated—of course—but they soon met up with pirates, and the resourceful captain yelled out that they had plague on board, and the pirates disappeared. Before landing in Palestine all the nobles changed into their servants' cast-offs, to save being pestered by the Saracens, but when they landed they found that they could get away with nothing —all were penned up for the night in filthy caves, and not only did they have to pay a penny each to go in—but another penny for the privilege of being released. They must have been feeling rather upset by the time their tour began, with a Franciscan saying mass and warning them how to behave afterwards—nobles were urged not to scratch their coats of arms on the Holy Sepulchre!

In a rapid fortnight's tour they saw everything there was to see, noting with some displeasure that the garden of Gethsemane was badly overgrown.

On his return to Italy, Tiptoft went to Padua and Ferrara to study. He did some translations from the Latin and from Italian into English which were to be printed later on. He collected a huge store of books, and went to Florence, where he walked about alone, in ordinary dress to avoid being fêted as a visiting nobleman, and attended lectures by famous Greek scholars. He made a trip to Rome to give a congratulatory oration to Pius II, and all were overcome by his brilliant style.

He had time and enough to spare, for affairs in England were in a bad state; but in 1461, with Edward IV on the throne, and the discords resolved (for the time being) he reluctantly decided to return.

He was showered with honours and offices—knight of the Garter, Lord Treasurer, president of the Court of Chivalry. In 1467 he presided as M.C. and umpire at the famous joust between the King's brother-in-law Lord Scales and the Bastard of Burgundy. But in one of his offices he showed himself resolute, and sowed the seeds of hatred that finally led him to the scaffold. As Lord Constable he was given summary powers to deal with treason, and although he was absolutely fair, he was also swift and ruthless. Londoners began to mutter that whilst in Padua he had studied foreign ways of administering the law, and that his behaviour was un-English and cruel.

In 1467 he was sent to Ireland where there was trouble brewing. The English had little forces there, and it seemed that Desmond was gathering all too much power, and might be planning a revolution against the English. Tiptoft at once convened a Parliament and attainted Desmond of treason, executing him and (lest a war of revenge should have a leader) his two sons as well.

In 1470 Edward needed him back in England, for disaffection was rife, and Warwick and Clarence had to be dealt with. Tiptoft stamped out rebellion ruthlessly, and soon he was given the name 'the butcher'. When Warwick invaded in force, Edward was forced to fly the country, and Tiptoft, with the treasure

Edward would need, rushed across country to join him at the coast. Round about Huntingdon he found himself in the thick of Lancastrian troops, and he and his men disguised themselves and joined a band of shepherds. They would have got through had not one of the party bought a large quantity of bread at a farm and paid for it with a gold noble. The suspicious event was reported, and Tiptoft captured.

He was quickly judged guilty of high treason, and a specially elaborate scaffold was prepared for his death—the floor covered with carpets and the sides with fine tapestries. So great was the press as he walked from Westminster to Tower Hill, that at the foot of Ludgate Hill the procession could get no further, and he had to spend a night in the Fleet prison, whilst the execution was postponed to the following day.

Throughout this time he refused to accept that he had done anything wrong: all of his actions he had deemed necessary to preserve the state from danger. When he came to the scaffold finally, he asked his executioner to sever his head with three blows as a sign of the Trinity.

His books (including printed bibles he had sent for from Germany) were left to Oxford: they were worth then something in excess of £300. His estates were not forfeit, and his body was honourably buried, the head with the body, and not displayed to the general public, as his victims' had been, with the head impaled on the buttocks.

Perhaps it was in John Tiptoft that England learned to fear the Machiavellian politics the Renaissance was to bring, and to feel some self-respect for its own rather murky and chaotic manner of organising the state.

See R. J. Mitchell: *John Tiptoft* (Longmans, Harlow, 1938).

John Wyclif

John Wyclif was born around the year 1330, probably at Wycliffe, near Richmond in the North Riding of Yorkshire. He came of a respectable family, who were able to support him to Oxford, where he was to remain for the most part of his life. Vain and humourless, he was always ready to see the world in terms of those who were right and for Wyclif, and those who were wrong, eternally damned, minions of Antichrist, and against Wyclif. His one real skill was the ability to argue the hind leg off a donkey—not an attractive facility to us today, but for him it was the way to fame and security, security he was to badly need, for his basic intellectual extremism was to lead him into trouble at every stage of his life.

He was associated in his lifetime with four Oxford colleges. In 1356, he was a junior fellow of Merton, but soon moved on to become third master of Balliol. He won respect there, for in 1361 he was given the college's richest living of Fillingham in Lincolnshire, for which he resigned the mastership. Fillingham produced £20 a year, and for £5 he could get a curate to serve there for him whilst he continued his studies; having gained his M.A. he could now go on to study Theology.

He took lodgings in Queen's, where he was to remain, with one brief interval, for the rest of his academic career, and set to work. He was given a second living in 1362, the prebendal canonry of Aust, near Bristol, but as this produced only a little over £6 a year he didn't bother to put in a curate. He was justifiably brought to court over this in 1366, a bad beginning for one who was to make his name criticising the Church; as a negligent pluralist he was surely in no position to judge? One can only point out that most other scholars supported themselves in the same way—there was no other—and it was the *system* Wyclif criticised. He was to make his contribution as a scholar, not as a parish priest, and one of his justifiable grievances was that the authorities did little to support him in the way of life to which he had committed himself.

This grievance became very real in 1366. A largely monastic college had been set up in Oxford by the Archbishop of Canterbury, and the strong opposition of the secular scholars had made its life almost impossible; so, without any thought of the legal implications, its monk-principal had been ousted, and Wyclif was put in instead. Very soon the statutes were re-asserted, and Wyclif found himself ousted from Canterbury College, and in high dudgeon he appealed to the papal court. To pay the expenses he exchanged his rich living of Fillingham for one worth a third of its value —Ludgershall—and promptly lost the case, The Pope attempted to compensate him by making him a canon of Lincoln in 1371, promising the next prebend (to which the money of such a position was attached) that fell in. The promise was to be renewed in 1373, but when a prebend fell in in 1375, it was not given to Wyclif. He must have been very short of money for a number of years.

Yet his position surely merited more— even his enemies called him 'the flower of Oxford', without an equal in philosophy or disputation; he worked immensely hard —some forty volumes of his works have been published, and there are still some remaining in manuscript. A reasonable grudge is the most dangerous thing to allow to a man of genius.

At this time it became apparent that Wyclif's talents for argument were needed in the larger world of politics. England was desperately in need of money to finance the Hundred Years' War, and increasingly people were looking to the Church, immensely rich, and superficially doing little to help. In fact the King drew most of the papal taxation into his own coffers, and the control the Pope had over many of the most important positions in the Church in England was most frequently exercised in favour of the King's nominees; but to the uninformed observer the Church seemed to be getting away with doing nothing to help the country, and money was draining out to Avignon like life-blood. Edward III seemed in his dotage, and William of Wykeham (who had come from nothing) ruled the administration as Bishop of Winchester, with £2000 a year to his purse. The nobles, and particularly the Black Prince and his devoted brother John of Gaunt, felt the time was ripe for a little public pressure on the Church, just to see what would happen.

Wyclif was drawn into politics just at the time his reputation in Oxford was at its height—he took his doctorate in 1372— and his main duty was to provide the secular powers with firm arguments about the nature of authority in Church and State. He looked immediately to the doctrines expressed a generation ago by another English scholar, Fitzralph, who had enunciated the principle that authority rested upon grace. By this he meant that 'dominion'—that is political power and ownership of property—depended upon the virtue of the man exercising it. A dangerous doctrine, especially in the hands of a man who habitually took every argument to its extreme.

In 1374 Wyclif was sent to Bruges to negotiate as a member of a team with papal commissioners about taxation. He was given very generous expenses, and the living of Lutterworth (equal in value to Fillingham) for his services to England, but seemed to expect a reward from the Pope as well. Some said he expected the bishopric of Worcester, but not only did he not get that, he was also denied the prebendary promised in respect of his canonry of Lincoln.

It is commonly asserted that Wyclif spent a good part of the year 1376 preaching round the London churches for Gaunt against William of Wykeham's administration, but recent studies have shown that sermons surviving from this period show no trace of such activities. He was certainly up to something for, in the following year, when the clergy struck back under the leadership of William Courtenay, Bishop of London, it was against Wyclif himself. In February 1377 Wyclif was called to St. Paul's for trial, but went guarded by the dukes of Lancaster and Northumberland, and the trial had hardly begun before a riot broke out, and Wyclif escaped. He was not to get away so easily though, for his enemies the Benedictines (whom he called 'black dogs') had sent excerpts from his works to the Pope, who smartly condemned them in May of the same year.

The bulls were late arriving in England, and Wyclif was not summoned to appear for a second time until December 1377. Meanwhile the chancellor of Oxford was ordered to send a report into court, but far from agreeing with the papal condemnation, he said that though Wyclif's views may sound ill to the ears of 'sinners and ignoramusses', that was no good reason for suppressing them. Furthermore, when Wyclif finally condescended to appear for trial in March of the following year, not only had the king's mother quietly arranged that no decision should be reached there, but also a conveniently timed London mob broke the whole thing up. Wyclif was still of considerable use to the crown—he appeared in the parliament in Gloucester in October 1378 to state the official case in a sordid matter of sanctuary-breaking, when not only had the royal officials murdered the escapee in Westminster Abbey, but also a sacristan who had tried to defend him.

The unhappy election of two rival Popes that marked the beginning of the Great Schism made life considerably easier for Wyclif, and allowed him to develop his most outrageous ideas in the last years of his life relatively free from interference. Treatises flowed from his pen with phenomenal speed, and no care at all for style; the language grew ever more virulent, the thinking markedly more revolutionary.

He wrote of the truth of Holy Scripture, establishing this holy word of God as the basis of all truth, the fount of all authority. What was not there had no right to exist— was the work of the devil. Everything must be judged by reference to Scripture, and if found wanting, must be destroyed. Going on to analyse the church he followed Bradwardine and Augustine, and took their ideas to extremes, elaborating a rigid doctrine of predestination. With one mighty sweep he cut away the very basis of the existence and authority of the church on earth: the Pope might be damned eternally—who knows?—but one certainly can do nothing to save one's soul by following his instructions. The labourer in the field might be predestined to go to Heaven, whilst his parish priest was consigned from the beginning of time to Hell, so who gives respect to whom? The behaviour of the clergy certainly seemed to Wyclif to suggest that this was often the case.

Proceeding to write on the office of the king, Wyclif enunciated the (to him) only possible area of reform: a return must be made to apostolic poverty and apostolic humility, and only the king and his lay lords can achieve this by disendowing the church and destroying its hierarchy. For Wyclif, the king is God's vicar on earth, not the Pope, and he must act up to his responsibilities.

Next Wyclif wrote about the historical roots of the power of the papacy, demonstrating with a rare skill the lateness in time of the establishment of many of the most important constituents of papal power. He also lectured and wrote on the sacrament of the Eucharist, contradicting official dogma by asserting that Christ was spiritually present after the words of consecration, rather than physically.

He had reached the limit—and perhaps he himself half knew it at this stage. Late in 1380 the chancellor of Oxford convened an all party committee of twelve to examine his teachings on the Eucharist, and a majority of seven denounced it. The news was taken to him as he was teaching, and although an observer declared him to be 'confused', he said that neither the chancellor nor any of his fellows could weaken his opinions. He appealed to the king, but was quietly informed that he had reached the bottom of the well of political protection. Nevertheless he issued in May 1381 a *Confession* defending his views, before

finally agreeing to retire to Lutterworth later on that year. The outbreak of the Peasants' Revolt in June may have been one of the causes prompting his retirement—many people looked to his views as a factor in the making of this tragic demonstration, though in fact they had nothing at all to do with it.

He left behind in Oxford a number of brilliant students who continued to preach and teach his doctrines, in and out of the university. The most notable of these were Nicholas Hereford and Philip Repingdon. They tried hard, but they did not have the kind of protection that Wyclif enjoyed, and within a year Courtenay had pretty well wiped out Wyclif's party in Oxford.

The cause continued in Lutterworth. Despite a stroke in 1382, Wyclif continued to write at high speed—three major treatises came out that year, quite apart from his great summary work containing all his thinking, the *Trialogus*. The work on the translation of the Bible that had begun sometime late in his Oxford career under the direction of Nicholas Hereford was completed. Not satisfied with this word-for-word translation, a new flowing version was begun by Wyclif's secretary John Purvey, who was also busy translating and paraphrasing his master's views into acceptable English.

On 28 December 1384, Wyclif was hearing mass in his parish church when he had a stroke for a second time. Paralysed, without the use of his tongue, the very instrument of his success, he lay for three days, dying with the end of the year.

In 1415 the Council of Constance condemned his doctrines and ordered his exhumation, but his pupil Repingdon, now a faithful son of the church, was at this time bishop of Lincoln, in whose diocese Lutterworth lay. He left his master in peace, and it was not until 1428 that Wyclif's bones were dug up and burnt, and his ashes scattered in the river, by Richard Flemyng, another scholar who had once come under his spell.

Although Oxford continued obstinately

to remember his fame as a philosopher with pride, Wyclif's works were far more widely used in Bohemia, where the Hussites collected them with care, even sending over copyists to England to bring back more. The Wyclif scholar of today must travel to the libraries of Prague, Vienna and Stockholm to read their subject's works in the original texts in many cases. At home the lesser luminaries of Oxford, whom Courtenay had not bothered to catch, went on with their missionary work all over the country, and found a receptive audience already there. The Lollards, humble folk who had come to much the same conclusions as Wyclif by a much shorter and less complicated route, felt a great pride that the cleverest man in Oxford had thought the same as them. They accepted his Bible with joy, and read and copied it right through a century and a half, until the Reformation rediscovered him.

See K. B. McFarlane: *John Wycliffe and the beginning of English Nonconformity* (English Univ. Press, London, 1953).

Envoy

A peasant rogue.

'Sir, for God's sake do not take it ill of me if I tell the truth, how I went the other evening along the bank of this pond and looked at the fish which were playing in the water, so beautiful and so bright, and for the great desire I had for a tench I laid me down on the bank and, just with my hands, quite simply, and without any other device, I caught that tench and carried it off; and now I will tell thee the cause of my covetousness and my desire. My dear wife had lain abed a right full month, as my neighbours who are here know, and she could never eat or drink anything to her liking, and for the great desire she had to eat a tench I went to the bank of the pond to take just one tench; and that never other fish from the pond did I take.'

(qu. from Maitland's *The Court Baron*. Vol. 4 in the annual series of the Selden Society.)

INDEX OF PROPER NAMES